1966—
The Year Black Power Challenged the Civil Rights Movement

SIMON & SCHUSTER
New York   London   Toronto   Sydney   New Delhi

LOWNDES COUNTY FREEDOM ORGANIZATIO

Mass Meeting, May 3, 1966, to nominate candida
for the November 8, 1966 general election.

LOWNDES COUNTY

SHERIFF -- put (x) before one name

-- -----MR. JESSE 'NOTE' FAVORS

X------MR. SIDNEY LOGAN, JR.

-- ---OTHER (write in name)

SAYING IT LOUD

MARK WHITAKER

ONE MAN - ONE VOTE

Simon & Schuster
1230 Avenue of the Americas
New York, NY 10020

First Simon & Schuster hardcover edition February 2023

SIMON & SCHUSTER and colophon are registered
trademarks of Simon & Schuster, Inc.

For information about special discounts for bulk purchases,
please contact Simon & Schuster Special Sales at
1-866-506-1949 or business@simonandschuster.com.

The Simon & Schuster Speakers Bureau can bring authors to
your live event. For more information or to book an event, contact
the Simon & Schuster Speakers Bureau at 1-866-248-3049
or visit our website at www.simonspeakers.com.

Interior design by Lewelin Polanco

Manufactured in the United States of America

1   3   5   7   9   10   8   6   4   2

Library of Congress Cataloging-in-Publication Data is available.

ISBN 978-1-9821-1412-1
ISBN 978-1-9821-1414-5 (ebook)

In memory of
C. Sylvester Whitaker Jr.
(1935–2008)
and
Jeanne Theis Whitaker
(1926–2021)

Contents

PART 2

Author's Note

When writing about Black people individually or as a community, or about anything relating to them as a race, I've capitalized the word Black, in keeping with widely accepted practice since 2020. The word used in that sense was generally not capitalized in the era covered here, however, so I've left it lowercase when it appeared that way in source material.

Although the word Negro seems archaic today, it was commonplace at that time, and thus appears throughout this narrative in that context.

While I find the "N-word" as offensive as anyone, I believe that seeing how it was used in the past, by white people and also by Black people, is important to understanding our racial history. So that distasteful word does appear in this book, but only in quotations as originally uttered or written.

I've spelled nonviolent and nonviolence in the modern unhyphenated fashion, which was also used at the time by the Student Nonviolent Coordinating Committee. But if those words appeared with hyphens in quoted material, I've retained the hyphens.

Mark Whitaker
New York, NY
January 17, 2022

The Road to Black Power

In the middle of Alabama, U.S. Route 80, the highway that links Selma and Montgomery, narrows to two lanes as it passes through Lowndes County, deep in the former cotton plantation territory known as the Black Belt. For decades, the deadly reach of the Ku Klux Klan made this slender stretch of open road, surrounded by swamps and spindly trees covered with Spanish moss, one of the scariest in the South. During the historic civil rights march between those two cities in 1965, fewer than three hundred protesters braved the Lowndes County leg, whispering as they hurried through a rainstorm about rumors of bombs and snipers lurking out of sight. When the march ended, cars transporting demonstrators back to Selma drove as fast as they could through Lowndes County, without stopping.

One car didn't make it. Viola Liuzzo was a thirty-nine-year-old mother of five from Detroit who had answered the Reverend Martin Luther King Jr.'s call for whites to join the Selma march. After it was over, she was helping drive marchers back from Montgomery along with a young Black volunteer named Leroy Moton. As the two headed back to Montgomery after a drop-off in Selma shortly after nightfall, a red-and-white Chevrolet Impala pulled alongside Liuzzo's blue Oldsmobile on Route 80. A spray of bullets exploded into the driver's side window, and the car careened off the road and into a ditch. Moton passed out, and when he came to Liuzzo was slumped lifeless on the bench front seat, her foot still on the accelerator. Moton raced through the darkness to report the attack—which, it would soon emerge, was carried out by four Alabama Klansmen, one of them a paid informant for the FBI.

Two days later, as newspapers across the country ran front-page updates on the murder of the first white woman to die in the civil rights struggle, five young Black organizers from the Student Nonviolent Coordinating Committee slipped unnoticed into Lowndes County on Route 80. The five were there to bring SNCC's mission of voter registration to the county, an impoverished backwater with the largest percentage of Black residents in the state, but where not a single Black had cast a ballot in more than sixty years. The group's leader was Stokely Carmichael, a lanky New Yorker with a long, angular nose and heavy-lidded but expressive eyes. His voice mixed the lilt of Trinidad, where he lived until age eleven; the urgency of the Bronx, where he spent his teens; and the polish of Howard University, the distinguished historically Black college from which Carmichael graduated. Over the next eight months, SNCC organizers proved successful enough that white farmers punished Black sharecroppers who registered to vote by evicting them from their land. So it was that, as the year 1965 ended, Carmichael and his comrades found themselves back along Route 80, erecting tents for displaced families while sharecroppers armed with hunting rifles kept watch for night-riding Klansmen.

On the second to last day of December, Carmichael was putting up tents on a six-acre plot that a local church group had purchased by the side of Route 80 when a blue Volkswagen Beetle drove up. A thin, mocha-skinned young Black man dressed in denim overalls stepped out of the car. Carmichael recognized Sammy Younge, a student at Alabama's Tuskegee Institute who had become active in campus organizing. Over the previous year, Younge had participated in several SNCC protests, and the two men had become friends. But the last time Carmichael had seen the young collegian, at a birthday party Younge threw for himself in November, he had experienced a change of heart. Drunk on pink Catawba wine, Younge cornered Carmichael and confessed that he was through with activism and wanted to return to partying and preparing for a comfortable middle-class career. Younge "was high that night, and we had a talk," Carmichael recalled. "He said he was putting down civil rights . . . and he was going to be out for himself. . . . So I told him, 'It's still cool, you know. Makes me no never mind.'"

Now Younge seemed eager to join the struggle again. "What's happening, baby?" Carmichael said, greeting the student with his usual teasing ease. "I can't kick it, man," Younge said, referring to the organizing bug. "I got to work with it. It's in me." Carmichael chatted with Younge for several minutes, then invited him to stay overnight to help with the tent construction. The next day, Younge approached Carmichael again and confided a new dream. He wanted to attempt in Tuskegee's Macon County what Carmichael was trying to do in Lowndes County: register enough Black voters so they could form their own political party and elect their own candidates to local offices.

In Carmichael's territory, that fledgling party already had a name: the Lowndes County Freedom Organization (LCFO). It also had a distinctive nickname: the "Black Panther Party," after a symbol that the LCFO had adopted to comply with an Alabama law requiring that political parties choose animal symbols that could be identified on ballots by voters who couldn't read. "Well, all you have to do is talk about building a Black Panther Party in Macon County," Carmichael counseled. "See how the idea will hit the people and break that whole TCA thing," he added, dismissively referring to the Tuskegee Civic Association, a group of elders who had long claimed to speak for Macon County Blacks. Then Carmichael gave Younge a last word of encouragement. "My own feeling was that it would," Carmichael recalled saying, before he watched Younge climb into his Volkswagen and drive back to Tuskegee.

Although neither Younge nor Carmichael knew it at that moment, they were both about to become major players—one, as a martyr; the other, as a leader and lightning rod—in the most dramatic shift in the long struggle for racial justice in America since the dawn of the modern civil rights era in the 1950s. Over the following year, the story would stretch from Route 80 in Lowndes County across the United States. It would unfold to the east, in that bastion of the Black privilege in Tuskegee; to the northeast, in SNCC's home base of Atlanta; and due west, on another highway linking Memphis, Tennessee, and Jackson, Mississippi.

To the north, the story would involve a slum neighborhood of Chicago that the Reverend Martin Luther King Jr. would select as his next battlefront. Far to the west, two part-time junior college students from Oakland, California, would take inspiration from the black panther experiment in Alabama to launch a radical new movement of their own. After a decade of watching the civil rights saga play out in the South, a restless generation of Northern Black youth would demand their turn in the spotlight. Before the year 1966 was over, the story would alter the lives of a cast of young men and women, almost all under the age of thirty, who in turn would change the course of Black—and American—history.

IN THE STUDY OF THE SEISMIC ERA KNOWN AS THE 1960s, NUMEROUS books have been devoted to individual years. In most cases, this approach has served to weave together different political and social threads that intersected throughout that remarkable decade. But this book will tell the story of the birth of Black Power through the framework of 1966 for more specific historical reasons. First, it was unquestionably the year when the movement as we remember it today took full form. In the spring of 1966, Stokely Carmichael assumed the helm of the Student Nonviolent Coordinating Committee and began to redirect SNCC's focus from peaceful voter registration in the South to a far more sweeping and radical agenda that questioned nonviolence, mainstream politics, and white alliances. During the summer, Carmichael exchanged the defiant chant of "Black Power!" with a crowd in rural Mississippi in a scene that transfixed the media and made him a nationally recognized figure virtually overnight.

In the fall of 1966, Huey Newton and Bobby Seale conceived

the "Ten Point Program" founding document of the leather-clad, gun-wielding Black Panther Party for Self-Defense that we remember today. Throughout the year, Dr. King fought an uphill battle to bring his nonviolent, integrationist strategy to Chicago, a flawed campaign that undercut the aura of success surrounding King's more moderate agenda. In Georgia, Julian Bond, SNCC's longtime communications director, waged a year-long battle to take a seat in the state legislature after he was banished for opposing the Vietnam War. For young Blacks across the country, it was a humiliating spectacle that deepened their cynicism about the prospects for achieving justice through the two-party political system.

While men received most of the press coverage for their roles in this drama, formidable women played key roles. In the same wild, all-night meeting that resulted in Stokely Carmichael ousting civil rights icon John Lewis as SNCC's chairman, Ruby Doris Smith Robinson, a tough-minded Spelman College graduate, was elected to the number two position of executive secretary. Caught in the middle of one of the year's most painful episodes—the expulsion of the last remaining whites from SNCC—was Dottie Miller Zellner, a white New York City native who was one of the group's longest serving and most loyal staffers. Waiting offstage was Kathleen Neal, the daughter of a Black scholar from Texas who dropped out of Barnard College in 1966 to work for SNCC, the first step in a journey that would lead to her becoming a globally recognized name and face as the wife of Black Panther leader Eldridge Cleaver.

For millions of young Blacks, it was the point at which "Black Consciousness," as they referred to it, became both a state of mind and a badge of identity. Students of language conventions identify 1966 as the year when Blacks in significant numbers began to reject the label "Negro." Looking back on this period, Gene Roberts, the white "race beat" reporter for *The New York Times*, recalled fighting a running battle with his copy desk editors in Manhattan over his decision to stop using that term when referring to young Black militants. By summer, *Ebony* magazine, the monthly chronicle of Black trends and newsmakers, officially recognized the popularity of the

Afro hairstyle with a cover story on "The Natural Look." While almost all the Black Power leaders cited Malcolm X as an influence, it wasn't until the middle of 1966, a year and half after Malcolm's assassination, that his bracing words and powerful life story became known to Blacks and whites of all ages and incomes with the publication of the bestselling $1.25 paperback edition of his posthumous autobiography.

In 1966, the relatively new tools of modern polling captured an ominous turn in racial attitudes. Three years earlier, on the eve of the March on Washington, *Newsweek* magazine had commissioned pollster Louis Harris to conduct a groundbreaking opinion survey which showed evidence of a widening national belief in racial progress. But when *Newsweek* had Harris conduct another such poll in the summer of 1966, it registered a stark reversal. Half of Blacks said that change wasn't happening fast enough, while 70 percent of whites complained that it was coming too fast. After watching TV news footage of another summer of urban race riots, two thirds of whites told Harris's pollsters that they now opposed *any* form of Black protest, even nonviolent. "They're asking too much all at once," Sandra Styles, a twenty-three-year-old commercial artist from Arlington, Virginia, told a *Newsweek* reporter. "They should try the installment plan."

That shift in public opinion, in turn, propelled a change in the political winds that would shape American life for the next half century. Two years after the Democratic Party under Lyndon Johnson had captured dominant control of all three branches of the U.S. government, a white "backlash vote" against Black Power and urban unrest produced huge gains for Republicans in the 1966 midterm elections and set the stage for Richard Nixon's comeback law-and-order presidential campaign of 1968. In California, a riot in the Hunters Point neighborhood of San Francisco and an eleventh-hour uproar over a speech by Stokely Carmichael on the University of California at Berkeley campus helped elect Ronald Reagan as governor, putting Reagan on a path to win the White House and further remake the modern conservative movement. In Alabama, the appeal of an even more openly white supremacist brand of politics was demonstrated when George Wallace, the term-limited segregationist governor, encouraged his wife, Lurleen, to run in his place, and the total political novice won in a landslide.

As a narrative framework, focusing on the events of 1966 also makes it possible to reconstruct not just what happened, but *how* it happened. This book attempts to capture the rich and often messy way that this historic pivot unfolded "in real time," to use a current expression. No doubt, the sort of broad social forces emphasized by academic historians played an important part. The insidious economic and structural racism of the North differed from the more overt Jim Crow racism of the South. The rising generation of young Northern Blacks didn't share the religious and deferential traditions of their Southern elders.

Just as important, however, was the timing and sequence of events, and the role of happenstance, both fortunate and tragic. So was the personality of the key players, all of whom had compelling strengths but also conspicuous flaws. As was the case with the earlier civil rights era, white print and television reporters occupied a prominent place in the story. But this time, journalists weren't welcome witnesses but bewildered outsiders looking on at an uprising that granted them little access and that they were ill-equipped to understand.

Although the Black Power movement continued to gather force and generate headlines into the 1970s, signs of the flameouts and power struggles that proved its eventual undoing were already apparent. For all his dashing good looks and irreverent charm, Stokely Carmichael by the end of 1966 had succumbed to the self-involvement and emotional fragility that would end his tenure as SNCC's chairman after only one year. At the end of 1966, Eldridge Cleaver was just leaving prison after seven years. But already Cleaver's jailhouse writings, published in *Ramparts* magazine and later collected in his bestselling book, *Soul on Ice*, showed a penchant for self-promotion and competitive egotism that would eventually lead to a destructive feud with Huey Newton after Cleaver joined the Black Panthers. Sensational press coverage of the Black Power phenomenon was already feeding poisonous jealousies, while the FBI was preparing to launch a new campaign of surveillance and dirty tricks that would cripple the movement from that point on.

Yet visible, too, were more positive and prophetic legacies that resonate to this day. The core of Carmichael's original conception of Black Power—the idea of harnessing the clout of Black voters to elect Black officials in areas where Blacks represented a decisive percentage of the population—has since become manifest in cities and localities across America, and helped lay the groundwork for the nation's first Black president. The initial mission of the Black Panther Party for Self-Defense—to monitor the way police dealt with Blacks in inner-city neighborhoods—looks prescient in the era of #BlackLivesMatter. Many of the tactics and symbols of the Black Power movement were borrowed or adapted, consciously or unconsciously, by the women's liberation movement and the gay rights movement. Fifty years later, they find echoes even in elements of Trump-era white nationalism, and in roiling debates over the meaning and impact of so-called identity politics.

At the time, some of the best analytical writing about the Black Power movement came from two insightful white scholars: social critic Christopher Lasch and Eugene Genovese, the historian best known for showing how Blacks survived the horrors of slavery by creating their own private social structures. Lasch and Genovese both predicted that the revolutionary political aims of Black Power were bound to fail in a country where the militants, unlike their heroes in Cuba and China, could claim to speak for only a fraction of the Black minority, let alone the larger white majority. But the two scholars also perceived that Black Power spoke to a yearning beyond politics—for a new, distinctly Black culture to replace the one that millions left behind when they moved from the South to the North in the Great Migration of the early and mid-twentieth century. By the end of 1966, glimmers of that new culture could be seen in the first demands for Black Studies programs on college campuses, in the emerging Black Arts Movement, and in the first celebration of the new holiday tradition of Kwanzaa. A half century later, the cultural legacy of Black Power pervades our entire society in the innovations of hip hop music; in other Black aesthetic influences on art, fashion, sports, and language; and in heated debates over how to teach Black history, or whether to teach it at all.

By the end of 1966, much of the tumultuous story of Black Power had yet to be written. But it was already eerily foreshadowed, just as Sammy Younge's fate was as he drove away from Lowndes County along Route 80 back toward Tuskegee on the eve of that New Year—the last time his friend Stokely Carmichael would see him alive.

PART 1

A Murder in Tuskegee

When Sammy Younge left Tuskegee Institute on a late night run to buy a jar of mayonnaise and a pack of cigarettes on the first Monday of 1966, he didn't expect his life to be in danger. Slender, long-necked, and baby-faced, Younge had the recognizably privileged look and manner of a child of the Black middle class, along with a winning smile and wide doe eyes that had attracted a succession of girlfriends by the time he was twenty-one. Sammy was not only a student at Tuskegee Institute but also a hometown boy. He had grown up in the small, stately Alabama city for which the school was named, a community of some two thousand whites and five thousand Blacks that prided itself on a reputation for racial harmony amidst the civil rights maelstrom raging in the Deep South.

Younge's father, Samuel Leamon Younge Sr., was chief of occupational therapy at the city's Veterans Administration Hospital. Born in Tuskegee, the elder Younge attended Talladega College, another historically Black Alabama school a two-hour drive to the north. There, he met Sammy's mother, Renee, a fair-complexioned native of Charleston, South Carolina, who hailed from a long line of mixed-race "free people of color." After a brief courtship, Samuel married Renee and took her back to Tuskegee. She found work as an elementary school teacher and they moved into the six-room red-brick house, several blocks from the Institute, where they raised two sons, Samuel Jr. and Stephen.

Members of Tuskegee's tight-knit Black elite were brought up to believe that the key to survival in white America was to embrace the self-help philosophy of the Institute's famous founder, Booker T. Washington. "Brains, prosperity and character for the Negro will settle the question of civil rights," Washington declared shortly after the school opened in 1881, a view that put him at odds with W. E. B. Du Bois and other Black leaders who advocated a more frontal attack on racial injustice. To Washington, that meant getting educated at Black schools and entering Black trades and professions. For graduates of the Institute, it meant celebrating Tuskegee's most renowned products, the Black airmen who fought Nazi pilots in the skies over Europe during World War II. For students and staff, it meant taking pride in the fictionalized description of the school as an oasis of "roads gracefully winding, lined with hedges and wild roses that dazzled the eyes in the summer sun" in *Invisible Man*, the acclaimed novel by one of the school's most illustrious alumni, Ralph Ellison. In America's Black newspapers, the Tuskegee elite were held up as examples to the race. Two years earlier, the *Pittsburgh Courier* had run a picture of Samuel L. Younge Sr. himself as he passed out collection envelopes for a Red Cross fund drive to a gathering of primly dressed hospital employees.

In this culture of Black middle-class conformity, Sammy Younge Jr. stuck out from his childhood days as a bit of an aimless soul. At the Catholic elementary school in town, he developed a reputation for playing hooky and "always getting into it with the Sisters," a classmate named Laly Washington recalled. Sent to a prep school in Massachusetts for high school—a not uncommon privilege for well-off Black Tuskegee youth—Younge was suspended for buying beer off-campus. He returned home and graduated from Tuskegee Institute High School, where he spent much of his time hanging out with a thrill-seeking crowd who called themselves "the Unbelievables" and took ninety-miles-per-hour joyrides to Montgomery in the Younge family's black Dodge sedan.

As graduation neared, Younge confessed to Laly Washington a sense that he was disappointing his parents. He said he was not "living up to what they wanted him to be," as she put it, and was serving as a bad example for his little brother, Stevie. So as his classmates went off to college, Younge joined the Navy. But after a brief stint aboard an aircraft carrier patrolling the waters off Cuba, that plan was cut short, too. Younge began to suffer from a congenital ailment that caused him to have one kidney surgically removed and left the other partially damaged. He was granted an honorable medical discharge and went home to Tuskegee, where he enrolled at the Institute as a freshman in the spring term of 1965.

It was on the night of March 7 of that year that Younge began to find a sense of purpose as he and his classmates watched television news coverage of "Bloody Sunday," the shocking scene of policemen tear-gassing and stampeding voting rights marchers as they tried to cross the Edmund Pettus Bridge out of Selma, Alabama. Among the victims, the Tuskegee students recognized John Lewis, the twenty-five-year-old Alabama native who had become chairman of the Student Nonviolent Coordinating Committee. Lewis had grown up in the small farming town of Troy, just an hour's drive south of Tuskegee. His father, Eddie Lewis, was a sharecropper and part-time bus driver, and his mother, Willie Mae, took in laundry. From a young age, Lewis dreamed of becoming a preacher, and he practiced by reciting Bible verses and Sunday school lessons to the chickens he tended on the farm. In his last year of high school, his mother brought home a brochure from a small religious school in Nashville, Tennessee, called the American Baptist Theological Seminary that offered students free room and board in exchange for work on campus. Accepted to the school in 1957, Lewis discovered seminars on the philosophy and practice of nonviolence taught in a church basement by James Lawson, a Nashville minister who had studied the tactics of Mahatma Gandhi as a Methodist missionary in India.

In 1960, as the movement that began with Black college students integrating drugstore lunch counters in Greensboro, North Carolina spread to Nashville, Lewis seized the chance to put Lawson's teaching

into practice. He became a leader of the Nashville sit-in movement
and signed up for the first Freedom Rides that sent young protesters
south on buses to test the enforcement of federal laws banning seg-
regation at public depots and rest stations. After a convoy of Freedom
Riders was savagely attacked in Birmingham, Alabama, Lewis joined
a second wave that made its way to Montgomery, where another mob
descended and Lewis was knocked bloody and unconscious by a blow
to the head with an empty Coca-Cola crate. After a Black cab driver
took Lewis for treatment by a local Black doctor, Lewis rejoined the
Freedom Riders, who made their way to Jackson, Mississippi, where
scores were arrested and sent to a notorious state prison known as
Parchman Farm.

By 1963, Lewis had gone to jail dozens of times and become
legendary within the Black student protest movement for his moral
and physical courage, a bravery made all the more conspicuous by
his quiet manner and slight, five-feet-five-inch build. When one of
the first chairmen of SNCC, Charles "Chuck" McDew, abruptly quit
that summer, the fledgling group summoned Lewis from Nashville
and chose him by acclamation to take McDew's place. Lewis assumed
that role just in time to represent SNCC at the March on Washington. On the steps of the Lincoln Memorial, he delivered a speech that
became famous for its call for "one man, one vote," but also notorious among SNCC's rank and file when march organizers pressured
Lewis to take out language criticizing the administration of President
John F. Kennedy for offering "too little, too late" in its proposed civil
rights legislation.

Although SNCC had started the 1965 voting rights campaign in
Selma, at the last minute its members voted to boycott the march to
Montgomery in protest over what they saw as the unnecessary risk of
violence and the way that the Southern Christian Leadership Conference, the older civil rights group led by Martin Luther King Jr.,
had taken over strategy and planning. Lewis chose to join the Sunday
march anyway, and he was at the front of the procession, wearing a
tan raincoat and a collegiate backpack, when he was approached by a
TV reporter for comment. "We're marching today to dramatize to the

nation and to dramatize to the world the hundreds of thousands of Negro citizens who are denied the right to vote," Lewis said. Then, with the TV cameras still rolling, a phalanx of blue-uniformed Alabama state troopers, their faces covered with gas masks, advanced on the six hundred marchers and ordered them to retreat. Instead, the protesters began to kneel in prayer. Hurling tear gas, the troopers shoved violently into the marchers and knocked Lewis to the ground. A trooper struck him on the head with a nightstick as police horses thundered overhead. "I thought I was going to die on that bridge," Lewis recalled. But unlike the beatings Lewis had suffered in the past, this one was witnessed by some 48 million Americans on national television, thanks to a CBS Special Report and other TV coverage of the attack.

THE DAY AFTER BLOODY SUNDAY, SAMMY YOUNGE JOINED MORE than a hundred outraged Tuskegee students who turned out for a hastily convened meeting of a campus activist group called the Tuskegee Institute Advancement League (TIAL). The group voted to send a delegation to the state capitol in Montgomery with a petition condemning the Selma attack. Younge was chosen to raise transportation funds, and he threw himself into the task with newfound passion. He went from dorm to dorm with a plastic bucket and collected $1,200 in just a few days, enough to pay for several buses to bring students to the capitol that Wednesday morning.

On Tuesday, Dr. King led another procession to the Pettus Bridge in Selma, but then ordered a retreat in the face of armed police assembled on the other side. After what become known as "Turnaround Tuesday," King declared a temporary halt as a lawsuit was filed to lift a city injunction against the march. Hearing about the stand-down order in Selma, the Tuskegee students voted to proceed with their trip to Montgomery anyway. Before dawn the next day, seven hundred boarded buses for the forty-mile drive west to the Alabama capital, clutching paper bags packed with bologna sandwiches and apples.

If the students appeared on their way to "a picnic," as TIAL president Gwen Patton described the departure, the first day in Montgomery became more like a soggy encampment. When the group arrived at the capitol building, they discovered that George Wallace, Alabama's segregationist governor, had no intention of coming outside to accept their petition. The students also hadn't bargained on the antipathy of conservative Black ministers who denied them access to their churches to use the bathrooms. Stuck outside all afternoon, the students resorted to forming walls of picket signs to surround anyone who needed to answer nature's call. Later they jokingly referred to the demonstration "the toilet revolution." As darkness fell, so did a steady rain, and all but some sixty students drove back to Tuskegee rather than face a sleepless night out in the cold.

After being inspired to go to Montgomery by the attack on John Lewis, the Tuskegee protesters encountered SNCC's second-in-command, executive secretary James Forman, when they arrived at the capitol. A heavyset man with bushy, unkempt hair and an utterly haphazard style of dress, Jim Forman, as he was known to everyone, was thirty-six years old and had come to his activism by a more circuitous route than most of his younger comrades. Born in Chicago, Forman was sent as an infant to live in rural northern Mississippi with a grandmother he knew as "Mama Jane" and whose four-room house had no electricity, indoor plumbing, or even an outhouse. He was given his first reading lessons at home by his Aunt Thelma, a schoolteacher, and didn't begin formal education until the second grade, after he moved back to Chicago to live with his mother, Octavia, and her husband, a man named James Rufus. Only years later did Forman learn that his birth father was a jitney cab driver named Jackson Forman who sometimes stopped to refuel his taxi at the gas station run by his stepfather.

A bright but restless student, Forman struggled to fit in as he bounced from a Catholic elementary school to a public high school, then to a vocational school and a stressful three-year stint in the segregated Air Force. Discharged from the military, he enrolled at the University of Southern California in Los Angeles, where he was falsely accused of robbery, beaten by a white prison officer, and briefly hospitalized for a psychological breakdown. Only after returning to

Chicago did Forman start to find a sense of mission as he enrolled at Roosevelt University, a haven for Black military veterans. He became student body president and a disciple of the distinguished Black sociologist St. Clair Drake. Further graduate study at Boston University convinced Forman that he wanted to become involved in the civil rights movement, and after the federal government intervened to force the desegregation of high schools in Little Rock in 1957, he headed south to organize in Arkansas.

In 1961, Forman was helping poor Blacks register to vote in southern Tennessee when he came to the attention of the sit-in leaders who had started SNCC and Ella Baker, the veteran civil rights leader who had encouraged them to form their own organization of college-age students and recent graduates. Forman was hired for the job of creating a proper headquarters for the nascent network of field organizers, and he proved to possess a unique talent for administration. Moving to Atlanta and taking over SNCC's first office in a tiny room on Auburn Avenue, Forman created a payroll and bookkeeping system and began hiring a staff. He formed a communications department to deal with the press and a research operation to dig up property records and other documents that could assist organizers as they went into Klan-infested rural areas. "Write it down," became Forman's watchword as he demanded that visiting fieldworkers produce affidavits memorializing all of their activities. He also enforced a code of strict egalitarianism, insisting that no job was too small for anyone at SNCC. Any volunteer, Black or white, who showed up at the Atlanta headquarters expecting to be sent immediately into the field would instead be handed a broom, then watch as Forman himself pitched in to sweep the floors and mop the bathroom.

AFTER SNCC VOTED TO PULL OUT OF THE 1965 MARCH FROM Selma, Jim Forman decided to head straight to Montgomery and organize a separate demonstration at the capitol. When he learned that the Tuskegee contingent had arrived in Montgomery as well, he saw an opportunity to combine the two protests and instruct the students in the discipline of nonviolent protest. "Everybody sit down," Forman shouted when police protecting the capitol went into V-formation and seemed ready to attack. In the middle of the night, he persuaded one of the uncooperative Black churches to open its doors and allow the students to come out of the rain and sleep on a concrete basement floor.

When Forman first observed Sammy Younge among the students outside the capitol, he didn't know what to make of him. "In the early part of the day, he was an amorphous personage to me," Forman recalled. Forman also had no idea that Younge was also a military veteran who was missing a kidney and taking a unique health risk by spending the night out in the rain. The next morning, as Forman saw Younge board a bus back to Tuskegee, he was disappointed. "I'm going to try to get students on the campus to come back here," Younge said, "because we have to have a unified student body." Forman shrugged and murmured, "Okay man," assuming that he would never see the earnest college boy again.

But Younge made good on his promise. As the Montgomery protest stretched into the following week, he returned several times, bringing reinforcements and impressing Forman with his efforts to boost morale and maintain order. The following Tuesday, Younge helped SNCC organizers assemble more than a thousand demonstrators to picket the capitol again. In a scene reminiscent of Bloody Sunday, mounted police stampeded the protesters and flayed them with long sticks designed to have a wider reach and nastier sting than billy clubs.

Other SNCC leaders took notice of Younge. One was Willie Ricks, a short, moon-faced Georgia native with a rousing speaking delivery and a pioneering fashion sense. Ricks was known for wearing dark sunglasses and all-black slacks and shirts at a time most SNCC organizers still favored blue jeans and denim jackets. He was also a hard man to impress. "Mr. Say ain't the man, Mr. Do is the man," Ricks liked to say, expressing his disdain for civil rights workers who talked big but didn't work hard in the trenches. Ricks recalled how Younge was "baptized" in the struggle in Montgomery, and turned out to be one of only "five or ten out of hundreds" committed enough to "take it beyond the marches."

Younge also caught the eye of Stokely Carmichael, the rangy, irreverent New Yorker who was spearheading a drive to register voters and organize a new independent political party in the Black Belt of Alabama. As a graduate of Howard University, the prestigious historically Black college in Washington, D.C., Carmichael knew all about the Negro elite. He marveled that Younge, as "a good-looking cat" with expensive clothes and his own car, was willing to jeopardize his "big man on campus" status for the sake of his political convictions. "He was isolated—you know, the same shit everybody goes through in the Negro college campuses," as Carmichael put it, with his glib sense of humor, in describing how Younge's activism was seen by many of his peers at the Tuskegee Institute. "He told them, fuck it, he was going with SNCC."

In the months after the protest in Montgomery, Sammy Younge became one of the most visible activists on the Tuskegee campus. Putting away his preppy sports coats and polished loafers, he dressed in denim overalls and his old Navy boots, and wore a puffy railroad engineer's cap over his long, loose curls. Friends noticed a change in the way he talked—with "a little hum in his voice at the end of a sentence, like a preacher," recalled Tuskegee classmate Ruby Taylor. Younge organized a picket of a local A&P supermarket that refused to offer summer jobs to Black students. He led a protest to demand use of the city swimming pool, prompting whites to throw manure into the water and crushed glass onto the diving board. Town officials shut down the pool, then claimed that they didn't have enough money to clean and reopen it. Later in the summer, Younge and other TIAL leaders tried to integrate three white churches. When five hundred Black students gathered at a Methodist church one Sunday, a white mob attacked them. A local café owner and suspected member of the Ku Klux Klan made a special point of chasing after Younge, thrusting a .32 caliber pistol into the tender side of his stomach where his kidney had been removed.

Yet when Younge returned to school in the fall of 1965, he appeared to lose interest in the struggle and typed out a letter of resignation from the TIAL. He dusted off his tweed jackets and spent most of the semester partying. One classmate remembered him climbing onto a dorm fire escape and serenading passing girls with Smokey Robinson tunes. Some friends attributed the change to the bomb threats that Younge's parents received as result of his activism. Others thought he might be afraid for his fragile health after his first stint in jail, while registering voters in a nearby Lee County. But others concluded that "the Tuskegee system got to him," as a classmate named George Ware put it, and that Younge didn't want to jeopardize a comfortable future in the Black middle class.

After moving off-campus in November, Younge threw himself a twenty-first birthday party and invited Carmichael. That was when he drunkenly confessed to his older friend that he was "putting down civil rights" because his privileged friends on campus made fun of him for working with SNCC. "I told him I thought there would be some people who would do that," Carmichael recalled, "but as far as I was concerned, we could still drink wine any time."

Only once during this fall period did Younge's desire to organize resurface—after Jonathan Daniels's killer was acquitted. Daniels was a young white seminarian from New Hampshire who had come south for the Selma march and become friendly with Stokely Carmichael. "We had some real good talks," Carmichael recalled of Daniels. "He was shocked and pained by the racism, injustice, and poverty he was seeing. And he really seemed interested in black culture." In August, Carmichael invited Daniels to participate in a protest in Fort Deposit, Alabama, against a storekeeper who was blocking voter registration efforts. The two were arrested for disturbing the peace and sent to the county jail in Hayneville with twenty other protesters. Carmichael posted bond so that he could raise bail money for the rest of the prisoners. He didn't witness what happened two weeks later when the others were released without explanation.

While some of the freed protesters searched for a phone to call for transportation, others went to a nearby grocery store to buy soda pop. As they approached, Tom Coleman, a local highway worker and part-time sheriff's deputy, stepped out of the store with a shotgun. Daniels moved to shield a seventeen-year-old Tuskegee student named Ruby Sales who was part of the group. Coleman opened fired, killing Daniels and wounding a Catholic priest from Chicago named Richard Morrisroe. Less than two months later, an all-white jury acquitted Coleman of murder charges after only two hours of deliberation, and the next day he was back playing dominoes in front of the courthouse where the trial took place. When word of the verdict reached Tuskegee, Sammy Younge was so upset that he rounded up a group of students to march into town in protest. Then he placed a coffin in the middle of the campus accompanied by a sign that read "Alabama Justice."

SHORTLY BEFORE CHRISTMAS, YOUNGE TOLD FRIENDS THAT HE was ready to plunge back into civil rights work. A week later, he was in Lowndes County, helping Carmichael put up the tents for the evicted Black sharecroppers who had registered to vote. When Younge returned to Tuskegee, he told friends about his dream of organizing a new independent Black political party, just as Carmichael was doing. He said he planned to start by registering as many new voters as possible in the surrounding rural areas, then to call a meeting to propose the idea of forming a Black Panther Party in Macon County.

In Alabama, voter registration offices opened for business only twice a month—one of the many obstacles the state had put in place to keep Blacks from participating in elections. The first Monday of 1966, January 3, was one of those dates, so Sammy Younge made plans to spend the day at the Macon County courthouse in downtown Tuskegee helping applicants fill out forms. When scores of Black citizens showed up at the courthouse, an elderly registrar tried to make them go away. The registrar said he was busy purging the voting rolls, or removing names of county residents who had died or moved way. When Younge protested and demanded to know the man's name, the registrar threatened to call the sheriff and pulled out a red and yellow pocket knife. "I'll take this knife and cut your guts out," the old man threatened. "Spill your guts all over the floor."

Retreating to a nearby diner, Younge found a pay phone and called SNCC headquarters in Atlanta. He asked workers there to notify the Justice Department, which under the new Voting Rights Act of 1965 was charged with preventing the kind of obstructionism exhibited by the ornery registrar. By the time Younge got back to the courthouse, an FBI agent had appeared, and he questioned everyone involved in the standoff. Under orders, the registrar began to cooperate, and Younge stayed at the courthouse registering new Black voters until he finished shortly after five in the afternoon.

A friend had invited Younge to a party that night, so he went to a liquor store to buy wine. The festivities started around eight in the evening and grew more animated as the night went on. Someone started playing bongo drums, and Younge danced with abandon. As more people arrived and food ran out, Younge and his latest girlfriend went out to buy pork chops and bread. When the meat was gone, someone found cans of tuna, but there was no mayonnaise to make sandwiches. So Younge volunteered to go out again, this time alone, and also agreed to pick up a pack of cigarettes for a partygoer who had run out.

At roughly a quarter to midnight, Younge pulled his blue Volkswagen Beetle into the Standard Oil service station in downtown Tuskegee. The station was a block from the Macon County courthouse where he had spent the day, with its century-old bell tower and decorative gargoyles. Outside the courthouse stood a granite statue of an infantryman in a gray uniform and crumpled hat—the sort of Confederate army memorial that could be found all over the South, recasting the Civil War as a noble Lost Cause battle for states' rights. Near the gas station was a Greyhound bus depot, and in between was an alley where four Black students sat inside a car that one of them had borrowed from his father for the night.

Parking his car on the street, Younge entered the gas station and approached the attendant, a frail-looking sixty-eight-year-old with a jutting chin and a beaklike nose named Marvin Segrest.

"I want to use the restroom," Younge said.

Segrest pointed to a bathroom outside, behind the station.

Younge said he wanted to use the public restroom inside the station.

Reaching below the counter, Segrest pulled out a .38 caliber silver pistol.

Younge asked if he could at least fill his car up with gas.

"No, just leave and don't come back," Segrest snapped.

As Younge exited the station, and went toward his car, Segrest pursued him, waving the gun.

"Come back over onto my property," the attendant called out when Younge reached the street.

"No, you can't shoot me from here," Younge shouted back. "You can't see me."

Ducking behind the car, Younge watched as Segrest attempted to take aim in the darkness. A bag of golf clubs lay nearby, waiting to be loaded onto a Greyhound bus that was pulling into the depot. Younge grabbed a club from the bag and ran toward the bus as Segrest fired and missed. "I'm going to get on the bus," Younge called out. "Come on the bus and shoot me."

Hoping to defuse the situation, the bus driver stepped down and tried to talk sense to Segrest. "You shouldn't shoot that boy," the driver said. "If you do, there's going to be trouble for you and everybody." Temporarily reassured, Younge came out of the bus as it pulled away. He went in the direction of his car, but before he crossed the alley Segrest fired another bullet that struck Younge just below his left eye. He slumped forward, his knees grazing the pavement before he rolled sideways onto his back.

A half an hour later, the phone rang at the home of Eldridge Burns, another Tuskegee student activist who lived with his parents off-campus. Burns had gone to sleep, and his mother picked up. "Sammy's been shot," the caller blurted. Awakened, Burns went to the Younge home near campus, and found Stevie Younge in hysterics. "They killed my brother," Stevie cried. "The white man got him." When Burns arrived at the Standard Oil station, several policeman were gathered, but no one could find Younge. Then a cab carrying another student activist pulled up, and the driver pointed to a shadowy figure in the alleyway. "What's that body doing over there?" the cabbie asked.

As the group approached the alley, they found a gruesome sight. Younge was sprawled face-up on the pavement, one arm across his chest and the other stretched out to his side. A pool of blood stretched all the way from the back of his head, where Segrest's bullet had entered under his eye, past the bottom of his shoes. More blood oozed from Younge's face, across his eyebrows, and down his chin. Next to the body lay the golf club Younge had grabbed outside the Greyhound bus. The white grip of the club was visible, but the shaft disappeared into the dark red puddle surrounding Younge's lifeless frame.

THE MURDER OF SAMMY YOUNGE JR. THAT JANUARY NIGHT WOULD be remembered, if it was remembered at all, as a footnote in most accounts of the civil rights struggle. President Lyndon Johnson made no mention of the case, as he had when two white civil rights sympathizers, James Reeb and Viola Liuzzo, were killed in Alabama the year before. Although *The New York Times* ran a front-page story on Younge's death by Gene Roberts, the Atlanta-based reporter covering the civil rights beat, most other newspapers around the country picked up a perfunctory United Press International wire service account that described Segrest as a "nice, quiet old man." Eleven months later, an all-white jury reached the same conclusion when Segrest went on trial. The defense argued that Younge had been rude to the old man on several previous visits to the gas station. "I'm going to kill him," Segrest told one witness that night. "He has harassed and deviled me all year, and I am sick and tired of it." After only seventy-one minutes, the jury took pity on Segrest and acquitted him of second degree murder.

Within Black America, however, the news of Sammy Younge's murder reverberated through a generation of young people who were reaching a breaking point of frustration with the gospel of nonviolence and racial integration preached by Dr. King. For Jim Forman, it added to a sense of despair and burnout that would soon lead him to pull back from his role at SNCC, opening the way for its take-over by younger, more radical leaders. Forman was in New York City on a fundraising trip when he heard a bulletin on the city's all-news radio station, WINS, about the killing of an Alabama civil rights activist named Sammy Younge Jr. Forman cursed under his breath, then phoned SNCC headquarters for confirmation and learned that the funeral was scheduled for the next day in Tuskegee.

As Forman flew to Atlanta to rendezvous with SNCC colleagues, he thought of other young Black men who had been wantonly murdered, only to have their white killers go free. His mind went to Emmett Till, the fourteen-year-old Chicago boy lynched while visiting his grandparents in Mississippi, after he was accused of flirting with the wife of a white shop owner. Forman thought of Mack Charles Parker, another military veteran, who was shot by a white mob and thrown off Louisiana's Pearl River Bridge after being falsely charged with raping a white woman. Forman recalled having the premonition, in that first week of the January, that "the year 1966 was going to be decisive, a turning point. I felt we were not going to remain tactically non-violent too much longer."

By the time Forman arrived at SNCC headquarters, he had lost the heart to see another young Black man in a coffin. "Cleve, I just don't want to go, I can't make it," he confided to Cleveland Sellers, SNCC's program secretary. "I'm just tired of going to funerals for civil-rights people." Sellers insisted that Forman had to show his face in Tuskegee, that it was his duty as SNCC's executive secretary. They set out on the two-hour drive from Atlanta with Stanley Wise, another young SNCC leader who like Stokely Carmichael had joined the organization as a student at Howard University. "That could be you," Forman recalled thinking as he stood over Younge's open casket the next day. In the pouring rain, the SNCC men followed Younge's family to a hillside graveyard. Tears in his eyes, Forman plucked a handful of fern leaves and threw them onto the casket as Younge's body was lowered into the muddy ground.

By 1966, Cleve Sellers was part of a SNCC faction that wanted to see the organization take a stand against the U.S. escalation in

Vietnam. With the murder of Younge, a Navy veteran, this group saw
an opportunity to force the issue. "The absolute absurdity of a man
having to die for attempting to do something as basically human as
using a toilet filled us with rage," Sellers recalled. "SNCC's members
could not help recognizing the gross contradictions between the freedom that Americans were killing and dying for in Vietnam and the
race hatred that motivated Younge's murder. The fact that Sammy
was a veteran made his death all the more galling." After the shooting, the antiwar faction drafted a statement and persuaded SNCC
chairman John Lewis to issue it at a press conference three days later.
A year before Dr. King would deliver a famous antiwar speech at Riv-
erside Church in New York City, the statement made SNCC the first
civil rights group to come out publicly against the Vietnam conflict.

   In tone as well as substance, the Vietnam statement marked a
stark departure. Instead of familiar civil rights appeals to the Bible and
the U.S. Constitution, it rang with the new language of international
human rights. The statement was drafted by Gloria Larry, an elegant,
French-speaking graduate of the University of California at Berkeley
who came to Alabama in 1965 to work in a SNCC school for Black
youngsters in Selma. Introduced to Carmichael, Larry was smitten by
his dashing looks and roguish charm. They became close, and he invited her to join his voter registration campaign in Lowndes County.
Larry had studied abroad in Paris, where she befriended young Africans battling French rule and embraced their anticolonial worldview.
"Sammy Younge was murdered because U.S. law is not being enforced," she wrote in the SNCC antiwar statement. "Vietnamese are
being murdered because the United States is pursuing an aggressive
policy in violation of international law. The U.S. is no respecter of
persons or laws when such persons or laws run counter to its need
and desires." Further on, Larry added an expression of "sympathy . . .
for men in this country who are unwilling to respond to a military
draft." As it would turn out, that nod to the draft resistance movement that was beginning to sweep Berkeley and other American
college campuses would make far more news than anything else in
SNCC's antiwar statement.

Sammy Younge was also the first Black activist to be killed while still enrolled in college. News of his murder less than a mile from the Tuskegee campus hit home with Black students, particularly children of the middle class. In the following weeks, thousands of them, many for the first time, marched in protest in Tuskegee and at numerous other historically Black colleges across the South. For friends who knew Younge personally, grief was compounded by indignation when word got out about what his killer, Marvin Segrest, was telling authorities. Segrest tried to make it sound as though Younge was drunk and out of control, rather than standing up for his rights. "Call him nigger, send him to the back, he wasn't going," Younge's friend Eldridge Burns fumed, imagining what unfolded between Younge and Segrest at the filling station. "He was going to sit up there and tell you he wasn't a nigger. You treat him like a man."

In New York City, news of the murder reached Kathleen Neal, a childhood friend of Younge's who came to know him when her father, a sociology professor from Texas, accepted a position at the Tuskegee Institute. Neal recalled that her father was the kind of cultivated Black man who "wanted his children to grow up knowing nothing about racial prejudice" and that he viewed Tuskegee an "ideal community" in that respect. From Alabama, the Neal family moved to Asia, where her father worked for the Foreign Service and Neal blossomed into a distinctively attractive teen with honey skin and wide-set, piercing blue eyes. Returning to America, she finished high school at George School, a private Quaker academy in Pennsylvania, and then enrolled at Oberlin College in Ohio, which her parents picked for her because of its long tradition of educating Blacks and women.

Neal found college boring after her years of traveling the globe, and she dropped out of Oberlin and moved to Washington, D.C. She took a job as a secretarial assistant at the Community Relations Service, a new agency designed to support Black urban neighborhoods launched under the 1964 Civil Rights Act. When Neal's parents nagged her to go back to college, she applied for transfer to Barnard College in New York City. But after hearing the news of Sammy Younge's murder just as the spring semester was about to begin, Neal left Barnard and starting working full-time for SNCC—the first step in an odyssey that would soon lead her to a radical new life under the married name of Kathleen Cleaver.

One more friend of Sammy Younge's was shaken by his death in a way that carried omens for the future. Stokely Carmichael was in Lowndes County when he got a phone call with the news in the middle of the night. Carmichael was told that a protest rally was planned in Tuskegee the following morning, and that everyone expected him to be there. But instead, the normally swaggering picture of self-confidence suffered what an Army therapist who later interviewed him for a draft physical characterized as an episode of psychological "decompensation"—otherwise known as a nervous breakdown. Carmichael thought back to his intimate conversations with Younge. His mind filled with memories of Jonathan Daniels, the white seminary student who was killed after Carmichael invited him to a protest. Carmichael recalled the long car ride to New Hampshire for Daniels's funeral, and how he broke down crying when he met Jonathan's parents. Overcome by feelings of guilt and depression, Carmichael couldn't bring himself to go to Tuskegee and rally its grieving community. "I didn't have any strength, man," he admitted later, "so I got me three bottles of wine and drank one for me and one for Sammy and one for Jonathan Daniels."

CHAPTER 2

Humiliated in Atlanta

Three days after Sammy Younge's murder, Julian Bond returned to his desk at SNCC headquarters in Atlanta to find a message from a twenty-five-year-old local radio reporter named Ed Spivia. Spivia wanted to get Bond's comment on the statement that chairman John Lewis had issued in the wake of Younge's killing condemning the U.S. escalation in Vietnam. Velvet-voiced and boyishly handsome, with a formal style of dress and speech that cloaked a mischievous wit and a dreamy love of writing poetry, Bond was accustomed to talking with the white press as SNCC's director of communications. But Spivia was contacting him in another capacity. The previous June, Bond had won a race to represent an Atlanta district in Georgia's House of Representatives, and he was scheduled to take his seat the next week. At Lewis's press conference, reporters asked him where Bond stood on the war, and Lewis said he couldn't speak for his colleague. So the enterprising radio reporter was calling to inquire directly: Did Bond agree with Lewis on Vietnam?

Bond had played no role in drafting the antiwar statement, and was attending a meeting at the local YMCA at the time of Lewis's press briefing. Still, he called Spivia back and earnestly answered his questions. "Yes, I do," Bond repeated as Spivia twice asked him to confirm on the record that he endorsed the Vietnam statement. "I'm not taking a stand against stopping world communism, and I'm not taking a stand in favor of the Viet Cong," he explained. "What I'm saying is that, first, that I don't believe in that war, that particular war." Then Bond went a step further. "I'm against all war," he said. "Because I'm against war, I'm against the draft."

Spivia bore down. Would Bond be willing to burn his own draft card? he asked. No, Bond ventured, he wouldn't do so personally, and he wouldn't encourage anyone else to. But he added that he thought how to protest the war should be "up to the individual," and that he respected anyone willing to accept the consequences of such a public step. "I would admire the courage of anyone who burns his draft card," Bond said.

Only days shy of his twenty-sixth birthday, Julian Bond was thoughtful beyond his years but still a political novice, and his guileless response to the persistent radio reporter betrayed both qualities. Known by his middle name, Horace Julian Bond was christened after his father, Horace Mann Bond, a distinguished educator who came from a long line of Black teachers and ministers. When Julian was five, his father was named president of Lincoln University, a historically Black college outside Philadelphia, and the family moved into a stately white house in the city's suburbs. For high school, Bond went to George School, the nearby Quaker academy that Kathleen Neal would later attend. As the school's only Black student at the time, he found it a lonely and sometimes insulting experience. After Bond began dating a white girl, a dean instructed him not to wear his varsity jacket when the couple left campus. But it was at George School, studying Quakerism's nonviolent teachings, that Bond discovered pacifism, the principled position reflected in his statement to Spivia that he was "against war."

After his father became a dean of Atlanta University, Bond enrolled at Morehouse College, where he majored in English and joined the civil rights movement. He participated in the lunch counter protests that swept the South in 1960, then served as one of the first volunteers for SNCC, the student-led organization that grew out of those sit-ins. In his last semester, Bond dropped out of Morehouse without earning a degree to take a job as a sportswriter for a local

Black newspaper. He began to moonlight as SNCC's communications director, a part-time job that in time became permanent. With little stomach for the dangers of field organizing, Bond was happy to interact with the press and to edit the SNCC newspaper, where he occasionally published his own poems. (*"I, too, hear America singing,"* began one of them, borrowing from Walt Whitman, *"But from where I stand/I can only hear Little Richard/And Fats Domino . . ."*) Already married, with a baby at home, Bond also needed the $85 a month that came with the job, which was the highest salary on SNCC's meager payroll.

In 1965, a Supreme Court ruling created eight new legislative districts in heavily Black areas across Georgia, and a record twenty-three Black candidates jumped into the race. At first, Bond had to be convinced that he was the right person to run in the new 136th District, an impoverished Black neighborhood in southeast Atlanta. Not only was Bond middle-class; he was so elite-looking that Royal Crown Cola had once hired him to model for an advertising poster. But his SNCC colleague Ivanhoe Donaldson convinced Bond that his clean-cut image was precisely what was needed to win over older Black voters. After SNCC offered to pay a $500 entry fee, Bond announced his candidacy and overcame his natural reserve to stump door-to-door. That June, he beat two older Black candidates with 82 percent of the vote and the highest turnout of any assembly race in the state.

Despite that political initiation, Bond was utterly unprepared for the furor that erupted over his Vietnam remarks. "Defiance of Draft Call Urged by SNCC Leader," read the front-page headline in the next day's *Atlanta Constitution*, the city's top morning newspaper, under the byline of veteran political reporter Bill Shipp. Instead of focusing on the news that SNCC had come out against the war, Shipp highlighted the draft card controversy. He quoted Bond as saying he would "admire the courage" of card burners without including his caveat about their having to face the consequences. Incensed by the news reports, Georgia's governor, lieutenant governor, and dozens of state lawmakers condemned Bond by the end of the day. A downstate Republican named Jones Lane vowed to prevent Bond from taking his legislative seat. This "is not because of race," Lane fumed. "It is because of un-American attitude."

Not recognizing the severity of Bond's predicament at first, older civil rights leaders were slow to come to his defense. Roy Wilkins, the imperious president of the National Association for the Advancement of Colored People, put out a statement insisting that Lewis and Bond didn't speak for "what is loosely called the civil rights movement" in denouncing the war and condoning draft resistance. Pressed for comment while on vacation in California, Dr. King, a pacifist himself, made only vague statements about the right to free speech. In Georgia, those tepid remarks provided cover for influential white moderates. *Atlanta Constitution* publisher Eugene Patterson, a civil rights supporter who had condemned the 1963 Birmingham church bombing in which four young Black girls died, and resisted FBI efforts to publish dirt about King's infidelities, wrote a scathing editorial. "The lost faith in America that was reflected in the SNCC fulminations does not reflect Negro thought," Patterson assured his readers.

By Sunday night, it had become clear what awaited Bond when the state legislature convened the following morning. Plotting over a meal of barbecued wild hogs at Atlanta's Henry Grady Hotel, anti-Bond legislators agreed on how to make their case. They planned to invoke a dusty provision that allowed the assembly to punish "disorderly behavior or misconduct" with "censure, fine, imprisonment or expulsion." Across town, Bond huddled with his SNCC colleagues and ten other Blacks elected to the new legislature. Bond was "really shaken" and "very, very scared," according to John Lewis's account. Some of the Black legislators urged Bond to issue what one report characterized as "a balancing patriotic statement." But already white lawmakers had signaled a statement wouldn't be enough. "This boy has to come before us humbly, recant, and just plain beg a little," one white legislator had publicly suggested. By midnight, it seemed that "every other Negro in the delegation was against Julian," according to Ivanhoe Donaldson. But then Jim Forman came into the room and made a passionate case for not backing down. Bond should not have to beg, Forman pointed out, for a seat to which the voters of his district had overwhelmingly elected him.

THE GEORGIA STATE CAPITOL IN ATLANTA WAS A CORINTHIAN-columned structure crowned by a gold-encrusted dome, on top of which rose a torch-bearing statue known as "Miss Freedom." In front of the building stood statues that spoke to darker chapters in Georgia's past. One likeness was of Tom Watson, a Gilded Age populist who soured into a white supremacist and anti-Semite; another was of General John Brown Gordon, a Confederate Army hero later suspected of secret membership in the Ku Klux Klan. In the House of Representatives chamber on the second floor of the building, rows of worn wooden desks faced an ornate dais. Above was a public gallery that for a century was segregated by race. In 1961, Bond had joined a group of Black protesters who quietly snuck into the whites-only area before capitol guards chased them away. "Mr. Doorkeeper, get those niggers out of the white section of the gallery," a segregationist legislator bellowed as he pointed up from the House floor.

On the morning of Monday, January 10, 1966, Bond returned to the capitol to take his assigned seat in that same chamber. On a back-row desk sat a small metal name plate printed "136th—Julian Bond." Bond was clad soberly in a three-piece blue suit, with a white shirt, thin dark tie, and a pocket watch dangling from his vest. Surprised, one white lawmaker quipped to Roy Reed of *The New York Times* that he expected Bond to be "bearded and unkempt," instead of looking, as Reed put it, "as if he was on his way to a college dance." As soon as Bond entered the room, he was escorted to his desk and instructed to remain seated while the 204 other elected legislators rose to be sworn in. While the oath of office was read, Bond tried to look as calm as possible. He pressed his fists against his chin and gazed into space, an outbreak of red hives across his mocha-colored face providing the only evidence of his inner distress.

After that mortifying spectacle, Bond was dismissed from the chamber while the House took up a petition for his ouster signed by more than seventy legislators. Exhausted from a sleepless night of drinking bourbon and chain-smoking Salem cigarettes, Bond attempted to take a nap in an empty back room. He placed three chairs together and struggled to straddle his lanky frame across them, then gave up and stretched out across a Formica-covered table. In the hallway outside, Jim Forman bucked up scores of pro-Bond demonstrators. Bond's lawyer and brother-in-law, Charles Moore, phoned the two Black candidates who had lost the race for the 136th district and persuaded them to come to the capitol to testify on their rival's behalf. Meanwhile, Bond's father, Horace Mann Bond, fetched soup and crackers and fretted to newsmen about his son's fragile state of mind. "He's taking this harder than I wish he had," the elder Bond told the *Atlanta Constitution*'s Bill Shipp. To *Newsweek* magazine's Marshall Frady, he regretted that his son had ever gotten mixed up in politics. "My God, I didn't raise my boy to be a Georgia legislator," said Horace Bond. "I'd hoped he would go into a more academic occupation."

When Julian Bond was summoned into the packed House chamber for a rules committee hearing that afternoon, the scene resembled a criminal trial. He was asked to climb to the dais in the front of the chamber to be questioned by a Republican former lawmaker named Denmark "Dennie" Groover, who had been assigned the role of prosecutor.

"Do you admire the courage of persons who burn their draft cards?" Groover asked, eyeing Bond disdainfully over the glasses perched on his nose.

"I admire people who take an action," Bond replied carefully, "and I admire people who feel strongly enough about their convictions to take an action like that knowing the consequences they will face." Bond's voice grew firmer as he added he would never burn his own draft card or urge others to take such a step. "I have never suggested or counseled or advocated that anyone burn their draft card," he insisted.

But Dennie Groover had a surprise in store. He had acquired a tape of Ed Spivia's radio interview with Bond, and he played it over the House loudspeakers. Now everyone there could hear the exact words Bond had used: "I'm against all war. . . . I don't think people ought to participate in it. . . . Because I'm against war, I'm against the draft."

A hush fell over chamber, as if the existence of the tape was proof of guilt, no matter how measured Bond's tone. His words were "treasonous" and provided "aid and comfort to the enemy," Groover declared as soon as the tape finished playing. Next, a rotund, downstate oilman named Bobby Pafford came to the dais. Referring to SNCC as "Snick"—the way the group's title was often spelled in the press—Pafford denounced "the infamous Mr. Bond" as "one whose Snicking pursues not freedom for us but victory for our enemies" and had despoiled the "fresh air and pleasant living known as Georgia." At six in the evening, the rules committee went into private session and an hour later announced its verdict—23-to-3 for expulsion. The vote came as no surprise to the legislators and newsmen waiting outside. "I don't even care if he's innocent of making those remarks," a Savannah Republican named Arthur J. Funk admitted to *Newsweek*'s Frady. "All these people tend to think that way, and every day he's on the floor is a disgrace." Another lawmaker demonstrated his contempt by swiping the metal name plate off Bond's desk and announcing that he was going to "take this tag home and hang it on my outhouse door."

The full House vote came quickly, and it was crushing: 184-to-12 for expulsion. Bond stared "at the tally board through a blur of tears," according to his biographer John Neary. In the middle of the night, Jim Forman sent a telegram to Liz Sutherland, the head of the SNCC office in New York City, describing the scene. "Everyone, including Julian, is in a state of shock," Forman wrote. The next morning, twenty-three U.S. congressmen wired telegrams to Georgia governor Carl Sanders protesting the ouster. Dr. King announced that he would cut short his California vacation and lead a protest march through the streets of Atlanta.

But by then, it was clear that the battle was lost, and that a long war to win back Bond's seat lay ahead. The next day, when Bond met with Marshall Frady at Paschal's restaurant, a local SNCC hangout, he was in such a state of fatigue and disbelief that he couldn't finish his tomato sandwich. "It was the worst thing I'd ever been through in my life," Bond confessed. "It was all like a play with everything unreal. I couldn't believe it was happening." Still, Bond vowed to keep fighting. "I intend to do everything I can to take that seat," he said.

IN THE MONTHS LEADING UP TO 1966, JOHN LEWIS HAD TRAVELED the country in his role as SNCC chairman, meeting with donors and capitalizing on the fame he achieved on Bloody Sunday. Playing down internal tensions, Lewis tried to keep SNCC associated in the public mind with Dr. King's strategy of nonviolence and search for legislative remedies to racial injustice. Lewis saw this as a reflection of his own personal beliefs but also as a fundraising necessity. By the beginning of 1966, SNCC was running a $200,000 deficit, hadn't made payroll in several months, and was so far behind on its office bills that the phone company had cut back service at the Atlanta headquarters.

Now, even Lewis sensed that what had happened to Sammy Younge and to Julian Bond was shaking support for the old civil rights verities among his generation of activists. "The irony hit me very, very hard," Lewis recalled thinking as he saw the American flag draped over Younge's casket. "Here was a man who had served his country, a military veteran, and what had it gotten him?" A week later, Lewis was furious as he watched Bond leave the Georgia capitol in tears. "I couldn't believe this . . ." Lewis recalled thinking. "Once again, we were getting screwed. Was it any wonder that people in the movement were bailing out right and left, abandoning all hope of appealing to and working through a system that would do something like this?"

For the SNCC generation, Bond's ordeal also brought back bitter memories of the 1964 Democratic presidential convention in Atlantic City, and deepened the sense of disillusionment with mainstream party politics they felt after that experience. That drama had begun deep in rural Mississippi, when a group of brave local Blacks tried to register to vote for the first time. One was a stocky thirty-five-year-old native of Montgomery County with a resonant choir singer's voice named Fannie Lou Hamer. The twentieth child of Cotton Belt sharecroppers, Hamer received an early taste of Southern racism as a child when a white man poisoned her family's animal feed and killed off their mule and horses. She dropped out of school after the tenth grade to work on the farm, but knew how to read and do arithmetic well enough that she was later hired as a "timekeeper" on a plantation run by a sharecropping overseer named W. D. Marlow. When Hamer first attempted to register to vote in August of 1962, Marlow summoned her for a threatening lecture. "We're not ready for that in Mississippi now," Marlow said. "If you don't withdraw, I'll let you go." Hamer refused to stop and was kicked off the plantation, and had to scrounge for rental housing and a job at a cotton gin while she continued her quest to claim her voting rights.

Once Hamer overcame Mississippi's onerous literacy tests and poll tax requirements to become a legal voter, she threw herself into registering other Blacks with the help of organizers from SNCC. Excluded from the all-white primaries held by the state Democratic Party, the newly registered Blacks staged symbolic elections they called "Freedom Votes." That campaign led to an even more daring undertaking after President Kennedy was assassinated and his successor, Lyndon Johnson, announced his candidacy for the White House. The plan was to challenge the segregationist state delegation that was set to represent Mississippi at the 1964 convention in Atlantic City by sending a rival, democratically elected slate of Blacks and whites under a new banner: the Mississippi Freedom Democratic Party (MFDP). "All my life I've been sick and tired," Hamer told audiences as she barnstormed rural Mississippi, signing up new MFDP members by announcing her own candidacy for the U.S. Congress in the Democratic primary that June. "Now I'm sick and tired of being sick and tired."

Although Hamer lost that primary bid, she helped to recruit thousands of MFDP members and to bring 2,500 of them to a state nominating convention in early August at the Masonic Temple in Jackson, Mississippi. Joseph Rauh, a well-known white civil rights attorney, agreed to represent the MFDP, and reams of legal briefs and background papers were produced to support the challenge. Sixty-four

MFDP delegates were chosen, and on the last week of August they arrived in Atlantic City along with hundreds of hopeful supporters in a convoy of buses and cars. While the delegates checked into a small hotel where they shared beds and slept on the floor, scores of SNCC organizers kept a round-the-clock vigil on the oceanside boardwalk outside the convention hall.

In the absence of any suspense over who the Democratic nominee would be, the MFDP challenge became the biggest news story of the convention. When the credentials committee held a hearing on the matter, the major television networks carried it live. Dr. King spoke in support of the MFDP, but the highlight of the proceeding came when Hamer strode to a witness table to address the packed room of convention officials and reporters. Wearing a patterned dress, her hair curled, and her broad face gleaming under the TV lights, Hamer recounted the years of terror she had experienced seeking the right to vote. "We're going to make you wish you were dead," a white policeman told her after she was arrested and taken to a Montgomery County jail, where guards coerced two Black prisoners into beating Hamer on the hands and feet with a blackjack until her skin turned blue. "All of this on account of we wanted to register, to become first class citizens," Hamer told the rapt gathering. "If the Freedom Democratic Party is not seated now, I question America."

Still in Washington preparing to be crowned, President Johnson was irate that the Black delegates from Mississippi were disturbing the picture of party unity he hoped to paint, and threatening to provoke a walkout by white Southern delegates. As Hamer began her testimony to the credentials committee, Johnson forced TV networks to cut away by holding an unscheduled press conference at the White House at which he did nothing more than note the nine-month anniversary of Kennedy's assassination. Yet Hamer's testimony was so riveting that the networks re-aired it that evening, and she became even more of a national sensation. Just as it began to look as though the MFDP challenge might succeed, however, Johnson pressured members of the credentials committee to delay a vote and informed Minnesota senator Hubert Humphrey, whom he was considering for vice president, that he would get the nod only if he found a way of sidelining the Freedom Democrats.

Humphrey turned the job of coming up with a face-saving deal over to his political protégé, Minnesota attorney general Walter Mondale, who stood to be appointed to fill Humphrey's Senate seat if his mentor was tapped as Johnson's running mate. Mondale formed a subcommittee that, after long and tense deliberations, produced a short-term snub wrapped in a long-term promise. At future conventions, the Mondale group announced, the Democratic Party would no longer allow all-white convention delegations; and in the meantime, the MFDP would be offered two "at large" seats, which would allow a pair of Black delegates to sit on the convention floor without the right to participate in the nominating vote.

With tempers raging and nerves running raw, all the Black leaders present in Atlantic City crowded into a church near the convention hall to debate the token offer. Despite his televised pledge of support for the MFDP, Dr. King spoke in favor of accepting the compromise. He was joined by all the other veteran civil rights leaders in the room, including NAACP chairman Roy Wilkins, National Urban League president Whitney Young, and Bayard Rustin, the organizer of the March on Washington. Both furious and exhausted after the months of work they had put into supporting the delegate challenge, SNCC leaders told the room that the decision should be left up to the Freedom Democrats themselves. Fannie Lou Hamer spoke last, and in an unwavering voice made it clear that the Black delegates from Mississippi had no intention of accepting the demeaning consolation prize. "We didn't come all this way for no two seats," Hamer declared.

More insult was added to injury in the following days. Several white Mississippi delegates walked out of the convention anyway, rather than cast their votes for Johnson. Sympathetic Northern delegates slipped floor passes to MFDP members, but when they arrived to sit in the empty Mississippi seats the chairs had been taken away. On the boardwalk outside the convention hall, SNCC supporters continued to picket and sing freedom songs such as "We Shall Overcome" and "This Little Light of Mine." But their hearts were no longer in it, and many recalled that week in New Jersey as the moment when they gave up on trusting in white liberal allies and the two-party political system. "Never again were we lulled into believing that our task was exposing injustices so that the 'good' people of America could eliminate them," Cleve Sellers recalled. "After Atlanta City, our struggle was not for civil rights, but for liberation."

SIXTEEN MONTHS AFTER THAT ATLANTIC CITY DRAMA, JULIAN Bond's humiliation in Atlanta moved one of his friends in particular. Dorothy Miller, known to everyone as Dottie, was a petite Manhattan native with pixie-cut dark hair, bottle-thick glasses, and a New York City accent as distinctive as any Southern drawl. She had been one of the first white volunteers to be hired at SNCC's Atlanta headquarters, and for two years had worked side by side with Bond in the communications department, helping to put out press releases and the SNCC newspaper, as well as dealing with the press and taking affidavits from visiting field organizers.

Miller came to relish Bond's wry sense of humor, and to trust her private confidences to his ironclad discretion. She rented an apartment with Julian's sister, Jane, in a Black neighborhood of Atlanta, and they two women became like sisters. Jane and Julian formed part of a raucous, late-night interracial wedding party when Dottie Miller married one of SNCC's other early white volunteers, an intrepid field organizer from Alabama named Bob Zellner. After their wedding, the Zellners moved north to New England for several years, but they were back in Atlanta in the winter of 1966 and Dottie became part of the private support network that rallied around Bond, helping him to recover from his setback and prepare for the fight ahead.

Yet in a poignant irony, the removal of Dottie and Bob Zellner's friend Julian Bond from the Georgia legislature set in motion another year-long drama—one that would end with their own expulsion from SNCC. It began when Bill Ware, a SNCC organizer who had been working in the Deep South, moved to Atlanta to work for Bond's reinstatement. Raised near Natchez, Mississippi, a river town in the southwest corner of the state, Ware was one of ten children born to a farmer named Walter Ware and his wife, Cebelle, neither of whom attended school past the eighth grade. Ware's parents nonetheless had great reverence for education, and they encouraged their son to finish high school and seek a scholarship to St. John's University in Minnesota. After graduating, Ware served two years as a lieutenant in the U.S. Army, then enlisted in the Peace Corps in Ghana, where he got swept up in the revolutionary spirit of the anticolonial struggles spreading across Africa and South America. Stern-faced and a lean six feet, Ware grew a scruffy beard that made him look like an ebony-skinned Che Guevara.

After teaching high school in St. Paul for several years, Ware returned to Mississippi to join the civil rights struggle, and quickly acquired a reputation for both daring and grandiosity. In the summer of 1963, he worked for the Council of Federated Organizations (COFO) to set up mock polling places for the symbolic Freedom Votes held by Mississippi Blacks who were kept from participating in the all-white state Democratic primaries. When Ware tried to use a white gas station restroom, a Natchez police offer clubbed him in the face, leaving him with a bloody jaw that required thirty stitches. The policeman proceeded to arrest Ware for reckless driving, whereupon Ware sent a telegram to President Johnson demanding that the Justice Department send an observer to his trial. Once the Civil Rights Act of 1964 was passed, the local NAACP announced a march on the county courthouse, but then canceled the plan after Natchez officials put the local National Guard on alert. At a public rally, Ware called for proceeding with the march anyway, in defiance of NAACP leader Charles Evers, whose brother Medgar had been gunned down the year before by a white segregationist. Evers had to shout over Ware's bellicose interruptions, warning the crowd that "these outside agitators are going to get you killed."

In 1964, Ware joined SNCC for Freedom Summer, the bold experiment to recruit and train as many as a thousand volunteers, many of them white college students, to register voters and set up schools for young children across the state of Mississippi. At the last minute, however, SNCC organizers decided that it was too dangerous for whites to work in Natchez and surrounding Adams County, which had its own wing of the Ku Klux Klan and was the site of frequent racial assaults. Along with his abrasive personality and affection for foreign revolutionaries, that experience helped explain the contentious attitude that Ware brought with him to Atlanta in 1966, when he moved into an impoverished corner of the 136th district known as Vine City to support Julian Bond's effort to win back his stripped state House seat.

Working with a small team of organizers out of a two-room shotgun shanty, Ware soon shifted his focus from supporting Bond to what he boasted would serve as a new model for urban "political organization and education." Dubbing his effort the "Vine City Project," Ware set out to mobilize the neighborhood's some 3,500 residents, who were 99 percent Black and had a median income of less than $3,000 a year, to fight eviction notices and protest lack of heating and other slum conditions. Ware put out a newsletter called the *Nitty Gritty* and threatened primary challenges against entrenched local Black politicians, ridiculing one of them as "a white woman although her skin is black." At first, the Vine Street organizers received help drafting proposals from a white SNCC staffer named Jehudah "Mendy" Samstein, a one-time yeshiva student from New York City who had dropped out of graduate school at the University of Chicago to work as a SNCC field organizer and by 1966 was volunteering in the Atlanta office. Once the project was under way, however, Ware pushed for it to be run entirely by Black staffers. As the cold Atlanta winter turned to spring, that demand sprouted into a full-blown obsession. No longer limiting his complaints about whites to Vine City, Ware launched an aggressive and frequently insubordinate crusade to force SNCC to sever *all* its ties to white staffers and allies.

At the end of January 1966, however, no one following the broader civil rights struggle had any inkling of the anti-white insurrection brewing in Vine City. The eyes of the media and everyone else who kept track of the movement had turned to Chicago, where Dr. King was making the biggest news since his march from Selma.

CHAPTER 3

A New Front in Chicago

When Martin Luther King Jr. moved into a run-down apartment in the Chicago neighborhood of North Lawndale as part of a new Northern civil rights offensive in the winter of 1966, he announced that he was doing so because the surrounding area represented the very definition of a slum. Yet like every other Black urban neighborhood characterized by that blunt term, North Lawndale had a long and complicated history. It began in 1870, when a real estate firm called Millard and Decker bought up miles of rural acreage to the west of the city, divided it into small plots, and advertised the new properties under the made-up marketing name of Lawndale. When the Great Chicago Fire destroyed most of the downtown area a year later, displaced factories moved west, bringing with them an influx of European immigrant workers. The tractor company later known as International Harvester relocated to the area, and Sears Roebuck & Company opened a clearinghouse for its mail order catalogue business there in 1905. At the turn of the twentieth century, North Lawndale was a white ethnic neighborhood of Irish, Dutch, German, and, mostly, Czech immigrants, who built an ornate Bohemian Club and named the local elementary school after composer Antonín Dvořák.

By the decades after World War I, this first wave of immigrants had saved enough money to afford bigger homes with actual lawns in the adjacent town of Cicero and other suburbs to the west. In North

Lawndale, they were replaced by Jews from Russia and Poland. Moving up from the Maxwell Street ghetto that was often their first point of entry to Chicago, the Jews crowded into gray stone townhouses that were divided into "two-flats" and newly constructed buildings that contained as many as twenty or thirty apartments. By the 1930s, Jews made up more than two thirds of North Lawndale's population of 112,000, and their synagogues, social clubs, and kosher butcheries filled the thoroughfares of Douglas Boulevard and Roosevelt Road. Then, in the 1950s, the Jews began to depart for less congested and more affluent neighborhoods on Chicago's North Side and northern suburbs. Their place was taken by Blacks who had come to Chicago in the second, post–World War II wave of the Great Migration from the South. In that decade alone, the Black population of North Lawndale soared from 13,000 to 113,000, while its white population plummeted from 87,000 to 11,000.

"White flight" was the term commonly used to explain this rapid racial shift, but the exodus wasn't as spontaneous as that phrase suggested. It was accelerated by a small band of ruthless slumlords who exploited white fears and Black vulnerabilities with a noxious practice known as "contract selling." Playing on worries of falling real estate values as more Blacks moved into North Lawndale, the speculators pressed white homeowners to sell to them while they had the chance, then turned around and peddled the same properties to Blacks at huge markups. Instead of turning over deeds, the speculators offered contracts that required buyers to pay off the entire asking price before taking ownership. No equity was created, and repossession was threatened if payments were missed. The contract sellers got away with this scam because most Black strivers who dreamed of owning their own homes couldn't qualify for conventional mortgages as a result of "redlining"—the bank guidelines that deemed Black neighborhoods financially risky and identified stay-away zones with red lines on lending maps.

In 1963, the *Chicago Daily News* provided a glimpse into the slimy world of contract selling. The paper assigned a reporter named John Culhane to infiltrate the operation of Lou Fushanis, a Greek American former used car salesman who ran a deceptively named real estate firm called Friendly Loan Corporation. In a story entitled "I Was Hired to Sell Slums to Negroes," Culhane described how Fushanis sent him out with a salesman who tried to foist a house with falling plaster and broken toilets on a Black couple while the previous owners, who had been served an eviction notice for missed payments, were still living there. Culhane quit after two days, but not before he got Fushanis's assistant to describe how her boss cheated buyers. "He loads them up with payments they can't meet," the assistant explained. "Then he takes the property away from them. He's sold some of these buildings three or four times."

In the late 1960s, Chicago's contract selling hustle came to citywide attention after a Jesuit seminarian working in North Lawndale encouraged a group of victims to wage a campaign of payment strikes that forced the slumlords to renegotiate hundreds of contracts. Forty years later, Beryl Satter, a historian and son of a lawyer who represented those victims, revived the story in a 2009 memoir, *Family Properties.* In turn, Satter's book provided inspiration for "The Case for Reparations," an influential 2014 *Atlantic* magazine article by the Black author Ta-Nehisi Coates. Coates presented North Lawndale as Exhibit A in a manifesto that revived a national debate over whether Black Americans were owed some form of mass class action settlement for the devastating financial toll of three centuries of slavery, Jim Crow, and housing discrimination.

Yet when Dr. King chose North Lawndale as Ground Zero for his 1966 crusade—to address the crisis of slum dwelling and housing discrimination that afflicted Blacks in the urban North—he was in too much of a hurry to take much account of the neighborhood's unique history. When what became known as the Chicago Freedom Movement was in the planning stages, John McKnight, the head of the Midwest office of the U.S. Commission on Human Rights, urged James Bevel, King's point person in West Chicago, to take on the shadowy world of contract selling. "It didn't sell," Bevel informed McKnight after bringing up the proposal at an Atlanta meeting of the Southern Christian Leadership Conference, the clergy-led civil rights organization led by Dr. King. The SCLC preferred to prioritize "the poorest people" who could only afford to rent in tenements, Bevel explained, rather than Blacks who had enough money to purchase their own homes. In the view of historian Satter, this was a pivotal "miscalculation" that "would prove costly for King and his people" as they discovered how hard it would be to find arch-villains among Chicago's slum landlords, and how it easy it would be for Chicago's wily mayor, Richard J. Daley, to string King along with token concessions.

BY 1966, DR. KING HAD BEEN THE MOST VISIBLE LEADER OF THE American civil rights movement for a decade—ever since, as a twenty-six-year-old minister recently arrived in Montgomery, Alabama, he was elected to lead the inspiring boycott that forced an end to separate racial seating on that city's buses. In that period, King's growing acclaim, which now included a Nobel Peace Prize, had come to obscure the degree to which less-well-known lieutenants prepared the battlefields on which he commanded. One of those aides was James Bevel, an impassioned young SCLC official who was known to the general public, if he was known at all, for wearing a skullcap akin to a Jewish yarmulke, even though Bevel himself was an ordained Baptist preacher. Like John Lewis, Bevel came from a large Southern sharecropping family. Along with sixteen brothers and sisters, he grew up picking cotton in the fields of Itta Bena, Mississippi. Like Lewis, Bevel also attended the American Baptist Theological Seminary in Nashville and studied the practice of nonviolent resistance under James Lawson. In Lawson's church basement seminars, Bevel got to know Diane Nash, a Chicago native and student at Fisk University who would become his wife and another early leader of the Nashville sit-in and Freedom Ride campaigns.

In April of 1960, Bevel was among the sit-in leaders invited to the retreat at historically Black Shaw University in Raleigh, North Carolina, where Ella Baker, then an officer of the SCLC, encouraged the students not to form a youth branch of that group but instead to create the new organization that became SNCC. But unlike many others at that meeting, Bevel chose to keep working for the SCLC, and he went on to play a key role in planning protests for which Dr. King got much of the press attention. Bevel organized the 1963 Children's Crusade in Birmingham, Alabama, after King was jailed there, setting the stage for the demonstrations that shook the nation's conscience when police commissioner Bull Connor unleashed dogs and water cannons on the city's Black youth. Bevel also helped plan the 1963 March on Washington and the Selma voting rights campaign of 1965.

In the months after Selma, the SCLC split over which battles to take on next. While King aide Hosea Williams and others wanted to keep giving top priority to the South, Bevel pushed for a new focus on racial problems in the North. In May of 1965, he traveled to Chicago to conduct protest workshops at the invitation of Bernard Lafayette, another early sit-in leader who had taken a job with the American Friends Service Committee in the city. Once there, Bevel met the leaders of a local activist group called the Coordinating Council of Community Organizations (CCCO), which had been waging a campaign to integrate the city's public schools and to remove a recalcitrant white superintendent. Encouraged by Lafayette and impressed with CCCO's leader, a quiet former schoolteacher named Al Raby, Bevel lobbied King to make his next stand in Chicago. To establish a beachhead, Bevel took a leave from the SCLC and accepted a job as program director with a church network called the West Side Christian Parish that served the Black communities in and around North Lawndale.

Over the summer of 1965, King tested the waters in a half dozen other Northern cities, only to encounter tepid responses from local Black populations or pushback from power brokers such as Adam Clayton Powell Jr., the turf-conscious U.S. congressman from Harlem. Meanwhile, Bevel painted a picture of Chicago as a potential Birmingham or Selma of the North: a place where the SCLC could capture the imagination of the national media and the sympathy of white liberals by pitting noble protesters against conspicuous white villains, especially white slumlords and discriminatory housing firms that kept the Black population of the West Side living in graphically squalid conditions. "The real estate dealers in Chicago are the equivalent to Wallace and Jim Clark in the South," Bevel argued in one strategy meeting, referring to the segregationist governor of Alabama and the white police chief who ordered the Bloody Sunday attack in Selma. "These are the cats who are most vulnerable to an attack because there is one thing that everyone can see and understand—that is, you don't even need to philosophize about housing in Chicago, you can show that on television."

Other King advisers tried to counter Bevel's enthusiasm. "You don't know what Chicago is like," Bayard Rustin warned, pointing out the perils of tangling with Mayor Daley and his mighty political machine. "You're going to be wiped out." Stanley Levinson, the white attorney who served as King's lawyer and strategic sounding board, was concerned about the logistics of crusading in such a large Northern city. But after months of debate, King became persuaded that a combination of factors made Chicago his best Northern option: the chance to partner with Al Raby and CCCO; the built-in interest of the national press; and an all-powerful mayor who could enforce any deals that might be reached. So it was that on the first day of September 1965, King held a press conference with Andrew Young, the middle-class dentist's son from New Orleans who had become the SCLC's executive director, to announce plans for a Chicago campaign beginning in the new year. "If northern problems can be solved there, they can be solved anywhere," Young proclaimed.

James Bevel was given a budget of $10,000 a month to begin hiring staff on Chicago's West Side. But through the fall of 1965, King remained preoccupied with other business, and was also slowed down by injuries suffered when he tipped over on a chair and cut himself on a shattered water glass. It wasn't until the first week of January 1966 that he arrived in Chicago for a last-minute, three-day planning strategy session with Bevel, Al Raby, Andrew Young, and Ralph Abernathy, the SCLC official who had been King's friend and partner since they both led church congregations in Montgomery during the bus boycott. The group hoped to keep the meeting secret, but their cover was blown when Betty Washington, an enterprising reporter for the *Chicago Defender*, the influential Black newspaper, broke the news of the hush-hush gathering at the Sahara Inn motel near O'Hare Airport.

Emerging to brief the press in the motel's red-and-gold Gigi Room, King handed out a fifteen-page document that defined the "Chicago problem" vaguely as "economic exploitation . . . crystallized in the SLUM" and offered a sketchy three-phase plan to combat it. In the winter, King announced, there would be two months of recruitment and education. In the spring, there would be isolated protests against "agents of exploitation," followed in the summer by escalation to undefined "massive action." As King biographer David J. Garrow put it, "the verbosity of the document left reporters grasping for exactly what the movement had in mind." But to the relief of the reporters, King offered at least one piece of news that made for a good headline in the next morning's papers. To illustrate the plague of "slumlordism," as he called it, King announced that he would rent an apartment in a West Side tenement and live there part-time for the rest of the year.

WHEN KING FIRST RAISED THE IDEA OF MOVING TO CHICAGO, SOME in Al Raby's alliance urged him to rent on the South Side. The CCCO had its headquarters there, and the South Side was home to a deeply rooted Black community dating back to the first wave of the Great Migration. But as King's lieutenants admitted, they chose the West Side for dramatic effect. Touring the area, Ralph Abernathy was reminded of bombed-out buildings he saw as a platoon sergeant in World War II, with broken windows, rubble-filled yards, hallways stinking of feces and rotten food, and rats scurrying everywhere. Assigned the task of finding an apartment, King aide Bernard Lee was told to look for such an "epitome of filth and disrepair," as Abernathy put it. After rejecting eight apartments as unlivable, Lee settled on a run-down four-room flat renting for $90 a month in a three-floor walk-up building at 1550 Hamlin Avenue.

Afraid that the building's owner might back out of the deal once he learned the identity of the intended occupant, Lee signed the lease himself. But when word leaked out that the rental was for Dr. King, the landlord, Alvin S. Shavin, had an unexpected reaction. "I'm delighted to have him," Shavin said. "What else can I say?" Shavin dispatched four painters, two plasterers, and two electricians to spruce up the building in advance of King's arrival. Amused by the turn of events, the editors of the *Chicago Defender* suggested that King might solve the housing crisis on the West Side single-handedly by moving from tenement to tenement. "It Wasn't the Plan, but Dr. King Shows How to 'Cure' a Slum Building," teased the paper's headline.

To King's elegant wife, Coretta, the digs were more than dingy enough. In her autobiography, Coretta recalled the smell of urine in the unguarded lobby, a refuge for local winos, and a grim railroad layout that required passing through two bedrooms to get to a tiny kitchen with a broken refrigerator and a rotting gas stove. Ralph Abernathy's wife, Juanita, was so appalled at the apartment that had been rented for the Abernathys on the floor below that she insisted on moving to a Black-owned hotel. Still, the last-minute repairs featured prominently in news stories about the Kings' arrival in North Lawndale on the afternoon of Wednesday, January 26. Looking none the worse for wear, the elegantly dressed couple posed on an upholstered camelback sofa in the repainted living room, and cheerfully waved from patched-up windows to local residents who gathered to greet them in the streets below.

"Dr King, Mate, Live in Flat—for One Day," read the arch headline in the *Chicago Tribune* when Coretta left town after spending only one night in North Lawndale. By the time her husband flew out of Chicago the following day, it was clear that the city's powers-that-be weren't about to remind anyone of George Wallace or Sheriff Jim Clark, as James Bevel had predicted. When King dropped by police headquarters to discuss his plans for nonviolent protests, Superintendent Orlando Wilson politely served him coffee and asked if it was true that King had Irish ancestry. (King did, distantly, on his father's side.) On winter vacation in the Caribbean, Mayor Daley moved to steal King's thunder by announcing a detailed plan to eliminate all Chicago slums in one year. Daley pledged to increase housing inspections, to withhold city welfare checks to offending landlords, and to launch "the most massive and comprehensive rodent eradication program ever undertaken in this country." Known for his convoluted syntax, Daley even managed to produce a succinct sound bite for the press. "All of us, like Dr. King, want to eliminate slums," the mayor declared.

As Dr. King flew in and out of Chicago over the next few months, and moved his campaign to its second phase of targeted protests, North Lawndale's rental landlords continued to make for elusive adversaries. In February, King zeroed in on a six-apartment building at 1320 South Homan Avenue where a group of families with twenty children among them were braving freezing winter temperatures with no heat or hot water. Assuming what he described as "supralegal" trusteeship of the building, King persuaded the tenants to stop paying rent to the landlord and instead to write checks to the SCLC to fund repairs. On a chilly Wednesday morning, he and Coretta even donned sanitation crew jumpsuits and spent several hours sweeping up rotting trash that had been left to pile up outside the building.

But when reporters searched for the identity of the South Homan Avenue landlord, they discovered an eighty-one-year-old invalid who claimed to have lost more than $25,000 on the building and was looking for someone to take it off his hands. "King is doing the right thing," said the owner, John B. Bender. "I don't blame him a bit, I wish him luck." Bender called the property a "white elephant" and suggested that he would turn it over to anyone willing to pay $1,000 and assume an $8,000 mortgage. The following month, James Bevel organized a tenants league in the neighborhood of East Garfield and launched a rent strike against several buildings owned by a firm called Condor and Costalis. Instead of avoiding the strikers, landlord John Condor showed up at the tenants league's meetings and argued that the real culprits were "big boys" downtown, the redlining bankers who refused to give favorable terms even to white owners on the West Side. "We're with you, believe it or not," said Condor, who became the first major landlord to settle with the tenants a few months later. "Don't fight the wrong fight."

King had also envisioned the Chicago campaign as a way to keep pressure on Lyndon Johnson to make good on promises to put fair housing at the center of his next piece of federal civil rights legislation. By the time King moved into the flat in North Lawndale, however, the political ground in Washington had shifted. In early January, Johnson appointed Robert Weaver, an expert in housing finance, to the newly created post of secretary of housing and urban development, and trotted out his entire cabinet for the announcement in the White House Fish Room. Weaver was the first Black to achieve the rank of cabinet secretary. But when details of the president's new anti-slum program leaked out days later, only $2.3 billion had been set aside over a six-year period—an amount that King immediately dismissed as too small. Delivering his annual State of the Union Address, Johnson buried the details of the housing plan and the rest of the new civil rights bill toward the end of an hour-long speech. Ominously, LBJ began and ended the speech with a defense of his military escalation in Vietnam, and a less-than-convincing argument that he could continue to pursue his Great Society domestic agenda while wading deeper into a costly war in Southeast Asia.

AS DR. KING WAS GETTING HIS FOOTING IN THE FRIGID SNOWS OF Chicago that winter, Stokely Carmichael was hard at work in rural Alabama, registering voters and preparing to run candidates under the black panther banner of the new independent political party in Lowndes County. As he watched from afar, however, Carmichael sensed instinctively that the biggest threats to King's Northern strategy wouldn't be greedy slumlords or two-faced city officials, but white homeowners who lived close to Black ghettos. In Chicago's case, they were descendants of the European immigrants who once resided in neighborhoods, such as North Lawndale.

Carmichael understood white people like these because he had spent his teen years around them. Stokely had been born in the

Caribbean nation of Trinidad and Tobago to Adolphus Carmichael, a hardworking carpenter and construction worker, and Mabel "May" Charles, a free-spirited native of Monserrat. After only a few years of marriage, May tired of her husband's smothering family and fled to America, and a lovesick Adolphus took a job on a freighter so he could jump ship and join her. As a result, Carmichael and two younger sisters spent their early childhood in the care of his grandmother and three aunts on the island. When he was eleven, his grandmother passed away, and his parents brought the three children and one of the aunts to live with them and two younger siblings in New York City. At first, the eight members of the Carmichael family crowded into a three-room apartment in a building full of Caribbean immigrants in the South Bronx. A year later, Adolphus announced that he had scraped together enough money to buy the family their own home in Morris Park, a neighborhood of Italian and Irish immigrants in the north Bronx where they would be the only Black family in sight.

The property on Amethyst Street in Morris Park was, in Carmichael's description, a "serious, serious dump" and "the worst house on the block." But through a long, cold winter, he watched his father fix up the house until it shined like the gem for which the street was named. Adolphus tore down and rebuilt walls, framed new windows and doors, added rooms upstairs and down, and built a playhouse in the backyard. As the white neighbors looked on, Stokely recalled, "amusement turned to skepticism, skepticism to wonder, and wonder to respect. They were, after all, working people and respected industry and competence."

What Carmichael took away from those teen years in the Bronx was that everyone in the neighborhood, including his own parents, cared more about protecting their property and families than about any lofty goal of racial integration. He also learned that the same sort of white people who came to respect individual Blacks such as his parents—diligent, orderly folks who kept an attractive home and went to Methodist church every Sunday—could be driven into a frenzy over fears of the Black masses. "These were working people," Carmichael recalled. "Their identity revolved around four things: family, home, church and neighborhood, in no particular order. I knew that those neat little houses, as with my father, represented their only life savings, their most tangible material accomplishment, the American Dream. . . . Any perceived threat to any of these, real or imagined, and we talking war. Be the easiest thing in the world to whip up a mob to confront any 'invasion.'"

When Carmichael thought about what Dr. King was trying to achieve in Chicago, he recalled a phrase he learned in an engineering class: "If the only tool you have is a hammer, the whole world will look like a nail." For a decade, going back to the Montgomery bus boycott, the tools of the civil rights struggle had been nonviolent civil disobedience, public marches, freedom songs, and soaring appeals to Scripture and the Bill of Rights. When the task at hand was ending Jim Crow and securing voting rights, those tools had been effective. But this was different. This was a campaign for housing rights within a crow's flight of white ethnics who were worried that Blacks might do to their neighborhoods what their own immigrant parents and grandparents once did: move in and take over.

"Aye-yai-yai," Carmichael recalled thinking. "Right issue, wrong approach, wrong strategy, wrong solution."

CHAPTER 4

Two Toughs from Oakland

For Huey Newton and Bobby Seale, Telegraph Avenue was more than a four-and-a-half-mile road stretching north from their hometown of Oakland to the campus of the University of California at Berkeley. It was a link between two distinctly different worlds: between the rough ghetto streets where they grew up, and the steepled academic sanctuary so close by. For much of the early 1960s, what existed of a Black student movement in the San Francisco Bay Area was organized by activists from Berkeley, and Newton and Seale, part-timers at a junior college in Oakland, followed the lead of those self-important, middle-class leaders. But that began to change for good on the evening of Thursday, March 17, 1966, when Newton and Seale and a friend they called Weasel took a walk up Telegraph Avenue to look for secondhand albums by bluesmen T-Bone Walker and Howlin' Wolf at a record store near the university.

Walnut dark, with a protruding brow, heavy eyebrows, and a thick mustache, Seale, at age twenty-nine, looked the tough guy part of a metalworker who had served in the Air Force and been court-martialed for a confrontation with a colonel. But Seale also had a theatrical streak, with a sideline as a stand-up comedian and a knack for memorizing and reciting poetry. As the threesome proceeded up Telegraph Avenue, his companions urged Seale to entertain them with one of his favorite poems, written by a fellow student at Oakland's

Merritt College, Marvin Jackmon, a pioneer of the Black Arts Movement who went by the pen name of Marvin X. Entitled "Burn, Baby, Burn," Marvin's composition told the story of 1965 Watts riots in the style of the Beat poets.

Loud enough so that passersby stopped to listen, Seale recited jagged verses that began with an expression of Black weariness . . . *"Tired./ Sick an' tired/ Tired of being sick an' tired . . ."* and ended with an expression of the pent-up fury that had been unleashed on the Los Angeles police and their imperious chief, William Parker: *"Motherfuck the police/ Parker's sista too . . . / Burn baby burn/ In time they will learn."*

As the trio neared the Berkeley campus, Seale summoned another poem from memory, an anti–Vietnam War diatribe called "Uncle Sammy Call Me Fulla Lucifer" by a street poet named Ronald Stone. By this time, so many onlookers had gathered that Weasel borrowed a chair from a restaurant patio so Seale could climb up and address the crowd. The spirited performance drew calls for an encore, and Seale repeated the draft dodger's lament: *"Uncle Sammy don't shuck and jive me/ You school my naive heart to sing/ red-white-and-blue-stars-and-stripes/ songs . . ."*

Just as Seale reached this point in the poem, an off-duty police officer named George Williamson emerged from the crowd.

"You're under arrest," Williamson announced.

Seale climbed down from the chair. "What are you talking about, 'You're under arrest'?" he asked. "Under arrest for what?"

"You're blocking the sidewalk," the policeman said.

"What do you mean I'm blocking the sidewalk?" Seale protested. "I'm standing over here."

Three more policeman appeared and tackled Seale to the ground. Out of the corner of his eye, Seale saw Huey Newton, his baby-faced friend, throwing punches, several of which landed on the side of a policeman's head. Seale squirmed loose and a brief tussle took place before the officers subdued the two men and arrested them for disturbing the peace. At the police station, Newton and Seale phoned a friend at a campus group they belonged to, called the Soul Students Advisory Council (SSAC), and arranged to borrow $50 to post bail.

A few weeks later, Newton and Seale were driving around Oakland when they saw another police officer arresting a Black man on the street for no apparent reason. Newton wanted to jump out of the car and confront the cop on the spot, but Seale held him back. Instead, the two went to the SSAC office, got more cash, then proceeded to the police station and posted bail for the arrested man, who was so grateful that he broke down in tears.

Along with the Telegraph Avenue incident, the experience of bailing out the stranger led Seale to two conclusions. The first was how much more satisfying it was to stand up to police harassment and provide assistance to Black folks on the streets of Oakland than it was to engage in windy intellectual debates with other college students. The second was that anytime he got into trouble, he wanted his friend Huey Newton by his side. Newton "doesn't let anybody mess over his partners, or whoever he's running with," Seale recalled with admiration. "That's the way he is. . . . That's the way he gets with any human being who tries to hurt him or his friends. And his people and his family. That was a big thing."

A casual observer of the two might have been surprised that it was Seale who looked up to Newton. Seale was the older one, by more than five years, the Texas-born military veteran and skilled mechanic who had worked in factories that supplied sheet metal for the Gemini rockets. He was more physically imposing, standing several inches above Newton's slight, five-foot-seven-inch, 130-pound frame. Seale was also the extrovert, the actor in campus plays and performer in Oakland's coffeehouses—compared to Newton, who was shy and hated speaking in front of crowds. But Newton was the tougher fighter, with lightning-quick hands and a fearless readiness to take on all comers. He was the deeper thinker, a self-taught reader who had introduced Seale to the French existential philosophers Albert Camus and Jean-Paul Sartre and helped Seale understand Frantz Fanon, the French African psychiatrist and author who saw armed rebellion as a path to psychological liberation. Newton was also the more visionary of the two, the one who kept raising the idea of creating a new organization that could appeal not just to privileged college students but to the sort of struggling Black folks the two had grown up with in the Oakland ghetto. The "brothers on the street," Newton called them.

IT WAS NEWTON'S FAMILY, AND HIS PLACE IN IT, THAT ACCOUNTED for this unique combination of traits. His father, Walter Newton, was a mixed-race, Alabama-born jack-of-all-trades laborer and Sunday preacher who married his mother, a Louisiana native named Armelia Johnson, when she was just seventeen years old. When the couple's seventh and last child was born in Monroe, Louisiana, on February 17, 1942, Walter chose the name Huey Percy Newton, after the state's former governor, Huey Pierce Long. History would remember Huey Long by his nickname, the Kingfish, and his fiery populist appeal to Southern whites. But Walter Newton admired Long for the sly, roundabout way the governor sometimes turned the racist Jim Crow system to the benefit of Black people. When Huey was a boy, Walter told him the story of being in the front of a crowd when Long gave a speech decrying the fact that white nurses had to treat "half-naked" Black men in the state's hospitals. A frenzy ensued that led to hospitals hiring more Black nurses to tend to Black patients. "My father believed that Huey P. Long had been a great man," Newton recalled, "and he wanted to name a son after him."

In his father, Newton had the rare example of a Black man of his generation willing to stand up to whites in the South. Wiry and stern-looking, with pale skin, piercing eyes, and a brush mustache, Walter taught his children that "you can take a killing but you can't take a beating." Huey grew up hearing accounts of his father's stubborn bravery. In one often told story, Walter publicly accused a white businessman of cheating him. When the angry merchant appeared at the family's house, Walter calmly walked out and sat on the running board of the man's car, knowing the glove compartment contained a gun. "If you hit me a lick, the other folks will have to hunt me down because you'll be lying in the road dead," he warned the merchant. For Huey, his father's mystique was made all the more powerful by the shadowy circumstances of his birth, to an unwed Black woman and a white man in the brutal era after Reconstruction. "My father's father was a white rapist," Newton reported on the first page of his autobiography, later reflecting that Walter's mixed blood may have served as a shield in the South, making white men reluctant to attack someone who looked so much like them.

Yet Newton also learned another lesson from his father: about how difficult it was for a Black man with little education, no matter how honest or hardworking, to provide for his family. In Louisiana, Walter labored in a sugarcane mill, at a carbon plant, and as a railroad brakeman, stopping only on Sundays to preach at the local Baptist church. In 1945, when Newton was three years old, his father moved the family to Oakland just as the war was ending and California's defense plants were closing. Walter had to resort to odd jobs as a brickmason, plumber, and carpenter while the family moved from one tiny two-bedroom apartment to another. Often, the children subsisted on a daily diet of "cush," a dish of fried leftover cornbread mixed with gravy and onions. No matter how scarce money became, however, Walter always insisted on paying his bills on time. He dispatched his sons to deliver checks to his creditors in person so they could bring back stamped receipts. "My father's constant preoccupation with bills is the most profound and persistent memory of my childhood," Newton recalled. "For me, no words on the street were as profane as 'the bills.' It killed me a little each time they were mentioned, because I could see the never-ending struggle and agony my father went through trying to cope with them."

From his mother, Newton received lighthearted relief from the family stresses and encouragement for the sensitive and creative side of his personality. Still barely out of her teens when her children were young, Armelia often seemed more like a playmate than a mother, leading them in laughter-filled games of jacks and hide-and-seek. Early on, she recognized an artistic bent in her youngest child, and got him started on piano lessons that he continued for seven years. By junior high school, Newton was introducing friends to recordings of Tchaikovsky's *Nutcracker* and Rimsky-Korsakov's *Flight of the Bumblebee*. As a way of overcoming his shyness with girls—and covering up for a learning disability that kept him from mastering the skill of reading by sight—he memorized poetry. He was able to recite entire poems by Edgar Allan Poe and T. S. Eliot, as well as passages from the *Rubáiyát of Omar Khayyám* and the "tomorrow, and tomorrow, and tomorrow" soliloquy from *Macbeth*.

From his older brother Walter Jr., meanwhile, Newton learned to use his fists. As early as kindergarten, students had started taunting Newton for his "too pretty to be a boy" baby face, and for the middle initial he included when announcing his name. "Huey Pee Newton," they chanted. "Huey Pee goes wee, wee, wee." At first, Newton responded to the bullying by pretending to be sick so he wouldn't have to go to school. But the Newton family had a tradition that older children looked after younger ones, and Newton was "given" to Walter Jr., the second born, known to everyone as Sonny Man. Sonny Man started taking his little brother to school—and teaching him how to fight back when he was picked on. By elementary school, Newton had "the fastest hands on the block," he recalled. He became champion of the pretend prizefights that Black boys staged on Oakland street corners, boxing with towel-wrapped hands while winos placed nickel bets and rewarded the last one standing with a box of Cracker Jack.

Walter Jr. was also a hustler—a pool shark, gambler, petty thief, and ladies' man who took the lesson from his father's struggles that honest work was a sucker's game. By the end of junior high, Newton began to take after Sonny Man in that respect, too. He joined a dice-playing, parking-meter-cracking gang called "The Brotherhood" and, at age fourteen, spent a month in Juvenile Hall after an arrest for carrying a gun. For high school, Newton went to Oakland Tech, an imposing institution on the city's north side with large white columns and a distinguished roster of white and Black graduates that would include film star Clint Eastwood, baseball great Curt Flood, and Ron Dellums, the city's future mayor and U.S. congressman. Because of his struggles with reading, however, Newton scored only a 78 on a Stanford-Binet IQ test, the intelligence exam schools used to track students. He was placed in "slow" classes whose teachers made no effort to relate coursework to the lives of inner-city teenagers. "My high school diploma was a farce," Newton recalled. "When my friends and I graduated, we were ill-equipped to function in society, except at the bottom, even though the system said we were educated."

Fortunately, Newton had another older brother who exerted a more positive influence. Melvin Newton was the second youngest child in the family, four years older than Huey, and the most studious. It was Melvin who introduced Huey to poetry, and taught him hypnosis, a skill that Huey used to impress his friends by putting them into trances and making them bark like dogs. When Melvin graduated from high school, he continued to live at home while enrolling at Oakland City College. In high school, a guidance counselor informed Huey that he wasn't "college material," but watching Melvin pore over his philosophy and sociology books gave Huey other ideas. If he wanted to follow his brother's footsteps, Huey realized, he would need to learn how to read properly. So one day, he borrowed Melvin's copy of Plato's *Republic* and a dictionary. For several months, Huey spent hours each day slowly making his way through the dense text. He looked up words in the dictionary, sounded them out, then pieced together sentences and trained himself to scan paragraphs. Finally, like the prisoner freed from the cave in Plato's allegory, he was able to grasp the meaning of what had once looked like only shadows on a page.

A SPRAWLING WHITE EDIFICE WITH A SQUAT BELL TOWER AND A roof of Spanish tile, Oakland City College—renamed Merritt College in 1964—occupied most of a city block in an area known as the Flatlands. Once a high school for the children of Berkeley faculty, the complex was converted into a business school and then into a two-year college after World War II. In 1960, it became part of a sweeping overhaul of California's education system that created a three-tiered network of universities, state colleges, and junior colleges, thus guaranteeing access to higher education to any state resident who wanted it. Sociologists credited the California plan with beginning a nationwide boom in college enrollment that shifted the focus of American youth culture from the high school to the college campus. It also led to a dramatic increase in racial diversity of higher education in California that gave the state the nation's highest percentage of Black college graduates and made it the most fertile cradle of young Black activism since the South's lunch counter sit-ins and Freedom Rides.

By the time Newton started taking classes at Oakland City College, he was in open rebellion against his father's upright, churchgoing ways. He grew a scraggly, beatnik-style beard, and expanded his secret life as a petty burglar. He stole credit cards and pretended to be a gardener so he could break into affluent homes in Berkeley and the Oakland Hills. Newton also fell in with a tall, enigmatic student named William Brumfield who called himself Richard Thorne and was known for espousing a lifestyle of "non-possessive" free love between the sexes. Moving out of his family's house, Newton briefly roomed with Thorne, who later became notorious for organizing orgies as the leader of a group called the Sexual Freedom League. Then Newton moved into a boardinghouse known as Poor Boys Hall in a converted book warehouse near the community college. Curious about the life of Black students at Berkeley, he began to hang around the fraternity Phi Beta Sigma, where he heard about a group called the Afro-American Association (AAA) founded by a recent Berkeley law school graduate named Donald Warden.

Newton went to a meeting of Warden's group and was dazzled by the handsome, wide-eyed young lawyer with his confident opinions and encyclopedic knowledge of Black history and literature. It was a charismatic mixture that Warden came to via an unusual route. His father was a Pittsburgh postman and follower of Marcus Garvey who moved his family to a small town in western Pennsylvania in a misbegotten attempt to create a Black separatist colony. As a result, Warden grew up in a virtually all-white rural environment, a lonely experience that made him yearn to attend a historically Black college. He chose Howard University in Washington, D.C., where he came under the influence of E. Franklin Frazier, the sociologist and author of *Black Bourgeoisie*, a critique of Negro elites and their obsession with emulating well-to-do whites. In Frazier's analysis, this segregated "make believe" world was an obstacle to the fight for true equality and integration. But Warden drew the opposite conclusion from Frazier's writings: that Blacks should forget about blending into a white world. By the time he arrived at Berkeley's Boalt Law School in the late 1950s, Warden had fashioned himself into a modern-day Marcus Garvey in collegiate tweed, spreading a message that Blacks should reject assimilation in favor of creating their own world of Black culture and business.

Over the next year, Newton became an eager participant in the book study groups that Warden convened at a Chinese restaurant on Telegraph Avenue. For the first time, Newton was introduced to *The Souls of Black Folk*, by W. E. B. Du Bois; to *Up from Slavery*, by Booker T. Washington; to *Invisible Man*, by Ralph Ellison; and to writings of James Baldwin. On the weekends, he went to hear Warden engage in a ritual he called "street speaking," spouting nationalist views to anyone who would listen on the corners of the Fillmore District of San Francisco and Seventh Street in Oakland. Warden also hosted a weekly radio program, *We Care Enough to Tell It Like It Is*, on the Black soul music station KDIA, and later had a television talk show called *Black Dignity*.

In the spring of 1962, Newton's friend Richard Thorne came to an Afro-American Association meeting with an old acquaintance from childhood, a twenty-five-year-old military veteran who was living at home with his parents and taking classes at Oakland City College after being kicked out of the Air Force. Thorne briefly introduced Bobby Seale to Huey Newton, and several weeks later, the two met again at an AAA rally protesting the Kennedy administration's blockade of Cuba. Newton was having an intense argument with another protester about Frazier's *Black Bourgeoise*, and Seale was amazed to hear Huey cite specific page numbers and passages from the book. The two struck up a conversation, and for the first time they talked about their mutual fascination with guns. After the rally, Seale invited Newton to his house and showed him a .38 pistol he kept in a leather holster in his bedroom.

Around this same time, Newton grew disillusioned with Donald Warden. He concluded that the AAA leader was a physical coward after Warden scurried away when a group of white hecklers interrupted one of the group's meetings. Newton also came to believe that Warden was using his activism to troll for legal work, then overcharging poor Oakland residents for his services. The last straw, Newton recalled, was when he accompanied Warden to a meeting of the Oakland City Council after one of its members was quoted in the newspaper denouncing the AAA as a radical menace. When Warden got a chance to speak, he responded to the councilman's accusation by insisting that the AAA was merely a self-help group devoted to getting Blacks off welfare. "I was really sick when I saw what went down before the City Council," Newton recalled. "Warden talked about black folks as if they were a lazy bunch of people who hated ourselves and had no will to better our own situations."

By the summer of 1963, Newton had broken with Warden, but he was still intrigued when he heard that the AAA had organized a day-long conference entitled "The Mind of the Ghetto" at Oakland's McClymonds High School. One of the speakers was Cassius Clay, the brash, lightning-quick boxer from Kentucky who had won the light heavyweight gold medal at the 1960 Olympics. At the McClymonds conference, Clay talked not about fighting but about his decision to join the Nation of Islam—a conversion that he would only make public the following year, after knocking out heavyweight champion Sonny Liston, and that the new champ would later ratify by changing his name to Muhammad Ali.

Clay arrived at McClymonds High School with his new religious mentor, Malcolm X, the minister of the Nation of Islam mosque in New York City. Elegantly tall and slim, with short reddish brown hair and browline glasses that gave him a professorial air, Malcolm instantly impressed Newton with the breadth of his intellect and directness of his personal appeal. "Here was a man who combined the world of the streets and the world of the scholar," Newton recalled thinking after he heard Malcolm speak, "a man so widely read he could give better lectures and cite more evidence than many college professors. He was also practical. Dressed in the loose-fitting style of a strong prison man, he knew what the street brothers were like, and he knew what could be done to reach them. Malcolm had a program:

armed defense when attacked, and reaching the people with ideas and programs that speak to their condition. At the same time, he identified the causes of their condition instead of blaming the people."

Before Newton could figure out what group he wanted to join next, however, his association with the AAA came back to haunt him. Several months after the McClymonds High School conference, Newton went with his older brother Melvin to a party thrown by one of Melvin's friends. As Huey was eating a piece of steak and carrying on a conversation in the corner of the room, a man named Odell Lee, who Newton knew distantly as the husband of a high school classmate, approached him.

"You must be an Afro-American," Lee said to Newton.

Newton replied that he was no longer a member of the AAA.

Lee persisted, asking more pestering questions until Newton turned his back.

"Don't turn your back on me when I'm talking to you," Lee snapped, putting his hand on Newton's arm.

"Don't you ever put your hands on me again," Newton snapped, then spun away again.

When Lee moved to touch him a second time, Newton wheeled around and stabbed Lee several times with his steak knife. He pushed Lee to the wall, and saw that Lee's hand was bleeding. Once Newton determined that the wound wasn't life-threatening, he left the party with Melvin, assuming that no one there would dispute his street-justice right to protect himself against the chance that Lee might have had his own knife or gun. But several weeks later, Lee filed charges, and police arrived at the Newton family home with a warrant and arrested him for assault with a deadly weapon.

In his spare time, Newton had begun to frequent the law library at nearby San Francisco State College, reading up on criminal statutes so that he could defend himself in his sideline as a petty burglar. Newton had even represented himself several times in court, beating one rap for possession of stolen books by so flummoxing the witnesses that the judge dismissed the charges. In the Odell Lee trial, Newton tried to act as his own lawyer again, arguing self-defense, but

the largely white jury had none of it. Newton was found guilty of fel-
ony assault, and the judge revoked his bail and sent him to await sentencing at the county jail on the tenth floor of the Alameda County
Courthouse. Once there, Newton joined a hunger strike, and he
was caught passing notes between inmates. As punishment, guards
moved him to a tiny solitary confinement cell known to everyone at
the Alameda jail as the "Soul Breaker."

The name, Newton quickly learned, had less to do with the cell's
six-by-ten-feet dimensions, or with the absence of a window or a bed,
as with the fact that the only toilet was a hole in the ground. Before
long, occupants were wallowing in their own urine and feces and
usually willing to do anything to get out. But Newton stubbornly
refused to apologize for what he had done. He coped using a strategy
he had read about in a book about Mahatma Gandhi: to avoid having
to relieve himself, he ate none of the cold pea soup he was served for
food, and took only tiny sips from the milk carton full of water he
was provided for liquid. After fifteen days, guards sent Newton back
to a regular jail cell long enough to shower and visit with a doctor and
a psychiatrist. When he still refused to apologize, he was returned to
the Soul Breaker for two more weeks until he was sentenced to a six-
month jail term in another county jail in Santa Rita, fifty miles south
of Oakland. There, too, Newton ended up in a solitary confinement
wing called Graystone when he smashed a steel cafeteria tray over another inmate's head. But after surviving a month in the Soul Breaker,
Newton recalled, he had little trouble enduring Graystone—or the
months of solitary that he would be subjected to five years later, when
he returned to the Alameda County Courthouse jail as the one of the
most famous prisoners in America.

BY THE TIME NEWTON WAS RELEASED FROM THE JAIL IN SANTA
Rita, Bobby Seale had also broken away from Donald Warden and the
Afro-American Association. Instead, Seale had joined the Soul Stu-
dents Advisory Council on the Merritt College campus. Publicly, the
SSAC presented itself as a group dedicated to pressuring the college

administration to create more course offerings for Black students. But privately, its members also saw themselves as a wing of the Revolutionary Action Movement (RAM), an underground network of radicals who viewed Black America as an occupied colony and imagined themselves laying the groundwork for a war of liberation. In the early 1960s, several founders of the SSAC traveled to Cuba to meet with Fidel Castro and RAM's spiritual leader, an exiled Black nationalist named Robert F. Williams. A Marine Corps veteran and longtime NAACP official in North Carolina, Williams had come out in favor of armed self-defense after watching a local white man charged with raping a Black woman go free. He severed ties with the NAACP, and applied for a gun license to start a Black rifle club. The FBI responded by pursuing Williams over a trumped-up kidnapping charge, and in 1961 he fled to Cuba. From there, Williams published a memoir called *Negroes with Guns* that was widely read and circulated among young Black militants.

Once Newton got out of prison, he reconnected with Seale, who urged him to join the SSAC. But from the start, Newton and the campus radicals didn't get along. Kenny Freeman, one of the SSAC leaders, told Seale that he didn't trust Newton because he came from a "bourgie family" and drank too much. Since Freeman himself came from a much more middle-class background than Newton's, he and Seale saw this as a snide way of making fun of them and taking them for ignorant "field niggers," as Seale put it. Eventually Freeman accepted Newton into the group, but the relationship soured again after Newton and Seale were arrested on Telegraph Avenue. The SSAC spread word around campus that the two had stolen $50 from them, rather than borrowing the money to post bail. They also tried to embarrass Newton and Seale by revealing that they had accepted a $100 donation from a white man—journalist Robert Scheer, an editor at the San Francisco magazine *Ramparts*, who had announced a longshot antiwar candidacy for the U.S. Congress.

Yet ironically, given the dog-eared copies of *Negroes with Guns* that the SSAC members liked to pass around, it was the issue of firearms that led to a final rupture. In early 1966, Newton conceived the idea of staging an SSAC rally in front of Merritt College on May 19, the birthday of Malcolm X, the Nation of Islam leader who had so impressed him at the McClymonds High School conference in 1963 and who had become even more of a hero to him and other young admirers after he was assassinated in early 1965. To dramatize Malcolm's message about the right of Blacks to defend themselves, Newton imagined, the student marchers would carry guns. In his law library research, he had discovered that California had an "open carry" statute that allowed citizens to carry firearms as long as the weapons were visible. He believed that a display of guns would show college administrators that the group was serious about its demands, and would also get press attention that would attract new recruits. To make that point, Newton and Seale showed up at an SSAC meeting to discuss the plan with one of Seale's pistols and scores of supporters they had rounded up on the Oakland streets.

Some two hundred people attended the SSAC meeting, where Newton presented his arguments for the Malcolm X birthday march. But the exchange quickly degenerated into more shouting about stolen funds, and it became clear that the campus radicals, for all their big talk about revolution, had no stomach for seeing how police and college officials would react to a procession of armed Black students. With a loud exchange of insults, Newton and Seale announced that they were quitting the SSAC, and stormed out of the meeting with their entourage. "So Huey and I jumped up, and we said, 'Well, fuck it. We resign,'" Seale wrote in his autobiography, claiming that on their way out they vowed: "We're going to the black community and . . . organize an organization to lead the black liberation struggle."

In reality, Newton and Seale were still more than six months away from taking the first steps toward forming such an organization. For his part, Newton had a different memory of how they felt after splitting with the SSAC. "This left us where we had been all along: nowhere," he recalled. But by the spring of 1966, the two had at least identified one of the symbols for which they would become known: the gun. As Seale put it his book, Newton's answer to the squeamish campus radicals was: "No, you must pick up guns, because guns are key." Meanwhile, unbeknownst to Newton and Seale, a second symbol with which they would become forever associated—the black panther—was about to leave its first mark on history at the other end of the country, more than two thousand miles away, deep in the Black Belt of Alabama.

CHAPTER 5

The Black Panthers of Lowndes County

A dolphus Carmichael died suddenly in January of 1962, just days after his son Stokely returned to Howard University to begin the second semester of his sophomore year. Stokely had spent the Christmas holiday at home in Morris Park, and his father had seemed his usual fit, driven self. Ever since Stokely had arrived in America at the age of eleven, Adolphus had worked so hard that his son often went days without seeing him. At dawn, Adolphus left for his primary job as a carpenter. After work, he had another part-time job, and then he moonlit as a cab driver at night. By the time Adolphus got home, the rest of the family was usually asleep. On the weekends, he was consumed with religious services and repairs on the Bronx house.

As a result, the few times father and son got to spend leisure time together were etched in Stokely's memory. He could recall the phonograph records that he found Adolphus listening to in his rare moments of relaxation. His father's favorites were crooner Nat King Cole and Louis X, the witty calypso singer nicknamed "the Charmer" who later earned a very different reputation as Nation of Islam leader Louis Farrakhan. Decades later, Stokely would recall how excited his father was after returning from a stint on a merchant ship that went all the way to Africa. The ship happened to dock in Ghana on the first day of Parliament under the country's new Black president, Kwame Nkrumah, and Adolphus managed to sneak into the gallery. With wonder, he told his son about how Nkrumah and his cabinet entered the hall dressed not in the top hats and tails of the British colonizers, but in the tattered coats and cloth caps that they had been forced to wear in prison during their fight for independence.

On the first Sunday after Stokely got back to school in Washington, D.C., his mother, May, phoned him with the awful news. Adolphus had awoken that morning saying he didn't feel well enough to go to church. Staying in bed, he asked May to fetch him a glass of water. With the first sip, Adolphus gagged and seized up with a heart attack. May called an ambulance, but by the time the medics arrived, it was too late. Later, Stokely channeled his grief into an angry commentary on the toll of racism, telling a reporter that Adolphus went to his grave at the age of forty-two "trying to prove that an honest, hard-working black man could make it in white America." Yet on the day of the funeral, Stokely was so undone that he couldn't look into the casket. "I want to remember our father the way I left him last week," he told his mother and sisters.

Still only twenty years old, Stokely Carmichael had faced two unique challenges in a youth otherwise free of the worst kind of hardship faced by many American-born Blacks. One was the need to adjust over and over again to new places and cultures. First, it had been the playful but obedient world of Black children in colonial Trinidad. Then, it was life as one of the few Black teens on the streets of the north Bronx. Next, it was the clubby universe of privileged Blacks at Howard University. Those jarring transitions had made Carmichael a quick study, a gifted mimic—and a social chameleon who could assume quite different personalities with different people in different situations.

Carmichael's other challenge was coping with separation from both of his parents as a child, while he stayed with his grandmother and aunts in Trinidad, and then with the distance of his workaholic father once he arrived in the United States. Now, Adolphus Carmichael was gone permanently before Stokely entered adulthood. Combined

with his fierce ambition, it was a loss that propelled Stokely into a series of intense mentorship relationships with older male role models,
each of whom he sought to emulate—and then outdo—on his path
to becoming the national face of Black Power.

BAYARD RUSTIN WAS THE FIRST ROLE MODEL. AT AGE FIFTEEN,
Carmichael was admitted to Bronx High School of Science, a competitive magnet school then housed in a Gothic-columned building on
184th Street. The school accepted gifted students from all five boroughs
of New York City and counted among its alumni such luminaries as the
writer E. L. Doctorow and the singer Bobby Darin. In his sophomore
year, Carmichael became friends with a white classmate named Gene
Dennis, whose father was general secretary of the American Communist Party. One day, Dennis brought Carmichael to a meeting of white
radicals into which strode a tall, imposing Black figure. The man had
a wide face and sharp cheekbones, a thick fringe of gray-flecked hair,
and a tenor voice that resonated with a strange but unforgettable self-
taught British accent. "He might not have been wearing anything so
dramatic as a cape, but in manner and gesture he *looked* as if he should
have been," Carmichael recalled of his first impression.

"Who the hell is *that*?" Carmichael asked Dennis. "That's Bayard Rustin, the socialist," his friend answered. Carmichael would
soon learn that Rustin's political identity was more complicated than
that: Rustin was a socialist only in the pro-labor sense, after ending a
youthful flirtation with communism. He was also a committed pacifist who had studied Gandhism in India and a homosexual who had
defied attempts by some civil rights leaders to sideline him after he
was arrested for having sex with a man. In later years Rustin championed gay rights. Yet what struck Carmichael was how grandly and
unapologetically Rustin embodied his racial identity. "It was his *blackness* that had inspired," Carmichael recalled.

While Carmichael was in his senior year at Bronx Science, Rustin
organized a Youth March for Integrated Schools in Washington, D.C.,
and Carmichael volunteered to recruit New York City students. The

trip changed his life. While picketing with the mostly white crowd outside the U.S. Capitol, Carmichael noticed a cluster of Black protesters. He approached, and they identified themselves as members of the Nonviolent Action Group, or NAG, based at nearby Howard University. The NAG students invited Carmichael to join them, and from that day on his college ambitions shifted. His mother had hoped that he would attend Harvard, but Carmichael informed her that his heart was now set on Howard.

Carmichael joined NAG as soon as he arrived at Howard, and soon after the group invited Bayard Rustin to the campus. The students prepared for the visit by reading Rustin's essays "The Negro and Non-Violence" and "Non-Violence vs. Jim Crow," his vivid account of being arrested in the early 1940s for refusing to give up his seat on a segregated bus bound from Kentucky to Tennessee, more than a decade before Rosa Parks made her famous stand in Montgomery. After Rustin's public talk to the NAG students, the students invited him to the tiny apartment that Carmichael rented off-campus, and Bayard stayed up until the wee hours regaling them with tactical advice and colorful personal stories.

In the fall of Carmichael's sophomore year, NAG persuaded Rustin to come to Howard to debate Malcolm X, who was then known to the students as the intriguing but somewhat frightening spokesman for the Nation of Islam. As a teenager, Carmichael had seen Malcolm speak in New York City, where he presided over the Nation of Islam mosque in Harlem, but this was his first opportunity to observe the man up close. Before the debate, NAG hosted a dinner, and when Malcolm appeared, the room turned "totally silent but strangely charged," Carmichael recalled. "There he stood, smiling almost diffidently in the doorway. Tall, slender, his horn-rimmed glasses glinting, the expression of his lean face alert, carrying himself erect, with a formality, a quiet dignity, in his posture, yet beneath it an unmistakable warmth. Without doing a thing for a moment he simply commanded the entire space."

Malcolm immediately disarmed the students with a self-deprecating quip about being detained by an interview with the campus newspaper. "Sorry if I'm a little late," he smiled, "but your young editors turned me every which way but loose." Refusing offers of food due to his religious practice of consuming only one meal a day, Malcolm patiently drank coffee while the others ate. Carmichael remembered one moment in particular from the dinner: when the only university official present, a dean named Patricia Roberts, asked Malcolm a probing question and he responded with a thoughtful answer and "a long, challenging look accompanied by his slightly ironic grin." In Carmichael's description, Dean Roberts, who would later be appointed by President Jimmy Carter as the first Black woman to serve in the U.S. cabinet under her married name of Patricia Roberts Harris, proceeded "to blush and emit something that sounded suspiciously like a soft giggle."

In his debate with Rustin that evening, advertised by the title "Integration vs. Separation," Malcolm electrified the standing-room-only crowd gathered in Howard's Cramton Auditorium. "Before you were American, you were *black*," he proclaimed, drawing a roar of approval from the mostly middle-class students preparing for lives in America's small integrated Black elite. "Before you were a Republican, you were *black*," Malcolm continued, drawing an even louder roar. "Before you were a Democrat, you were *black*," he went on, drawing the loudest roar yet. Meanwhile, Rustin seemed uncharacteristically soft-spoken and hurried in his plea for integration. Yet while everyone present agreed that Malcolm won the debate on style points, Carmichael and his fellow NAG members remained loyal to Bayard. "Malcolm did not 'convert' me or anyone else in NAG that evening," Carmichael recalled. The next spring, after Rustin was chosen to organize the 1963 March on Washington, he repaid that loyalty. He asked several of his NAG disciples to join the planning committee, assigning them key roles organizing transportation and other logistical details.

The first crack in the cult of Rustin came on the eve of that famous protest, as it became clear that the march had become "respectable," as Carmichael's friend and fellow student activist Cleve Sellers put it in a tone of disdain. Instead of a massive act of passive resistance, the

March on Washington turned into a huge rally staged for television, with a lineup of famous speakers addressing a cast of thousands on the Washington Mall. By then, Carmichael and other NAG members were spending their summers registering voters with SNCC in the Deep South, and they were outraged when the march organizers insisted on censoring parts of the speech prepared by SNCC chairman John Lewis.

For Carmichael's part, his final break with Rustin came the following summer, over his mentor's role in the drama surrounding the Mississippi Freedom Democratic Party at the 1964 Democratic convention in Atlantic City. Like the rest of the SNCC organizers, Carmichael was furious at the Black elders and white politicians who conspired to block the bid by Fannie Lou Hamer's delegation to replace the Mississippi segregationists. But Carmichael was particularly angry and disappointed with Rustin. Before the convention, Rustin had reached out to SNCC and the MFDP and promised that if they refrained from embarrassing displays of militancy, he would persuade Dr. King to support their cause. But when push came to shove, Rustin joined King in recommending that the MFDP accept the token offer of two nonvoting seats. "You're a traitor, Bayard, a traitor!" shouted the white SNCC veteran Mendy Samstein, then a close friend of Carmichael's, at a tense meeting with Rustin.

BOB MOSES, THE VISIONARY SNCC ORGANIZER WHO PLAYED A leading role in helping the MFDP mount its delegate challenge, was convinced that Rustin had a self-interested motive. At the time, Rustin was in negotiations to take a well-paid job leading a new labor-funded organization called the A. Philip Randolph Institute. Moses was convinced that Rustin didn't want to cross one of that institute's benefactors: Walter Reuther, the president of the autoworkers union and a key Lyndon Johnson and Hubert Humphrey supporter. Moses later pinpointed Atlantic City as the place where Carmichael disengaged "mentally and spiritually" from Rustin. "That broke the mentorship under Bayard," as Moses put it.

Bob Moses was in a position to comment on Carmichael's state of mind at the time, because he had replaced Rustin as Carmichael's newest role model. A small, bookish-looking man with a round face and thick glasses, Moses was every bit as quiet, unassuming, and thoughtful as he appeared. Raised in Harlem, he also attended a prestigious magnet school—Stuyvesant High School, then located on the East Side of Manhattan—and went on to win a scholarship to Hamilton College, a secluded, virtually all-white liberal arts school in upstate New York. From there, Moses was admitted to a doctoral program in philosophy at Harvard, but he dropped out after his mother died suddenly and his father suffered a psychotic breakdown. Moses was teaching math at a private New York high school, Horace Mann, when he saw a newspaper photograph of the four Black students who started the lunch counter sit-in movement in Greensboro, North Carolina, in early 1960. "The students in that picture had a certain look in their faces, sort of sullen, angry, determined," he recalled. "Before, the Negro in the South had always looked on the defensive, cringing. This time they were taking the initiative."

Moses continued to follow the sit-in movement as it spread through the spring of 1960, and during his summer vacation he traveled south to see how he could help. By then, the movement's leaders had formed SNCC and hired a full-time staffer, a white seminarian from New York City named Jane Stembridge, who set up shop in a corner of the SCLC office in Atlanta. Moses volunteered to help Stembridge collect mail and send out letters informing the world of SNCC's existence. At first, many of the group's student founders were suspicious of Moses, because he was older and seemed at once so serious and so eager. Some even thought he might be a government or communist spy. But Moses impressed Ella Baker, SNCC's patron saint, and by the end of the summer she sent him into the Deep South to look for volunteers. Baker gave Moses introductions to local activists in the Delta, including one, a sharecropper named Amzie Moore, whose efforts to register Black voters in Cleveland, Mississippi, inspired Moses with a new, near mystical sense of mission about the cause of Black voting rights.

The next summer, Moses returned to Mississippi to continue his registration crusade just as Carmichael was drawn into the Southern struggle for the first time, as part of a NAG group that answered the call for Freedom Ride reinforcements. The original Freedom Riders from the Congress of Racial Equality who set out to test the South's new laws desegregating interstate transportation facilities were savagely attacked by white mobs in Alabama. Charging into the fray, Carmichael and dozens of other Northern college students flew south and started boarding buses headed for Jackson, Mississippi. In Jackson, they joined John Lewis and James Bevel in a group of seventy-two Freedom Riders who were arrested for disorderly conduct.

Along with Lewis, Bevel and dozens of others, Carmichael was sent to the Mississippi state penitentiary called Parchman Farm. Although he had less experience with prison than many of the others, Carmichael immediately impressed the group with his courage and his wit. He outlasted everyone on a hunger strike, then laughingly told his cellmates that he never wanted to hear the words "hunger strike" again. That fall, Carmichael returned to Howard, but he kept hearing about Bob Moses from Freedom Riders who stayed in the South to join Moses's latest voter registration drive in Mississippi's McComb County. In one story, Moses endured a bloody beating to the head and then bravely brought charges against one of his attackers, a cousin of a local white sheriff. Hearing such tales of bravery, Carmichael became eager to return to the Delta and meet the inspiring leader who was said to live up to his biblical name.

Carmichael got his chance in the summer of 1962, when SNCC assigned him to Moses's latest campaign in Greenwood, Mississippi. Arriving at the SNCC Freedom House in Greenwood, Carmichael asked a bespectacled, soft-spoken organizer dressed in baggy overalls where he could find Bob Moses, unaware that the man was Moses himself. "I hadn't realized who I had been talking to," Carmichael recalled, "because Bob had absolutely no swagger about himself, no posturing, no ostentatiousness, no self-projection." Searching for a way get to know the enigmatic math professor, Carmichael kept Moses up all night peppering him with questions about Gödel's "incompleteness theorems." Moses was impressed that Carmichael wanted to understand the details of the complicated proofs, published by German mathematician Kurt Gödel in the 1930s, that showed the impossibility of finding axiomatic solutions to certain mathematical problems. "It took all night, but he went with me step-by-step, line-by-line," Moses recalled. "He had a real thirst for incisive intellectual knowledge and understanding the completeness of a certain level of logic." Carmichael had left Howard that spring thinking that he might major in philosophy, and now his introduction to Moses clinched that decision.

SOON CARMICHAEL BEGAN TO DRESS LIKE MOSES, IN FARMING dungarees and work boots, the better to fit in with Delta sharecroppers. The two continued their long philosophical discussions, particularly about Moses's favorite thinker, the French existentialist Albert Camus. Moses carried a frayed copy of Camus' *The Rebel* in his back pocket, and he expounded on the book's thesis that man is defined by what he does, not by what he says, and that challenging injustice can bring meaning to a seemingly arbitrary life. Carmichael marveled at further examples of Moses's unflappable courage. One day, Moses drove forty miles back to the SNCC headquarters in Greenwood after it came under attack by white vigilantes, then curled up in a corner and took a nap once the danger passed. More than anything, Carmichael was inspired by Moses's prowess as an organizer. Quietly and patiently, he won the trust of Blacks in the Delta with a humble willingness to listen, to explain, and to show respect for even the poorest and the most uneducated. "Boil it down to gravy, Bob was, first of all, a phenomenal organizer," Carmichael recalled. "You could not be around Bob long and fail to see how much he really loved our people and was totally dedicated to our liberation."

The next summer, Carmichael worked alongside Moses again in Mississippi, and the following spring, Moses made a special trip to Howard University, where Carmichael was finishing his senior year. Moses informed Carmichael and the other Howard activists of his ambitious plan for the summer of 1964: to recruit a thousand Black and white student volunteers to register voters and start health clinics and schools for young children across the state of Mississippi. Then Moses asked Carmichael to take charge of the operation across the fifty thousand square miles of the 2nd Congressional District of Mississippi, stretching from the middle of the state to its western border. Carmichael was "overwhelmed," he recalled, to be offered "the greatest honor and responsibility I'd had in my young life." For his part, Moses entrusted Carmichael with that responsibility, at the age of twenty-two, because he saw in the soon-to-be Howard graduate a unique mix of qualifications to handle the disparate players who would be part of the Freedom Summer experiment. Carmichael would be working with poor Delta sharecroppers, with middle-class Black students, and with privileged whites, most of whom had never experienced anything like the perilous conditions in the Deep South. "It was an almost impossible job," Moses recalled thinking. "You had to have energy, charisma, and intelligence to pull it off. Stokely had all three."

As soon as Carmichael graduated from Howard that June, he drove a carload of activists to a Freedom Summer training retreat that Moses held at the Western College for Women, in Oxford, Ohio. Dressed modestly in dungarees strapped over a white T-shirt, Moses conducted three days of workshops to prepare some eight hundred volunteers—a majority of whom were white—for what awaited them in Mississippi. The topics ranged from the details of the state's election laws to the protocol for responding nonviolently to attacks by the Ku Klux Klan. At a workshop on the last day, Moses invoked Albert Camus' *The Plague*, comparing the United States to the fictional town that doesn't realize it has been infected by a fatal epidemic. "The country isn't willing to admit it has the plague, but it pervades the whole society," Moses explained to the rapt volunteers, just as a SNCC aide approached him and whispered alarming news into his ear.

Two days earlier, an interracial trio of volunteers who had come to the Ohio retreat from Mississippi—James Chaney and his white co-workers Andrew Goodman and Michael Schwerner—had returned to investigate the firebombing of a church in Neshoba County. Now the three men were missing. When word reached Ohio that the trio's car had been found abandoned by a roadside, Carmichael volunteered to join a search party that included Cleve Sellers, several other male organizers, and Bob Moses's wife, Dona. Driving to Mississippi and slipping into Neshoba County under cover of darkness, they spent the next few nights hunting through a landscape thick with gnarly trees, bristled scrubs, and reedy swamps. Deer flies and mosquitoes buzzed around their heads, snakes slithered in the mud underfoot, and guard dogs barked ferociously from white farmhouses in the distance.

The group ended their search several days later, when FBI agents arrived to take over the investigation. While Carmichael's stay in Neshoba County didn't last long, he would remember it as the most harrowing experience he had in his years in the Deep South, and one that changed for good his views on the civil rights movement's prohibition against armed self-defense. Asked about the episode in later years, Carmichael said he had only one regret. "I sure would not venture into those swamps and woods again unless I was well armed," he said. "And I'm talking superior firepower too."

Two months later, three bodies were found buried in an unmarked berm in Philadelphia, Mississippi. Klansmen had buried the trio of organizers after executing them in brutal fashion. Goodman and Schwerner had been shot in the heart, and Chaney had been castrated and riddled with three bullets. Moses was devastated by the news, and by the grim responsibility of comforting the parents. That was followed by the crushing experience of the Mississippi Freedom Democratic Party in Atlantic City, and by tense disputes with Jim Forman over SNCC's future. Forman wanted to follow up on Freedom Summer with more splashy campaigns and a new fundraising push, and he kept pressuring Moses to become more of a "media person," as Moses put it scornfully. For his part, Moses simply wanted to return to the quiet, self-effacing work of organizing county by county in the South.

The conflict came to a head at a SNCC planning retreat held at a theological seminary in Atlanta in February of 1965. Abruptly, Moses stood up and angrily confronted the other leaders, including

Forman, John Lewis, and Carmichael. "He said that some of us needed to leave, get out now," Lewis recalled. "*Leave*, he said. Leave the movement because we were becoming nothing but creatures of the media." Then Moses pointed the finger of blame at himself, for allowing others to make him the object of hero worship. To put a halt to all that attention, Moses announced, he planned to renounce his last name. He wanted to be known from then on only by his middle name, which came from his mother's family. "My name is no longer Robert Moses or Bob Moses," he declared. "I am Bob Parris now." Then Moses stormed out of the seminary, never to take part in another SNCC meeting or campaign again.

In his later accounts of what happened next, Carmichael insisted that it was this strange, sudden retreat by Moses that made him want to step into his mentor's shoes. "I felt a responsibility to carry on the work Bob had given so much of himself to," he wrote in his autobiography. "I just got into that Bob Moses bag," Carmichael said in another interview. "I had to see what I could do in the place no one else would go." In the memoir, Carmichael also suggested that by the time Moses quit, he had begun to envision how—and where—he would take that work a step further. After the debacle in Atlantic City, Carmichael wrote, he had started thinking about how to create "a second model" for maximizing the impact of newly registered Black voters, and had decided that it shouldn't be in Mississippi but next door, in Alabama.

BY THEN, CARMICHAEL AND EVERYONE ELSE AT SNCC WAS ALSO FOL-lowing the evolution that Malcolm X had undergone since splitting with the Nation of Islam the previous year. Raised by followers of Marcus Garvey, the Jamaican-born nationalist who urged Black Americans to seek their own colony separate from whites, Malcolm Little had converted and joined the Nation of Islam while serving a prison term for larceny and adopted its practice of rejecting his given last name as a symbol of spiritual rebirth. For a decade, he was the most visible national spokesman for Elijah Muhammad, the Nation of Islam leader who espoused a version of that faith that included not only a message of Black separatism but also the belief that white people were degenerate "blue-eyed" devils created in a breeding experiment by a mad Black scientist. Following President Kennedy's assassination in late 1963, however, Muhammad had suspended Malcolm for declaring that the murder represented "chickens coming home to roost." For Malcolm's part, the controversy represented an opportunity to make a clean break from Elijah Muhammad after a period of growing disillusionment with the self-styled prophet's predatory and hypocritical practice of seducing young female assistants and followers.

In March of 1964, Malcolm officially left the Nation of Islam, and two months later he embarked on a pilgrimage to Mecca and got a taste of the true multinational and multiracial spectrum of the Islamic faith. He also witnessed firsthand the way that the newly independent countries of former colonial Africa were putting aside tribal and ideological differences to form an alliance called the Organization of African Unity. Returning to America, Malcolm rented out a large meeting space on the second floor of the Audubon Ballroom north of Harlem to give a speech in which he announced plans to form a new American movement based on the African model called the Organization of Afro-American Unity (OAAU).

Malcolm's speech that day would be most remembered for his call to American Blacks to seek freedom, justice, and equality "by any means necessary." Many interpreted those words as a call to violence, but in fact they came immediately after Malcolm argued that the African example demonstrated the need for peaceful cooperation and compromise. "Those who formed the organization of African states have differences," Malcolm told an audience of six hundred at the Audubon Ballroom. "They represent probably every segment, every type of thinking. You have some leaders that are considered Uncle Toms, some leaders who are considered very militant. But even the militant African leaders were able to sit down at the same table with African leaders whom they considered to be Toms, or Tshombes, or that type of character. They forgot their differences for the sole purpose of bringing benefits to the whole."

Malcolm's OAAU address was also notable for its point-by-point presentation of his new agenda. Malcolm read aloud a statement entitled "Basic Aims and Objectives of the Organization of Afro-American Unity" that contained echoes of the Declaration of Independence. Then he elaborated five areas of action: "Establishment" (seeking alliances among Black groups), "Self-Defense" (demanding the right to bear arms for purposes of self-protection): "Education" (emphasizing Black-run rather than integrated schools), "Politics and Economics," and "Social." In this last category, Malcolm included everything from a call to celebrate Black culture and history, to an appeal to Blacks to take personal responsibility for fighting drug use and crime, even while standing up to police abuse and corruption. In a notably prescient passage, he singled out new law enforcement measures that had recently been promoted by then New York governor Nelson Rockefeller. "The no-knock law, the stop-and-frisk law," Malcolm argued, "that's an anti-Negro law."

In the fall of 1964, Carmichael began hearing more and more praise for Malcolm as the latter embarked on another tour of Africa and Europe and was greeted as an honored visitor wherever he went. At a hotel in Nairobi, Malcolm ran into John Lewis, who was touring Africa after accompanying other SNCC leaders on a trip to Guinea. "After a long talk with Malcolm," Carmichael recalled, "even John Lewis came back from Africa sounding like a Pan-Africanist revolutionary." Several months later, Fannie Lou Hamer joined a group of young Mississippi Blacks who traveled to New York City and heard Malcolm speak at a church in Harlem. "He made a hell of an impression," Carmichael recalled. "The youth came back elated, just *elated*, talking about nothing but Malcolm." Meanwhile, Malcolm charmed Fannie Lou Hamer with his gentlemanly warmth and show of respect for her courage. "Even good Christian Mrs. Hamer had a crush," Carmichael recalled, quoting Fannie Lou as saying: "Stokely, he so handsome and so kind."

As a college student, Carmichael had remained loyal to Bayard Rustin when Rustin debated Malcolm X at Howard University, but even then he saw how Malcolm's rhetoric captivated his classmates.

Now, Carmichael realized that after breaking with the Nation of Islam, Malcolm was positioned to play a more strategic role in expanding the civil rights struggle beyond the South. "I knew we in SNCC would have to begin looking seriously to the ghettos in the North, for the kind of grass roots organizing we'd been doing in the South," Carmichael recalled. "Malcolm would be key." Although no public negotiations had taken place, talk began within SNCC of a potential alliance with Malcolm's new OAAU movement. "Malcolm had always, always, been respectful and supportive of us in SNCC," Carmichael recalled. "Of all the civil rights groups, I knew he felt closest to us, to the SNCC spirit."

As a sign of respect—and a precursor to further talks—SNCC's field secretaries in Alabama, Silas Norman and Fay Bellamy, invited Malcolm to speak at Selma's Brown A.M.E. Chapel on February 4, 1965. By then, the Southern Christian Leadership Conference had joined the Selma voting rights campaign at the invitation of local activists, so the SCLC's Reverend Fred Shuttlesworth and Dr. King's wife, Coretta, also spoke at the church. Predictably, newspaper reports portrayed Malcolm as a dangerous fanatic in comparison to the more moderate civil rights veterans. With his talk of demanding "the right to the ballot . . . by whatever means is necessary," one press account concluded, Malcolm was advocating "the road to violence." But Carmichael, who was still in Mississippi, heard nothing but raves about Malcolm from the young Blacks who attended the Brown Chapel event. "Sure his presence there had upset some people," Carmichael recalled, "but the grassroots Africans in Selma had been really responsive."

Two and a half weeks later, Carmichael was driving with other SNCC organizers from Mississippi to Selma when they heard a bulletin on the car radio: "Former Black Muslim leader Malcolm X has been shot and killed." The passengers in the car listened in stunned silence, trying to process the news as well as the shocking reports of who had done the deed. According to the radio bulletin, Black men had stormed the stage at the Audubon Ballroom with shotguns and fired on Malcolm in front of a packed house that included his wife and children. Although three members of the Nation of Islam would be apprehended and sent to prison for the murder, Carmichael instinctively felt that there must be more to the plot—a suspicion that in time would be borne when two of the men were exonerated and scholars gathered evidence of a plot organized out of the Nation of Islam mosque in Newark.

Carmichael also sensed immediately that Malcolm's death wasn't a loss only for Black America. If white authorities had had anything to do with organizing or turning a blind eye to a murder plot, Carmichael thought, they would come to regret it in dealing with a new generation of Blacks who were no longer prepared to take directions from Dr. King and other older civil rights leaders. "See," he reasoned, "Malcolm was the only figure of that generation, the *only* one, who had the natural authority, the style, language, and charisma, to lead and discipline rank-and-file urban youth. The only one who commanded that kind of respect. Over and over you saw it. Time and again. Many times you saw a crowd of angry Africans fixing to tear the place up, and the only person who could reason with them, cool them out, was Malcolm. That was because the masses knew him and trusted him. Now they'd killed him. Bad mistake."

Five days after Malcolm X's assassination, the civil rights struggle took another fateful turn when a sixteen-year-old Black demonstrator named Jimmie Lee Jackson was shot dead by white policemen not far from Selma. With the support of Dr. King, the SCLC conceived a plan to take Jackson's body on a march from Selma to the state capitol of Montgomery, as a way of honoring his death and dramatizing the call for federal voting rights legislation. It was then that SNCC's leaders voted to pull out of the march, even though they had begun the Selma campaign. For Carmichael, boycotting the march meant that he could move forward with his plan to take the organizing skills he learned from Bob Moses a step further, by moving to Alabama and organizing voters to form an all-Black political party. But in so doing, Carmichael would have to rely on groundwork laid by yet another older role model, one whose name would be far less remembered by history than Bayard Rustin, Bob Moses, or Malcolm X.

A WIRY WHIPPET OF A MAN, RECOGNIZABLE FROM A DISTANCE BY
a crumbled fedora he wore atop his dark, lively face, John Hulett was
a man of few words, but those words came fast. "I can probably say
twice as much in half the time," Hulett liked to joke, flashing one of
his toothy grins. Born in 1927 in the Lowndes County town of Gor-
donville, Hulett grew up on a family farm where he learned to shoot
and skin rabbits, a skill that came in handy whenever he was out of
a job. After high school, Hulett moved to Birmingham to work in a
furnace factory. He joined the foundry workers union and became
a follower of Fred Shuttlesworth, the Baptist minister renowned in
Black Birmingham for his charismatic preaching style and brave re-
covery from a near fatal dynamite attack on his home. Shuttlesworth
was head of the Birmingham office of the NAACP until Alabama
authorities banned that organization from the state, whereupon he
founded a new civil rights group called the Alabama Christian Movement for Human Rights (ACMHR). Joining the ACMHR, Hulett
registered voters, protested for better roads and playgrounds in Black
neighborhoods, and served as a bodyguard for Shuttlesworth and for
Dr. King when he came to town. At age thirty-two, Hulett returned
to Lowndes County to care for his ailing father, but he never lost the
instinct to organize.

A flat, humid stretch of former cotton fields that had grown so
poor and violent that it became known as "Bloody Lowndes," Hulett's
birthplace was "the very heart of darkness," in the words of journalist
Andrew Kopkind, when it came to circumstances for the local Black
population. Blacks outnumbered whites by the largest margin in the
state—four-to-one, or roughly twelve thousand to three thousand—
yet eighty-nine white families owned 90 percent of the land. Average
household income among whites, many of whom were illiterate, was
a modest $4,400; for Blacks, it was a much sparser $935 a year. Black
men toiled as farmhands for a little as $3 a day, while Black women
commuted more than forty miles each way to work as domestics in
Montgomery. Among whites, election fraud was so common that in

1964 almost 20 percent more ballots were cast for local offices than there were eligible white voters. Confronted with poll taxes and literacy tests, Blacks had gradually given up on exercising their voting rights, until not a single Black registered to vote for sixty years.

By 1965, Hulett and his wife, Eddie Mae, had joined a charity group in Lowndes County called the Daylight Savings Club. After passage of the Voting Rights Act that summer, the couple showed up at a club meeting with a daring proposal: to go to the county courthouse in Hayneville and demand the right to vote. Word of the plan spread, and by the time Hulett acted on the morning of the first day of March, thirty-eight fellow club members and churchgoers gathered at the courthouse. While the others waited in the parking lot, Hulett walked into the office of the registrar, a burly car salesman named Carl Golson.

"Don't you know how to knock when you come into an office?" Golson grunted.

"I came here to get registered," Hulett replied. "I didn't come here to knock."

Golson told Hulett to go away, and he did—only for that day. Two weeks later, he returned with more than forty applicants, only to find that Golson had moved to the courthouse jail. The new registration site was a dank, windowless space with a naked light bulb hanging from the ceiling and a jail cell door looming ominously in the background. Golson allowed seventeen people to fill out forms and take a literacy test before dismissing the rest, then waited several weeks before approving only two new voters—Hulett and a blind preacher.

On March 21, 1965, Dr. King led the Selma marchers across the Edmund Pettus Bridge and onto the road toward Montgomery. Two days earlier, Hulett and twenty-seven other Black residents of Lowndes County acquired the key to an abandoned department store and met there to form a new group that, inspired by Fred Shuttlesworth, they named the Lowndes County Christian Movement for Human Rights (LCCMHR). Hulett was elected chairman, and plans were made to hold Sunday meetings every week at the Mount Gillard Missionary Baptist Church in the nearby town of Whitehall. So Hulett's

voting rights crusade was well under way the next week when he
and another member of the LCCMHR, a bricklayer named Robert
Strickland, went to watch the Selma march pass through Lowndes
County and met Stokely Carmichael.

After withdrawing from the Selma march, SNCC had freed its
members to make personal decisions about whether to participate.
That was how chairman John Lewis found himself on the Edmund
Pettus Bridge on Bloody Sunday, while executive secretary Jim Forman was in Montgomery with Sammy Younge and other student
protesters from the Tuskegee Institute. For his part, Carmichael saw
no point in trying to upstage the sainted Martin Luther King Jr. "I
said, the people *looove* Dr. King, don't oppose him," he argued during
SNCC's internal debates. Instead, Carmichael proposed the idea of
piggybacking on the march to lay the groundwork for a new, Bob
Moses–style organizing campaign in Lowndes County.

Carmichael argued that Lowndes County was a ripe target because it had so many Black residents, but also because it was so notoriously backward and Klan-infested that other civil rights groups had
stayed away. "As far as movement was concerned, this was virgin territory, bro," as he put it, "with no organizational rivalries to deal with,
precisely because it was a terrorist stronghold." Carmichael found an
ally in his SNCC colleague Bob Mants, who had initially accompanied Lewis on Bloody Sunday. "We're going into Lowndes County
together, bro," Mants told Carmichael. "I'm with you."

As the Selma march reached Lowdnes County, Carmichael and
Mants trailed behind, chatting with locals who turned out to watch
and to staff an overnight tent encampment. Along Route 80, they
came across John Hulett and his bricklayer friend, Robert Strickland.
When Carmichael asked for their names and addresses and told the
two men that he planned to come back after the march was over,
Strickland was skeptical. As a teenager, Strickland had served five
years in prison for shooting a local white boy who tried to attack him.
Ever since, he had kept a shotgun on his front porch, and he didn't
think much of Dr. King and his pious talk about nonviolence. "You
one of them non-violence folks, huh?" Strickland asked Carmichael.

"Well, in this county, turn the other cheek and these here pecker-woods will hand you back half of what you sitting on. If you do come back, you're going to have to find a different way to come in here, young fella." When Carmichael insisted that he and Mants planned to come back "by any means necessary"—a reference to Malcolm X that was probably lost on the grizzled mason—Strickland responded with a dubious smile.

Carmichael and Mants did return to Lowndes County the next week—along with SNCC organizers Scott B. Smith, Judy Richard-son, and Willie Vaughn—and made good on their promise to look up John Hulett. But Hulett remained wary. He had seen organizers from the SCLC pass through the county before, never to return. Hulett wondered if the young SNCC workers had the stomach for the dangers they would face in Lowndes County. To prove themselves, Carmichael and his comrades offered to pass out leaflets advertising the next meeting of the LCCMHR, which was scheduled to take place at the Mount Gillard church that Sunday. They took a stack of leaflets to a local segregated high school, hoping to urge students to spread the word to their parents.

No sooner did the SNCC workers arrive in the schoolyard than five cars pulled up, and out stepped fifteen sheriff's deputies, local men authorized by the county sheriff to carry guns. When one of the deputies ordered the strangers off the property, Carmichael walked to the dusty car the group had arrived in, pulled out a walkie-talkie, and pretended to call SNCC headquarters. "If you're going to arrest me, do it," Carmichael told the deputies coolly. "If not, don't waste my time. I have work to do." The deputies backed off and drove away, and the awestruck Black schoolchildren mobbed the strangers, eagerly snatching up leaflets. By that Sunday, reports of the schoolyard standoff had rippled across the county. More than five hundred people showed up to meet the SNCC workers who dared to stand up to the sheriff's men. Farmers Matthew and Emma Jackson were so inspired that they offered Carmichael the use of an empty house they owned nearby, a four-room shanty without indoor plumbing that the SNCC workers moved into and nicknamed "Freedom House."

THE CHANCE ENCOUNTER WITH JOHN HULETT ON THE SELMA
march, Carmichael realized, had given his ambitious plans for Lowndes County a providential head start. "You have any idea how long
that would have taken as an organizer?" Carmichael remarked, thinking back to his arduous work in Mississippi. "Without the march? Dr.
King handed all that to us on a platter, and we took it." The day after
the church meeting, Carmichael and Hulett were back at the county
jail with another seventy-five prospective voters. Over the following
months, the SNCC outsiders and the Christian Movement insiders
divided up organizing work. The youngsters went door-to-door visiting sharecroppers on their front porches and in their kitchens, while
the elders spread the word through churches and local Black civic
organizations.

At first, it was slow going. Most Lowndes County Blacks were
afraid to stick their necks out, particularly once they heard what happened to the Jackson family after it became known they were helping
the organizers. Whites stopped buying Matthew Jackson's crops, and
the Jackson children were fired from their jobs as a bus driver and a
schoolteacher. At the jailhouse, Carl Golson intimidated Blacks who
showed up to register by laying a loaded pistol and an open whiskey
bottle on the sign-up table. By May, only twelve more applications
had been approved. Even after the Justice Department intervened
to force the county to abandon literacy tests and widen the applica-
tion window to four days a month, Golson rejected almost half the
238 applicants who stepped forward, disqualifying them for errors
as small as misspelling street addresses or placing signatures in the
wrong place.

On a torpid day in early summer, John Hulett approached a wooden
sharecropper's shack to find a young girl standing on the porch. "Baby,
tell your mother to step to the door," Hulett coaxed. When the mother
appeared in the door frame, Hulett introduced himself and asked if
she had heard about the drive to register voters. Hulett tried to explain
what could be accomplished if Blacks were able to elect their own

county officers, from extending access to running water to building better schools. "Uh-huh," the woman muttered, not seeming to understand or care. "You don't need to be afraid," Hulett promised. "If we stand together, there ain't nobody can turn us 'round." But the woman remained mute until he went on his way. Only the following Sunday, when the woman and her husband showed up at the weekly Christian Movement meeting wearing their finest church clothes, did Hulett see that his organizing visit had paid off.

Then in August, events in Washington, D.C., quickened the pace of Black voter registration across the South. In the ornate President's Room on Capitol Hill, surrounded by leaders from both political parties and pillars of the civil rights establishment including Dr. King, President Johnson signed the Voting Rights Act of 1965 into law. Three days later, Attorney General Nicholas Katzenbach announced that he would send federal "examiners" to nine Southern counties with the worst records of voter intimidation. By the next morning, federal officials were on the ground, overseeing the registration of more than 1,100 Blacks within twenty-four hours across Alabama, Mississippi, and Louisiana. In Lowndes County, scores of Blacks arrived in Hayneville to discover that examiners had moved the registration center from the county jail to a more welcoming federal post office in Fort Deposit, seventeen miles away. Over the next three days, more than two hundred applicants made their way to Fort Deposit, ignoring a pickup truck with a rifle sticking out of the cargo bed that someone had parked outside the post office.

With federal help on hand, and after earning the trust of Hulett and the other locals, Carmichael decided to introduce his idea for a new Black political party. At a Sunday meeting of the Christian Movement, Carmichael gave an impassioned speech about the folly of registering Blacks only to have them vote for segregationist Democrats who ruled the state. "There's no room for Negroes in the same party of Wallace," Carmichael declared, invoking the hated name of the state's governor, George Wallace. Still furious over the Atlantic City convention experience, Carmichael told the crowd that President Johnson and the Democrats in Washington were "the most treacherous enemy of the Negro at the national level. They step on us, take our vote for granted and are completely irrelevant."

Hulett and the others were intrigued by Carmichael's pitch, but they wanted to know how a third party would work. So Carmichael asked Jack Minnis, the head of SNCC's research department in Atlanta, for help. Disheveled, obsessive, and always surrounded by clouds of cigarette smoke, the thirty-nine-year-old white Oklahoma native was renowned for his ability to unearth local records that were helpful to SNCC field workers. Over the next few days, Minnis pored through all twelve volumes of the Alabama Code of Laws until he found what he was looking for: an obscure statute that laid out instructions for forming new political parties at the county level. Dating from the post–Civil War era, the law was originally designed to help vanquished Confederates make a comeback, but no one had made use of it in decades.

In a letter to Carmichael, Minnis spelled out the details: to become official, a new party had to hold a nominating convention in the spring, then win 20 percent of the vote in at least one race in the fall. "It's going to take a major educational effort, I'm sure, between now and next November," Minnis cautioned, but he advised that it could be done. After a spirited debate over whether getting mixed up in party politics was "white people's business," Hulett's group voted to move forward with Carmichael's plan, and Jack Minnis informed them of one additional detail. Alabama law required political parties to select animal symbols that could be recognized by illiterate voters. Like its counterparts across the country, the state's Republican Party chose an elephant. Alabama Democrats, however, had rejected the donkey, their party's traditional symbol, in favor of a rooster.

To find an appropriate symbol for the new Lowndes County party, Minnis assigned Ruth Howard, a young Black volunteer in the Atlanta office. Howard proposed a dove, but Minnis rejected that image as too meek. Then the idea of a panther emerged, inspired by the athletic mascot of Clark University, a nearby historically Black college. Howard asked Jennifer Lawson, a SNCC staffer with a gift for illustration, to sketch a panther. At some point, Lawson's drawing was shown to Dottie Zellner in the Communications Department, and she suggested making the whiskers more prominent and inking the entire panther black. By the time everyone had weighed in, this interracial team of women had produced an image that would become world famous as a symbol of virile Black nationalism: a slithering black panther, with a serpentine tail, bared teeth, and sharp claws protruding from two enormous paws.

IN LATE DECEMBER, 1965, THE SNCC NEWSLETTER THE *STUDENT Voice* announced the founding of the new party, to be called the Lowndes County Freedom Organization, and the story was accompanied by an illustration of the prowling black panther. Carmichael and his comrades began blanketing the county with leaflets contrasting the panther and the new party's motto—"One Man, One Vote"—with the crowing rooster of the Alabama Democrats and their segregationist slogan: "White Supremacy for the Right." Over the coming months, excitement generated by the panther symbol kept scores of Blacks from leaving the county even as white farmers evicted sharecroppers who registered to vote. Along Route 80, SNCC workers erected the shelter for displaced sharecroppers they christened "Freedom City"—a compound of ten Army surplus tents crammed with sixty cots and plywood floors to keep the tents from sinking into the swampy ground. Through the winter, Freedom City also became a hub for political education, as SNCC workers, using hand-drawn storybooks, conducted workshops to teach the squatters how elections worked and what various county officials did.

By the end of January, more than two thousand Lowndes County Blacks had registered to vote, the most since Reconstruction a century earlier. The rest of the civil rights world had also taken notice. In Selma, Hosea Williams, the aide to Dr. King who was in charge of the SCLC's registration efforts in the South, called a meeting at the St. Paul Methodist Episcopal Church to urge new voters to support reform-minded Democrats. "If any Negro is crazy enough to talk about a third party, he's out of his mind," Williams fumed. "We may mess around here and create a monster in Alabama. It will be detrimental to generations of Negroes unborn." But in a theatrical maneuver, Carmichael arrived at the church before Williams and used the illustrated pamphlets to make the case for a third party. "If you're registered in the Democratic Party, you back this," Carmichael exclaimed, waving the Democratic Party leaflet with the white rooster in one hand. In the other hand, he held up a black panther flyer. "You ever seen a panther?" Carmichael asked the crowd with a mischievous smile. "He can't be tamed, and once he gets going, ain't nothing going to stop him. He's a mean cat."

As if to prove Carmichael's point, the Alabama Democrats met the next week and showed how little clout the reformists touted by Hosea Williams actually possessed. Chief among the racial moderates was Attorney General Richmond Flowers, who was courting Black voters in a bid to replace George Wallace as governor, a race in which Flowers was expected to face Wallace's wife, Lurleen. Flowers argued for changing the party's flagrant slogan of "White Supremacy for the Right," but he managed to get it watered down only to the slightly tamer "Democrats for White Supremacy." After the vote, a party veteran made fun of the new linguistic niceties to Marshall Frady of *Newsweek* magazine. "No candidate is going to be elected any more hollering nigguh, nigguh, nigguh," the pol snickered. "Or knee-gro, that is. We can't even *say* nigguh anymore."

According to the obscure election law that Jack Minnis had unearthed, would-be new parties were required to hold nominating conventions on the first Tuesday of May, Alabama's primary day. At a Sunday meeting in April, LCFO members declared their candidacies for seven county offices. John Hinson, a brick mason, announced for school board and handed out homemade brochures. Alice Moore, a forty-two-year-old sharecropper's wife, already had a campaign promise ready for her tax assessor campaign. "Tax the rich to feed the poor—that's my slogan," Moore declared. In a healthy sign of competition, there were two candidates for county sheriff: Jesse Favors, a railroad worker, and Sidney Logan, a World War II veteran who was one of the few Blacks in Lowndes County to own his farm. Meanwhile, John Hulett announced that he wouldn't run for office, telling the crowd that he wanted to remain free to oversee the election process and to deal with any last-minute hurdles.

Hulett didn't have to wait long. The election law also required that nominating conventions be held close to established polling places. So Hulett wrote the county sheriff, Frank Ryals, to request use of the yard outside the courthouse in Hayneville. At the last minute, Ryals denied the request, claiming that that he couldn't guarantee protection against vigilantes. Hulett responded by convening an emergency meeting of the LCFO, at which members voted to proceed with the convention anyway. Carmichael volunteered to send a letter to Assistant Attorney General John Doar asking the Justice Department for help. "If we do not hear from you, or if the U.S. government does not find itself able to protect the participants, we shall be forced to look to such resources as we can muster on our own," Carmichael informed Doar, dropping a not-so-subtle hint that the conventioneers might arm themselves.

On the Saturday before primary day, Charles Nesson, a twenty-seven-year-old aide to Doar in the Justice Department, arrived in Lowndes County to mediate. What if there's shooting? Nesson asked when Hulett informed him of the decision to proceed with the nominating convention. "We are going to stay out there" and "die together," Hulett replied, as a stricken look crossed Nesson's face. At the weekly church meeting of the LCFO the next day, Nesson pleaded again for the convention to be delayed, but Hulett refused to back down. "We are going to have it," Hulett insisted. Shaken, Nesson left the church and returned later that night, as the meeting was about adjourn, with news that Richmond Flowers, the moderate state attorney general, had ruled that the convention could take place as long as it was moved from the courthouse to the nearby First Baptist Church.

TUESDAY, MAY 3, 1966, WAS THE KIND OF SUNNY SPRING DAY cherished by Black Belt natives, when the hickory trees are in bloom and the clay soil in the fields has yet to be baked hard and gray by the summer sun. For some two thousand Black residents of Lowndes County, it would be remembered as the day when they voted for first time in their lives. Of that number, more than half went to the Hayneville courthouse and cast ballots in the Democratic primary. Some did so out of fear of reprisals; others because they owed a white candidate a favor. Still others didn't know that they had any other choice. For sixty-four-year-old Iona Morgan, who put on a red dress and one of her best church hats for the occasion, it came as a surprise that voting was so easy. "It wasn't nothing bad," Morgan marveled as she left the courthouse. Willie Bolden, an eighty-one-year-old grandson of slaves, came out feeling a head taller than his official height of five-foot-three. "It made me think I was sort of somebody," Bolden beamed.

Meanwhile, at the First Baptist Church a half mile away, some nine hundred Black citizens stood in line to vote in the nominating convention of the first Black Panther Party. On the sloping lawn outside the church, seven wooden tables were piled with ballots for each office at stake. The candidates stood behind the tables, so voters could look them over. Church volunteers explained how to mark the ballots and offered help for the aged and the blind. In the distance, an impromptu choir sang spirituals and freedom songs. Wearing his trademark crumpled fedora, John Hulett passed out balloons stamped "Vote for the Lowndes County Freedom Organization" and grinned with relief at the strong turnout and the absence of violence. But in a quiet corner of the churchyard, a sixty-seven-year-old veteran of World War I pulled three shotgun shells out of his denim overalls to show a reporter that he was prepared for any trouble. "I remember when the minister got shot here," the man said, referring to Jonathan Daniels, the white seminarian who was killed after being released from the Hayneville jail. "We gonna protect our friends this time."

At half past seven o'clock, as the sun was setting, the nominees were announced. The one contested race, for sheriff, had been won by Sidney Logan, the burly forty-one-year-old farm owner. Asked by a reporter why he wanted to be sheriff, Logan said that he had dreamed of running for the office ever since one of Frank Ryals's deputies blocked the door to the county jail the first time he tried to register to vote. "Go home," the deputy commanded. How did Logan feel now that he would be running against Ryals in the general election? the reporter asked. "I don't go out to lose," Logan replied.

Before the crowd dispersed, Willie Ricks, the fiery SNCC organizer from Georgia, climbed the steps of the church to speak. "When people talk about Selma, they tell you there's some bad white folks down there," Ricks shouted, his arms thrusting from a black denim coat he wore over a black shirt and black slacks. "When they talk about Wilcox County, or Greene County, they tell you there's some bad white folks down there." Pausing for effect, Ricks drew a loud roar with his punch line: "But when you mention Lowndes Country, they say, 'There's some bad niggers down there.' We gonna show Alabama just how bad we are!"

With the indispensable help of John Hulett, Stokely Carmichael had indeed pulled off a miracle in Lowndes County. Not only had the two men succeeded in increasing the number of registered Blacks from zero to more than two thousand in the space of one year; they had done the unthinkable and founded a Black political party from scratch in the heart of the Jim Crow South. Still, if Bayard Rustin and Bob Moses had been advising Carmichael, they might have counseled caution. Rustin, the hard-nosed political realist, might have suggested waiting for the results of the November election before proclaiming victory. Moses, the humble organizer, might have wanted to see if the Black Panther Party experiment could be duplicated in other counties across the region. But like Moses's denim overalls, humility and patience were about to go out of style. In the rush of events to follow, the tentative triumph in Lowndes County would be touted as a model for nothing less than a racial revolution, and become a calling card in the fastest ascent of a major Black leader since Martin Luther King Jr. rocketed to national fame in Montgomery a decade earlier.

CHAPTER 6

A Coup in Kingston Springs

F ive days after the nominating convention in Hayneville, Carmichael drove with a carful of SNCC comrades to Kingston Springs, a small town outside of Nashville, for one of the organization's occasional week-long retreats. Some 150 field organizers and staffers from the Atlanta and New York offices were gathering at Bethany Hills, a scenic religious camp in the Tennessee woods, to discuss future plans and to conduct the annual election of SNCC officers. By this time, the attendees knew they would be selecting a successor to executive secretary Jim Forman, who was exhausted and suffering from ulcers after five years in his job and had announced plans to step down. Carmichael claimed that he expected John Lewis to be reelected as chairman, in spite of scattered grumbling that Lewis had grown out of touch with the organization's increasingly militant mood.

During the drive to Tennessee, Carmichael insisted, he barely thought about the upcoming summit. Instead, he talked about the prospect of opening a new organizing front in Washington, D.C., his old college stamping ground, now that Dr. King had signaled that the civil rights movement was headed north by planting his flag in Chicago. "I truly wasn't paying that much attention" to internal politics, Carmichael maintained. "SNCC had never, to my knowledge, voted any of its two executive officers out. And I thought that if it came to an election, the general sentiment in John's favor would prevail, easily."

Lewis, who arrived in Kingston Springs badly jet-lagged after an overnight flight from Europe, had a different memory. "As soon as I got back from the airport," he recalled, "I learned that Stokely had been mounting a campaign for the chairmanship." Lewis professed to be shocked that anyone in SNCC would engage in such "behind-the-scenes campaigning," given the group's ethos of "utter openness." But Lewis was also worn out after a year on the speaking circuit since his heroics on Bloody Sunday. During one trip to San Francisco, Lewis had averaged more than three appearances a day. When he returned to Atlanta, he discovered that Penny Bartlett, a San Francisco volunteer, had sent an alarmed memo to headquarters. "Re: Health of the John Robert Lewis, Esq," Bartlett wrote. "Speaking as one who acted as chauffeur this past weekend, may I recommend for your observation that John Robert Lewis is *tired* . . . and that he needs a Rest. I had the illusion most of the time that I was driving a hearse, because the person contained therein resembled a corpse more than any other thing, so great was his exhaustion."

Upon hearing the rumors of Carmichael's maneuvering, Lewis recalled, his first impulse was to step aside and let someone else take over. But then he told himself that SNCC was at such a critical juncture in sorting out issues he cared about—nonviolence, integration, and white alliances—that he had no choice but to soldier on. "I finally decided that I had an obligation to stay, to stand up for the SNCC I believed in and for the vision of America that I could still see," Lewis recalled. "Maybe if I stayed around for another year, I could hold the group together and we could stay on course."

If Carmichael and Lewis already appeared to be on a collision course as they arrived in Kingston Springs, no one at the retreat had any doubt about who would be elected to take over for Jim Forman as executive secretary. The consensus choice was a formidable young woman who for the previous five years had been Forman's assistant: Ruby Doris Smith Robinson, a twenty-four-year-old Spelman College graduate known for her blunt honesty, brisk administrative efficiency, and proud early adoption of the all-natural Afro hairstyle. The promotion stood to make Smith Robinson the highest-ranking woman in the civil rights movement at that point. But in a sign of prevailing sexism of the day, the press would give only passing notice to that remarkable achievement—and even less to Ruby Doris's subsequent role in the tense behind-the-scenes struggles that took place within SNCC as a consequence of what unfolded that week in Kingston Springs.

IN THE DECADES AFTERWARD, THERE WOULD BE ONLY ONE BIOGraphy of Ruby Doris Smith, who changed her last name to Robinson when she married Clifford Robinson in 1964. In that slender but invaluable volume, University of Tennessee historian Cynthia Griggs Fleming suggested that to understand her complicated subject it was necessary to start with her physical appearance. Smith's dark skin, broad features and full figure were a source of psychological conflict for her, Fleming maintained, in an era when Black women were judged by white standards of beauty. Even SNCC program director Cleve Sellers, who wrote in a memoir that he was "closer to her than I was to my own sister," described Ruby Doris as being of "medium height with plain features." Yet from her earliest childhood photos, Smith was to the contrary quite striking by the Black-is-beautiful aesthetic she would help to pioneer, with glowing skin, full lips and bright, wide-set eyes.

Smith's parents J. T and Alice Smith, were both natives of rural Georgia who, instead of migrating north, settled in Atlanta. The Smiths managed to buy their own house in the working-class neighborhood of Summerhill, where Alice ran a beauty shop and J.T. started a furniture moving business and was ordained as a Baptist minister. Like North Lawndale in Chicago, Summerhill was a once predominantly Jewish enclave that by 1942, when Ruby Doris was born, had become increasingly segregated by race. Although she would tell stories of hurling stones at white neighbors from a distance, she and her childhood friends mostly kept their distance. "I didn't recognize their existence, and they didn't recognize mine," Ruby Doris recalled. "You wouldn't even think of going into a white restaurant."

J. T. Smith was a stern taskmaster who pushed his seven children to do well in school and to keep up appearances. As a student at Price High School, Ruby Doris obliged by making the honor roll and serving as head majorette in the marching band. Donning a white evening gown, she even attended a debutante ball held at the Atlanta Auditorium. But her mother Alice exerted a less conformist influence. Using the pseudonym of "Sarah," Ruby Doris spoke about her mother to Josephine Carson, a white novelist who wrote about the lives of female civil rights leaders. Over her husband's objections, Alice turned their house into a refuge for Black prisoners who had escaped from chain gangs. "My mother always kept a suit of men's clothes in the house and a package of things—a little silver money, matches, names and telephone numbers, maybe of certain preachers around the South who could help—you know?" Ruby Doris recalled. "Didn't matter what he did or who he was—he was a Negro man off the chain gang and if they caught him, they'd beat him to death. So she helped him escape."

When Ruby Doris entered Spelman, Atlanta's renowned historically Black women's college, at the precocious age of sixteen, she followed her mother's independent-minded example. Founded by nineteenth-century white missionaries and funded by John D. Rockefeller, the stately red-brick campus was then known as a place where women went as much to catch the eye of a "Morehouse man" from the nearby men's college as to receive a first-rate education. But Smith defied that demure stereotype. She "was not the quintessential Spelman woman," Reverend Albert Brinson, a Morehouse contemporary, told biographer Fleming. "She was not the ladylike kind."

In the middle of her sophomore year, Smith saw television reports about the four Black students who were arrested for sitting at a whites-only lunch counter in Greensboro, North Carolina. Soon her older sister, Mary Ann, who attended nearby Morris Brown College, became a leader in the Atlanta sit-in movement, and Ruby Doris pleaded to be included. That spring, she was one of two hundred students chosen to stage the city's first sit-in at a cafeteria in the Georgia state capitol. Over the next year, she participated in dozens of similar demonstrations, often in the company of fellow Spelman students Marian Wright, the future civil rights lawyer, and Gwen Robinson, later a SNCC field secretary. Ruby Doris picketed an A&P supermarket that refused to hire Blacks, joined "kneel-ins" at Atlanta churches, and had a Coke bottle hurled at her while integrating a Woolworth's lunch counter.

Then, in the winter of 1961, an unexpected sequence of events propelled Ruby Doris into the heart of SNCC's inner circle. It began when activists in Rock Hill, South Carolina, staged a series of protests to commemorate the one-year anniversary of the first student sit-ins, and nine were arrested. The early leaders of SNCC decided to send four members to carry on the Rock Hill protest. Mary Ann Smith was chosen along with sit-in veterans Diane Nash, Charles Sherrod, and Charles Jones. At the last minute, Mary Ann had second thoughts, and her little sister volunteered to take her place. As soon as Ruby Doris and the three others sat down at a lunch counter at Good's Drug Store in Rock Hill, they were arrested and sent to the local prison. Bond was set at $100, but instead of paying the students elected to serve out a one-month sentence—the beginning of a defiant policy they called "jail, no bail."

For Ruby Doris, the month in Rock Hill's York County Prison marked an intellectual and psychological turning point. Anxious at first about serving such a long sentence, she found solace in singing, daily exercise, and constant reading. "After one night in jail," she recalled, "the four of us concluded that imprisonment was merely a state of mind. We knew then the statement was valid which says 'stone walls do not a prison make.'" Her charismatic cellmate Diane Nash, the twenty-two-year-old Fisk University graduate who had been among the first sit-in leaders, instructed Smith in the fine points of nonviolent philosophy. By the time she left the prison, she had read more than a dozen books, including *The Life of Mahatma Gandhi*; novels such as *Exodus*, *Elmer Gantry*, and *The Ugly American*; and *The Wall Between*, a gripping, real-life account of a Black family terrorized for trying to move into a white neighborhood in Louisville, Kentucky.

Just as liberating, Smith began to conquer her physical insecurities. In her interview with Josephine Carson, she confessed that she had gone through a phase of resenting white women because of "how the whole world had this white idea of beauty." On the day of her arrest in Rock Hill, she refused to set out for Good's Drug Store before putting her hair in curlers. In letters home from jail, she fretted about the impact on her waistline of greasy prison food and care packages of sweets. But all that changed by the time Smith was released a month later. In a news photograph of her return to Atlanta, where she was greeted as a hero by fellow activists at the airport, her hair had grown into a short Afro, and she beamed with contentment despite the eighteen pounds she had put on in prison. Reflecting on what she called "my African kind of beauty," Smith told Carson that "I had to find a new sense of my own dignity, and what I really had to do was start *seeing* all over again, in a new way."

AFTER ROCK HILL, SMITH SAW HERSELF AS AN ACTIVIST MORE than a student, so she dropped out of Spelman before finishing her junior year. Two months later, Freedom Riders from the Congress of Racial Equality were savagely attacked in Alabama. Diane Nash issued a call for "fresh troops" to take up the crusade to desegregate Southern bus depots. In Atlanta, Smith scraped together money to fly to Birmingham to join the second wave of Freedom Riders. They gathered to board a bus for Montgomery, but had to plead with several drivers before they found one brave enough to undertake the journey. When the Freedom Riders arrived in Montgomery, a mob of three hundred whites attacked them. John Lewis and his white comrade James Zwerg were beaten bloody. "Kill the nigger loving son-of-a-bitch," the assailants shouted as they chased after Zwerg. The Freedom Riders retreated to Montgomery's First Baptist Church for the night, and the next morning they embarked for Jackson, Mississippi. When they tried to use the white restrooms at the Jackson bus station, two dozen women were arrested for disorderly conduct and escorted to Hinds County Jail, where Smith kept up the spirits of the female prisoners by leading them in freedom songs and ballet exercises.

After several days, the women were awoken in the middle of the night and herded into a van. After a two-hour drive in the pitch dark, they passed through iron gates into a compound of drab, low-roofed buildings surrounded by scruffy cotton and vegetable fields. They had arrived at the notorious Mississippi prison Parchman Farm. The women were strip-searched, issued prison uniforms, and escorted to foul-smelling, bug-ridden cells. Several days later, during a brief stay in the prison infirmary, Smith looked out a window and saw some of the male Freedom Riders who were also sent to Parchman Farm—the group that included John Lewis, James Bevel, and Stokely Carmichael. Under the hot July sun, the men were doing the kind of chain gang work from which her mother, Alice, had once helped prisoners escape. "There were fifty, sixty Negro men in striped uniforms, guarded by a white man on a white horse," Smith told Spelman history professor Howard Zinn. "It reminded you of slavery."

While the female Freedom Riders were spared hard labor, they endured some of the same punishments as their male counterparts. When they ignored orders to stay quiet, guards took away their sheets, towels, and toothbrushes. After the women persisted in chanting spirituals and "The Star-Spangled Banner," their mattresses were removed, and they spent the remaining nights until they were released sleeping on hard bunk-bed metal.

Along with Carmichael, Smith was rewarded for her role in the Freedom Rides with an invitation to a week-long workshop that Ella Baker organized in Nashville for the emerging SNCC leadership. Just turned nineteen, she impressed everyone there with her calm, confident voice and hard-headed observations. Carmichael recalled that Smith was one of the few participants willing to point out that nonviolence would be a hard sell among rural Southern Blacks who kept shotguns on hand to protect against the Klan. "The overwhelming majority of our people are not believing in non-violence and we know that," she said, by Carmichael's account. "So if we are going to make this a mass movement like we say, we have to understand that." That August, Smith spent several weeks working for Bob Moses's voter registration drive in McComb County, Mississippi. But by the end of the summer, she decided that she wanted to go back to college. When Spelman insisted that she reapply for admission, she received a letter of recommendation from none other than Dr. King, who had committed to helping jailed Freedom Riders complete their college educations. "Her moral character is above reproach," King wrote to Spelman officials.

Back at Spelman, Smith started working in her spare time at SNCC's headquarters in Atlanta. By then, it had moved from the corner of SCLC office where Bob Moses licked envelopes to spartan digs across the street. The space rented for $20 a month and was so small it had only a partial address: 197 1/2 Auburn Avenue. Smith met James Forman, who had just taken up his new post as SNCC's executive secretary. Putting her to work as his assistant, Forman began to impose order on an operation that until then had consisted of little more than a map of fieldworker locations and a phone ringing with calls from reporters. He created a payroll system for issuing weekly checks, a financial ledger to keep track of contributions and expenses, and the communications department headed by Julian Bond. As Bond put it, Forman "molded SNCC's near-anarchic personality into a functioning, if still chaotic, organizational structure, and insured that most of its parts functioned smoothly most of the time."

Yet as everyone who worked for SNCC during this period recalled, Smith deserved as much credit for the transformation as Forman. Over the next three years, until she graduated from Spelman in 1965, she worked part-time and took occasional leaves from school as she assumed more and more administrative responsibility. By the spring of 1962, Smith was in charge of dispensing all of SNCC's money, from signing and mailing checks to approving expenses. Eventually she was appointed to the personnel committee and put in charge of vetting new hires. She was also given control of SNCC's most sought after—and fought over—assets: its automobiles. When Forman got a deal for twenty-three new tan Plymouth sedans from Black autoworkers union officials in Detroit, adding to a ragtag array of used cars already in the field, he put Smith in charge of access to the shared collection of vehicles that was known within SNCC as the Sojourner Motor Fleet.

As SNCC grew from an informal network of student volunteers to a full-time staff of more than ninety by early 1964, Smith became universally respected—and feared—for her forceful personality as much as her crack efficiency. After hours, she bonded with the troops by dancing to soul music and playing whist. When staffers faced a personal crisis, she could be sympathetic and "soft as cotton," as her Rock Hill prison mate Charles Jones put it. But everyone knew that Smith could also be tough as nails. As Jack Minnis, the head of the research department, put it, "She had a 100-percent-effective shit detector." Relentless in tracking expenses, she caught a field officer who put in for reimbursement for sixteen new tires in the space of four months. She also had no time for unprofessionalism, particularly if it cost SNCC money. Once a member of the Freedom Singers, a folk group that traveled the country raising money for SNCC, missed a flight back to Atlanta from San Francisco. How was he supposed to get home? the singer pleaded when Smith refused to fund a new ticket. "Walk back," she snapped, before hanging up the phone.

THEN CAME FREEDOM SUMMER IN MISSISSIPPI, ANOTHER TURN-ing point that added to Smith's authority but also shifted perceptions of her within SNCC. When the idea of enlisting more than a thousand Black and white students from across the country to organize in the rural Delta first came up, Smith opposed it, voicing concerns about training so many outsiders all at once. She went along with the decision once it was made, however, and spent the summer in the Atlanta office dealing with the financial and emotional turmoil created by so many young people from such different backgrounds. In field offices across Mississippi, disputes broke out over who should perform tasks as small as a typing reports, with Black volunteers resenting whites who flaunted superior clerical skills. But the sharpest resentments came over romantic entanglements between veteran Black male organizers and white female volunteers. In accounts of Freedom Summer, several white women accused Smith of snubbing them out of displeasure over all the men who were "talking black and sleeping white," as the expression went among SNCC's Black female staffers. "She had a tremendous, tremendous amount of anger" toward white women, Anne Romaine, one of those volunteers, told biographer Fleming.

Yet SNCC's most veteran white female staffers told another story. If Smith had once resented white women because of her anger over Caucasian standards of beauty, she had gotten over it by the time Dottie Miller met her in the years preceding Freedom Summer. Although they didn't become close at that time, Miller looked up to Smith for her "unbelievable management skills," as she later described them. Meanwhile, Ruby Doris respected Dottie for her no-nonsense work ethic. On one slow afternoon, they found themselves singing "Just a Closer Walk with Thee" and other freedom songs with a group of staffers in the office. On another occasion, the two traveled together to Norfolk, Virginia, to march arm-in-arm in protest over the killing of a civil rights worker named William Moore. Over time, Smith signed off on hiring two other white women who became key members of Julian Bond's communications team: Mary Elizabeth King, a protégé of Ella Baker, and Sandra "Casey" Hayden, a Texan who was married to Tom Hayden, one of the founders of the Students for a Democratic Society, the white-led social justice and antiwar group.

By January of 1964, enough women of both races were working in the Atlanta office that they banded together to demand more nonsecretarial duties, and Smith joined a sit-in outside of Jim Forman's office. In a photo of the protest, she can be seen sitting on the floor with Mary King and three Black female staffers, her legs elegantly folded on a newspaper, holding up a sign that read: "NO MORE WORK til Justice Comes to Atlanta Office." That November, King and Hayden pressed the issue of women's roles even further at a week-long staff retreat at a Methodist church in the Gulf Coast town of Waveland, Mississippi. The two circulated an unsigned "position paper" that cited eleven examples of indignities suffered by female SNCC staffers—from being cut out of decision making, to being called "girls" and asked only to "take minutes"—and asserted that a "woman in SNCC is often in the same position as that token Negro hired in a corporation." Although Smith viewed the sexism debate as secondary to the retreat's announced goal of strategic soul-searching, she did nothing to block the writing or discussion of King and Hayden's paper, which would later be seen as an exhibit of how women's experience in the civil rights and antiwar movements helped fuel the feminist movement.

To the extent that Smith was bothered by sexual politics within SNCC, it was more with the behavior of some of her Black male colleagues. During the work strike at the Atlanta headquarters, she made clear that the women's demands were physical as well as professional. As Stanley Wise recalled, her position was: "Women would do absolutely nothing until men recognized that, first of all [they] couldn't grab your butts, couldn't grab your breasts." Smith was also upset with an office affair that her boss, Jim Forman, was having with a white staffer. Still married to his Black wife, Mildred, Forman took up with Constancia Romilly, known as "Dinky," a daughter of author Jessica Mitford and Edmond Romilly, a British socialist who died flying an Allied bomber during World War II.

Nor was Smith happy with SNCC's most notorious incident of male chauvinism. At a wine-fueled bull session at the end of the Waveland conference, Stokely Carmichael made fun of all the papers that had been presented at the meeting. When he came to King and Hayden's sexism manifesto, he asked rhetorically: "What is the position of women in SNCC? The position of women in SNCC is prone!" Some of the women present, including Mary King herself, said that they understood Carmichael to be joking, and that everyone roared with amusement. But Smith didn't view Carmichael's "prone" remark as a laughing matter. When she heard Stanley Wise repeat the story sometime later at the Atlanta headquarters, she came out of her office and slapped Wise in the face.

If a change did come over Smith in 1964, it was less a result of Freedom Summer than the tensions that emerged in the months afterward. In September, just as SNCC's leaders were recovering from everything that happened that summer, the singer Harry Belafonte invited them on a trip to the African country of Guinea. Welcoming a respite,

John Lewis and Jim Forman chose a delegation that included Smith, Bob Moses, and Fannie Lou Hamer. Lodged in a scenic seaside villa, the group toured the African countryside by day and feasted on lavish meals at night. They were feted at the sprawling palace once occupied by French colonizers that had been taken over by Ahmed Sekou Touré, the first African leader to win independence from France. But after three weeks, Forman and Smith were abruptly called back to Atlanta for an executive committee meeting that had been convened by Court-land Cox, the SNCC officer they left in charge. Lobbied by Freedom Summer volunteers, most of them white and from the North, to con-tinue working for SNCC, Cox had decided to take up a request by eighty-five of them to become full-time staff members. Worried about how such a sudden influx of still largely untested organizers would change the character of the organization, Forman and Smith opposed the proposal, but it was approved after a series of heated meetings.

Over the next year, that expansion led to a factional battle that started with disagreements over strategy and grew increasingly per-sonal. On one side was a group of Black and white staffers, many of them Northerners, who wanted to stick with SNCC's traditional nonhierarchical, improvisational model of organizing. On the other was a mostly Black and Southern contingent that favored exerting tighter central control and taking a stronger stand on national issues such as voting rights enforcement and the Vietnam War. In February of 1965, at the Atlanta staff meeting where Bob Moses announced that he was quitting and changing his name to Bob Parris, Cleve Sell-ers was elected SNCC's program director. Taking aim at the type of organizers Moses had come to exemplify, Sellers described them as "philosophers, existentialists, anarchists, floaters and freedom-high niggers." He found an ally in Ruby Doris, who opened an executive committee meeting in Holly Springs, Mississippi, two months later by criticizing staffers who "just float and don't do any work." From then on, the intramural squabble had a label: the "Hardliners" versus the "Floaters."

By then, Ruby Doris also had personal reasons for her impatience with time-wasters. Without telling anyone at work, she had married her sister Catherine's brother-in-law, a taciturn mechanic named Clifford Robinson. The two began dating and wed so quietly that most of her SNCC colleagues learned about it only when she began using her husband's last name. In the spring of 1965, she gave birth to a boy she named Kenneth Touré Robinson—in honor of the leader she had met in Africa—and she went back to work after only two weeks. Several times, she brought the baby to the office and breast-fed him during meetings. But on most days, Ruby Doris dropped little Kenneth off with her mother, Alice, first thing in the morning, and picked him up late at night. Although she never complained, she began to suffer hemorrhoids and digestive problems that sent her to the hospital several times. On at least one occasion, she shut the door to her office and vented her frustrations by hurling empty Coke bottles at the wall.

BY THE TIME OF THE KINGSTON SPRINGS RETREAT IN 1966, SNCC'S leadership was also dealing with another rebellious faction. Bill Ware, the Mississippi organizer who had moved to Atlanta to help Julian Bond, had launched his crusade to rid SNCC of whites. Over the winter, Ware received a $3,000 donation for his organizing work in Vine City. Instead of turning the funds over to SNCC headquarters, he used the money as leverage to demand a hearing before the executive committee. When Jim Forman grudgingly agreed to this manipulative deal, Ware worked with other Vine City staffers to compose an eight-page single-spaced memo.

Presented as a "position paper" for the "SNCC Vine City project," the document said little about that neighborhood and instead launched into a long list of arguments about the damage that whites were doing to the Black cause. White organizers patronized and intimidated Black co-workers, the paper argued. Whites had no feel for the inner-city Northern neighborhoods that were the next civil rights frontier, it continued, and their very presence kept Blacks from appreciating their own history and celebrating their culture. Drawing on Ware's experience in the Peace Corps in Ghana, the paper compared Black Americans to African nations that were throwing off white colonial rule—ignoring the fact that Blacks were in a majority in those countries, and that many of the colonizers supported the transition to independence. Ware's manifesto called for SNCC to become 100 percent "black-staffed, black-controlled and black-financed," without addressing the question of how the bills would be paid. "If we are to proceed toward true liberation," the paper concluded, "we must cut ourselves off from white people."

When Ware presented his position paper to SNCC's executive committee in March, however, he got a cold reception. Already angry about the withheld $3,000 donation, Forman dismissed the separatist arguments and refused Ware's request to tape-record the meeting, suspecting a scheme to leak a transcript to the press. Despite their reputations as firebrands, Stokely Carmichael and Willie Ricks sided with Forman. Ricks viewed Ware and his group as posers who hadn't paid sufficient dues in the field. "They talked about nationalism and that kind of thing on the inside of SNCC," Ricks recalled, "but they did not have an organization in the community." Carmichaels saw Ware and his followers as political "opportunists" who were using a "Blacker than thou" stance to get attention, according to an interview Carmichael later gave to historian Clayborne Carson.

Although Ruby Doris Robinson, as she now called herself, was friendly with some of the Vine City organizers, especially her fellow Spelman alumna Gwen Robinson, she also backed Forman in the debate over Ware's manifesto. She knew better than anyone how dependent SNCC was on white donations, and was instinctively allergic to Ware's impractical rhetoric. Folks who preferred to "sit around talking about white people" than do real work, Robinson called the Vine City separatists, according to Freddie Greene Biddle, a Mississippi native who was one of Ruby Doris's closest female confidantes within SNCC. After the March meeting, Ware's relations with the SNCC brass were so strained that he didn't attend the Kingston Springs summit. Yet, as it turned out, his presence still hung over the meeting, as the future of white participation became a major focus of a SNCC retreat for the first time.

The Kingston Springs meeting was SNCC's first organization-wide retreat since the one in Waveland, Mississippi, in November of 1964, and much had changed in the interim. After the influx of white Freedom Summer volunteers, more than 170 SNCC members gathered for the Waveland meeting—a new high in numbers, and in racial diversity. During that week, Danny Lyon, a New Yorker who dropped out of the University of Chicago to become SNCC's staff photographer, captured moving images of Black and white organizers in intense workshop discussions and joyous after-hours dance sessions. But in the subsequent year and a half, many of the white volunteers had left SNCC to go back to college or to join anti–Vietnam War groups such as the Students for a Democratic Society. Realizing that his own future was limited in a Black-run organization, Lyon had moved on to work that would bring him acclaim as a photographer who immersed himself in distinct American subcultures, from a Midwestern motorcycle gang to a rural Texas prison.

While Southern protests and federal legislation had dominated headlines about civil rights in the months after Waveland, other seismic events had changed the mood of Black America. The week-long riot in the Watts neighborhood of Los Angeles exposed smoldering tensions between Blacks and white-run police forces in the urban North. After renouncing the name Cassius Clay and joining the Nation of Islam, heavyweight boxing champion Muhammad Ali linked Black nationalism to the antiwar movement by signaling that he would refuse to serve in Vietnam. In New York, poet LeRoi Jones shed his identity as a Greenwich Village hipster and moved to Harlem to launch the Black Arts Movement. Across America, more and more young Black women were emulating the Afro hairstyle that Ruby Doris Robinson and other female civil rights workers first adopted by necessity, because they were in jail.

SET ON 350 ACRES IN THE TOWN OF KINGSTON SPRINGS, TWENTY miles west of Nashville, the Bethany Hills religious camp consisted of rustic, dormitory-style cabins strewn around a large lake, with a two-story lodge in the middle of the property. The lodge had a mess hall on the first floor, and an open, pine-paneled meeting room up-stairs with large windows looking out on the surrounding woods. Originally built as a convalescent retreat for tuberculosis patients, the site had been purchased in the 1940s by the Disciples of Christ, an ecumenical alliance of Tennessee churches. Since then, it had been converted into a facility that was rented out to church youth groups and other organizations with religious affiliations, and named after the town where Jesus stayed on his way to Jerusalem.

On the Sunday before the retreat began, John Lewis drove to the Bethany Hills camp straight from the airport after an overnight flight from Norway. It was the second time in eighteen months that Lewis had spent a long stretch of time abroad, away from the churning strategic debates within SNCC. After the group trip to Guinea in September of 1964, Lewis stayed behind for two more months touring Africa. This time, Lewis had accepted paid invitations from several European student groups without consulting his colleagues, then used SNCC funds to pay for Stanley Wise to travel with him to organize his schedule and answer his mail. Before leaving, Lewis wrote a prickly memo to the other members of SNCC's executive committee defending the trip. "The European tour that I am making is not one for fun or folly, but it is another attempt to win friends for the struggle," Lewis wrote. "I have made a decision, call it what you may, unilateral, dictorial [*sic*], or, an over use of executive powers, that SNCC should make an investment in this venture, by making funds available to provide transportation for Stanley Wise, to accompany me on the European speaking tour."

Arriving in Kingston Springs, Lewis found a different SNCC from the one he was used to describing in his travels. The spirit of interracial cooperation that early SNCC leaders called the "circle of trust" was all but gone, and the organization was more divided by race than ever. For the more than 120 Black participants, the retreat was a time of "good feelings and a renewed sense of hope," recalled Cleve Sellers. The Black staffers played spirited games of volleyball, and took cooling swims in the lake. During workshops in the central mess hall and long walks through the woods, they discussed a new set of ideas and attitudes they called "Black Consciousness." In his account of the retreat, Sellers defined the term as a new "way of seeing the world." On a cultural level, it meant rejecting the label Negro and celebrating Black America's ties to Africa. On a political level, it involved a rethinking of SNCC's priorities that Sellers captured in this earthy description of the position that he and others took in debates over integration:

> "Blacks are not being lynched and dumped into muddy rivers across the South because they aren't 'integrated,'" we countered. "Black babies are not dying of malnutrition because their parents do not own homes in white communities. Black men and women are not being forced to pick cotton for three dollars a day because of segregation. 'Integration' has little or no effect on such problems. Look at those 'integrated' towns and cities in the Midwest. Niggers up there have it just as bad as we down here. The real issue is power; the power to control the significant events which affect our lives. If we have power, we can keep people from fucking us over. When we are powerless, we have about as much control over our destinies as a piece of dog shit."

In a presentation early in the conference, Ivanhoe Donaldson also made a pragmatic argument for a new focus on Black Consciousness: its value as a recruiting tool. At a time when SNCC was losing membership, the posthumous publication of *The Autobiography of Malcolm X* and Muhammad Ali's embrace of the Nation of Islam had captured the imagination of young Blacks across the country. To remain in the "vanguard," Donaldson argued, SNCC needed to reflect the new mood. Other SNCC leaders threw out ideas for how SNCC could capture the nationalist zeitgeist. Ella Baker suggested convening workshops on "revolutionary ethics" and inviting Third World leaders to speak. Cleve Sellers called for campus recruiting exclusively on historically Black colleges. Stanley Wise questioned whether SNCC leaders should speak at white campuses at all. Perhaps SNCC press releases should be sent only to Black publications, Wise proposed, and not to the white press.

For the forty or so white attendees, meanwhile, the week in the Tennessee woods was a tense experience. In his account of the meeting, historian Clayborne Carson argued that if Bill Ware had been there, he might have pressed his anti-white views with obnoxious aggressiveness. That might have forced Jim Forman to stand up for his white colleagues. Instead, in Ware's absence, it was Forman who put forth one of the ideas in the Vine City Project manifesto. He proposed that from then on, white staffers focus on organizing in white communities, and leave work in Black communities to Black staffers. Forman asked Jack Minnis, SNCC's white research director, to draft a resolution putting forth the new policy, and it passed with both Black and white support. Minnis later explained that he supported the proposal because he saw some logic in it and also respected the will of SNCC's Black majority. But other accounts made clear just how upsetting the deliberations were. "That hurt a lot of people, white and black alike," recalled John Lewis, who opposed the resolution. "It hurt me terribly." Even Sellers, who supported the motion, described how "painful" its passage was. "I witnessed several members leave the discussions with furrowed brows and tears welling in their eyes," he recalled.

On the last full day of the conference—Friday the 13th—the attendees assembled for the annual election of SNCC officers. As the sun set, everyone gathered in the central mess hall. They formed a sprawling semicircle, with some staffers sitting on chairs and others squatting on the floor or standing against the walls. By then, the outcome of the election for two of the top three posts was a foregone conclusion. Jim Forman had thrown his support behind Ruby Doris Robinson to take his place as executive secretary. Still only twenty-one, Cleve Sellers had done well in his first year as program secretary—the job of overseeing field organizers—and had wide backing for a second term. But after a week of late-night gripe sessions, significant opposition had surfaced to John Lewis's reelection as chairman.

Although Carmichael may have had more interest in the post

than he let on, his candidacy was ultimately the result of a draft more than an organized campaign. As Sellers told it, he and six other staffers took Carmichael aside and urged him to run. After the success of the Black Panther Party convention in Lowndes County, they argued, Carmichael had the track record and the media profile to represent SNCC's new direction. The draft-Stokely delegation also included Ruby Doris Robinson, a sign that Carmichael had support at the Atlanta headquarters and among SNCC's female staffers. In Carmichael's words, "This wasn't no undertow, Jack, it was a groundswell."

As the Friday evening meeting got under way, frustrations with Lewis poured forth. After expressing personal fondness for Lewis and respect for his bravery, speaker after speaker raised questions about his priorities. Why had Lewis spent so much time traveling abroad, they asked, rather than focusing on SNCC's work at home? Why was he so eager to present himself as the hero of the Selma march, when SNCC had pulled out of that protest? Why did Lewis still sit on the board of the SCLC at a time when SNCC was questioning Dr. King's agenda? And why was he so eager to do business with Lyndon Johnson when SNCC was challenging the president on everything from lack of voting rights enforcement to the war in Vietnam? For more than four hours, the discussion rambled on, in a tone that grew steadily more heated and profane. "It got very low and nasty, very bitter and mean," Lewis recalled. "People stood up and said we needed someone who could grab Lyndon Johnson by his balls and tell him to kiss our ass. We needed someone who would stand up to Dr. King and tell him the same thing. That was a phrase I heard several times—'kiss our ass.'"

When it came to a vote, however, Lewis's critics fell short. Lewis proudly stood his ground, reminding everyone of his years of service to SNCC and all the money he had raised. His remaining allies came to his defense, invoking all the police beatings Lewis had endured, and the twenty-four times he had gone to prison. Many of those who were on the fence didn't want to go on the record. So when a vote was taken shortly after midnight, scores of staffers abstained, and Lewis beat Carmichael by a comfortable margin of 60-to-22. Exhausted, people drifted back to the cabins to go to sleep. So only about half of the staff was left when, sometime after one in the morning, a SNCC veteran named Worth Long burst into the mess hall.

A NORTH CAROLINA NATIVE WITH A ROUND FACE AND CLEAR horn-rimmed glasses, Long had resigned from SNCC after organizing stints in Arkansas and Alabama to pursue the study of folklore, an interest he acquired while serving in the Air Force in Korea and Japan. But Worth was still well-liked and respected enough to be invited to SNCC retreats, and his opinion carried weight even though he no longer had an official vote. Although Long hadn't been present for the election, he was upset when he heard about the chairmanship outcome, and now he took the floor to argue that John Lewis was no longer the best man to lead SNCC. Worth also raised a procedural objection. The election hadn't been sufficiently democratic, he argued, since almost half of SNCC's membership hadn't participated. For the results to be legitimate, Long argued, more members needed to vote.

"Instant chaos" was how Sellers described what happened next. Lewis critics raced through the dark woods to wake people up and bring them back to the mess hall. Jim Forman seconded Long's objection about the insufficient number of voters. Another turning point came when Fay Bellamy, a widely respected veteran of the Selma voting rights campaign, stood up and unloaded on Lewis. A blunt-spoken Pennsylvania native and Air Force veteran, Bellamy was in the camp of staffers who privately viewed Lewis as "a bit of a handkerchief head," in her words—slang for Blacks who were too eager to ingratiate themselves with whites. Bellamy later described her opinion of Lewis at the time as someone who was "certainly brave enough" but who spent too much time "fronting" in Washington and "didn't seem like he had a clue" about what was going on with his troops in the field. "Every time LBJ called," Bellamy quipped, "he'd rush his clothes into the cleaners and be on the next plane for Washington."

Yet, in an ironic twist, the final path for John Lewis's ouster was paved by a white staffer: research director Jack Minnis. Although friendly with Lewis, Minnis had come to share the criticisms of his leadership, and also to admire Carmichael during their work together launching the Black Panther Party in Lowndes County. As the chaotic debate in the Bethany Hills mess hall raged on, Minnis pulled a small group that included Carmichael, Sellers, and several others into a corner. Minnis pointed out that if Sellers and Robinson both resigned their posts, Lewis would have to stand down as well, and another vote for all three offices could take place. The others agreed with the maneuver, and told Carmichael to keep his mouth shut while it played out. "Don't say anything at all," Sellers whispered to Stokely as the huddle broke up.

Returning to the center of the room, Sellers asked to speak. "There seems to be some question in the minds of some as to whether or not the vote just taken was legitimate," he said. "For that reason, I submit my resignation so that another vote can be taken." Ruby Doris wasn't included in the secretive huddle, but she grasped what was happening and also offered to step down. At that point Lewis, who had been struggling to contain his emotions, erupted. He saw what was afoot, he said, and he would not resign from a post to which he had been duly reelected. According to Sellers's account, Lewis tried to appeal to SNCC's Southerners by suggesting that he was victim of a plot by "troublemaking Northerners."

Then Lewis brought up the circumstances of his rise to the SNCC chairmanship three years earlier. Lewis argued that he never asked for the job in the first place, but was talked into it—and that much was true. When Chuck McDew, SNCC's previous chairman, quit unexpectedly just before the March on Washington in 1963, Jim Forman sent an emergency telegram to Lewis, who was organizing in Nashville, and asked him to come to a meeting in Atlanta where he was anointed chairman with no opposition. Yet few of the Kingston Springs attendees knew that history, and bringing it up now made Lewis look like he thought the post was his birthright. From then on, in Sellers's words, the meeting "quickly degenerated into arguing, fussing and cussin'." By five-thirty in the morning, Lewis realized that he no longer had enough support to prevail, and he relented and resigned.

As the morning sun began to peek through the mess hall windows, a second vote was taken. Ruby Doris Robinson and Cleve Sellers were unanimously reelected to their posts, and this time Carmichael won the chairmanship by a wide margin. Dazed and drained, Lewis staggered back to his cabin and slept for several hours. When he awoke, he wondered if the events of the previous night had actually taken place. It was only when Lewis made his way back to the mess hall and found a gathering of mournful allies that the finality of the vote sank in, and his emotions welled up. Lewis had had his head gashed open during the Freedom Rides and been beaten by police in Selma. He had survived Parchman Farm and dozens of other prisons. But this "hurt more than anything I'd been through," he recalled. "My life, my identity, most of my very existence, was tied up in SNCC. Now, so suddenly, I was put out to pasture."

IN THE FOLLOWING WEEKS, LEWIS ACCEPTED A FACE-SAVING post as head of a newly created Bureau of International Affairs, and refused to complain to the press. "I'm here today, and I'll be here tomorrow and that's all I can say," he responded when contacted by Gene Roberts of *The New York Times.* Lewis even agreed to "swallow some pride, some self-respect, some dignity," as he put it, and accompany Carmichael to a fundraising dinner in Washington, D.C. But Lewis's private resentment lingered, and it wasn't directed at Stokely Carmichael. Lewis blamed Jim Forman. In a score-settling feud played out in their respective autobiographies, Forman accused Lewis of standing in the way of a new generation of leaders, while Lewis described Forman as being so driven by "the factor of ego" that he couldn't stomach giving up his number two post without bringing Lewis down with him.

Improbably, given how chaotically it unfolded, Lewis even suggested that Forman had orchestrated the middle-of-the-night rebellion in Kingston Springs. "I've thought a lot over the years about why Worth Long did what he did. And long ago I came to suspect that Jim Forman was in part responsible," Lewis wrote. "Even Stokely's

ascent, in large part, was, I believe, due to Forman's engineering behind the scenes. Putting Stokely out there, with all his fireworks and
histrionics, was a good cover for Forman to see me removed."

While Lewis and his allies nursed their wounds, SNCC's new
leadership met in Atlanta. A resolution passed in Kingston Springs
had replaced SNCC's unwieldy twenty-one-member executive
board with a new ten-person Central Committee. The change put
even more power in the hands of Ruby Doris Robinson, who was
given control of all fundraising and widespread authority over hiring
and firing. The next week, she and Carmichael made their debut before the national media at a press conference announcing that SNCC
would boycott President Johnson's proposed conference on civil
rights. After Robinson read a statement, Carmichael took questions,
and he gave the press a taste of the kind of vivid, inflammatory language that would become his trademark. "We see integration as an
insidious substitute for white supremacy," Carmichael said, echoing
the rhetoric that filled the air in Kingston Springs. "The goal of integration is irrelevant. Political and economic power is what black
people have to have."

In what would become a familiar pattern, Carmichael's statement generated another wave of newspaper stories when reporters
approached other civil rights leaders for comment. *New York Times*
correspondent Austin Wehrwein tracked down Dr. King in Chicago,
where he was forging on with his Northern campaign. In a carefully
worded response, King expressed sympathy for the "deep discontent,
frustration, disappointment and even despair" that was leading young
Blacks to question integration, but insisted that "large numbers of
Negroes" were still "trying to get into the mainstream of American
life." But in another sign of things to come, *Times* editors put a less
nuanced headline on a story that ran on the paper's front page and
was picked up around the country. "Dr. King Disputes Negro Separatist," the headline read.

By the third of June, so many alarming stories had appeared about
the Kingston Springs results that SNCC's New York office put out

a "special bulletin" disputing the reports. The changing of the guard "did not constitute a pattern of 'takeover' by 'anti-white extremists,'" the statement insisted. There was no "schism" within SNCC, and the new Central Committee still included John Lewis and Jim Forman and one white veteran—Jack Minnis. "Organizing the strength of Negroes as a group force does not constitute 'reverse racism' or black nationalism as the press would define it: in a purely negative sense of 'hate whitey,'" the statement continued. To drive home the reassuring message, the bulletin informed SNCC supporters that its new leader's top priority would remain overseeing fieldwork in the South. "Chairman Stokely Carmichael will be devoting most of his time this year to traveling around our Southern projects, strengthening the staff," the New York office reported.

True to that initial promise, Carmichael began a tour of SNCC's Southern offices with Cleve Sellers and Stanley Wise. But three days later, on Monday, June 6, the three were in Little Rock, Arkansas, conferring with field secretary Ben Grinage, when a local lawyer rushed into the room. The attorney had just heard a radio bulletin that James Meredith, the man who came to national attention as the first Black student to enroll at the University of Mississippi, had been shot and was being reported dead.

After all the civil rights heroes they had seen cut down, the young SNCC leaders were more sickened than shocked. "I felt cold, suddenly numb from the top of my head to the soles of my feet," Carmichael recalled. "Weary to the bone. Another man done gone." Sellers described feeling a "dull, aching pain that seemed always to be lurking in the pit of my stomach." How did it happen? the two asked gravely. The attorney responded that the radio report offered few additional details about the attack on Meredith. "All I know," Sellers recalled the lawyer saying, "is that some white fella shot him in the head while he was walking down some Mississippi highway."

CHAPTER 7

Showdown at the Lorraine Motel

James Meredith had always been a maverick, and it was consistent with that personality that he chose the posh Peabody Hotel in Memphis, Tennessee, as the starting point for a march across the poorest parts of Mississippi. A grand Italianate structure in the heart of downtown, the hotel had long been a gathering place for the white businessmen who owned and financed the Black-tilled farmlands and cotton fields to the south. "The Mississippi Delta begins in the lobby of the Peabody," was a saying in that clubby crowd. So Meredith, himself born on a hardscrabble farm in the Delta town of Kosciusko, appeared to be making a quirky symbolic statement when he set off from the entrance to the hotel on the hot Sunday afternoon of June 5, 1966.

Four years earlier, Meredith had exhibited that same idiosyncratic streak when, inspired by what he described as a revelation of "divine responsibility," he applied to become the first Black student to attend the University of Mississippi. That solitary act sparked a crisis that escalated into a tense standoff between segregationist governor Ross Barnett and Attorney General Robert F. Kennedy, the dispatch of five hundred federal marshals to the Ole Miss campus, and a bloody riot that ended with two people dead. Once admitted, Meredith ate alone in the dining halls and studied at night as white students bounced basketballs on the floor above his dorm room. Now he was playing the daring maverick again. Calling his foray a "March Against Fear," Meredith left his law studies at Columbia University to walk across his state, 220 miles from Memphis to Jackson, to inspire Mississippi's Black citizens to claim their new voting rights.

Meredith was also dressed the part of an eccentric loner. A pocket protector clipped to his short-sleeve, checkered brown shirt made him look like an engineering student, while a yellow pith helmet perched atop his small head gave him the air of a tourist embarking on safari. In his hand, he held an ivory-tipped ebony walking stick that he had received as a gift from a tribal chief during a visit to Sudan. The stick came with a traditional African blessing, Meredith told reporters: "We Shall Arrive." As he set off from the Peabody Hotel toward Highway 51, the fabled north–south thoroughfare that stretched from northern Michigan all the way to New Orleans, Meredith was accompanied by a small entourage that included a local officer of the NAACP, a white Episcopal priest whom he had just met on a flight from New York, and a young R&B record promoter named Claude Sterrett.

When the group reached the Mississippi border, they stopped and returned by car to Memphis for the night. The next morning, they drove to the spot where they left off and resumed the march. A procession of state troopers, sheriff's deputies, and two FBI agents trailed behind. Along the highway, a Black woman in a cotton dress called out: "We're praying for you." A car sped by and a white man shouted out the window: "I hope to hell you die before you get there." Fifteen miles into Mississippi, the group passed through the town of Hernando. As they exited to the south, a Black man standing on the side of the road called out to Claude Sterrett that someone was waiting ahead to stage an ambush. Sterrett scurried to warn Meredith, who was reading a newspaper as he walked, catching up on reports of his quixotic crusade. "Well . . ." Meredith muttered with a distracted shrug.

"James," a voice called out from the water oak trees by the side of the road. "James. I just want James Meredith." As the marchers turned to see where the voice was coming from, a short, stocky white man wearing sunglasses emerged from a thicket of honeysuckle and waved a shotgun. "James, he's got a gun!" someone shouted. Meredith dove to the ground, his pith helmet and sunglasses flying. He tried to crawl to the shoulder of the highway, to hide behind the police cars. The shooter opened fire, first hitting the pavement and then striking Meredith with a spray of ammunition. "Who, who?" Meredith cried out as blood began to seep from the back of his head. "Is anybody getting any help for me?"

Police rushed to apprehend the assailant, who was so drunk he didn't try to resist and puffed on a pipe as he was taken into custody. He was a forty-year-old unemployed Memphis man named Aubrey James Norvell whose last job had been as a clerk in his family's hardware store. Five minutes after the shooting, at about half past four, an ambulance arrived and rushed Meredith to Bowld Hospital in Memphis, where doctors determined that the more than sixty wounds to his head, neck, back, and legs were serious but not life-threatening. Meredith had been spared by the fact that Norvell's 16-gauge shotgun was loaded not with bullets but with No. 6 birdshot, the tiny pellets used to hunt duck and quail in the Tennessee woods.

Because of an erroneous news report, however, millions of Americans that evening heard that James Meredith was dead. The Associated Press, the wire service relied on by newspapers and radio and TV stations to cover events outside their territories, had staffed the Meredith March with a young local reporter named Ron Alford. Alford had left the march as it reached Hernando and gone to file a story from the newsroom of the Memphis *Commercial Appeal*. He heard about the shooting only when someone phoned from the scene and spoke to a newsroom editor. Listening in on the call, Alford misunderstood the word "head" for "dead," and filed a report to that effect to the AP's regional office in Nashville. A 6:33 p.m., the wire service sent out a bulletin over its ticker machines that civil rights icon James Meredith had been killed—just in time to be picked up by the network evening news broadcasts.

The AP correspondent wasn't the only reporter who missed the shooting. *New York Times* reporter Roy Reed had stopped at a country store just south of Hernando to buy a bottle of soda pop and only realized that something had happened when he saw people running back up Highway 51. At *Times* headquarters in New York City, Claude Sitton, the veteran civil rights reporter who had been promoted to national editor, saw a picture on the photo wires of Meredith writhing on the side of the highway. "Where's Roy Reed?" Sitton asked, wondering why he hadn't heard from his reporter on the scene.

Reed redeemed himself, however, when he found a pay phone to call in his report. By that time, the AP had moved its story reporting Meredith's death, and Reed was able to inform Sitton that he had just seen the wounded victim alive. "Hold on!" Sitton shouted, instructing an assistant to call WQXR, the local radio station owned by the *Times*, which broke the news that Meredith hadn't been killed. Meanwhile, the initial reports of Meredith's death had reached his wife, Mary June, at the couple's apartment in Manhattan, and she broke into sobs and had to be sedated. When the WQXR bulletin ran and the AP story was corrected, Mary June was still too woozy to respond in more than a whisper. "I want Jay home," she said softly, calling Meredith by his nickname. "I want him to come home."

DR. KING WAS MEETING WITH HIS SCLC STAFF IN ATLANTA WHEN they heard the first reports that Meredith had been shot and killed. A stunned silence fell over the room, followed by expressions of fury, as King later put it, at "this latest evidence that a Negro's life is still worthless in many parts of his own country." A smaller gathering of executive staff convened and decided that the best way for King to honor Meredith would be to carry on his March Against Fear. In New York, Floyd McKissick, the longtime lawyer for the Congress of Racial Equality who had recently been elected CORE's president, reached the same conclusion. By the time King and McKissick conferred by phone, they had learned that Meredith was alive but far too wounded to resume his march, so they decided to proceed with the plan to take his place.

The next morning, McKissick took a plane to Atlanta, then accompanied King on a flight to Memphis. When the men arrived at
Bowld Hospital, they were ushered into Meredith's room—number 511B—and spent the next hour laying out their proposal. The
back of Meredith's head was shaved where dozens of birdshot pellets
had been removed, and he was under heavy medication, so it took a
long, rambling discussion before he gave his blessing. Just as King
and McKissick were about to leave, a nurse came into the room and
announced a new visitor. "Mr. Meredith, there is a Mr. Carmichael
in the lobby who would like to see you and Dr. King," the nurse said.
"Should I give him permission to come in?"

The night before, after hearing about the shooting from the lawyer in Little Rock, Carmichael had learned that Meredith was alive
but hospitalized. Relieved, he resolved to make the 140-mile drive
to Memphis with Cleve Sellers and Stanley Wise. When the trio was
ushered into Room 511B, Carmichael went to Meredith's bedside,
took his hand, and made a showy declaration of sympathy. But Meredith was fading, so after several minutes the civil rights leaders left
the room and huddled in the corridor outside. King and McKissick
sketched out a plan to bring all the top civil rights groups together to
carry on Meredith's march. The objective would be to reinforce the
voting rights message and put pressure on Congress to pass the new
civil rights bill that President Johnson had proposed in his 1966 State
of the Union Address. Roy Wilkins, the president of the NAACP, was
arriving in Memphis that night, along with Whitney Young, the head
of the Urban League. Together with King's SCLC and McKissick's
CORE, they would account for four of the so-called Big Five civil
rights groups. SNCC was the fifth. So where did SNCC stand? King
asked its new leader. Was Carmichael on board?

Less than two months into his tenure as chairman, Carmichael
knew that he should check with SNCC's Central Committee. He
imagined how Ruby Doris Robinson would react. She would say
that SNCC's resources were stretched too thin to get involved with
a halfhearted sequel to the Selma protest. "Another march? Is y'all
crazy?" he could hear the Spelman grad saying in her Georgia drawl.

"Now I know Howard University done ruined more good Negroes than whiskey." In his autobiography, Carmichael would insist that before giving Dr. King an answer, he flew to Atlanta to get consent from the Central Committee.

But that didn't happen. Within hours after visiting Meredith in the hospital, Carmichael appeared with Dr. King at a press conference announcing plans for a joint march. In a photograph that ran in newspapers the next day, Carmichael was seated by Dr. King's side, dressed in white shirt sleeves and looking like an earnest disciple. Not until three days later, according to SNCC minutes, did Carmichael and Sellers meet with Robinson and the other leaders in Atlanta. At that point, the march was too far along for doubters to do anything but tell Carmichael that he was on his own. "We don't want to hear anything more about this march," Sellers recalled someone on the Central Committee saying. "Don't call us for help!"

What did occur that morning was that Carmichael met with Sellers and Wise and laid out a vision for how they could turn the march to SNCC's advantage. Meredith's planned route passed close to the rural areas where Carmichael had worked during Freedom Summer. If the march returned there, he argued, SNCC workers could use their local knowledge to stage a massive voter registration drive. Local sharecroppers and Black youth would recognize them and be eager to help. For Carmichael, it also presented a chance to counter the wild radical image that had been painted of him after Kingston Springs, to show what he actually meant when he talked to the press about mobilizing Black political power. "Hey, *telling* them hadn't worked at the press conference," he recalled arguing. "We'd need to *show* the media. I wanted this march to *demonstrate* the new SNCC approach in action."

Once Carmichael confirmed that SNCC was on board, he and Sellers and Wise joined Dr. King and McKissick in a caravan of four cars that drove to Hernando that afternoon. As dozens of reporters followed them, the leaders made a symbolic start to the new march at the spot where Meredith was shot. They held a brief prayer service, linked arms, and sang "We Shall Overcome." On the opposite side of the road, comedian Dick Gregory, dressed in a jeans jacket and a cowboy hat, led a separate march in honor of Meredith. Gregory had flown to Memphis with his wife, Lillian, and was leading a small procession back toward Tennessee. "If one shot from the bushes can scare a nation, we're in trouble," Gregory told reporters. Meanwhile, police cars filled both sides of the highway, trailing the two marches in opposite directions.

King's group had advanced only fifty yards, to the top of a small hill, when three state troopers got out of a patrol car and ordered them off the road.

"Stay off the pavement," an officer named L. Y. Griffin barked.

King gave Griffin a puzzled look. "It's your duty to give us protection . . ." he said.

"Off the pavement," Griffin repeated.

"We marched on the pavement from Selma to Montgomery . . ." King said, recalling the scene in Alabama the year before.

"You had a permit for that," Griffin snapped. "I don't care if you march to China, as long as you march on the side of the road."

"Can't you ask us . . ." King began, before another trooper cut him short by thrusting an arm into his chest. King staggered back, and was saved from falling to the ground by Carmichael and McKissick.

After pulling King to his feet, Carmichael lurched in the direction of the troopers.

"Get Stokely, somebody, lay on him," King called out, worried that Carmichael was about to do something rash.

So as not to be overheard, King took the others behind an ice cream stand for a ten-minute conference. He urged them to obey the stay-off-the-road order, and teasingly chastised Carmichael for "breaking discipline" by trying to lunge at the troopers. "I am sorry, Dr. King," Carmichael replied quietly. When the group resumed walking along the muddy edge of the road, King took credit for keeping Carmichael out of trouble. "I restrained Stokely—non-violently," he chuckled. When the leaders reached the Coldwater River a few miles ahead, they stopped for the day and boarded cars back to Memphis. That evening, Roy Wilkins and Whitney Young joined them for a unity rally at the Centenary Methodist Church, a congregation now led by Reverend James Lawson, the expert in nonviolent protest with whom John Lewis and James Bevel had once studied as seminary students in Nashville.

As the Big Five leaders rose to address a packed house of more than a thousand, they already seemed to be haggling with one another. Wilkins and Young went first. They called for channeling anger over Meredith's shooting into pressure for the new civil rights bill, and appeared to make reference to press reports of SNCC's new separatist direction. "If you want to start hating all white men, you will waste your energies," Wilkins warned. When Carmichael's turn came, he sounded as if he felt personally attacked. "I'm not trying to beg the white man for anything I deserve," he shouted. "I'm going to take it." Then Carmichael mocked the idea of expecting help from Washington by contrasting the way the government had protected Meredith when he integrated Ole Miss with his lonely fate on Highway 51. "When they needed Meredith, they sent in federal troops, but when they didn't need him, he was just a nigger in the cotton patch," Carmichael shouted. "We need power!"

In his speech, McKissick showed more militancy than anyone had ever seen from his predecessor at CORE, James Farmer. He talked about the false image created by the Statue of Liberty of an America open to all races. "They ought to break that young lady's legs and throw her in the Mississippi," McKissick shouted. Speaking last, King tried to end the rally on a positive note with one of his familiar, uplifting sermons. "We can transfer a dark yesterday into a bright tomorrow," King preached. The crowd shouted "Amen," just as they had to all the other speakers, oblivious to the jabs that were being exchanged.

When the rally was over, the Big Five leaders drove back to the Lorraine Motel on the west side of Memphis to hash out terms for the march and to draft a joint manifesto.

"So, you expect any problems?" Stanley Wise asked Carmichael on the way.

"Can't think of any," Carmichael responded with his usual cool bravado. "Why?"

"Well, you know, it'll be your first summit," Wise said. "Representing SNCC among the Big Negroes . . ."

For all his surface nonchalance, Carmichael had been mentally preparing all day for the summit meeting. He reminded himself of the lesson he learned as an activist at Howard University: when dealing with older authority figures, come prepared with detailed proposals. He tried to envision how the discussion would play out. Wilkins and Young would favor a conservative approach, he predicted, and be arrogant about it. Carmichael didn't know McKissick well yet, but he sensed that Floyd might be open to SNCC's bolder ideas. That would leave Dr. King in the middle, trying to play peacemaker but also positioned to break a stalemate.

Despite what the press was writing about their rivalry, Carmichael had a great deal of respect for Dr. King. Like Ruby Doris Robinson, Carmichael had received help paying for college from the SCLC after the Freedom Rides, and he had always been grateful. The two men had come to know each other personally when Carmichael chauffeured Dr. King around rural Mississippi, and they had bonded over a shared love of soul food and talent for mimicry. Carmichael admired King's willingness to face physical danger and go to prison, unlike Wilkins and Young and other establishment leaders who operated from the safety of office buildings and hotel suites. Most of all, Carmichael respected how much ordinary Black folks loved Dr. King, and how much he loved them, no matter what their station in life.

IF THE PEABODY HOTEL WAS A CROSSROADS FOR THE WHITE EStablishment in Memphis, its Black counterpart was the Lorraine Motel, a mile to the south on Mulberry Street. Once known as the Marquette Hotel, the property had been purchased in 1945 by Walter Bailey, a local Black businessman, and renamed for his wife, Loree, and the swing era hit "Sweet Lorraine." Bailey rebuilt the property as a two-story motor inn with a drive-in parking lot, a swimming pool, a restaurant, and a reception hall for parties and weddings. Advertisements in the "Green Book," the Jim Crow guide to Southern hotels that welcomed Blacks, made the motel a popular destination for tourists. Meanwhile, its proximity to the Stax Records recording studio and the jazz clubs of Beale Street attracted top Black musicians and other entertainment stars. For years, Dr. King had stayed at the Lorraine Motel whenever he visited Memphis. He appreciated the warm hospitality of the Baileys as well the confidence that any business he engaged in on the premises, official or otherwise, would be kept private from the world outside.

King had reserved a conference room for the meeting, and he was already seated at a large table along with McKissick and SCLC aide Bernard Lee when Carmichael entered with Cleve Sellers and Stanley Wise. Carmichael explained that SNCC's Central Committee had sent the trio as a delegation, and King nodded his okay. Wilkins and Young arrived last, both dressed in suits and carrying briefcases. Young, the handsome, salt-and-pepper-haired chief of the Urban League, greeted everyone with an affable smile, while the tall, balding president of the NAACP maintained a grim expression.

To break the ice, Carmichael stood up and greeted the two men so effusively that Sellers later joked that he might as well have asked for their autographs.

"Mr. Wilkins, Mr. Young. A pleasure, gentlemen," Carmichael oozed. "An honor to meet you. An *honor*, Mr. Wilkins. Just looking forward so much to working with you . . ."

Wilkins responded with a pinched smile, and Carmichael thought he spied a glint of amusement in Dr. King's eyes.

When the men all sat down around the conference table, Wilkins shot Sellers and Wise a haughty look.

"Martin, didn't you say this was a meeting of the *leadership*?" Wilkins asked.

"I said of the national organizations," King replied. "Each group has one vote."

"Martin, you know we talk with generals," Wilkins sniffed. "Not with rank and file."

King couldn't suppress a grin. "The young people are very democratic," he said, defending the presence of the two SNCC aides.

Wilkins glowered at Carmichael. "Well, *John* certainly never felt a need to surround himself with an *entourage*," he said, referring to John Lewis.

"That was his biggest problem," Stanley Wise muttered under his breath.

Feigning more humility, Carmichael explained that he was so new to his job that the Central Committee had decided to send a delegation. Even Whitney Young seemed amused by this unctuous display, but Wilkins remained stone-faced.

"As long as you all understand now," Wilkins said sternly. "SNCC has one spokesman and one vote. That clear?"

"Yes, sir. Thank you, sir," Carmichael agreed. "Understood, yes sir."

After that, the meeting began cordially enough. The leaders all agreed on the goal of carrying on Meredith's march, and that each of the five organizations would contribute according to its particular strengths. Carmichael said that SNCC could provide boots on the ground and knowledge of the Delta. As Young nodded assent, Wilkins said the NAACP and the Urban League would take the lead in raising money and linking the march to Johnson's new civil rights bill.

The bill was in serious peril, Wilkins warned. Threatened by its fair housing provisions, real estate interests were mounting fierce opposition. Sam Ervin, the conservative Democrat who chaired the Senate Judiciary Committee, had come out against the bill on the grounds that its federal penalties for race crimes would be better addressed by a constitutional amendment—something the wily North Carolinian knew would never happen. But Meredith's shooting had shaken leaders of both parties, Wilkins argued, and given the bill new momentum. Everett Dirksen, the Republican Senate minority leader, had told reporters that "such a ghastly act on the highway" was bound to add new "spirit and steam" to the legislation. Emanuel Celler, the Democratic sponsor in the House, seemed newly optimistic. "There are times," Celler said after Aubrey Norvell's attack on Meredith, "when the civil rights movement has no greater friend than its enemy."

To take advantage of the moment, Wilkins lectured, the Big Five would have to be careful about the message they conveyed during the march. The NAACP and the Urban League could help keep politicians in Washington and wealthy white donors in line, but only if the agenda remained focused on the new bill, and nothing was done to embarrass the Johnson administration. Reminding everyone of the NAACP's standing as the oldest of the Big Five, Wilkins insisted that he would need firm assurances on these points before risking the group's reputation and political capital.

WHEN CARMICHAEL'S TURN CAME TO SPEAK, HE IGNORED THE legislative battle in Washington and focused on the realities of rural Mississippi. He reminded everyone that James Meredith had set out to inspire Black people to vote. If the Big Five were going to carry on his crusade, Carmichael argued, shouldn't that work be continued? Shouldn't the priority be registering poor Blacks in the Delta, rather than just giving white supporters another opportunity to march? Then Carmichael painted a picture of SNCC's vision of the march. At every town on the road to Jackson, a registration center would be set up at the local courthouse. Every night, a public rally would take place. Local Black youth would be invited to speak, so they could gain experience they might use to run for office one day.

As Carmichael went on, he could see Wilkins frowning every time he questioned the necessity for white participation. But Carmichael was getting murmurs of approval from McKissick, and Dr. King was doing more listening than talking. At one point, King did speak up to stress "the morality of making the march completely interracial," as he later put it, but he also seemed intrigued by Carmichael's vision of registering voters and inspiring Black youngsters.

Then Carmichael gambled on raising an issue that he knew could tilt the rest of the meeting in one direction or the other. Arriving at the Lorraine Motel that evening, he had run into Earnest Thomas, one of the founders of the Deacons for Defense and Justice. The Deacons were a group of Black men who had banded together to provide armed protection for civil rights workers after a series of Ku Klux Klan attacks on CORE organizers in Louisiana. The Deacons were highly controversial within the movement, because they carried guns and were viewed by some as violating the commitment to nonviolence. But they had won the respect of others by keeping a low profile and patrolling from a distance. In the motel lobby, Thomas recognized Carmichael and approached him with a distressed look. As soon as the Deacons had heard about Meredith's shooting, a contingent had traveled to Memphis to offer help. But they were being given "the runaround," Thomas complained, and told that their participation would have to be approved by the Big Five.

Carmichael promised Thomas that he would bring up the matter, and now he placed it squarely on the conference table. He could see Roy Wilkins brighten when the Deacons were mentioned. "Bro Wilkins perked up," Carmichael recalled. "I knew he was hoping this would be the wedge that would separate SNCC from CORE and SCLC. So I had to hit that one hard." Carmichael's words grew more vivid and passionate. Why was Meredith shot? Carmichael asked. Because he was a Black man walking through the Deep South without protection. If the shooter's gun had been loaded with buckshot instead of birdshot, they'd all be attending a funeral instead of planning a march. This wasn't a parade down Broadway or a walk around the Reflecting Pool, he said. This was the Mississippi Delta. As far as SNCC was concerned, it would be irresponsible and immoral to put marchers on its roadways without armed backup. "We needed the Deacons," Carmichael concluded, "not the other way around."

The room was silent for a moment, then Floyd McKissick spoke. Recalling that the Deacons had originally been formed to support CORE's work in Louisiana, he said that he refused to tell them to go home. Finally, after listening quietly, Dr. King weighed in. He didn't dwell on the fine points of nonviolence, although aides would later explain that his answer reflected his private distinction between aggression and self-defense. Instead, King said matter-of-factly that he would accept the presence of the Deacons as long as they agreed to the goal of keeping the march peaceful.

That's when the yelling started. Wilkins shouted at King that he was making a grave mistake and risking the credibility of the march and the movement. Then Wilkins lit into Carmichael. "And as for me, I was impudent, inexperienced, arrogant and ignorant of history," Carmichael recalled, describing the tongue-lashing. "I didn't understand the movement or the delicate dynamics of coalition. Didn't even understand politics. A foolish young upstart, dangerous to himself and the movement."

Sometime after midnight, McKissick tired of the rancor and excused himself. But as he left the room, he announced his support for SNCC's positions on the two most contentious issues: the involvement of the Deacons, and the focus on organizing local Black youth. "It's getting real late, and I'm going on to bed," McKissick said. "But I'm with Stokely on both counts." Once it became clear that the generals were divided two-against-two, and that Dr. King was leaning against him, Wilkins became even more enraged. For two more hours, he continued to argue loudly with Carmichael, as the conference room grew hazy with cigarette smoke.

With the two o'clock hour approaching, the discussion turned to drafting a joint manifesto for the march. Carmichael pressed for language that would take a swipe at President Johnson for not doing more to enforce existing civil rights legislation. Two weeks earlier, Carmichael had announced that SNCC would refuse to participate in an upcoming White House conference that Johnson had entitled "To Fulfill These Rights." For the manifesto, he proposed language that turned that phrase against the president. "This march will be a massive public indictment and protest of the failure of American society, the government of the U.S. and the state of Mississippi to 'fulfill these rights'" read Carmichael's draft.

Wilkins blew up again. How could they turn on LBJ, he fumed, after all he had done to push through the Civil Rights Act and the Voting Rights Act? What good would it to do antagonize the White House when they still needed its support for the new bill? At some point during this exchange, Carmichael mockingly referred to Johnson as "that cat, the President," and this was too much for Wilkins.

"Don't give me any of 'that cat the President' crap, Stokely," he snapped.

Wilkins stood up, stuffed the papers he had strewn on the conference table into his leather briefcase, and clasped it shut. Whitney Young also got up to leave. Under the circumstances, Wilkins informed King, the NAACP and the Urban League had no choice but to "wash their hands" of the march.

"Yeah, like Pilate before you," Cleve Sellers snickered, as Carmichael shushed him and Wilkins and Young grimly exited the room.

The next day, Whitney Young took the private skirmish public. On only two hours sleep, he flew to Kentucky for a ceremony honoring his father, who was retiring as president of the Lincoln Institute, a historically Black boarding school east of Louisville. James Driscoll, a reporter for the Louisville *Courier-Journal*, asked for an interview about the Meredith March. Sitting on a folding chair in the school library, an exhausted Young let his frustrations show. He explained the position of the Urban League and the NAACP—that the march should focus on passage of the new civil rights bill. But he said the Big Five had split over Carmichael's vision of trying to mobilize Black political power without white help. "It's not a matter of white versus black, but of good people versus bad people," Young said wearily, adding that he saw it as "completely unrealistic" to think that Blacks could achieve their goals on their own in a country where they accounted for only 10 percent of the population.

Although the fractious meeting at the Lorraine Motel was only fleetingly mentioned in the news reports at the time, the withdrawal of the NAACP and the Urban League from the Meredith March had a critical ripple effect on the events to come. For the press, it provided an irresistible new angle—about growing divisions within the movement—that drew even more attention to the march. For SNCC, it gave the new leadership far more influence over the march's tactics—and eventual route—than they would have had otherwise.

For Stokely Carmichael, it meant that he would be seen side by side with Dr. King for the next two weeks. Overnight, those images would make the handsome, provocative new SNCC chairman look to the world like King's generational rival—or potential heir. As Gene Roberts of *The New York Times* pointed out, it was a status that even Malcolm X, who had met and been photographed with Dr. King only once, never enjoyed during his lifetime. "Reporters and cameramen drawn to a demonstration by the magic of Dr. King's name stay to write about and photograph Mr. Carmichael as he demonstrates and talks alongside the older civil rights leader," Roberts wrote. "This is an advantage that Malcolm X never had as he exalted the Negro and attacked the 'duplicity' and 'hypocrisy' of the white man."

CHAPTER 8

A Cry in the Mississippi Night

For the first few days, the Meredith March resembled a pale imitation of the Selma march, just as Carmichael had imagined Ruby Doris Robinson predicting. Because sleeping accommodations had yet to be arranged, protesters assembled every morning at the spot on Highway 51 where they left off the day before, walked several miles, then drove back to Memphis for the night. Dr. King left the march for the first of several visits to his slum apartment in Chicago. Evidence of how Vietnam and urban race riots had soured the mood of the country kept surfacing. As the marchers locked arms and sang spirituals, a Black girl on the roadside mocked them with a new verse to a familiar freedom song. "I love everybody, I love everybody, I love everybody in my heart," the girl sang. "I just told a lie, I just told a lie, I just told a lie in my heart." An antiwar protester from Coney Island came up with a variation on "The Ballad of the Green Berets," the patriotic hit single of 1966. His version compared the elite Marines to the Ku Klux Klan. "Amorphous" was the polite term used to describe the atmosphere by Unitarian minister Homer Jack, a veteran of Selma and other previous marches. "The Movement is changing so rapidly," a bewildered Jack told a reporter, "that one has to run fast to keep up."

Reporters were hard pressed to come up with fresh story angles. During one particularly slow day, Gene Roberts went to the front of the procession to question Carmichael and McKissick about their views on white support for the civil rights cause. Carmichael responded with typical breeziness. "I'm for the Negro" he said. "I'm not anti anything." McKissick labored with metaphors as he tried to distinguish between white support and white control. "We've received a lot of help from white liberals and we appreciate it," he said. "But the situation is sort of like when you are sick and your neighbor comes in to help you. You need his assistance, but you don't want him to run your house or take your wife." By evening, word had reached the SCLC about the potentially embarrassing line of inquiry that Roberts was pursuing. When the march reached Batesville, Mississippi, Ralph Abernathy took to the pulpit of a local Black church to make a loud declaration of the SCLC's support for white alliances. "If you got any notions that Negroes can solve our problems by ourselves, you got another thought coming," Abernathy thundered. "We welcome white people." He paused for a few seconds to let Roberts jot down the quote. "Ain't that right?" Abernathy called out to the Black locals, many of whom must have wondered what all the fuss over white people was about.

The pace picked up, however, as Carmichael's plans for a rolling voter registration drive came together. Four circus tents arrived, rented by Andrew Young from an Atlanta company for $100 a night, allowing the marchers to stay overnight in the Batesville churchyard. The next morning, some two hundred marchers, joined by three hundred locals, converged on the Panola County courthouse in Batesville and watched as fifty Blacks were added to the voter rolls. "Registration is all right," a 106-year-old retired farmer named El Fondren declared as he hobbled out of the courthouse on a cane. Two young Blacks swept the old man onto their shoulders and paraded him through the cheering crowd. From then on, an advance team of SNCC workers leapfrogged ahead each morning to identify new campsites. Drawing on contacts from the Bob Moses days, they recruited locals to help with cooking meals, gaining access to indoor toilets, and providing transportation to registration centers. At each town, the Deacons for Defense scouted for discreet spots where they could stand guard.

The advance work paid off when the march reached Grenada, a small town of twelve thousand halfway between Memphis and Jackson. SNCC workers received permission to erect the big tops on a campground near the Enid Federal Dam, and to register voters at the courthouse in town. Bradford Dye, an up-and-coming local attorney, was assigned to negotiate the details. Dye gave approval for nighttime registration hours and a rally in the town square. Then he quietly spread word among Grenada's white population not to cause any trouble, in hopes that the marchers would go about their business and leave quickly.

On the sultry morning of Tuesday, June 14—Flag Day—several hundred marchers departed from the Enid Dam campsite and proceeded along Highway 51 toward Grenada. Outside the town, someone had painted a crude warning on the pavement, ironically misspelling a taunt to illiterate Blacks. "Red nigger and run," the message said. "If you can't red, run anyway." Yet when the marchers entered the Black section of town, they received a rapturous welcome. People stood in the doorways of tin-roofed houses and in narrow yards teeming with sunflowers to get a glimpse of Dr. King, who had just returned from Chicago. "Mr. Charlie ain't going to give you a whippin tonight," a marcher called out, using a Southern Black term for white law enforcement, and dozens of locals emerged from their shanties to join the procession. "I was just looking, and all of a sudden I was marching," marveled a woman named Tessie McCain. Observing the scene, a state trooper muttered to a reporter that he could see "about a mile of niggers."

In the white section of town, homeowners watched warily from columned porches and behind stately elm trees as the procession passed by. Arriving at the county courthouse downtown, the marchers went to integrate its bathrooms. After the Civil Rights Act, Jim Crow–era "White" and "Colored" signs had been replaced with less blatant placards that read "Men's 1" and "Men's 2," and "Women's 1" and "Women's 2." "We're going over to the toilets marked 'No. 1' and see if it ain't a little better," McKissick announced. But all the signs had been taken down, so the Black integrators left nothing to chance by splitting up to use all four restrooms.

In the town square, perspiring marchers sat down in the shade of a Confederate memorial. Hovering above them was a statue of a skinny Rebel soldier holding a canteen in one hand and a musket in the other. "To the noble men who marched neath the flag of the stars and bars," read an inscription. Below the statue was a bas-relief of Jefferson Davis, the seccessionist president. Robert Green, a Black psychology professor from Michigan State University who had taken a leave to serve as the march's liaison officer, climbed onto the base of the monument. Because it was Flag Day, Green stuck a small replica of the Stars and Stripes in an oval frame surrounding Davis's bearded face. "We want old Jeff Davis to know that the South that he repre-sented will never stand again," Green called out to the crowd. "This is not the Confederacy, this is America. We're tired of seeing rebel flags. Give us the flag of the United States, the flag of freedom."

On the other side of a line of state troopers, grim-faced white townspeople watched as an elderly bishop of the African Methodist Episcopal Zion Church prayed for their salvation. "We don't exactly hate them," the preacher said of the whites. "We just hate what they do." Under his breath, one of the onlookers threatened earthly retri-bution to Paul Good, a freelance journalist covering the march for the journal *New South*. "I saw two of my niggers in there and they won't have no jobs tomorrow," the man groused. "They get in that march an' that's it. They'll be on relief tomorrow."

After sunset, the marchers were still in the square when some five hundred local Blacks arrived to register to vote. Despite Bradford Dye's promise of nighttime hours, the courthouse was closed. After a short negotiation with the town police, Dr. King told the crowd to go home and to return the next day in even greater numbers. In the morning, as the rest of the marchers moved on to the next town, a SNCC contingent stayed behind in Grenada and spent all day sign-ing up new voters. By the time they were finished, the number of registered Blacks in Grenada County had nearly doubled, from 697 to more than 1,300. The spirit of accommodation wouldn't last long. Soon after the SNCC workers departed, police arrested several Blacks who tried to integrate the town movie theater. Still, Carmichael was elated with the Grenada results. SNCC had never registered so many Blacks in such a brief period of time, even during Freedom Summer or in a whole year in Lowndes County. Reporters had also been shown that the Meredith March could produce concrete results. The next day, the headline on Gene Roberts's front-page story for *The New York Times* read: "Negroes Win Voting Gains on Stop in Grenada, Miss."

For the moment, at least, the march also brought Carmichael and Dr. King closer than ever before. As they walked together in the ninety degree heat, and shared a circus tent at night, Carmichael saw a human side to "Da Lawd," as he and other young organizers teasingly called the great man behind his back. King was relaxed, talkative, and eager to tell funny stories. It "was almost like a holiday for Dr. King," Carmichael recalled thinking, as though he had been let "out of a straightjacket." King seemed relieved to be away from SCLC business and Washington politics, and Carmichael was reminded that for all his renown and responsibilities, King was still only thirty-seven years old, closer in age to him than to elders like Roy Wilkins.

As the two walked side by side at the front of the march, Carmichael described the Black Panther Party experiment in Lowndes County, and the moving nominating convention in Hayneville. Under a beige panama hat, King listened and responded with probing questions. At the nighttime rallies that ended each day's march, Carmichael would give a fiery speech, then King would follow with words that began to echo Carmichael's, only in more measured language. "Little by little, he began to agree that it *might* be necessary to emphasize Black Consciousness," Cleve Sellers recalled thinking as he listened to the subtle shift in King's tone. "He also agreed that our commitment to independent, black organizations *might* just work."

Carmichael also couldn't help feeling moved by the deep affection that the Black folk of the Delta showed for Dr. King. Every day, people lined Highway 51 to wait for him, then jostled to get a closer look as the march approached. "There he is! Martin Luther King!" someone would shout, and everyone would link arms and form a protective cordon as he passed by. King would smile shyly, sometimes shake a hand, and promise reassuringly that "a new day's coming."

In one of these expectant crowds, seven elderly Black women waited in the shade of a tree and cupped their hands against the sun's glare to catch a glimpse of King.

"I see him. I see him," one of the women cried out.

As the woman rushed forward to touch King, she knocked Carmichael to the ground.

"Oh, my!" the woman apologized. "Son, you all right? You ain't hurt, is you?"

"No'm," Carmichael answered. "I ain't hurt. Entirely my fault. I should know better than standing between Dr. King and his people."

"You sure got that right, son," the woman replied.

The success of the voter registration drive in Grenada buoyed King's spirits, and made him more open to SNCC's tactical suggestions. Taking advantage of the moment, Carmichael made a pitch to reroute the march into Leflore County, where he had worked first with Bob Moses and then during Freedom Summer. Carmichael wanted the Black folks there to get to see Dr. King in person. He also knew that the deeper into the Delta the march went, the more SNCC alone would know the terrain and be able to steer events. So it was on that on Wednesday, June 15, before departing for another two-day visit to Chicago, King informed reporters that the Meredith marchers wouldn't proceed all the way to Jackson along Highway 51 as planned. Instead, they would swing southeast along Route 7 toward the Leflore County seat of Greenwood, Mississippi—Carmichael's old stamping ground.

TO MOST OUTSIDERS WHO HAD HEARD OF IT, LEFLORE COUNTY was notorious as one of the poorest and most violently racist pockets of the South. From the 1870s until the 1950s, forty-eight documented lynchings took place there, the most of any county in Mississippi. It was in the Leflore town of Money, just ten miles north of Green-wood, that a mob of white men tortured, shot, and drowned Emmett Till on suspicion that the fourteen-year-old boy from Chicago had flirted with the wife of a local grocery store owner. Although Blacks made up two thirds of the county's population, they owned less than 8 percent of its land. For almost a century, poll taxes, literacy tests, and contrived constitutional quizzes had kept most of the county's Blacks from ever voting.

Yet for Carmichael, Leflore County was a place of magical mem-ories. During his summers there, he had relished visits to sharecrop-per homes, full of laughter on wooden porches and shared meals cooked in cramped kitchens. As his biographer Peniel E. Joseph put it, Carmichael came to admire the "unassuming dignity and grace" with which even the most impoverished and unlettered Blacks in the county carried themselves. "I met heroes," Carmichael recalled of his time in Greenwood. "Humble folk, of slight education and modest income, who managed to be both generous and wise, who took us in, fed us, instructed us and protected us, and ultimately civilized, edu-cated, and inspired the smart-assed college students."

As Mississippi governor Paul Johnson saw it, the detour into Le-flore County could only spell trouble, and he didn't want any more responsibility for preventing it. Four years earlier, as lieutenant gov-ernor, Johnson had made a name for himself by trying to block James Meredith's entrance to Ole Miss. "Paul Stood Tall" was his campaign slogan when he ran for governor. But since then, Johnson had evolved into a "new breed segregationist," as *Newsweek* described him. Pro-jecting a image of reasonableness, Johnson had originally offered po-lice protection for the march named after his onetime adversary. But now, in a hastily called press conference, the governor announced that he was cutting back the number of state troopers assigned to the Meredith March from twenty to four. He complained that the march had become little more than a publicity stunt and fundraising vehicle for Dr. King. "We're not going to wet nurse a bunch of showmen all over the county," Johnson griped to reporters. "They are using a very few people to get out and march in the hot sun while the leader goes to a country church to pass the hat and raise money, which is what he is down here for."

As the state troopers pulled back, two carloads of white youth tailed the procession as it turned south onto Route 7. "Look at that black boy walk!" one of the passengers called out to a young marcher. "You mean, that nigger?" another sneered. When SCLC organizer R. B. Cottonreader parked a supply truck near a cotton gin along the roadside, a white man waving a snub-nosed revolver ordered him to leave before one of the remaining state troopers intervened. In the *Greenwood Commonwealth*, the local newspaper, an editorial welcomed Dr. King by comparing him to Joseph Stalin and Mao Tse-tung.

The marchers received more troubling news as they neared the Greenwood town limits: Byron de la Beckwith was back in town. Three years earlier, the fertilizer salesman from Greenwood had shot Medgar Evers, the NAACP's Mississippi field secretary, as Evers got out of his car in the driveway of his Jackson home. An all-white jury failed to reach a verdict, and de la Beckwith went free. Medgar's older brother Charles had since taken over his post at the NAACP, and at first had joined his boss Roy Wilkins in refusing to participate in the Meredith March. "I don't want this to turn into another Selma where everyone goes home with the cameraman and leaves us holding the bag," Charles explained to the press. But after Grenada, Charles was so impressed by the voter registration gains that he decided to join the march. Hearing that news, de la Beckwith slipped back into Greenwood and started lurking around the campsite that was being prepared for the marchers before police chased him away.

The campsite was on the grounds of Stone Street High School, a segregated school in a Black neighborhood of Greenwood known as Baptist Town. Carmichael knew the school officials from his summers in Greenwood, and had reached out for permission to pitch the circus tents on the athletic field. On the morning of Thursday, June 16, Carmichael was driving by to inspect the installation when he saw the town's police commissioner, B. A. "Buff" Hammond, and nine of his men arguing with Bob Smith of SNCC and Bruce Baines of CORE as they spread tents out on the field.

Carmichael parked his car and approached Hammond, whom he also knew personally from his earlier stints in Greenwood. "Is there a problem?" he asked.

Hammond replied that Smith and Baines were trespassing on town property.

Carmichael explained that school officials had given their okay. "That ain't no problem," he said, nodding at the tents. "We'll put them up anyway."

Carmichael started to pitch in, and Hammond ordered him to stand back. As soon as Carmichael placed his hand on one of the tents, a policeman yanked his arm away and held a billy club aloft as if ready to strike. The officer pulled Carmichael's arms behind his back and handcuffed him, while two other policemen did the same to Smith and Baines. Then the three men were dragged off to jail in full view of dozens of onlookers, including Bob Fitch, the staff photographer for the SCLC, who snapped a photo of the scene that was then distributed by the AP to newspapers across the country later in the day.

Carmichael passed the next six hours in the Leflore County Jail before he was released on $100 bail. Usually he made a point of maintaining his customary air of cool bravado and playful humor while spending time in prison, but this time he was furious. Buff Hammond had never treated him so disrespectfully when he was a lowly student organizer, Carmichael thought. But now that he was getting national attention, the police chief seemed to take pride in showing him up. "What's a man going to do?" Hammond later told reporters, defending the arrest. "There are times when you have to hold your head up."

While Carmichael fumed in prison, another location was found to pitch the tents. It was Broad Street Park, a block-long lot with a scruffy ball field a half mile away from the Stone Street School in Baptist Town. This time Hammond's men looked on stern-faced as the big tops went up, but they kept their billy clubs holstered. Meanwhile, Willie Ricks and other SNCC organizers fanned out across Greenwood to spread word that there would be a rally that night, and that Carmichael would speak as soon as he got out of jail. By evening, the park was packed with more than three hundred Black locals, many in their teens and twenties, as well as some two hundred marchers. The turnout was the largest for a nighttime rally since the Meredith March began, despite the absence of Dr. King, who was back in Chicago.

FOR WILLIE RICKS, IT WAS THE KIND OF CROWD HE HAD WAITED for all week. The sharp-tongued organizer known within SNCC as "Reverend Ricks" hailed from Chattanooga, Tennessee. His family name came from his father's birthplace in Colbert County, Alabama, where generations of white plantation owners called Ricks gave that surname to their slaves. Raised on a sharecropping farm, John D. Ricks married another Alabama native named Eileen Neloms, who went by the nickname "Casey." The couple moved to the Black west side of Chattanooga, where John poured concrete for a living and Casey tended to nine children.

One of five boys in the family, Ricks was a distracted and rowdy student, and dropped out of school in the seventh grade. By his teens, he was waiting tables at a Chattanooga hotel and spending his free time hustling in pool halls and stealing hubcaps and pig iron off the back of passing trains. Then in 1960, the Nashville sit-in movement spread to Chattanooga, and Ricks began to tag along to protests with his twin sister, Betty Joyce, and other students from predominantly Black Howard High School. At a demonstration against the city's police commissioner, someone passed him a microphone, and for the first time he experienced the rush of rousing a crowd. He had always admired two skills as a youth, Ricks liked to say: "conning," or talking people out of their money, and "preaching" of the kind he heard during summer visits to Alabama. With a mic in his hand, Ricks recalled, "my preacher desire began to come out."

Ricks caught the attention of the Reverend C. T. Vivian, the future top lieutenant to Dr. King who had a congregation in Chattanooga, and Vivian suggested that Ricks volunteer with SNCC. He went to work at SNCC's Atlanta office, where he was put in charge of recruiting Spelman College students. Over the next few years, Ricks played a supporting role in one historic civil rights protest after another. In Birmingham, he helped organize the schoolchildren who went up against Bull Connor's dogs and fire hoses. In Selma, he tended to a beaten woman on the Edmund Pettus Bridge on Bloody Sunday, before joining Jim Forman in his second-front protest in Montgomery. At a protest in Tuskegee after Sammy Younge's death, Ricks captured the frustration with nonviolence that so many felt in the wake of that murder. "The only way we can stop whites from killing is to start buying the rifles they kill us with," he proclaimed from the roof of a car to an angry crowd of five hundred Tuskegee students.

Along the way, Ricks acquired the "Reverend Ricks" nickname, even though had never been ordained and hadn't read much of the Bible. Colleagues called upon him whenever they needed to fire up a crowd, as the reserved Julian Bond did when he ran for the state legislature in Atlanta. During the Birmingham campaign, Ricks would sometimes warm up for Dr. King and try to steal some of his thunder. King didn't appreciate the competition, and Ricks became one of the few young organizers who got under his skin. After Ricks tried to stir up a crowd during the delicate deliberations after Bloody Sunday in Selma, King scolded him at a public meeting. "Come here, son," King said. "I've been out here fighting a long time, and I know what I'm doing. You can't hurt me." Cain may have slain Abel, King continued, but Ricks couldn't touch him. "You remember that," King said. "I was Martin Luther King before you were Willie Ricks, and I'll be Martin Luther King long after you're gone."

Yet ironically, the new battle cry that Ricks was thinking about that night in Greenwood owed its origins to Dr. King. During the 1963 Children's Crusade in Birmingham, King had heard the story of a white policeman who saw a little Black girl demonstrating with her mother and asked the child: "What do *you* want?" The child looked into the policeman's face and replied with one word: "Freedom." King liked the story so much that he began to work it into sermons that he gave across the country, which became known as his "Freedom Now" speeches. Then the line became the basis for a chant at civil rights rallies. "What do we want?" speakers would shout. "Freedom Now!" crowds would yell back.

When Willie Ricks joined the Meredith March, he began to experiment with a new version of that refrain. In small churches and segregated schools along Highway 51, he told Black listeners that the point of registering to vote wasn't to gain freedom, but to amass enough *power* to change their circumstances. "What do we want?" he called out. Then, instead of "Freedom Now!," Ricks shouted: "Black Power!" Ricks would repeat the question, and the crowds would take up the chant: "Black Power!" People became so excited that Ricks bragged to his SNCC colleagues about his new discovery. "They're going wild for it," he reported. "I left the people hollering 'black power' and they're still screaming."

At first, Carmichael was skeptical. "Stokely tried to get me thrown off the march for exaggerating," Ricks told SNCC historian Clayborne Carson. In his autobiography, Jim Forman took credit for encouraging Ricks to use the new slogan when he came through Atlanta on the way to the Meredith March. "Hey Jim, I got an idea," Ricks said, according to Forman. "Suppose when I get over there to Mississippi and I'm speaking, I start hollering for 'Black Power'? What do you think of that? Would you back me up? You think it would scare people in SNCC?" Forman claimed that he gave Ricks his blessing. " 'Black Power'—sure, try it," he replied. "Why not? After all, you'd only be shortening the phrase we are always using—power for poor black people. 'Black Power' is shorter and means the same thing. Go on, try it."

By Ricks's account, Carmichael became convinced once he accompanied Ricks to a church meeting early in the Meredith March and witnessed the effect of the new chant firsthand. By June 10, three days into the march, the slogan was on Carmichael's mind when he returned to Atlanta to brief SNCC's Central Committee. Minutes of the meeting describe Carmichael speaking of "people relating to the concept of Black Power." On June 16, six days later, Carmichael was ready to take what Willie Ricks had started and push it a dramatic step further, just as he had done along the way with Bob Moses and John Hulett.

By dusk, Ricks had built a makeshift stage in Broad Street Park in Baptist Town. He surrounded a flatbed truck with generator-powered floodlights, and recruited local Black teens to stand guard on the back of the truck. First Floyd McKissick addressed the crowd, then Ricks said a few words. But this time, Ricks held himself back and waited for Carmichael to arrive. Finally, as darkness fell, Carmichael appeared. He wore a brown paisley shirt, and his chest and face were tanned dark brown after two weeks of walking in the Alabama sun.

As Carmichael climbed onto the back of the truck, Ricks whispered into his ear. "Drop it now," Ricks said. "The people are ready. Drop it now."

When Carmichael emerged from the line of Black youth on the truck, it was as though he had stepped into the lights of Broadway. Gazing down at hundreds of moonlit faces looking up at him, he raised his right arm and clenched his hand into a fist. Then he clutched a small silver microphone and spoke in a voice filled with anger not only at the infuriating events of the day but at all the indignities he had suffered and witnessed in five years of working in the South.

"This is the twenty-seventh time that I have been arrested," Carmichael shouted, "—and I ain't going to jail no more!"

The crowd cheered and clapped, and Carmichael repeated the line with even more urgency. "I *ain't going* to jail no more!" he cried.

Another cheer rose up.

"The only way we're going stop them white men from whupping us is to take over," Carmichael continued. "We've been saying 'Freedom Now' for six years and we ain't got nothing. What we're gonna start saying now is: 'Black Power'!"

"Black Power!" the crowd roared back.

Next to Carmichael on the truck, Willie Ricks waved his arms from side to side, like a conductor uniting soloist and orchestra in a thunderous concerto. Five times, Carmichael repeated the refrain, stabbing the night air with his right index finger, and five times a chorus of hundreds of voices answered from the field below him.

"We want Black Power!" Carmichael shouted.

"Black Power!" the crowd cried.

"We want Back Power!"

"Black Power!"

"We want Black Power!"

"Black Power!"

"We want Black Power!"

"Black Power!"

"We want Black Power!"

"Black Power!"

Then Carmichael rephrased the refrain as a question, and the answer came back even louder.

"What do you want?" Carmichael asked.

"Black Power!" the crowd screamed.

"What do you want?"

"Black Power!"

"That's right," Carmichael shouted. "That's what we want, Black Power! We don't have to be ashamed of it. We have stayed here. We have begged the president. We've begged the federal government—that's all we've been doing, begging and begging. It's time we stand up and take over. Every courthouse in Mississippi ought to be burned down tomorrow to get rid of the dirt and the mess. From now on, when they ask you what you want, you know what you tell them? What do we want?"

"Black Power!" the crowd roared again, as Willie Ricks took over, leading yet another round of the chorus.

"What do you want?" Ricks cried.

"Black Power!" the crowd shouted.

As Carmichael climbed down from the truck, his eyes were gleaming and his dark face was bathed in sweat. On the dusty ball field below, older veterans of a decade of civil rights protests watched the raucous spectacle in uncomfortable silence, unaware that they were witnessing the moment that would change their movement forever.

PART 2

Tear Gas Over Canton

U ntil Stokely Carmichael shouted "Black Power!" over and over
again on that hot June night in Greenwood, Mississippi, those
two words had never gained traction as a racial rallying cry. In 1954,
novelist Richard Wright wrote a book entitled *Black Power* about his
travels through Africa, but its publication came and went without
much attention. In May of 1966, Congressman Adam Clayton Powell Jr. gave a little-noticed commencement address at Howard University in which he urged graduating students to "seek black power,
what I call audacious black power, the power to build black institutions of splendid achievement." When Carmichael included the two
words in earlier descriptions of political empowerment, he was dismissed by white journalists accustomed to relying on insights from
older, integration-minded Black leaders. Just a few weeks earlier,
Bruce Biossat, a columnist for the Scripps-Howard newspaper chain,
assured his readers that "one Negro of responsible status dismissed as
'ludicrous' the talk by SNICK's new leader, Stokely Carmichael, of
building a countervailing 'black power structure' to extract necessary
concessions from a nation which is 9-to-1 white."

Then, in the late hours after the Greenwood rally, the Associated
Press—the wire service that drew Black leaders to Mississippi with
its erroneous report that James Meredith had been killed—moved
another history-bending story over its ticker machines. Written by

James Bonney, a reporter from the AP bureau in Jackson, the story was only ten short paragraphs, but its lead was dramatic. "'We want black power! We want black power!' The 1,000 Negroes chanted it again and again," the story began, nearly doubling the actual size of the crowd in Broad Street Park. The account went on to conjure up Stokely Carmichael, his militant message, and his dramatic arrest on what Bonney called "the most troubled day for the march since James H. Meredith . . . was shot and wounded on June 6."

The next day, the AP story was picked up by more than two hundred American newspapers and run under blaring headlines such as "Mississippi Marchers Chant: 'We Want Black Power!'" Across the country, the words "Black Power!" leapt off the pages of some the biggest urban dailies in the land, from the New York *Daily News* to the *Chicago Tribune* and the *San Francisco Examiner.* The AP story also ran in small regional newspapers all the way from Hawaii (the *Honolulu Star-Bulletin*), to northern Wisconsin (the *Fond du Lac Commonwealth Reporter*), rural Missouri (the *Moberly Monitor-Index*), the New Jersey shore (the *Asbury Park Press*), and the Louisiana bayou (the *Lake Charles American Press*).

From that story on June 17 until the Meredith marchers reached Jackson nine days later, references to "Black Power" appeared in at least seven hundred more press accounts. The cry was the headline of a story in the next issue of *Newsweek*, the newsmagazine that had gained in circulation and reputation on its older and larger rival, *Time*, partly on the strength of its coverage of the civil rights movement. Written by Peter Goldman, a masterful wordsmith whose fascination with the Black struggle later inspired him to write a book about Malcolm X, the *Newsweek* story ended with a vivid description of Carmichael's speech and "the new politics that Carmichael proposed to substitute for the old."

Not to be outdone by *Newsweek*, *Time* briefly considered putting Carmichael on the magazine's cover. Known for recognizing news figures with painted portraits framed by the magazine's unmistakable red border, *Time*'s art department commissioned a likeness from Jacob Lawrence, the acclaimed Black painter known for depicting figures from Black life and history in a style that mixed the influence of French Cubism with the hues of Harlem. After traveling south to meet with Carmichael for a sitting, Lawrence produced an image that drew inspiration from the line drawing of the Lowndes County black panther. In Lawrence's portrait, Carmichael's face appeared inked in all black, while an un-inked panther crawled over his shoulder. The portrait was considered for a *Time* cover in early July, but discarded in favor of a portrait of the prime minister of Indonesia. By that point, *Time*'s editors had decided to weigh in on the Black Power juggernaut with a more disapproving take, leading their July 1 issue with a story entitled "Civil Rights: The New Racism." The new slogan, *Time* scolded, represented nothing less than "a racist philosophy that could ultimately perpetuate the very separatism against which Negroes have fought so successfully."

ONLY THREE DAYS AFTER THE GREENWOOD SPEECH, THE SUDDEN spotlight on Black Power also led to another first for Carmichael: a guest appearance on a national television news show. In Washington, that week, *Meet the Press*, the influential Sunday program hosted by moderator Edwin Newman on NBC, scored a coup by booking James Meredith for his first interview since the shooting. Scrambling to compete, *Face the Nation*, the CBS show hosted by gravel-voiced correspondent Martin Agronsky, invited Carmichael to leave the Mississippi march and travel to its studio in Washington. In keeping with the group interview format of both programs in those days, Agronsky was joined by two other reporters: John Hart, a chiseled-jawed young CBS correspondent, and Jim Doyle, a ruddy-cheeked reporter from the blue-collar Irish neighborhood of Dorchester, Massachusetts, who was covering the Meredith March for *The Boston Globe*.

As Doyle would later admit, the main goal of the "Sunday shows" was to provoke guests into saying something that would make news for the evening news broadcasts and the next morning's newspapers. With that in mind, Agronsky and his two panelists tried to get Carmichael to break ranks with Dr. King by grilling him on the issue of nonviolence. A month earlier, on the day of the nominating convention in Lowndes County, Carmichael had given an interview to a socialist weekly called *The Militant.* He was asked what his new Black party would do if Alabama officials blocked its seven candidates from running in the fall election. "We're out to take power legally." Carmichael replied. "But if we're stopped by the government from doing it legally, we're going to take it the way everyone else took it, including the way Americans took it in the American Revolution."

In his first question, Agronsky seized on the American Revolution quote, ignoring Carmichael's caveat about taking power legally. "This would seem to say that you are advocating taking power by force and violence—by the overthrow," Agronsky said. "Is that what you want?" Carmichael began to explain the logic behind forming Black political parties, but the reporters kept returning to the question of nonviolence. What did Carmichael mean by saying in Greenwood that "every courthouse in Mississippi ought to be burned down"? Doyle asked. "Are you talking in violent analogies because you want to see a violent Negro uprising?" When Carmichael argued that nonviolence was "tactical" and refused to disown the use of force under any circumstances, Agronsky asked in an indignant tone: "How can you not reject violence and be the head of the Student *Nonviolent* Coordinating Committee?" Hart even tried to get Carmichael on the record endorsing urban race riots. "If the means are irrelevant," Hart asked, "is there a condition under which you can see a usefulness in a Watts riot or a Chicago riot?"

Dressed conservatively in a light gray suit, his hair neatly cropped, Carmichael delivered answers that were "cogent but not incendiary," Doyle recalled, and avoided "picking a fight with King." But under the barrage of questions about nonviolence, Carmichael failed to give the television audience a concrete picture of the Lowndes County experiment—of how it came about, and what it was meant to achieve. Only toward the end of the program did he point out that getting ahead by acquiring local political power was nothing new in America, as shown by white immigrants in cities where they had large presences. "The Irish did that in Boston . . . just like [Italian] people did it in New York with La Guardia," Carmichael said. In what could have been the start of a useful debate, John Hart posed an obvious question: What about all the places where Blacks *didn't* outnumber whites? "What kind of real leverage do you have in Mississippi, in states where you do have these counties—against the remaining power structure on a state level?" Hart asked.

But by that point, the half hour broadcast was over.

"I sincerely regret that our time is up," Martin Agronsky interrupted.

"I also regret that," Carmichael said, looking startled that the interview had flown by so quickly.

Within the confines of the CBS studio, Jim Doyle thought that Carmichael had artfully dodged the efforts to stir up controversy. Meanwhile, across town, James Meredith made news on *Meet the Press*, announcing that he had recuperated sufficiently to rejoin the Mississippi march by the end of the following week. But Doyle's editors saw Carmichael's responses to the persistent questions about nonviolence, no matter how measured, as the sexier of the two stories. When *The Boston Globe* ran an AP account of the two news programs the next day, its headline focused on Carmichael rather than Meredith. "Rights Violence Can Be Justified, SNCC Man Says," the headline read.

BACK ON THE GROUND IN MISSISSIPPI, DR. KING WAS CONFRONTED with the challenge of how to respond to Carmichael's new battle cry. Absent on the night of the Broad Street Park rally, King returned to Greenwood the next day and at first tried to align himself with the Black Power message but with more nuanced language. Speaking at the Leflore County Courthouse, he pointed to a cluster of white policemen and told the crowd: "We're going to put black men in those uniforms" but added that "we need power" to do so. "We've got to organize ourselves in units of power," King declared that evening

at another Broad Street Park rally that ended in a mood of festive
unity, with Hosea Williams of the SCLC passing a collection plate and
SNCC's Cleve Sellers dancing the frug as a transistor radio played
rock 'n' roll.

When the march moved on from Greenwood, however, the atmosphere grew tense as it became clear how fast the new slogan was
spreading. On the way to Belzoni, the next town on the route, march
organizer Robert Green tried to revive the "Freedom Now" chant.
"What do we want?" Green called out to Black youth along the highway. "Black Power!" the young people shouted back several times.
"Let's have a little 'Freedom!'" Green implored. After watching Carmichael's appearance on *Face the Nation*, King returned to Atlanta and
huddled with SCLC staff. By Monday evening, King had decided to
issue a statement distancing himself from the new slogan. "It is absolutely necessary for the Negro to gain power, but the term 'black
power' is unfortunate because it tends to give the impression of black
nationalism," King told reporters, thereby providing another opportunity for stories with "Black Power" in the headline.

With Carmichael still on his way back to Mississippi from Washington, King made a move to reclaim the Meredith March spotlight.
He announced that he would make a hundred-mile detour to Philadelphia, Mississippi, to commemorate the three civil rights workers murdered during Freedom Summer. But if King's side trip was
meant to reaffirm the effectiveness of nonviolent protest, it backfired
badly. Philadelphia was the seat of Neshoba County, where whites still
outnumbered Blacks five-to-one at the time. When *New York Times*
reporter Joseph Lelyveld visited the town six months after the murders, a grocery store owner assured him that a "responsible majority"
of Philadelphia's white population felt nothing but "friendliness and
neighborliness" toward the town's Blacks. But the brutal slaying of
James Chaney, Andrew Goodman, and Michael Schwerner had laid
bare the town's dark secret: Philadelphia was also home to a coven
of some 150 Ku Klux Klansmen who burned crosses, fire-bombed
churches, and otherwise terrorized the Black community with the
tacit acceptance of that white majority.

According to a federal conspiracy indictment that was awaiting a trial date in the summer of 1966, the Freedom Summer murders had been made possible by Philadelphia's top two lawmen. Lawrence Rainey was the town's burly, tobacco-chewing police chief, and Cecil Price was his double-chinned, Stetson hat–wearing deputy. The two officers had deliberately released the three organizers from the Neshoba County Jail, where they were detained on a minor traffic charge, so that nineteen Klansman could finish them off. Yet even after the buried bodies were dug up and the policemen were charged, Lelyveld found whites in Philadelphia openly referring to the murdered civil rights workers as the "nigger and a couple of nigger lovers."

Traveling from Belzoni to Philadelphia, marchers led by Dr. King gathered at the Mount Nebo Baptist Church in the Black section of town. Singing freedom songs, they crossed the railroad tracks and headed toward the Neshoba County courthouse. As dust from the red-clay streets rose under their feet, a black sedan side-swiped the procession with a loud screech of brakes. Next, a red convertible swerved toward the marchers, followed by a blue ragtop. "I wouldn't dirty my goddamned car with you black bastards," a woman shouted from the blue car's passenger window. From the back of a passing pickup truck, a man swung a wooden club and struck several protesters. When the marchers stopped briefly to pray at the county prison, more club-wielding white men closed off both ends of the street, and a young boy turned a fire hose on the bowed heads before a shopkeeper shooed him away.

In the center of town, Cecil Price and ten of his men were waiting at the steps of the marble-columned courthouse, armed with pistols and nightsticks.

"You can't go up those steps," Price barked to the marchers.

"You're the one who had Schwerner and those fellows in jail?" King asked.

"Yes, sir," the deputy sheriff replied unapologetically.

Wearing thick sunglasses under the noonday sun, King led the congregation across the street, where they knelt in prayer and he offered a pointed remembrance. "In this county, Andrew Goodman,

James Chaney and Mickey Schwerner were brutally murdered," King declared. "I believe in my heart the murderers are somewhere around me at this moment."

"They're right behind you!" a young voice called out from a crowd of white onlookers.

"They ought to search their hearts," King continued. "I want them to know that we are not afraid. If they kill three of us, they will have to kill all of us."

"Hey, Luther!" another white onlooker taunted. "Come up here alone and prove it!"

The moment the short service ended, Price stepped forward and arrested one of the protesters, a local Black pastor, for a months-old traffic violation. But the deputy sheriff and his men did nothing when some three hundred of the white onlookers stampeded toward the marchers as they walked away from the courthouse. One man attacked with a five-foot club; another swung a large metal hoe. In the melee, a TV cameraman was knocked to the ground, and a Black protester suffered an epileptic seizure. Only when a few young Black locals fought back, throwing punches and hurling bottles and stones, did Price and his officers move in to break up the confrontation. When the marchers reached the safety of the Black section of town, Dr. King was badly rattled. "This is a terrible town, the worst I've seen," he told reporters. "There is a complete reign of terror here."

As if to prove King's point, the violence continued that night after he and the other marchers left to rejoin the Meredith March. Night riders staged an armed attack on the small storefront office of SNCC field secretary Ralph Featherstone. A tall, soft-spoken aspiring schoolteacher who had joined SNCC during Freedom Summer, Featherstone had been part of the search party that raced to Neshoba County after the three civil rights workers went missing. Along with Carmichael and Cleve Sellers, Featherstone spent several terrifying nights hunting through the surrounding swamps while trying to avoid detection by the Klan. So when he was appointed to run the SNCC office in Philadelphia two years later, he made a point of bringing a shotgun.

At eight o'clock on the night of King's visit, several cars drove past the storefront and a shot was fired through the window. From inside, a shotgun fired back and struck one of the attackers in the head and neck. Featherstone later denied having fired the gun, but that's not the impression he gave the FBI office in Jackson when he called to report the attack. "We are armed and returning fire," Featherstone told the FBI agent who answered the phone. "You can do what you want about it." Reconstructing the scene later for *Ramparts* magazine, reporter Andrew Kopkind spoke to a man he identified anonymously as the organizer who had "fired back" from the storefront office. The organizer's knowledge of leading civil rights figures and their positions on nonviolence suggested that the source was almost certainly Featherstone himself.

"Ralph Abernathy says, 'If you fight back, you're a coward,'" the organizer told Kopkind. "That's crazy. It's just a question of being a man. What's my non-violent response to a guy shooting at me in the dark and running away through the streets? Do I go limp somewhere inside the house? What the hell am I supposed to do? The assumption of non-violent protest is that the other guy has a conscience you can appeal to. That's not true in Mississippi. People get hung up when Martin tells them to be non-violent down here. Nobody wants to hear that non-violent stuff anymore. The real issue isn't violence *versus* non-violence; it's self-defense *versus* accepting anything white people want to do to you—including death."

When word of the events in Philadelphia reached the Meredith March, the contrast between Dr. King's humiliating retreat and Ralph Featherstone's armed resistance only fueled the growing arguments over nonviolence. "The assault in Philadelphia filled the debate with urgency," reported Roy Reed of *The New York Times*. "Several young Negroes said they would defend themselves if attacked." Trying to save face, Dr. King announced that he would return to Philadelphia later in the week to stage another protest and vowed to "straighten the place out" with "all our non-violent might." But when King sent a telegram to Lyndon Johnson asking for protection by federal marshals, the president demurred. LBJ wired back that he had received assurances from

Governor Paul Johnson that "all necessary protection can and will be provided" by Mississippi state troopers, and that Assistant Attorney General John Doar would be on hand to monitor the situation. So on the afternoon of June 23, the Meredith marchers set out in a heavy rainstorm from Yazoo City toward their next destination—Canton, Mississippi—relying on nothing more than the good word of "Paul Stood Tall" Johnson, the man who had tried to block federal marshals from escorting James Meredith into the University of Mississippi.

THE SEAT OF MADISON COUNTY, CANTON WAS KNOWN FOR ITS red-brick Greek Revival courthouse, admired as one of the most elegant in the state. Blacks had last voted there in significant numbers during the era of Reconstruction, when Election Day violence became routine and town officials armed with slingshots fired stones from the courthouse roof to break up racial brawls. In more recent decades, Canton had become known in Black America as the place where a Delta bluesman named Elmore James took a job in a local electrical factory and used spare parts to build guitars that produced a distinctively aggressive sound. James went on to minor stardom on the Chicago blues scene and served as an inspiration to Jimi Hendrix. By 1966, most of Canton's Blacks lived in the northwest corner of the city, and it was there that organizers made plans to pitch their circus tents on the grounds of a school called the McNeal Elementary School for Negroes.

Shortly after six in the evening, Carmichael and King arrived with two hundred rain-soaked marchers at the Canton courthouse only to discover that town officials had declared the Black school off-limits and arrested an advance party for trespassing. Undeterred, Carmichael rose to address a crowd of a thousand locals who had gathered to greet the visitors. "They said we couldn't put tents on our own black schoolyard; well, we're going to do it now," Carmichael declared. Singing freedom songs, the protesters walked fifteen blocks to the McNeal school, picking up more locals along the way, until by the time they reached the schoolyard they numbered more than two thousand. The sky was so full of dark, purple rain clouds that the canvas tents had to be unloaded from a U-Haul truck by flashlight. So at first, the marchers didn't see more than sixty state highway patrolmen who had assembled behind the school. Wearing military police helmets and gas masks and carrying automatic rifles, the patrolmen rounded the corner of the building and announced their presence with a clack of gun bolts.

Climbing onto the back of the U-Haul truck, Carmichael urged the marchers to continue putting up the tents. "The time for running has come to an end," Carmichael shouted. "You tell them white folks in Mississippi that all the scared niggers is dead! They've shot all the rabbits, now they'll have to deal with the men!" At ten past eight—the hour of sunset in late June in Canton—the city attorney hoisted a bullhorn and issued a stern warning. "You will not be allowed to erect that tent on this lot," the official barked. "If you continue doing so, you will be placed under arrest." In the schoolyard, marchers stopped singing "We Shall Overcome" and joined in a defiant response. "Pitch the tents!" they cried. "Pitch the tents!"

At a quarter to nine, the patrolmen advanced, hurling tear gas canisters and filling the schoolyard with a thick fog of acrid white smoke. Gasping for air, the protesters scattered in all directions. Dozens dove to the ground and pushed their faces into the grass to avoid inhaling the fumes. A patrolman kicked a stout, thirty-year-old Black woman named Odessa Warwick in the back. "Nigger, you wanted your freedom, here it is!" the officer snarled. A Catholic priest from Chicago was struck with the butt of shotgun, and a freelance photographer from Florida was hurled into a ditch by the road. An eight-year-old child who had been brought on the march by a young couple from Toronto passed out from the fumes. A young white girl who tried to appeal to a helmeted patrolman was met with derision. "Can't you see I'm a human being like you?" she pleaded. "Can't you see it?" As soon as the girl was out of earshot, the patrolman snickered: "I couldn't see it, friend. I couldn't see it."

For Carmichael, defiance dissolved into desperation. As the patrolmen advanced, a gas canister struck Stokely in the chest, knocking him to the ground. His eyes welled up and he struggled to breathe. His mind raced back to the first time he had been tear-gassed, during a protest in Cambridge, Maryland, when he was a student at Howard University. On that occasion, Carmichael felt like he was about to die before he lost consciousness and woke up in a local hospital. "Gas in my lungs was always my weakness," he recalled. "It felt like Cambridge, Maryland all over again." When Carmichael got up, he appeared "hysterical," in the words of Renata Adler of *The New Yorker*. Tears streamed down his face as he wandered in circles, shouting randomly to marchers. "Don't make your stand here," he called out. "I can't stand to see any more people get shot."

Paul Good, the freelance journalist covering the march for *New South*, described a similar scene. "Start movin', baby," Good heard Carmichael shout through the fog of gas. "They're gonna shoot again. They're gonna shoot again. The people . . . get the people outa here."

Seeing Carmichael so unnerved, King and McKissick tried to bring him to his senses.

"Keep calm, Stokely," McKissick snapped.

"Stokely, let's go to the nearest house and talk," King counseled, "We can't accomplish anything out here on the street."

By nine o'clock, the highway patrolmen had cleared the schoolyard and carted the tents away on a truck. The marchers faced the prospect of spending the night out in the rain before a Catholic mission offered shelter. As Carmichael saw it, after promising state protection, Governor Johnson had sanctioned "a planned, vicious attack" and "a demonstration of naked, brute strength for its own sake." Yet this time, unlike civil rights confrontations in the past, the federal government showed little sympathy for the victims. President Johnson remained silent, and his emissary on the ground, John Doar, threw up his hands. "What can I do?" Doar told reporters. "Both sides refuse to give an inch."

Doar's boss, Attorney General Nicholas Katzenbach, put out a statement blaming the marchers for trespassing on the schoolyard and refusing to avail themselves of several nearby campsites. For

King, the rebuff showed how badly his relationship with the Johnson administration had frayed, and how much harder that strain would make it for him to counter the Black Power message. "Yes, I heard that terrible statement," King lamented when reporters asked about Katzenbach's remarks. "It's terribly frustrating and disappointing. The federal government makes my job more difficult every day . . . to keep the movement non-violent."

The next day, King made his announced return to Philadelphia with three hundred marchers, and this time the day passed without major incident. Whites who lined the route shouted "Go to hell" and "You're a nigger," and reporters counted three bottles and two eggs among the objects thrown. But the only injury was suffered by reporter Murray Kempton of the *New York Post*, who was struck on the foot by one of the hurled bottles. But back in Canton, more generational discord bubbled up. March organizers had originally planned to spend two nights at the McNeal Elementary School, and more than a thousand young protesters showed up on the second day expecting to try to pitch the tents again. When they arrived, they discovered that march elders had cut a deal. In exchange for permission to hold a rally in the schoolyard, they had agreed to send the tents ahead to the next stop, Tougaloo College outside of Jackson.

"This is a proud moment for us," Ralph Abernathy told the restive crowd.

"No it ain't," someone shouted.

A chant went up: "Get the tents!"

Another King aide tried to explain the decision to send the tents ahead. "I know you want to know what happened," he said.

"We know what happened," a Black youngster shouted. "You sold us out."

THE NEXT DAY, MORE MELODRAMA ENSUED AS JAMES MEREDITH rejoined the march. Meredith had planned to arrive in Canton and walk to Tougaloo College. When he discovered that the marchers had moved on a day early, he insisted on sticking with his original plan. So

King, Carmichael, and McKissick had to drive back more than twenty miles to accompany Meredith on foot, lest the press photograph him marching alone again. Then, with just two miles left to Tougaloo, Meredith abruptly announced that his legs were tired. He asked for a car to take him and Dr. King the rest of the way, leaving Carmichael and the others to keep walking. At the college that night, Meredith refused to address a huge rally that drew more than eight thousand people and included such Hollywood celebrities as Marlon Brando, Burt Lancaster, and Sammy Davis Jr. "The whole thing smells to me," Meredith grumbled when he first arrived in Canton, and he radiated the same cantankerous attitude for the rest of the day.

Meredith was in a much better mood, however, as the march reached Jackson on the morning of Sunday, June 26. Despite oppressive heat and humidity, thousands of Black residents turned out in their churchgoing best to watch Dr. King walk eight miles from Tougaloo College to the state capitol. Hundreds of state patrolmen and city police lined the route. TV and newspaper cameras were everywhere, and the procession kept stopping as people jostled to be photographed with Dr. King. A young entrepreneur sold ten-cent bottles of Coke for a quarter. A Black girl enviously eyed Jackson residents who watched the parade from their front lawns, sipping cold water, and waving miniature Confederate flags. "I'd almost join the white folks on the side," the girl joked, "if they would give me a drink." Still complaining of weakness in his legs, Meredith rode alongside the procession in a car. Nearing the capitol, he let out a gasp of delight at the huge crowd assembled around the building, inside a two-hundred-foot-wide area cordoned off by National Guardsmen, Jackson police, and Mississippi hunting and fishing rangers. "It's everybody," Meredith exclaimed. "You can't do better than that."

On the surface, the Jackson rally resembled the historic end to the Selma march at Alabama's capitol in Montgomery the year before. On that day, thousands had listened as Dr. King delivered his famous "How Long? Not Long!" speech, promising that "the arc of the moral universe is long but it bends toward justice." This time, a crowd estimated at between twelve and fifteen thousand looked on as

King predicted that the Meredith March would "go down in history as the greatest demonstration for freedom ever held in the state of Mississippi." Alvin Poussaint, a thirty-two-year-old Black psychiatrist who spoke on behalf of the Medical Committee for Human Rights, declared that "the civil rights movement is doing more for the mental health of Negroes in this country than anything else." Charles Evers of the NAACP wasn't present because his boss, Roy Wilkins, continued to refuse to endorse the march manifesto negotiated at the Lorraine Motel. But at the last minute, Whitney Young signed the document and was added to the program of speakers.

Despite the show of unity, however, there were omens that this would be the last civil rights gathering of its kind, at least until Black America was briefly reunited in grief after King's assassination two years later. King's speech betrayed growing pessimism about the slow pace of racial progress in the South and the harsh resistance he was encountering in the North. The bright dream he had conjured up during the March on Washington "has turned into a nightmare," King declared, as widespread Black poverty persisted "in a vast ocean of prosperity." Carmichael sounded cockier than ever, after succeeding in registering some forty thousand new Black voters across Mississippi. Blacks "must build a power base in this country," he told the crowd, that would "bring white people to their knees every time they try to mess with us." Meanwhile, a band of SNCC organizers led by Willie Ricks wandered through the crowd snatching up tiny American flags that other civil rights groups had handed out. Instead, they distributed Lowndes County Freedom Organization pamphlets with the black panther logo and the party's motto: "Move Over, or We'll Move Over on You."

Introduced to the new militant slogan and symbol for the first time, even older Black residents of Jackson seemed intrigued. Along the route to the capitol, Molly Gray, a sixty-one-year-old domestic, sat under a mimosa tree in her front yard and offered cold water to thirsty marchers. A group of SNCC workers drove by in a pickup truck and shouted out: "Say 'Black Power.'" Gray emitted a bemused giggle that suggested she didn't exactly know what that meant, but she played along anyway. "Black power," Molly called back, saluting the youngsters with a shake of the ice cubes in her glass.

The Meredith March also foreshadowed deepening misunderstanding between the Black Power forces and the national media. During the march, the Associated Press hadn't just misreported Meredith's death and the size of the crowd in Greenwood. The wire service made several other errors that added to confusion about the Black Power message. During his tear-gas-induced frenzy in Canton, Carmichael had called out: "Now is the time to separate the men from the mice!" Instead, the AP reported that Carmichael said: "Now is the time to separate the men from the whites!" The media's obsession with looking for division among the civil rights groups also became a running joke. "Dissension in the press!" marchers called out mockingly when they overheard an argument break out on a press truck. "A split! A split!" Playing along, some of the reporters raised their fists and shouted: "Press Power!"

Summing up the march for *The New Yorker*, Renata Adler made a wry observation about the effect that the misleading press coverage was having on Carmichael. Instead of dispelling the distortions, Adler wrote, Carmichael seemed to take perverse pleasure in feeding them. As Adler put it: "Stokely Carmichael, the young chairman of S.N.C.C., argued most persuasively for black power, and when, as he saw it, he was continuously misrepresented by the press, he became obdurate and began to make himself eminently misrepresentable."

For Gene Roberts of *The New York Times*, it would only be when he arrived in Vietnam that he fully grasped what he had witnessed covering SNCC in the years leading up to the Meredith March. In 1968, Roberts was named the *Times* bureau chief in Saigon. When he saw the impact that serving in the hot-fire war zones of Asia had on young servicemen, he was reminded of the stress and exhaustion he had seen among SNCC organizers in places like Leflore County, Mississippi, and Lowndes County, Alabama. "They only had to look around and see people getting killed, and beaten up, and brutalized," Roberts said. "The whole situation wasn't likely to produce people

who saw a middle-ground solution. It was almost guaranteed to rad-
icalize them."

For all its success in registering voters, the Meredith March had
revived that trauma in the streets of Philadelphia and in a schoolyard
in Canton. It had turned a gentle soul like Ralph Featherstone into
an angry warrior ready to return fire on night-riding vigilantes. And
in just a few weeks, the march had begun to transform the Stokely
Carmichael who Gene Roberts had come to know over the years, the
irreverent but still thoughtful and approachable disciple of Bayard
Rustin and Bob Moses. "Before the Meredith March, you could have
a reasoned conversation with Stokely," Roberts recalled. "But that
changed, very quickly."

CHAPTER 10

"Starmichael" on Tour

On the last day of the march to Jackson, James Meredith turned thirty-three, and four days later Stokely Carmichael turned twenty-five. After the rally at the state capitol, some 1,500 marchers gathered at Tougaloo College to celebrate the dual milestones. Carmichael acted "all over shy" as everyone sang "Happy Birthday," by the account of Renata Adler. But another reporter used a different adjective to describe Carmichael several hours later. According to Nicholas von Hoffman of *The Washington Post*, sometime after midnight a tired reporter was enjoying a smoke outside the Student Union building when Carmichael emerged on the terrace. "All right, treacherous one, take that cigar out of your mouth!" Carmichael called out. He pulled a water pistol from his denim overalls and squirted the reporter in the eye. "I'm going to give you some black power-r-r-r!," Carmichael cackled. "Carmichael was so high," von Hoffman reported, "that when he spied the Southern Christian Leadership Conference's Rev. Hosea Williams coming through the darkness to conduct a staff meeting in the union lounge, he whooped 'Black Power!' and shot the older man in the face. 'My God!' Williams hollered after being hit by the water. 'And he's a national civil rights leader!'"

Bob Moses, Carmichael's onetime role model, was also present for the festivities that night. After quitting SNCC and changing his name to Bob Parris, Moses had devoted his time to speaking at anti–Vietnam War rallies. At the last minute, Moses decided to travel to Jackson for the end of the Meredith March, and he stayed with the other civil rights leaders at Tougaloo College. But for all their personal history, Carmichael made no attempt to speak with Moses at the birthday party, and the far-off glimpse Moses got of Carmichael was the last he would see of his former protégé for more than a decade.

Shortly afterward, the government mailed Moses a draft notice, despite his relatively advanced age. He fled to Canada, using his high school French to cross the border into Montreal and assuming a new identity as a night watchman named "Robinson." Several years later, Moses moved again, to Tanzania, where he lived for almost a decade before returning to the United States. Yet looking back decades later, he would recall that he already sensed on that night in Jackson that Carmichael was embarking on a new course as a national celebrity and would-be global freedom fighter that he would have difficulty navigating. As a former math teacher, Moses used the language of physics to answer the question: What happened to Stokely? "You're dealing with the idea of gravitational force, or a geometry that has its own curvature," Moses explained. "If you move into that gravitational force field, you face currents that you have no control over."

Ruby Doris Robinson was also in the birthday crowd at Tougaloo College. Along with Jim Forman, she had traveled from Atlanta for the last leg of the march into Jackson. During the speeches at the capitol, she and Forman showed support for the cry that Carmichael and Willie Ricks had unleashed by standing in front of TV cameras and shouting "Black Power!" But when the revelry was over, and Carmichael embarked on a nonstop speaking tour for the next two months, Robinson returned to SNCC headquarters to deal with its consequences. She watched as fundraising dried up, and the Internal Revenue Service hit SNCC with a suspicious audit. During Freedom Summer, Carmichael's flamboyant knack for drawing media attention had earned him a nickname within SNCC, Ruby Davis recalled, and now she thought it was more appropriate than ever. The nickname was "Stokely Starmichael."

If that label invited comparisons to a rock star, so would the frenzied reception that Carmichael received wherever he went in the summer of 1966. And as with some rock acts, it was his exciting tone that drew crowds, while critics struggled to decipher the meaning of his words. The wildly different assessments of Carmichael that emerged in those months stemmed in part from his chameleon-like tendency to show different sides of his personality to different people. At times, he could still be the humble, denim-clad organizer, or the clean-cut Howard intellectual. At others, he was now something new: an insolent militant in dark sunglasses.

But the shifting images of Carmichael and his new message also reflected the way the American media was changing. By 1966, reporters at some of the country's top publications were beginning to experiment with injecting more personal voice and point of view into their stories, a practice that would later be dubbed "the New Journalism." One of them was Renata Adler, the precocious twenty-eight-year-old summa cum laude graduate of Bryn Mawr College who had been sent south to cover the Selma march by *The New Yorker* and returned for the Meredith March. In Adler's novelistic description, Carmichael was a figure in a contentious family saga—the leader of the "radical children" of SNCC rebelling against "the older, conservative relatives" of the NAACP as the "worried parents" of the SCLC looked on. For another *New Yorker* writer, Jacob Brackman, Carmichael was a master of the "put-on"—the art of keeping people guessing about whether you're serious or not. As a case in point, Brackman cited Carmichael's tongue-in-cheek proposal that Harlem "send one million black men up to invade Scarsdale," the wealthy white suburb north of New York City. Carmichael "could get away with it simply because the put-on is so elusive," Brackman argued. "The victim is never precisely sure what's happening."

Nicholas von Hoffman, a dashing former community organizer who had become a star feature writer for *The Washington Post*, also captured that prankster quality in his account of Carmichael's squirt gun attack at Tougaloo College. Likewise, Andrew Kopkind, a freelancer for left-wing journals such at *The New Republic, The New Statesman,* and *Ramparts*, saw Carmichael as more of an improv performer than an angry radical. Carmichael was an "unscarred," middle-class "child of Camus," Kopkind wrote, who was "not deeply cynical enough" to assume the mantle of Malcolm X or "evoke the radical funkiness" of the Black street. "There is something stagey about his public appearances," Kopkind observed in *The New York Review of Books.* "Until now, at least, he has had too good a time."

In Black America, Carmichael's image was filtered through the lens of *Jet* and *Ebony*, the magazines that by the 1960s had eclipsed the influence of Black newspapers such as the *Chicago Defender* and the *Pittsburgh Courier.* Filled with photographs and newsmaker profiles, those publications found an ideal subject in the theatrical new SNCC chairman. Within weeks of the Meredith March, Carmichael was on the cover of *Jet*, his face twisted in a defiant snarl. In keeping with its boosterish worldview, the weekly downplayed the growing disagreements within the civil rights movement. Entitled "What Black Power Really Means," a story inside made it sound as though all of Black America's best-known political leaders were embracing the new mantra in one fashion or another.

Carmichael, Floyd McKissick, and Adam Clayton Powell Jr. were all quoted by *Jet* as insisting that Black Power meant nothing more than fighting for local political power, just as the Irish and Italians had done. That definition was echoed by Carl Stokes, a Cleveland attorney who would run successfully for mayor in the next year, making him the first Black to lead one the country's ten largest cities. "To the extent that this new movement is intended to shake the Negro into political action, and to excite pride in being black, I support it," Stokes said. Even Dr. King found good things to say to *Jet*'s readers about the slogan, stressing its psychological benefits. "The Negro is in dire need of a sense of dignity and a sense of pride," King said, "and I think 'Black Power' is an attempt to develop pride."

At *Ebony*, *Jet*'s monthly counterpart, executive editor Lerone Bennett Jr., who was also an accomplished historian, assigned himself the job of profiling Carmichael. In a story entitled "Architect of Black Power," Bennett traced the roots of Carmichael's message to his childhood in Trinidad, where he had become accustomed to seeing Blacks in positions of authority as civil servants, policemen, and teachers. He linked Carmichael to the memory of Malcolm X by taking him to the African National Memorial Bookstore in Harlem, where Malcolm frequently spoke and where Carmichael had browsed the stacks as an impressionable teenager. "Malcolm X is still living," the bookstore's owner, Lewis Michaux, exclaimed as Carmichael arrived. "When you walked in, Malcolm smiled."

Bennett also highlighted a class dimension to Carmichael's message that had been largely lost on white observers. Black Power was a "call for the black middle class to come home," Bennett explained— to reject the priority of integrating a handful of "special Negroes" into white society in favor of fighting for "the overwhelming majority of poor sharecroppers and slum-dwellers of the North and South." As Carmichael himself told Bennett, describing a phenomenon that he had experienced firsthand when his family moved from the South Bronx to Morris Park: "Integration never speaks to the problem of what happens to the black school or the black community after two or three people move out 'to integrate.' That's the problem that we must force America to speak to; that's the problem Black Power speaks to."

While painting a more substantive portrait of Carmichael and his message than anything found in the white press at the time, Bennett also offered less flattering snapshots that only a Black reporter might have captured. In addition to "Starmichael," he informed *Ebony*'s readers, Carmichael had another nickname inside SNCC. He was called "the Magnificent Barbarian" because of his penchant for outrageousness. Illustrating that quality, Bennett described a scene he witnessed as he drove with Carmichael to Lowndes County in a Ford micro-bus. Stopping at a gas station, Carmichael recognized a SNCC fieldworker with his white girlfriend. "Man, with all the pretty black girls in this town, what are you doing shacking up with that white broad?" he called out. Then Carmichael turned to Bennett and proceeded with this crude line of talk, acting as though he was gossiping with a fraternity brother instead of talking to a veteran journalist on the record. "All my black nationalist friends are shacking up with white broads—and not only that, they are ugly, fat white broads that nobody else wants," Carmichael sneered. "It's time out for part-time revolutionaries. It's time for cats to live what they believe."

The mainstream white press, meanwhile, remained less interested in exploring the nuances of Carmichael's ideas than casting him as a disruptive new character in a messy civil rights drama. Four days after the Jackson rally, Carmichael's name was back on the front page of *The New York Times* when John Lewis abruptly announced that he was quitting SNCC. With his usual gentlemanly reserve, Lewis insisted that his resignation had nothing to do with the events of Kingston Springs, and that he merely wanted more time to study and write. Asked by an AP reporter to comment on Carmichael and the Black Power message, Lewis would only go so far as to say that "there is a danger in SNCC of fumbling the ball." The next day, Carmichael held a press conference in Washington to criticize President Johnson's new civil rights bill, and reporters pressed him for a response to the Lewis news. When Carmichael tried to declare the questions off-limits, many of the reporters lost interest and walked out of the church where the press conference was held.

Over the Fourth of July weekend, Floyd McKissick handed Carmichael another opportunity to make headlines when he invited Stokely to give the keynote address at CORE's annual convention in Baltimore, after Dr. King pulled out due to a scheduling conflict. Before a boisterous crowd of delegates at the Knox Presbyterian Church in West Baltimore, Carmichael rehearsed applause lines that he would use throughout the summer, many of them designed to deflect criticism by highlighting white hypocrisy. On integration, he declared that if whites were serious, residents of the Westchester suburbs would send their kids to school in Harlem. On nonviolence, he asked what right America had to tell Blacks they couldn't arm themselves when it was waging war in Vietnam. On the meaning of Black Power, Carmichael took the at once defiant and evasive position that the slogan encompassed the right not to have to explain what it meant to whites. "We will define our own terms, whether they like it or not," he proclaimed.

Just as newsworthy as those remarks, meanwhile, was an endorsement that Carmichael received from his warm-up act at the CORE convention: Fannie Lou Hamer, the hero of Atlantic City. Hamer amused
the crowd with salty jabs at the previous generation of civil rights leaders, dismissing them as "Ph.D.s" and "chickeny black preachers who
sold out blacks during Reconstruction [and] are doing it again." Then
she brought the delegates out of their pews and onto their feet by invoking Carmichael's new mantra. "The black people in the United
States are starting to move to black power," Hamer exclaimed.

A few days later, the NAACP held its annual convention in Los
Angeles, and Roy Wilkins responded to the news from Baltimore by
raising his attacks on Carmichael to a new level of alarm and disdain.
Addressing a plenary session, Wilkins predicted that Black Power
would lead to "black death" by driving away white financial support
and inviting political backlash. "It is a reverse Mississippi, a reverse
Hitler, a reverse Ku Klux Klan," Wilkins warned. Invited to address
the convention on its second day, Vice President Humphrey echoed
his host by condemning "racism of any color." In an apparent bid to
embarrass SNCC, Wilkins issued a "memorandum" to the convention
that documented instances when the NAACP had provided money to
post bail for Carmichael and to settle lawsuits resulting from Sojourner
Motor Fleet car accidents. Reflecting how angry Wilkins may still have
been with Dr. King over the fight at the Lorraine Motel, the memorandum described a $5,000 loan that the NAACP had given to a "desper-
ate" SCLC during the Selma march—a revelation that *The New York
Times* pointed out marked "the first indication for the public record
that relations between the NAACP and Rev. Dr. Martin Luther King
Jr.'s leadership council were strained because of money transactions."

WITH BATTLE LINES OVER THE BLACK POWER MESSAGE SO PUB-
licly drawn, Carmichael spent the rest of July looking for high-profile
allies. In North Philadelphia, he appeared at the Episcopal Church of
the Advocate with Nina Simone, the soulful singer known for protest anthems such as "Mississippi Goddam," her cry of despair over

the murders of Freedom Summer. Dressed in dungarees, Carmichael seized the occasion to focus on Black Power's cultural dimension. "We need a black renaissance," he insisted, pacing back and forth behind the pulpit. "We need to love black art, black music, black jazz, black spirituals." As the overflow mixed raced crowd stomped the floor in agreement, he proclaimed: "I'm getting tired of looking at television and seeing Tarzan beating up black people. I want to see some of those black people beat the hell out of Tarzan and send him home." Following Carmichael to the stage, Nina Simone had tears in her eyes. "I have been thinking some of those things I heard tonight since I was three years old," said Simone, who had been raised in a poor Black family of six children in rural North Carolina.

In Washington, Carmichael donned a dark jacket and tie to join Congressman Adam Clayton Powell Jr. for the announcement of a planned Black Power summit over Labor Day weekend. Dressed more rakishly in a wide-lapeled, three-button white suit, Powell gleefully sided with Carmichael against his own civil rights peers. A "new breed of cats" was chasing out "our pasteurized Negro leadership which should be put out to pasture," Powell chortled. Reminding everyone that he had used the phrase Black Power before Carmichael, Powell answered predictable questions about the phrase's meaning with a prescient generational and demographic analysis. Black Power did not mean "that black people will take over the whole nation," Powell explained, but it did represent a mindset of "tough, proud young Negroes who categorically refuse to compromise" and who were bound to become more of a "controlling force" in America's cities "as they become blacker."

Shortly after the Greenwood, Mississippi, speech, Carmichael had received word that Elijah Muhammad, the leader of the Nation of Islam, wanted to meet with him. Traveling to Chicago at the end of July, Carmichael titillated the press by suggesting that he might "join hands" with the Nation of Islam. But when Carmichael and Cleve Sellers visited the sect's sprawling headquarters on the South Side of Chicago, they were quickly dissuaded from any further thoughts of an alliance by Elijah Muhammad's eccentric ramblings and demands that they convert to his faith. During a long meeting in his ornately furnished office, the self-proclaimed prophet meandered in a soft, raspy voice about lost Black civilizations, blue-eyed devils, and "some stuff about a mothership," Sellers recalled.

That night, Carmichael and Sellers were invited to Elijah Muhammed's house for dinner with his most famous convert, Muhammad Ali. The heavyweight champion was "full of energy and fun . . . charm, and high spirits," Carmichael recalled, despite being in the early stages of a battle to keep his boxing license after announcing that he would resist the draft as a conscientious objector. Before leaving Chicago, Carmichael also met briefly with Dr. King and invited him to his planned Labor Day summit with Adam Clayton Powell Jr. At their respective appearances on different sides of town, Carmichael and King avoided any mention of each other. By the fall, however, the idea for a Black Power summit would fall apart, after a series of delays and the start of a mounting scandal over Powell's estrangement from his third wife and his taxpayer-funded junkets to the Bahamas.

Moving on to Detroit, Carmichael switched back to a more provocative tone at a huge rally at Cobo Hall, the venue where King had given an early version of his "I Have a Dream" speech months before the March on Washington. Wearing the dark sunglasses that would become his sartorial trademark from then on, Carmichael proclaimed "Negroes should refuse to fight in Vietnam" and that any Black American who volunteered for the war was no better than a paid "mercenary." Then he mocked white campus liberals with a comic exaggeration that drew loud laughs and cheers from the crowd. "I'm going to tell you what a white liberal is," Carmichael exclaimed. "You talking about a white college kid joining hands with a black man in the ghetto, that college kid is fighting for the right to wear a beard and smoke pot, and . . . we fighting for our lives. That missionary comes to the ghetto one summer, and next summer he's in Europe, and he's our ally. That missionary has a black mammy, and he stole our black mammy from us. Because while she was home taking care of them, she couldn't take care of us."

When NBC's *Today* show invited Carmichael to participate in a special two-hour broadcast devoted to "Black Leadership," he resorted to yet another gambit: blaming the brouhaha over Black Power on the white media. "It seems to me that Black Power would not cause this disturbance unless the white press wants it to," Carmichael asserted. Following up on that line of analysis, *Newsweek* devoted an entire page to examining the conflicting ways that the media had characterized the new buzz words. *The Wall Street Journal* had denounced Black Power as "the Wages of Hatred." Cartoonist Bill Mauldin of the *Chicago Sun-Times* depicted it as a mugging, in which a Black youth dressed in a "Black Power" T-shirt stood over an older Black man with a knife in his back. "This is just a little nudge, dad," read the caption. "You're going too slow." Meanwhile, *The Boston Globe* editorialized that Black Power simply stood for old-fashioned "bloc voting" and might be "a change for the good." James "Scotty" Reston, the influential *New York Times* columnist, also shrugged off the Black Power talk as a typically American special interest group ploy. "Negroes . . . have learned that it's the squeaky wheel that gets the grease," Reston wrote, "and they're likely to demand more and more grease, like everybody else."

In another corner of the *Times* editorial pages, humor columnist Russell Baker made bemused fun of the whole controversy. Baker imagined himself returning to Washington after a six-week absence to find that everyone in town had forgotten about the topic that obsessed the capital before he left: auto safety. Before getting back on the dinner party circuit, Baker phoned a friend to find out what everyone was talking about now.

"Be a pal, will you," Baker asked the fictional friend. "Put me in touch with what I'm supposed to be excited about."

"Well, the big thing right now is Black Power," the friend explained.

"What's Black Power?" Baker asked.

"Nobody knows what it is," the friend said. "That's why it's so big."

"How can I get excited about something if nobody knows what that something is that I'm excited about?" Baker asked.

"That's the whole trick," the friend replied. "What you do is say, 'The trouble is that everybody misunderstands what Black Power really is.' Then you tell them what it really is and what Stokely Carmichael really means. You'll be right in the Washington swing before you can say 'Roy Wilkins.'"

"Who is Stokely Carmichael?" Baker imagined himself asking.

"The Robespierre of the civil rights movement," replied the fictional friend. "Use that line. It'll get you off an analogy invoking the French Revolution."

YET IN MAKING SUCH GENTLE FUN, BAKER HAD NO IDEA THAT THE next day the *Times* would make the most consequential error yet in the media coverage's of the new Black Power phenomenon. In its Friday, August 5, edition, the paper devoted a "Man in the News" profile to Carmichael. Entitled "Black Power Prophet," the profile traced Carmichael's intellectual journey from college philosophy major to Camus-quoting organizer to rabblerousing Delta orator. It also captured Carmichael's malleable mannerisms—how "in the south, his speech lost some of its Caribbean–New York clip and became almost a drawl"—as well as his good looks and capacity for teasing charm. "His fine-cut face is friendly," the story observed, "and he carries his tall frame with a slump-shouldered grace suggesting that he doesn't take himself too seriously."

In a graver tone, however, the profile also informed *Times* readers that Carmichael was "said to have played a leading role in the preparation of a position paper on the new black philosophy, which was used to reverse the SNCC central committee's policy on whites." On the front page, *Times* editors ran a separate story on this position paper, under a dramatic headline: "Black Power Idea Long in the Making." Describing the document as "the first detailed explanation of the thinking behind the 'black power' concept to become available to the public," the story suggested that it showed that SNCC had officially decided to sever all ties with whites. "If we are to proceed toward liberation, we must cut ourselves off from the white people," read a quote from the paper.

Gene Roberts had the byline on the front-page story, and it bore some signs of his usual careful reporting. Unlike the unnamed author of the "Man in the News" profile, Roberts took pains to describe the position paper as "written last winter by dissident members of SNCC and still confidential." However, Roberts went on to report that the paper's arguments had since been embraced by Carmichael and Jim Forman and made official policy. Roberts quoted John Lewis several times in the story, suggesting that his source for this confirmation may have been SNCC's still bitter former chairman.

The trouble with the *Times* scoop was that the vaunted "position paper" wasn't an official or confidential document at all, or one that Carmichael had any part in producing. It was the Vine City Project memo written by the militant Bill Ware, a manifesto that all of SNCC's top leaders had rejected when Ware tried to foist it on them in that spring. Since then, however, the memo had been suspiciously printed in a formal-looking ten-page pamphlet, with the title "Black Power" on the cover, and disseminated by an organization called the "United States National Student Association." That name sounded innocent enough, but more scrutiny would have revealed that the organization was a once genuine student group formed in the 1940s that by the 1960s was secretly funded by the CIA. So the *Times* editors may have fallen for a government-supported gambit, abetted either by disgruntled former SNCC officials or by Ware's militantly anti-white faction, that was calculated to embarrass and undercut Carmichael.

By seizing on the inflammatory Ware memo and making its contents front-page news, *The New York Times* created the impression that Black Power was a more narrowly focused anti-white phenomenon than it actually was—at least at that delicate point in its evolution. That impression, in turn, helped accelerate a sudden falloff in white support for the civil rights cause in the late summer of 1966. The proof of that plunge would come in a comprehensive new national poll on racial attitudes released in August, following another wave of urban race riots and a searing spectacle that unfolded in a park in southwest Chicago.

CHAPTER 11

A Rock in Marquette Park

For three straights weeks in late June and early July of 1966, a blistering heatwave scorched most of the United States east of the Rocky Mountains. In New York City, a thermometer at LaGuardia Airport registered 107 degrees on July 3—a record for that date at the time. In St. Louis, temperatures topped 100 degrees for five straight days, and an overworked coroner lamented: "It's like the plague." In Dayton, Ohio, an appliance salesman reported that "people are buying as if air conditioners are going out of existence." In Chicago, half of the city's three million residents fled each day for temporary relief at the nearest beaches, parks, golf courses, and zoos. But that didn't keep the region from enjoying a grim distinction: of eleven states that saw a dramatic rise in deaths by heat stroke that summer, Illinois had the sharpest, with a 28.3 percent spike.

After spending most of June on the Meredith March in Mississippi, Dr. King returned to Chicago with plans to restart his Northern offensive with a huge rally in Soldier Field on Sunday, July 10. SCLC planners announced that they expected to draw a crowd of 100,000 to the football stadium, where they intended to announce an ambitious new front in the Chicago campaign. Instead of slum conditions, the target would be discrimination by real estate agencies and banks against Blacks who wanted to buy homes in white neighborhoods.

In part, this shift to "open housing" reflected King's frustration that his initial focus on the tenements of North Lawndale hadn't produced more results. But he also conceded that he was looking for a more confrontational strategy to blunt the wildfire appeal of Stokely Carmichael's Black Power message. Warning that the civil rights movement might be "very, very close" to a permanent rupture, King told Gene Roberts of *The New York Times* that he needed to be "militantly non-violent" to answer "the cry, 'black power,' which whether they mean it or not, falls on the ear as racism in reverse." King's aim, he told Roberts, was to mount an offensive "that avoids violence, but becomes militant and extreme enough to disrupt the flow of the whole city."

Yet on the day of the Soldier Field rally, the temperature rose to 98 degrees, and fewer than 50,000 people showed up. B. B. King, Mahalia Jackson, and a group of ten singing nuns warmed up a scattered crowd that hardly needed it, as humid air rising from Lake Michigan made the U-shaped stadium with its Doric-columned entrances feel like an outdoor steam bath. Speaking under a black parasol to block the sun, King laid out a list of demands that started with open housing and also included more jobs, better schools, and a civilian review board to monitor the city police. As a Black youth sprinted across the field waving a bedsheet scrawled with "BLACK POWER" in capital letters, King acknowledged the slogan's psychological appeal. "We want to be proud of our race," he declared. "We should not be ashamed of being black." But King decried the divisiveness of Black Power rhetoric and insisted that racial progress remained a two-way street. "Our power is in our unity," King declared. "The Negro needs the white man to free him from his fears. The white man needs the Negro to free him from his guilt."

In another sign of King's hopes for reviving the Chicago campaign, his wife, Coretta, agreed to move back to the slum apartment in North Lawndale, and to bring their four young children from Atlanta. Hearing her parents making plans, three-year-old Bernice King pleaded to join the family at the Soldier Field rally. When the speeches

were over, "Bunny," as Bernice was nicknamed, joined some five thousand sweaty marchers on a three-mile trek to City Hall. But along the
way, she dozed off in the heat and had to be carried on the shoulders
of King aides Andrew Young and Bernard Lee. So she wasn't awake
to witness a clever publicity stunt her father had planned. Dr. King
knew it was Sunday, and that City Hall would be mostly empty. So he
Scotch-taped a copy of his demands to the door—a gesture designed
to recall his namesake, Martin Luther, who launched the Protestant
Reformation by nailing ninety-five theses to the door of a church in
Wittenberg, Germany.

On Monday morning, Mayor Richard J. Daley invited King and
his aides back to City Hall for a closed-door meeting. The mayor
tried to shift the discussion away from open housing back to slum
conditions—boasting that the city had repaired more than 100,000
tenement apartments—and blasted the proposal for a police review
board. On Tuesday, another meeting ended without agreement, and
Daley and King gave dueling press conferences that showed how testy
their relations had become. "We are demanding these things, not requesting them," King told reporters in a weary voice. Red-faced, the
mayor dismissed King as a naive outsider. "Dr. King is very sincere
in what he is trying to do," Daley sputtered, but "maybe, at times, he
doesn't have all the facts on the local situation. After all, he is a resident of another city."

That night, King and Coretta ate dinner at the home of gospel
singer Mahalia Jackson on the South Side. Afterward, Jackson drove
the couple to a nighttime rally at the Shiloh Baptist Church. From
the car window, King spied a group of youth sprinting unusually fast
down the street. "These people—I wonder if there is a riot starting,"
he recalled thinking to himself. Arriving at the church, King learned
the source of the commotion, which had started on the West Side
earlier in the day as another result of the brutal heatwave.

As temperatures soared into the high nineties for a third straight
day, youngsters opened the fire hydrants surrounding a housing project called the Jane Addams Homes. An ice cream truck broke down,
and kids raided the stranded vehicle for popsicles. The truck driver

called the police, and to punish the perpetrators the cops locked the fire hydrants. An angry crowd began hurling bricks and bottles, setting off a confrontation that resulted in the arrest of seven youths, including a sixteen-year-old who was beaten with billy clubs as he was taken into custody. Hearing all of this, King drove to the police station where the seven arrestees were detained and bailed them out. "I told Mayor Daley something like this would happen if something wasn't done," King was heard to mutter.

On Wednesday morning, police in blue helmets fanned out across the West Side, shutting down fire hydrants and warning residents to stay indoors. As night fell, the oppressive heat gave way to a dramatic thunderstorm, filling a dark sky with flashes of lightning. When the storm was over, Black residents poured into the streets, attacking police with bricks, bottles, and Molotov cocktails. As the skirmishes continued into Thursday, two Black protesters were killed, including a visitor from Mississippi who was shot in the back. A police captain was clipped in the shoulder by sniper fire, and six more police were injured. At the Shiloh Baptist Church, Dr. King and Chicago clergymen pleaded for nonviolence, only to watch as scores of gang members who had showed up for the meeting stormed out.

Invited to speak to a rally on the North Side, Coretta King couldn't find a babysitter and took along her four children. When the family arrived back at the North Lawndale slum rental, they found a UPI reporter named Charles Krohn waiting for them. As Mrs. King readied the children for bed, gunfire filled the street below, and the four siblings rushed to see what was happening. "Get away from that window," Coretta called out. "You want to get your head shot off?" Krohn described the scene in his wire story that night, and the next morning Coretta awoke to the sensational headlines in newspapers across the country. "Want Your Head Shot Off?" shouted one headline; "Mrs. King Fears for Her Children's Lives," exclaimed another.

Not until Friday did the rioting ease, as temperatures dropped into the seventies and more than four thousand National Guardsmen dispatched by Illinois governor Otto Kerner filled the streets. With no air-conditioning, King's apartment still felt like an oven when Justice

Department officials John Doar and Roger Wilkins, the nephew of NAACP president Roy Wilkins, arrived for a late-night meeting. They found King huddled with the heads of Chicago's Black gangs, and Wilkins recalled waiting for "four *hot* hours, four sweaty hours" as King tried to negotiate a cease-fire. Finally, in the wee hours, the leader of the Roman Saints gang agreed to stand down and the others followed suit—thus ensuring that the "Fire Hydrant Riots," as they were being called, didn't spill into the weekend.

As the violence subsided, however, the sniping between Daley and King continued. At another petulant press conference, the mayor accused unnamed members of the SCLC for inciting the riot. "I don't think you can charge it directly to Martin Luther King," Daley fumed. "But surely, some of the people that came in here and have been talking for the last year of violence . . . they're on his staff and they're responsible in great measure." In a phone call to the White House, Daley badmouthed King to President Johnson, calling him "a goddam faker." Meeting again with Gene Roberts at the North Lawndale apartment, King described his challenge as producing enough results to keep sympathizers in line and the new Black Power forces at bay. "Somehow, there has to be a synthesis," King said. "I have to be militant enough to satisfy the militant yet I have to keep enough discipline in the movement to satisfy white supporters and moderate Negroes."

When Dr. King went back to Atlanta after the Chicago riots, he was greeted with more headlines about the spread of Black Power. Worried about the bad publicity, Stanley Levinson, King's lawyer and adviser, suggested taking out a full-page advertisement in *The New York Times*. Written by Levinson and published with King's byline, the statement ran under the headline "It Is Not Enough to Condemn Black Power." Those words were "an unwise choice," King argued, but their appeal would only grow if more progress didn't take place on the issues he was tackling in Chicago. "In the face of the cries of Black Power we helped to summon 60,000 Negroes in the sweltering slums of Chicago to assemble non-violently for protest—and they responded magnificently," King asserted, exaggerating the size of the

Soldier Field crowd by at least ten thousand. "The burden now shifts to the municipal, state and Federal authorities and all men in seats of power. If they continue to use our non-violence as a cushion for complacency, the wrath of those suffering a long train of abuses will rise."

AS THE SITE OF HIS NEW OPEN HOUSING CAMPAIGN, KING CHOSE a working-class immigrant area of Chicago that had remained overwhelmingly white while nearby enclaves such as North Lawndale turned increasingly Black. In the 1960 Census, a third of the roughly 100,000 residents in three of the neighborhoods—Gage Park, Chicago Lawn, and Belmont Cragin—were identified as coming from white "foreign stock," while only seven households were listed as "Negro." To prepare for the campaign, the SCLC sent out "tester teams" that identified thirty-one local real estate agencies that refused to show houses in those white neighborhoods to Blacks. So as July ended, King announced that the campaign would begin with an all-night vigil at one of the worst offenders, the Halvorean Realty Company in Gage Park.

The next day, King left town to give a speech in North Carolina, so he didn't witness the unsettling start to the open housing drive. On a late Friday afternoon, CCCO head Al Raby and fifty protesters arrived at Halvorean Realty to set up camp for the night. As the sun set, hundreds of white residents appeared, hurling debris and shouting slurs. The vigil was canceled and the protesters retreated to the South Side. In the morning, a procession of some five hundred marchers set out again, led by Raby and Jesse Jackson, a twenty-four-year-old Chicago divinity student who had become King's newest disciple. As the protesters made a loop through Gage Park and Chicago Lawn and back to the South Side, another huge crowd of whites bombarded them with bricks, bottles, and angry taunts at every step along the way.

On Sunday, the marchers took the precaution of driving to the protest zone. They left their cars in Marquette Park, a municipal park just south of the neighborhood of Gage Park, and started out on foot. A third huge crowd of whites swarmed around them, throwing cherry bombs and sharp objects. "White Power," the locals chanted, and "Burn them like Jews." Several hundred Chicago police officers were on hand, but fewer than twenty arrests were made. After promising to keep an eye on the cars in Marquette Park, policemen stood by as vandals torched and overturned dozens of the vehicles and pushed two of them into a lagoon.

The following Thursday, Dr. King returned to Chicago and announced that he would lead the next march. "My place is in Gage Park," he proclaimed in a church speech on the South Side that was carried live on local radio. But the next morning, August 5, white counter-protesters arrived first at Marquette Park, the staging area for King's Gage Park march. By three in the afternoon, they numbered close to a thousand. Scores waved Confederate flags and banners making racist taunts such as "The Only Way to End Niggers Is to Exterminate." When a convoy of cars carrying some six hundred Black demonstrators arrived from the South Side around four o'clock, the park rang with cries of "Go home niggers," and "Two, four, six, eight, we don't want to integrate."

At roughly five o'clock, Dr. King stepped out of a car in Marquette Park "We want Martin Luther Coon," someone in the mob shouted. Policemen surrounded King with plastic shields to protect him from a barrage of bottles, eggs, and cherry bombs. Suddenly, a small rock pierced the human wall and struck King on his right temple. He fell to one knee and remained on the ground for several seconds. "I think so," he responded when he was asked if he was all right. "It hurts, but it's not an injury." King rose and marched on, but not before press photographers captured the moment. In the coming days, that image of a dazed-looking Dr. King kneeling on the ground in Marquette Park would run in *Newsweek* and hundreds of newspapers, adding to national concerns about his Chicago campaign and the white fury it had unleashed.

By the end of the afternoon, well over a thousand angry white hecklers filled Marquette Park. Sharp objects and racist shouts continued to fly as the Black marchers made their way through the park and into the Gage Park business district. "Hate! Hate! Hate!" the white crowd chanted when the marchers tried to strike up a freedom song. "King would look good with a knife in his back," taunted one sign. "Go home, Communist, go home," directed another. "You dirty nigger loving priest!" a local resident shouted from his front porch at a white clergyman who joined the march. A knife was thrown in King's direction, striking a teenage marcher in the shoulder and sending him to the hospital for stitches. In two hours, thirty protesters were injured, and the Chicago police at last got off the sidelines and made forty arrests.

As sunset approached, Chicago's deputy police chief, Robert Lynskey, concluded that the only way to get the marchers out of the area safely was on city buses. As the protesters boarded the buses around seven o'clock, Lynskey saw what looked to him like an army of whites amassed on a hilltop in Marquette Park. "There must be 2,500 people up there," he exclaimed. Even after the buses left, calm wasn't restored until well after dark. Back in the sanctuary of the South Side, King expressed shock at what he had witnessed. "I have never in my life seen such hate," he told reporters. "Not in Mississippi or Alabama. This is a terrible thing."

Drained and suffering from headaches after the rock attack, King came down with a raging fever the next week as he presided over an SCLC convention in Jackson, Mississippi. In his absence, Jesse Jackson assumed temporary leadership of the Chicago protest. At a rally at the Warren Avenue Baptist Church on the West Side, Jackson got carried away and raised the prospect of taking the open housing campaign across city lines to Cicero, the notoriously racist suburb to the west of North Lawndale. "I counted the cost!" Jackson cried out from the pulpit. "I'm going to Cicero!"

Everyone in Chicago recognized immediately how much trouble Jackson's promise could cause. Fifteen years earlier, a race riot had broken out in Cicero when a Black family tried to move in. Even in 1966, the town had a "sundown law" prohibiting the presence of Blacks after dark. That spring, a Black teenager who went to Cicero for a job interview had been beaten to death when he didn't leave in time. The sheriff of surrounding Cook County warned that a civil

rights protest in Cicero would make "Gage Park look like a tea party."
Within days, Governor Kerner announced that he had put 3,500 National
Guardsmen on alert in the event that the SCLC made good on
Jackson's threat.

Although Cicero would later be remembered as the site of an epic
civil rights clash, it became a bluff that neither Dr. King nor Mayor
Daley could afford to call. After a week of headlines about the looming
crisis, Chicago business leaders intervened. Led by Ben Heineman,
the president of the Chicago and North Western Railway, they
brought emissaries from the SCLC, Al Raby's CCCO, and the mayor's
office together at the posh Palmer House hotel. By the end of August,
a face-saving deal was announced. King agreed to "defer" a march to
Cicero. In exchange, Daley promised to appoint a blue-ribbon commission
to study how to expand the city's public housing and to secure
wider access and better bank terms for Black homebuyers.

When Daley and King signed the Palmer House agreement, the
mayor called it "a historic day for Chicago," and King heralded the
promised blue-ribbon panel as "the most significant program ever
considered to make open housing a reality for a metropolitan area."
But when King spoke before at a church rally that evening to trumpet
the deal, he was cut off repeatedly by chants of "Black Power!" SNCC
members passed out flyers that read: "WAKE UP, BROTHER: DE-
CIDE FOR YOURSELF—WHO SPEAKS FOR YOU? King says
we should celebrate a 'significant victory' tonight because he got
some concessions from the city. These concessions were just more
empty promises from Daley, a man who has lied and lied to the black
man in this city for years. Many people are calling it a sellout." When
a reporter asked James Bevel, the lieutenant who had persuaded King
to come to Chicago in the first place, what he thought of the Palmer
House accord, Bevel couldn't hide his disappointment. "I don't
know," he responded wearily. "I'll have to think about it."

To register his own disapproval of the deal, Bob Lucas, the head
of the local CORE chapter, announced that he would lead a march to
Cicero anyway. That protest happened in the first week of September,
bringing 250 marchers into Cicero for two hours and resulting in

thirty-two arrests and several injuries to white hecklers who charged National Guardsmen who were armed with clubs and bayonets. Once King and his SCLC aides left town at the end of the summer, Lucas was left to deal with a local civil rights community that had only become more disgruntled and divided by race, not less, in the aftermath of the vaunted Chicago Freedom Movement. "After King left the city in late August of 1966, having failed really in Chicago, we began to notice a wider split between the blacks and the whites in the civil rights movement," Lucas recalled. "As long as Dr. King was here, that was sort of held at bay, out of respect for him. But after he left, it really began to manifest itself to the point where blacks literally asked whites to leave the movement and to leave meetings."

IN LATE AUGUST OF 1966, A COMPREHENSIVE NEW NATIONAL POLL showed a similar widening and hardening of racial attitudes on both sides of the American color line. The poll was commissioned by *Newsweek* editor Osborn Elliott, a forty-two-year-old Harvard graduate and Navy veteran who was descended from New York City's Dutch settlers. With his bow ties and prep school cuff links, Elliott looked like the sort of well-born establishment figure long associated with *Time* magazine, where he had worked for a decade. But after moving to *Newsweek* and being promoted to its top job in the early 1960s, "Oz," as everyone called Elliott, had proven to be a remarkably progressive and far-sighted editor. In particular, he had gained attention for *Newsweek* by combining two of his strongest interests: the civil rights movement, and the growing field of public opinion research.

In advance of the March on Washington in 1963, Elliott had commissioned a wide-ranging survey of Black and white attitudes from Louis Harris, the up-and-coming pollster who had worked for President Kennedy. The results were published in a special issue of *Newsweek* entitled "The Negro in America"—the first of a series of groundbreaking reports on race that the magazine would produce during the decade. While confirming the persistence of racist prejudice in the South, that poll showed growing nationwide support for what were seen then as the goals of the civil rights struggle. A majority of both Black and white Americans opposed Jim Crow discrimination, supported the push for integrated schools and Black voting rights—and expressed deep admiration for Dr. King.

In August of 1966, after devoting a cover story to the Meredith March and a long article to the Chicago riots, Elliott wanted to see how attitudes on both sides of the color line had changed in three years. He asked Harris to conduct another poll that would be featured in a thirty-two-page *Newsweek* cover story entitled "Black and White: A Major Survey of U.S. Racial Attitudes Today." Harris dispatched 113 Black pollsters to interview a total of 1,059 Blacks, while another white team questioned 1,088 white Americans. What the pollsters found was ominous. Despite the passage of two historic civil rights bills in the years since the first Harris poll, Blacks and whites had very different views of the state of race relations—and in key areas, the mood had turned dramatically for the worse.

One major disparity was over the pace of progress. Although a majority of Blacks confirmed that their lives had improved since 1963 in many areas—from jobs and schools to access to public accommodations and voting rights—half complained that the change was happening too slowly. Among a group identified as a "leadership sample" of Black politicians, business leaders, and civic activists, the rate of unhappiness was even higher: 84 percent. Analyzing this apparent paradox of dissatisfaction amidst advancement, *Newsweek* described it as a "revolution of rising expectations"—similar to the phenomenon that historians identified among the emboldened bourgeoise battling the entrenched aristocracy during the French Revolution.

Among whites, however, views on the speed of racial progress had shifted in the other direction. Seventy percent of whites agreed when asked if Blacks "are trying to move too fast"—compared to 64 percent in 1963. Posed a similar question—whether "Negroes were asking for more than they were ready for"—the percentage answering yes jumped from 54 percent in 1963 to 64 percent in 1966. "The Negro hasn't given all these civil rights laws a chance to work," W. F. Schell, a retired sixty-five-year-old machinery salesman from Moscow, Idaho, told a *Newsweek* reporter. "They are demanding too much, too fast." A seventy-one-year-old white woman from Dayton, Ohio, was even more blunt. "They're so forward," she said. "If you give them a finger, they'll take your hand."

Sharp differences also stuck out over the urban riots that had swept America since 1963—first in Harlem in 1964, then in Watts in 1965, and in 1966 from Chicago to Cleveland to Lansing, Michigan. While only 15 percent of Blacks said they would participate in a riot, a third thought the uprisings had "helped the Negro cause" by calling attention to the problems of inner cities, and almost two thirds predicted more riots to come.

Not surprisingly, three quarters of whites described the riots as "harmful" to the Black cause. But more startlingly, the violence in America's streets had turned white opinion decisively against *any* form of civil rights protest. By a margin of 64 to 24 percent, the whites interviewed said they now opposed even *peaceful* Black demonstrations. Additional reporting by *Newsweek* reporters suggested how much TV coverage of the riots had contributed to this shift. "People who weren't prejudiced before, are now," remarked a Seattle mechanic. "When I see these demonstrations on TV, it makes me think of them [Blacks] as savages."

The widest gaps were over police and housing. Asked if police officers were generally "fair," well over half of whites agreed, compared with only a third of Blacks. On housing, more than two thirds of both races expected racial integration to continue. Yet in spite of that expectation, almost half of whites didn't want to see Blacks move into *their* neighborhoods. That opposition was fiercest, *Newsweek* noted, among the sort of working-class whites who had assaulted Dr. King in Chicago. "Most of all, his home is his castle—and his fortress," the magazine observed. "A 54 percent majority would object to having a Negro move in next door—and the lesson of Chicago is that even the prospect can make whites fighting mad."

Despite King's setbacks in Chicago, he was still seen by Blacks as their most admired leader, with nearly 90 percent approval. Meanwhile, only 19 percent of the Blacks polled had a favorable view of Stokely Carmichael—in part, no doubt, because many still hadn't heard of the new SNCC chairman. Yet the cry of Black Power, only two months old, was already gaining traction. "Though interpretations of the idea vary widely," the poll found, the concept was "favored" by a quarter of all Blacks and almost a third of "low-income and younger" Blacks. Tellingly, favorable response to the Black Power slogan was highest—almost 50 percent—among the poll's "leadership sample" of Black political, business, and social leaders.

If what lay ahead were the racial earthquakes associated with the late 1960s, the *Newsweek* poll registered their early rumblings. In the short run, the Harris survey also served to heighten those tremors by providing the rest of the press with opinion data that would shape coverage of the civil rights story for the rest of 1966. And by August, whether Oz Elliott and other media leaders knew it or not, each new piece of evidence they produced about the impact of the Black Power message was being delivered to two of the most powerful men in America: J. Edgar Hoover of the FBI, and an increasingly aggrieved President Lyndon Baines Johnson.

CHAPTER 12

A Dynamite Bust in Philadelphia

I n August of 1966, Frank Rizzo, the deputy commissioner of Pennsylvania's largest city police force, was temporarily in charge while his boss was on summer vacation. A jowly, tough-talking son of Italian immigrants, Rizzo would later become nationally known as Philadelphia's police chief and two-term mayor. Notorious for his homophobic boast that he could "make Attila the Hun look like a faggot," Rizzo left a legacy so tainted with racial controversy that a subsequent mayor ordered a bronze statue of him removed from the steps of the city's main office building. But in 1966, Rizzo was still largely unknown outside Philadelphia, and had appeared in local headlines mostly for his run-ins with Black protesters who were picketing to integrate a city school for fatherless boys.

On the morning of August 13, just in time to make the front pages of the afternoon *Philadelphia Bulletin*, Rizzo summoned the press for a dramatic announcement. The previous night, his men had moved to disrupt what Rizzo described as a suspected plot by SNCC to blow up one of Philadelphia's most prized historic landmarks. Someone he identified only as an "informant," Rizzo said, had provided evidence of "warehouses of arms, ammunition and dynamite . . . powerful enough to remove Independence Hall."

Operating on that tip, twenty-man police teams had staged late-night raids on SNCC's local office and two other locations used by the organization around the city.

Although no explosives were found at those three sites, Rizzo reported, police had discovered two and a half sticks of dynamite during a fourth raid on an apartment at the corner of North 16th Street and Poplar Avenue in North Philadelphia. Three men and a woman were arrested on conspiracy and explosives charges and detained with bail set at $50,000 each. That afternoon, reporters went to North Philadelphia to gather more details and talked with Black neighbors who had emerged in the middle of the night to demand to know the grounds for the raid. An inspector named Millard Meers had told the suspicious crowd that the police were only looking out for the public's safety. "The dynamite could have caused a disaster in this neighborhood if it had gone off prematurely," Meers shouted through a bullhorn. "It could have injured any one of you."

Reporters soon established that only one of the arrested suspects was a SNCC member: a twenty-three-year-old recent recruit named Barry Dawson. Three others found in the North Philadelphia apartment belonged to different activist group called the Young Militants. Still, as word spread of Rizzo's bomb plot accusation, Fred Meely, SNCC's Philadelphia field secretary, placed an anxious phone call to Atlanta headquarters. Suspecting a "frame-up," as he put it, Jim Forman met with the other top SNCC leaders—including Stokely Carmichael, Cleve Sellers, and Ruby Doris Robinson—and they decided that Forman should go to Philadelphia immediately to help deal with authorities. But by the time Forman arrived, Meely had gone into hiding with two other SNCC members.

When a trial of the four suspects took place at the end of August, the bombing conspiracy case quickly fell apart. Dawson testified that the episode had started when a Black construction worker named John Jenkins stole nine sticks of dynamite from a job site. Jenkins intended to resell the dynamite but became worried and asked friends to help dispose of it for him. A mutual acquaintance passed several of the sticks to Dawson, who hid them in SNCC's office for several days. When Fred Meely found out, he ordered Dawson to dump the dynamite in the Schuylkill River. On the way there, Dawson panicked and threw the stash over the fence outside the building on North 16th Street. Dawson then alerted a friend who lived in the building—one of the Young Militants—and that man hid the two and half sticks of dynamite where the police found them: under a roach-infested couch.

All charges against the four arrested suspects were eventually dropped for lack of evidence. But while the strange episode would become a brief side note in the history of SNCC, it carried strong omens for the future relationship between the Black Power movement and the FBI. Declassified FBI documents later showed that the "informant" whom Rizzo touted to the press was on the bureau's payroll. It was this informant who discovered the two and a half sticks of dynamite in the paper bag thrown over the fence in North Philadelphia, apparently after tailing Dawson as he left the SNCC office. The FBI tipster notified Philadelphia police officers, who surveilled the scene and witnessed Dawson's friend take the bag inside his apartment building. The search warrant for the late-night raid was then obtained partly on the strength of a vague claim by a Philadelphia FBI agent that the informant had previously provided tips on "approximately 200 occasions that led to valid arrests."

WHAT ALMOST NO ONE INVOLVED IN THE PHILADELPHIA CASE knew at the time—including Frank Rizzo and his policemen—was that the FBI's involvement traced all the way to the White House. On August 5, a week before the Philadelphia raids, President Johnson had been preparing for his daughter Luci's wedding the next day, a black-tie affair that was broadcast on national TV. LBJ awoke to the front-page *New York Times* story linking Stokely Carmichael to Bill Ware's incendiary anti-white "position paper." In a heated phone call with Joseph Beirne, the vice president of the AFL-CIO, Johnson brought up Carmichael's name twice. "What makes Stokely Carmichaels?" the president fulminated. "We don't want a hell raiser."

A few days later, Johnson's personal assistant, Marvin Watson, reached out to FBI deputy assistant director Cartha DeLoach, known to everyone by his nickname "Deke." Watson told DeLoach that the president "was very concerned about the activities of Stokely Carmichael," and wanted to receive personal FBI reports on him "at least twice a week." DeLoach assured Watson that the bureau had "good coverage on Carmichael," even though until then the new SNCC chairman's name had appeared only occasionally in FBI files. It was only after Marvin Watson's inquiry that memos about Carmichael began to fly back and forth between FBI headquarters and its regional offices, many of them laced with reminders of "the interest of the President in the activity of Stokely Carmichael and his organization."

In the rush to provide twice-weekly updates for the White House, FBI agents at times merely rehashed newspaper stories and trivia dredged up from other government agencies. One memo included information from the immigration files on Carmichael's arrival from Trinidad at the age of eleven, including the fact that he had been four feet and seven inches tall at the time. Another memo contained a tangential revelation that, when Carmichael was organizing in Mississippi, a SNCC phone number listed under his name had been used by someone else who planned to attend a convention of the Young Communist League in San Francisco.

In mid-August, however, the FBI turned from providing personal background on Carmichael to circulating evidence that could be used against him. A memo dated August 10 reprinted a letter to Attorney General Nicholas Katzenbach from L. Mendel Rivers of South Carolina, the hawkish chairman of the House Armed Services Committee, calling for Carmichael to be punished for his statements critical of the draft. The South Carolina Democrat quoted the Detroit Cobe Hall speech in which Carmichael declared that "Negroes should refuse to fight in Vietnam" and asked if "criminal penalties" were being pursued by the Justice Department. "If no action is being considered," Rivers instructed Katzenbach, "please provide me with an explanation as to why it is not."

Two days before the Philadelphia arrests, a top FBI official named F. J. Baumgardner sent a memo to the bureau's head of domestic intelligence, William C. Sullivan, updating him on the informant tip about the bag of dynamite. But after Rizzo held his press conference, an "Addendum" was added to the memo instructing anyone who read it to keep the FBI's role hush-hush. "Arrest matter of local publicity but FBI not mentioned," the addendum read. "Philadelphia [office] advises against mentioning of FBI for fear of informant's safety." In the margins of the addendum, over the initial "D"—likely Deke DeLoach—was scribbled: "This is the type of information White House desires re Student Nonviolent Coordinating Committee."

NONE OF THIS WAS KNOWN TO CARMICHAEL, OF COURSE, WHEN he appeared a week later on a special ninety-minute edition of *Meet the Press* devoted to the state of the civil rights movement. In a booking coup, the producers persuaded all Big Five leaders to appear together for the first time since the eve of the Meredith March. Joining them as the sixth guest was Meredith himself. Still in Chicago, Dr. King was beamed in via satellite from the city's local NBC station. In the *Meet the Press* studio in Washington, the other leaders were positioned in two rows, with Roy Wilkins of the NAACP and Whitney Young of the Urban League in front. Behind them sat Meredith, Floyd McKissick of CORE, and Carmichael, dressed in a light-colored suit, his hair grown into a short Afro.

Despite their fight at the Lorraine Motel and subsequent sparring in the press, the leaders remained on good behavior. They resisted repeated invitations to trade personal attacks from five interrogators: *Meet the Press* host Lawrence Spivak, NBC News reporter Richard Valeriani, and newspaper columnists Rowland Evans, James J. Kilpatrick, and Carl Rowan. Carmichael denied having called Roy Wilkins an Uncle Tom and insisted that he would "never publicly denounce any black leader in this country." In turn, Wilkins shrugged off Carmichael's flamboyant rhetoric as so much clever marketing for SNCC.

"I think Mr. Carmichael—if he weren't where he is, he ought to be on Madison Avenue," Wilkins quipped. "He is a public relations man par excellence."

The panelists expressed subtle disagreements over nonviolence, but didn't have the public spat the journalists might have expected. It was McKissick, not Carmichael, who argued that Blacks should have a right to defend themselves, declaring that "if somebody hits us, then you better have an ambulance on the side." Meredith suggested that Blacks weren't asking for anything more than other gun-loving Americans, with their "frontier-style mentality." As usual, Dr. King warned that any talk of violence sent the wrong message. "The minute the nomenclature of violence gets into the atmosphere, people begin to respond violently," he said, "and in their unsophisticated minds they cannot quite make the distinction between defensive and aggressive violence."

NBC's Valeriani seized on the poll that had just been published by *Newsweek*. He confronted Dr. King with the finding that two thirds of whites had come to oppose all civil rights demonstrations, even nonviolent ones. "By continuing them, don't you do more harm than good?" Valeriani asked. King responded that blaming Blacks for demonstrating against racist conditions was like condemning "the robbed man," then tried to remind viewers of his inspiring Southern protests. He was "still convinced," King said, "that there is nothing more powerful to dramatize a social evil than the tramp, tramp of marching feet."

At this point, King had to leave the Chicago studio. After a commercial break, Spivak turned to Carmichael. "Will you tell us what you mean by Black Power," Spivak asked, "so that all of us can understand your meaning without misquoting you or distorting you?" But Carmichael once again deflected the invitation. "I am sorry you asked that question now," he responded, "because two days ago the Student Nonviolent Coordinating Committee decided we are not going to define the term Black Power anymore."

Yet this time, the panelists cited their own source of information about what Black Power meant: the *New York Times* story on SNCC's anti-white "position paper." Did Carmichael endorse the position paper? the reporters asked. What did the document mean when it stated that "the masses of white people" were "in reality 180 million racists"? Flustered, Carmichael pointed out that the paper wasn't an official document and didn't reflect the origins of the Black Power concept in SNCC's voter registration campaigns in the Delta. "We thought the work we have been doing for the past six years has been the basis for Black Power because this is all we have been working on in SNCC," he said. But by going on television without being prepared to talk about Black Power, Carmichael had lost another opportunity to give viewers a clearer understanding of his Lowndes County vision.

Unable to lure Carmichael into a discussion about Black Power, the panelists bore down on his opposition to the Vietnam War. What did he mean by calling Black draftees "mercenaries"? Spivak asked. Would Carmichael himself serve in the war? "No, I would not fight in Vietnam," Carmichael replied, "and I would urge every black man in this country not to fight in Vietnam." Toward the end of broadcast, Spivak circled back indirectly to the draft issue, asking Carmichael if he was a U.S. citizen, given his birth in Trinidad. Carmichael danced around the question several times, suggesting that no Black person was truly an equal citizen, before eventually giving a straight answer. "I am a citizen of the United States, if that is what you mean," he conceded. "A paper citizenship."

By declaring before a huge national television audience that he was a U.S. citizen but still wouldn't serve in Vietnam, Carmichael provided *Meet the Press* with a headline for the Monday newspapers. He also opened a wide new avenue of attack for his adversaries. The next flurry of FBI memos were full of details of Carmichael's statements on the draft and more calls from Mendel Rivers and others to prosecute him for sedition or teach him a lesson by sending him to Vietnam. After a two hectic months on the road, meanwhile, Carmichael returned to Atlanta to attend to business at SNCC headquarters, only to find himself in the middle of the next racial explosion of 1966.

Riot Comes to Summerhill

By the mid-1960s, Atlanta was advertising itself as "the city too busy to hate." That label captured a spirt of cooperation between the Georgia capital's white and Black business and political elites, but it ignored conditions in the city's poorest Black neighborhoods. One was Vine City, where Bill Ware and his followers had come to organize in early 1966 and stayed to launch their aggressive campaign to rid SNCC of whites. Another was Summerhill, a half-square-mile area south of downtown which, like North Lawndale in Chicago, was once a predominantly Jewish neighborhood that became increasingly Black and impoverished as middle-class Jews moved out in the post–World War II era of white flight.

In the period immediately after the war, most Blacks who settled in Summerhill were strivers like Ruby Doris Smith Robinson's parents. Mary Ann Smith, Ruby Doris's older sister, described the Summerhill of that era as a "mosaic" of Black and white, working-class and poor. But by the 1950s, Mary recalled, the races barely mixed, and the sight of a white face on Fraser Avenue, where the Smiths lived, or a Black face at a local high school football game was rare.

Then, in the early 1960s, Atlanta elected a pro-business mayor named Ivan Allen with a dream of bringing a professional baseball team to the city. Allen selected a site on the edge of Summerhill to build an $18 million stadium with surrounding parking lots and ready access to a new interstate highway that cut through the heart of the downtown. Atlanta-Fulton County Stadium helped lure the Milwaukee Braves to Atlanta and became the site of baseball history when Hank Aaron broke Babe Ruth's all-time home run record there in 1974. But by the time the Atlanta Braves played their first game at the stadium in April of 1966, the project had turned Summerhill into an isolated urban island. For Blacks who remained there, it lent an air of armed occupation to the presence of the Atlanta Police Department, a force so traditionally white that it would take a riot in Summerhill in the fall of 1966 for Black officers to be approved for patrol duty for the first time.

Harold Louis Prather was another Black Summerhill native who lived with his mother on Ormond Street two blocks from the baseball stadium. At twenty-five, Prather had drifted into a life of petty crime and been arrested several times for minor offenses. Shortly after one in the afternoon on Tuesday, September 6, he was driving around the neighborhood when two white police officers, Lamar Harris and R. H. Kerr, pulled him over for questioning about a recent carjacking. Rattled by the prospect of adding another arrest to his rap sheet, Prather jumped out of his car and raced toward his mother's house. Officer Harris gave chase, ordering Prather to stop. When Prather kept running, the policeman pulled his gun and opened fire, striking the unarmed suspect in the side and hip.

A resident of Ormond Street named Geneva Brown was getting out of a taxi several doors away when she heard the two shots, then saw Prather collapse on his mother's porch. "Mama, don't let them kill me," he cried out. Mrs. Prather appeared in the doorway and demanded to know who had shot her son. "He did, mama, he did," Harold replied, pointing to Harris as he approached the house. "You didn't have to shoot my child," the mother yelled. As Ormond Street filled with onlookers, Brown recalled, the policeman began to appear nervous. He holstered his gun and radioed for an ambulance that took Prather to Grady Memorial Hospital, where he was treated for a grave but not mortal wound.

As it happened, Mayor Allen had met that morning with Stokely

Carmichael. Carmichael led a SNCC delegation to City Hall to demand the release of several staffers who had gone to jail for picketing a
local Army induction center. Greeting the group, the mayor held out
his hand, but Carmichael refused to shake it. After Allen explained
that the Army center was under federal jurisdiction, the SNCC delegation tried to block him from leaving the meeting before eventually
standing aside. Carmichael returned to SNCC headquarters, where
around two in the afternoon he learned about the Summerhill shooting from a reporter for WAOK, a Black radio station. Racing to the
scene, Carmichael found a crowd of at least forty neighbors gathered
around Harold Prather's house, some of them already holding signs
scrawled "Stop Police Brutality." The locals asked Carmichael to help
them organize a larger protest and he agreed. "We're going to be back
at four o'clock," he promised, "and tear this place up."

Carmichael spent the next two hours working to gather a crowd
from across the city. He put out word of the planned protest on
WAOK and asked Bill Ware to bring a sound truck from Vine City. By
the time Carmichael returned to Summerhill at four o'clock—along
with Ruby Doris Robinson, Cleve Sellers, and Ivanhoe Donaldson—
more than four hundred demonstrators had filled the streets around
the Prather house. From the sound truck, Ware led chants of "Black
Power!" and passed the microphone to witnesses of the shooting. Despite his threat to "tear this place up," however, Carmichael left the
protest after only ten minutes. So he was no longer in Summerhill at
five o'clock when his adversary of that morning, Mayor Allen, arrived.

DAPPER AND ENERGETIC AT AGE FIFTY-FIVE, WITH A BOYISH FACE
framed by silver hair and horned-rim glasses, Ivan Allen brought a
fresh political image to Atlanta. After attending Georgia Tech, where
he was elected student body president, he had taken over an office
supply business from his father. In his first foray into politics in 1957,
Allen briefly flirted with a run for Georgia governor and tested familiar segregationist language about "preserving our Southern way
of life." But when he reset his sights on the Atlanta mayor's office in

1961, he ran as a racial moderate, forging alliances with Black business owners and civil rights leaders and promising to desegregate the city's hotels and restaurants.

To the relief of establishment figures of both races, Allen handily defeated his main opponent, Lester Maddox, the bald-headed, crudely segregationist restaurant owner who had gained notoriety by chasing Blacks out of his cafeterias with guns and baseball bats. Easily reelected four years later, Allen had grown used to being praised for his forward thinking and noble intentions. So he was completely unprepared for the reception he received in Summerhill, where he was viewed as the man who had demolished part of the neighborhood to build a baseball stadium and added to chronic overcrowding in the part that was left.

Allen arrived in Summerhill with a police officer who served as his chauffeur and bodyguard. By the time they got there, the crowd had grown so thick that the mayor got out of the car and walked the last hundred yards to Ormond Street. "Everybody, go to your homes," he pleaded. "Let's go home. Come on, let's go home." Around six o'clock, he climbed onto the roof of a police car to address the protesters, only to have one of them jump onto the vehicle and pull away his bullhorn. "Atlanta is a cracker town," the protester shouted. "It's no different from Watts. The mayor walks around on a plush carpet and wears $500 suits and eats big steaks, while we eat pigs feet and chitlins."

As Allen was standing on the roof of the patrol car, protesters rocked the vehicle back and forth. Losing his balance, Allan jumped to the pavement and fell to his knees. As he rose to his feet, he was showered with rocks, bottles, and chunks of pavement. "Cut loose with the tear gas," the mayor commanded, and police started hurling gas canisters that filled the streets with acrid smoke. One canister crashed through the window of a house, sending a twenty-two-year-old Black mother and her five children wheezing into the street. Walking through the haze, Allen held a white pocket square to his mouth as he pleaded once again for calm. "This is a great city," he called out. "Help keep it that way, and go home."

By seven o'clock, virtually the entire Atlanta police force—some 750 officers—had descended on Summerhill, along with as many as 150 state troopers. An armored car arrived, and police officers lined up to pull shotguns out of its hatch. "Why the shotguns?" the crowd chanted. "Why the shotguns?" Allen tried to offer reassurance. "They're not going to use them," he shouted. "They're here to protect you." But the demonstrators were unconvinced and they raged on as the sun set. By the time Allen left Summerhill around nine o'clock, sixteen injuries had been suffered by protesters or policemen, and more than a hundred demonstrators had been arrested and taken to jail.

Late that Tuesday night, Dr. King and Ralph Abernathy arrived in Summerhill and tried to comfort its seething residents. The next day, King put out a statement denouncing the violence but also trying to grapple with its roots. "While condemning riots, it is just as important to condemn the conditions that bring riots into being," his statement read. "A riot is the desperate language of the unheard." But even in his hometown, King's intervention couldn't stop a deteriorating war of words between Stokely Carmichael and Ivan Allen.

As Atlanta and the rest of the country awoke to front-page headlines about the Summerhill riot on Wednesday morning, the mayor accused the SNCC chairman of inciting the violence and then running away. "If Stokely Carmichael is looking for a battleground, he created one last night," Allen declared, "and he'll be met in whatever situation he wants to create." In return, Carmichael had SNCC circulate flyers in Black neighborhoods across Atlanta that picked at festering grievances against Allen and the Atlanta Police Department and gave a defiant answer to the accusations of cowardice. "The revolt was—and is—against the bestiality of a racist mayor and his corrupt police department," read the SNCC pamphlet. "Racist Allen has said that SNCC has run out of the black community. We are here. Here, baby!"

Prominent local journalists who in the past had denounced racist authorities in the Deep South took the side of Mayor Allen. In a front-page column, Ralph McGill, the pro–civil rights publisher of

The Atlanta Constitution, described SNCC's transformation from the days of John Lewis and Bob Moses to its new incarnation under Carmichael as a "Dr. Jekyll and Mr. Hyde" story. "SNCC is no longer a student movement," McGill lamented. "It is not now a civil rights organization. It is openly, officially committed to the destruction of existing society." In another column, Eugene Patterson, the paper's executive editor, fumed that "trying to reason with the Student Nonviolent Coordinating Committee is like preaching brotherhood to the Ku Klux Klan." From Washington, Vice President Humphrey called into a live interview that Allen gave to WSB-AM, a news and talk radio station. Humphrey praised the mayor for intervening in Summerhill and passed along congratulations from President Johnson. "If there is a hero on the domestic scene today, it's Ivan Allen of Atlanta," declared the garrulous veteran of Minnesota politics, reminding everyone that "I used be a mayor myself."

Ignored in all the media posturing, less militant Black residents of Summerhill strained to be heard. Some homeowners quietly tried to disassociate themselves from the rioting by affixing "Good Neighbor" stickers to their front doors. Others pointed out that they hardly needed Stokely Carmichael to incite them after years of police harassment. As Geneva Brown, the neighbor who had witnessed Harold Prather's shooting, put it: "This thing has been building for a long time. People have been shot around here and nothing was done about it. People were not told what to do, they were just mad."

If Allen and the police were fishing for more evidence to hold against Carmichael, he took the bait on Thursday. Returning to Summerhill, Carmichael went door-to-door asking residents to tell him what they had seen on the day of the shooting. As soon as he left Geneva Brown's house, a Black police officer knocked. The officer asked where she had gotten a Black Power sticker that was visible on her porch. "He said if Stokely Carmichael had put it up without my permission, they could lock him up," Brown recalled. Shortly after ten that evening, the police arrived at SNCC headquarters to arrest Carmichael on charges of "disorderly conduct" and "inciting to riot." Bail was set a stiff $11,000 and Carmichael immediately sent word through lawyers that he considered himself a "political prisoner" and had no intention of paying.

For Julian Bond, the spectacle was finally more than he could bear. Now in the ninth month of his battle to be seated by the Georgia state legislature, Bond was under growing pressure from white and moderate Black supporters to sever ties with Carmichael. Two days after the Summerhill riot, he announced that he was quitting as SNCC's communications director after five exhausting years. Accustomed to talking to the press on background, Bond went on the record to tell *Atlanta Constitution* reporters that SNCC had gone "kind of crazy" under Carmichael. He also vented his long-simmering grievance over the financial sacrifices he and his young family had made for the organization. "If I had money from all the paydays I've missed in the past five years," Bond groused, "I'd be a rich man."

Over the weekend, further proof arrived that racial tensions in Atlanta had boiled over beyond the control of any of the city's leaders. Around ten-thirty on Saturday night, two Black sixteen-year-olds, Hubert Varner and Roy Wright, were sitting on their bicycles outside a housing project in the northeast Atlanta neighborhood known as "Boulevard." A car carrying a middle-aged white couple passed by the two youths, then stopped and backed up.

"Hey, boy, did you say something?" the white man yelled at Varner, leaning over his wife from the passenger's seat.

"No," the teenager replied.

The white man lifted a pistol, pushed his wife aside, and fired out the car window. One bullet wounded Wright in the back, and another blew a fatal hole through Varner's head. By the time police arrived to investigate the drive-by shooting, some four hundred angry protesters had gathered in Boulevard, hurling bricks and bottles. More police arrived to clear the area, but the violent protests flared into the next day until the shooter, a forty-two-year-old logger with a nine-page arrest record, was found and taken into custody.

Meanwhile, in Washington, D.C., September brought the final demise of the Civil Rights Act of 1966. Decades later, it would be only dimly remembered that President Johnson introduced an ambitious sequel to the 1964 Civil Rights Act and the 1965 Voting Rights Act. Taking up where those bills left off, the new legislation would have beefed up federal oversight of voter registration sites, barred racial bias in jury selection, and addressed the rampant housing discrimination that Dr. King was attempting to expose in Chicago. In August, the House of Representatives had narrowly passed the bill after watering down its open housing provisions. But those changes didn't satisfy segregationist Senate Democrats, who resorted to the same filibuster tactics with which they tried to defeat the previous bills. In those cases, the filibusters failed when Senator Everett Dirksen of Illinois, the Republican minority leader, produced enough votes to end them. But this time Dirksen, whose constituents included the inflamed white homeowners of Chicago, backed away from the bill.

When a final vote to end the filibuster fell short and Senate Majority Leader Mike Mansfield was forced to withdraw the bill, Dr. King accused Dirksen of "sheer hypocrisy." The Republican was only too happy to pose as a civil rights champion when it involved the South, King fumed, but supporting the 1966 bill "would have affected him in his own Northern backyard, and this was indeed too close to home." But Mansfield didn't want to antagonize his Republican counterpart, so instead he blamed Stokely Carmichael, blasting SNCC for opposing the bill and muddying the civil rights agenda. In a veiled reference to Carmichael, the usually statesmanlike Democrat from Montana faulted "those who, in the name of racial equality, or perhaps more accurately in the name of a new racial superiority, have not advocated further civil rights legislation, but, in fact, have actively spoken and fought against measures the Administration has been trying to have enacted."

STILL IN JAIL IN ATLANTA, CARMICHAEL USED HIS EIGHT-DAY STAY behind bars to pen his own answer to Dr. King's famous "Letter from Birmingham Jail." In late September, versions of the piece were published in *Ramparts* magazine and *The New York Review of Books*. Entitled "What We Want," the *New York Review* essay began with a straightforward statement of the original Lowndes County conception of Black

Power. "Politically, Black Power means what it has always meant to SNCC: the coming-together of black people to elect representatives and *to force those representative to speak to their needs*," Carmichael wrote, adding the italics to make clear that he was talking about more than token representation.

As the essay went on, however, Carmichael made a more sweeping claim for Black Power as a rebuke to Dr. King's dream of racial integration. "Integration today means the man who 'makes it,' leaving his Black brothers behind in the ghetto as fast as his new sports car will take him," Carmichael wrote sarcastically. "It has no relevance to the Harlem wino or to the cotton-picker making three dollars a day." Blacks were better off, Carmichael argued, pursuing the "psychological equality" that came from proving that "black people are able to do things by themselves."

At other points, Carmichael went even further and called for the wholesale dismantling of America's white power structure. "For racism to die," he asserted, "a totally different America must be born." Borrowing language from Africa's independence movements, he wrote that "the colonies of the United States—and this includes the Black ghettoes within its borders, north and south—must be liberated." Yet nowhere in the long essay did Carmichael explain in any specific detail how that liberation might occur.

For all of their prestige, *Ramparts* and *The New York Review of Books* had little influence on broad public opinion. But at the end of September, after he posted bail in Atlanta, Carmichael was presented with his biggest national audience yet when he was interviewed for a prime-time CBS News special entitled "Black Power, White Backlash." The host was Mike Wallace, the former game show host and morning news anchor who had been promoted to a new position as a hard news feature reporter. The special would serve as a prototype for a new weekly newsmagazine called *60 Minutes*, which debuted a year later in the same time slot—Tuesday evening at ten o'clock—before it later moved to Sunday nights. Although not yet a household name, Wallace was already a skilled interviewer after years of hosting a nighttime talk radio show. He had also been a student of militant Black politics since producing a controversial 1959 syndicated TV special about the Nation of Islam, called "The Hate That Hate Produced," that first introduced Malcolm X to a national audience.

The CBS special opened with grainy footage of Carmichael shouting "Black Power!" again and again in Greenwood, Mississippi. The video had been shot by TV cameramen but didn't air at the time. Yet for many Black viewers, the scene was such a revelation that decades later they had the impression that they had watched it live. "I saw it that night, with my mother and father," the renowned Harvard scholar Henry Louis Gates Jr. told historian Aram Goudsouzian, the author of a book about the Meredith March. "I got goose flesh. It was like the top of your head was about to come off."

With his slick dark hair and grave smoky voice, Mike Wallace appeared on the screen and gave an evocative summary of how America's racial atmosphere had changed in just three months since Carmichael's Greenwood speech. "Summer 1966 was a season of revelation for the white man in the North," Wallace said.

> For the first time, he began fully to comprehend the intensity of his feelings and his fears about the black man. For years, he had watched smug and fascinated as the trials of the Southern black and white were played out for him like some morality play on the television screen. But he remained a spectator, only half involved. Then came summer 1966, and as riots crackled through his cities, the Northern white man came to realize the depth of his confusion, his animosity and his fear. Black Power was the catalyst, a phrase shouted by a twenty-five-year-old revolutionary on a Mississippi highway. It was a rallying cry to Northern blacks mired in frustration and bitterness, and a cry that sounded like a threat of violence, or vengeance, to a white man fed up with racial turmoil.

In the interviews that followed, Wallace found more sympathy for the Black Power message than that ominous introduction might have suggested. Dr. King said that he understood the appeal of the slogan even though he opposed it. "The cry of Black Power was a reaction to the reluctance of white people to make the kind of changes necessary to change the reality of the Negro," King told Wallace. Congressman Adam Clayton Powell Jr. defended the slogan against its crudest stereotypes. "It means dignity; it doesn't mean violence," Powell said. "It means integrity; it doesn't mean anti-white. It means pride in being black."

Even Daniel Patrick Moynihan, the white former Labor Department official who had written a controversial report linking Black poverty to a decline in two-parent households, said he understood where Carmichael was coming from. "I would hope there was something to hope for from a Stokely Carmichael," Moynihan told Wallace. "Whites get upset. Well, they want you to get upset. Who ever met a twenty-six-year-old social reformer who didn't want you to get upset?" Now a Harvard University sociology professor, Moynihan described the message of Black Power as: "Give us what is, by rights, the situation of any American. And if you don't, you're going to have trouble."

Yet from Carmichael himself, Wallace got a surlier explanation. For this TV appearance, Carmichael didn't wear a suit and tie, as he had for *Face the Nation* and *Meet the Press.* He received Wallace at SNCC headquarters dressed like an African head of state, in a multicolored dashiki that Ahmed Sekou Touré of Guinea had sent him as a gift. Hanging behind Carmichael's wooden desk was a poster of an American flag, hung upside down. A shadowy figure was visible behind the red stripes, making the flag look like a prison cell. Passing up another opportunity to tell the Lowndes County story, Carmichael launched into a demand that white slum owners voluntarily turn over their buildings to Black residents. Then he spent several more minutes arguing that the Vietnam draft was a "black urban removal program" deliberately designed by "the racist McNamara"—Johnson's secretary of defense Robert McNamara—to exterminate Blacks.

Wallace tried a softball question. "Mr. Carmichael," he asked, "if you had the opportunity to stand up in front of the white community and say anything you desired—to say, 'Understand me, white man'— what would you say?"

Carmichael rolled his eyes contemptuously. "I would say, 'Understand yourself, white man'," he said. "You have moved to destroy and disrupt. You have taken people away. You have broken down their systems, and you have called all that civilization. And we who have suffered from at this are now saying to you: '*You* are the killers of the dreams. *You* are the savages.' Yes, it is *you* who have always been uncivilized. Civilize yourself."

At the end of the CBS special, Wallace spoke with pollster Louis Harris. Since his in-depth survey for *Newsweek* over the summer, Harris had sent interviewers back into the field to re-ask two questions: about white views of Black demonstrations, and about white liberal support for the civil rights cause. On both fronts, Harris reported, the numbers had turned even more dramatically worse in less than two months. Whites now disapproved of any Black protest, even nonviolent, by more than *four*-to-one. And white liberal support for the Black cause had slipped to just 27 percent, down from 64 percent before the 1963 March on Washington, and 42 percent as recently as the weeks after the Meredith March.

When Wallace asked what issues were precipitating the plunge, Harris cited school integration, welfare, and competition for jobs. But by far the main factor, the pollster reported, was housing. "Where the shoe really binds and where the pinch is felt is on housing," Harris said. "The fear that whites have over Negroes moving into their neighborhoods is without question the deepest fear that abounds in white society today." Wallace asked what impact the racial sea change might have on the upcoming 1966 midterm elections. "Decisive" was Harris's prescient one-word reply.

IN ATLANTA, IT WAS A MOMENT OF DECISION FOR RUBY DORIS Robinson. For four months, SNCC's executive secretary had watched the controversy over Black Power sap fundraising and depress staff morale. Now she decided it was the time to bring her concerns into the open. As the ten-member Central Committee prepared to gather for its first retreat since Kingston Springs, Ruby Doris sat down to type up an "Organizational Report" for circulation before the meeting. After detailing the growing mismatch between SNCC's monthly expenses and its dwindling contributions, she offered a blunt assessment of the pros and cons of Carmichael's high-profile and incendiary rhetoric.

Robinson started the critique by offering a skeptical analysis of why Carmichael was getting so much press attention in the first place. "How could one individual make such a tremendous impression on so many people in such a short period of time?" she asked rhetorically, reflecting on all the media coverage that Carmichael had received since his elevation in Kingston Springs. "Actually it is very simple. He has been the only consistent spokesman for the organization and he has had the press not only available but seeking him out for whatever ammunition can be found—FOR OUR DESTRUCTION."

Then Robinson homed in on the impact of the Black Power message. "There can be no dissent on the fact that for the most part Carmichael has spoken for the masses of black people," she wrote. "At his best, he has said what they wanted to hear—and for many what they would like to say. But, there have been times . . . too many times, when he, like most of us, has not been at his best. Cliche after cliche has filled his orations . . . things that many like to hear but few understand . . . things that feed those who wish to destroy us . . . things that hurt men in the black communities where we organize."

To drive home her point, Robinson adjusted her typewriter to put the next sentence in capital letters. "CAUSE PEOPLE DON'T UNDERSTAND CLICHES," she typed, repeating the blunt assessment of Carmichael's rhetoric. "How do they apply to the lives of black people in a town where the SNCC worker is organizing a co-op or running political candidates or trying to explain the draft program, or preparing a campaign against police brutality? For the most part, they have no meaning and to give meaning means to devote hours to a dialogue that attempts to 'water down' what was actually said to what was really meant. Personally, I don't feel that we have the time to afford such a luxury."

Getting more specific, Robinson brought up the riot in Summerhill, just blocks from her childhood home on Fraser Street. She faulted Carmichael's decision to return to the neighborhood two days after the uprising, handing out Black Power stickers and pamphlets denouncing Mayor Allen as a racist. It was an impulsive bid for more publicity, she suggested, without a plan for what to do next. "There was absolutely nothing he could do short of leading an armed insurrection—which he was not prepared to do," Ruby Doris concluded harshly.

On the last weekend of October, SNCC's Central Committee met for two days in Knoxville, Tennessee. By then, all the members had read Robinson's tough critique, and Carmichael knew that he would have to address it when he delivered his Chairman's Report. Leading off the discussion on the second day, he struck a note of contrition. "Rhetorically, there have been a lot of mistakes made," Carmichael confessed, according to minutes of the meeting. He acknowledged he had spent most of his time since the Meredith March speaking in Northern cities where SNCC had no active programs. He hadn't bothered to study that terrain in advance, as SNCC had always done in the South. "One of the problems we have in the North is that we do not understand political machinery," Carmichael conceded. "A lot of mistakes have been made in the North because we do not understand this."

When Carmichael finished his *mea culpa*, Ralph Featherstone—the quietly intense schoolteacher who had likely fired back at night riders in Philadelphia, Mississippi—took the floor. Perhaps it was best, Featherstone suggested, that Carmichael take a break from public speaking for a while. Chastened, Carmichael promised to do so. After making good on a scheduled commitment in early December, he pledged, he would come off the road and devote himself full-time to overseeing SNCC's fieldwork and sorting out its chaotic finances.

Yet no sooner did Carmichael make that promise than two new developments thrust him back into the national spotlight. In late October, he received word that the Army had ordered him to report for a physical. Then the white leaders of the Students for a Democratic Society at the University of California at Berkeley invited Carmichael to give a keynote speech at a conference they were organizing entitled "Black Power and Its Challenges."

For a showman like Carmichael, the invitation to speak on the most famous stage for campus activism in the country at that time was an opportunity too good to pass up. Nowhere do the minutes of the Knoxville retreat indicate that he discussed the Berkeley appearance with the rest of the Central Committee. But it would turn out to be Carmichael's most consequential speech since the Meredith March—one that thrust him into the middle of a governor's race with powerful portents for American politics, and provided fodder for a West Coast outgrowth of Black Power that would come to eclipse both Carmichael and SNCC.

CHAPTER 14

Berkeley and the Backlash Vote

F ive days into 1966, Hollywood actor Ronald Reagan began his career in elective politics by announcing his candidacy for the governorship of California. Capitalizing on his long experience in performing for the camera, first as a minor movie star and then as host of the television show *Death Valley Days*, Reagan kicked off his campaign with a thirty-minute TV ad. Although the onetime liberal Democrat had burst onto the national political scene with a fiery right-wing speech at the Republican presidential convention in 1964, he projected a folksy image in this commercial. He strolled around a living room set, with logs burning in a fireplace, and pitched his crusade against "big brother, paternalistic government" in the manner of a friendly door-to-door salesman. At one point, Reagan picked up a bottle of ketchup and claimed that "social tinkering" had cost hundreds of jobs in the local foodstuffs industry and led to shortages of the beloved condiment on grocery shelves across California.

Square-jawed and twinkle-eyed, with an impressive mane of pomaded hair, Reagan quickly opened a wide lead in the polls over moderate, two-term Democratic governor Edmund "Pat" Brown. Newspaper columns attributed Reagan's rise not only to his movie star charm and antigovernment economic message but also to growing resentment among white Californians over racial strife, from the 1965 Watts riots to tensions over a fair housing bill that had been overturned by referendum but then reinstated by state courts. Yet at first, Reagan avoided direct racial appeals, in keeping with an overall strategy of painting a sweeping libertarian vision without offering many specifics. As one of his advisers put it, "We concluded that Reagan is communicating with people in great enough depth so that the average voter is satisfied."

As the race entered the home stretch, however, Brown closed the polling gap from fifteen points in mid-June to just three points by late August. As Reagan's lead shrank, he grew more forward in courting what pundits were calling the "white backlash" vote. He repeated a false claim that Brown was allowing anyone who came to California from out of state to qualify for welfare payments within twenty-four hours. He made a showy visit to a crowded tomato cannery to defend the right of California businesses to import seasonal workers from Mexico without offering benefits or protections. Still, the contest remained neck-and-neck for the next month—until an unseasonably hot day in late September, when a riot broke out in Hunters Point, a run-down Black neighborhood in southeastern San Francisco that had become another testament to the shattered dreams of the Great Migration.

A thumb-shaped peninsula sticking out into the San Francisco Bay, Hunters Point was a sleepy stretch of warehouses and fishing piers until World War II, when the U.S. Navy took over a dormant shipyard and launched a drive to attract Black workers from the South. By the end of the war, a third of the workers at the Hunters Point Naval Shipyard were Black, and the influx had increased San Francisco's citywide Black population six-fold, to more than thirty thousand. In the decade afterward, however, Hunters Point was hit with the same perfect storm that battered Black neighborhoods across America. The shipyard laid off workers in the face of falling demand and foreign competition; white residents fled to the suburbs; and Hunters Point was severed from the rest of the city by a new highway called the Bayshore Freeway. As their circumstances deteriorated, some children of the wartime migrants turned to petty crime.

So it was that, much like the Summerhill riot in Atlanta, the unrest in Hunters Point began when white police officers came upon Black youths joyriding in a stolen car.

Around two-thirty in the afternoon on Tuesday, September 27, teenagers Matthew Johnson, Clifton Bacon, and Darnell Mobley were cruising around in a carjacked 1958 Buick when it stalled out in a boxed-in three-way intersection. Just then, two policemen pulled up in a patrol car and recognized the license plate number from a stolen vehicle report. Panicking, the three youths jumped out of the Buick. Mobley ducked behind a nearby parked car, while Johnson and Bacon fled. One of the policemen, a white twenty-three-year veteran of the force named Alvin Johnson, got out of his vehicle, pulled his gun and called out to Matthew Johnson to stop. "Hold it, will you," the policeman shouted. "I just want to talk to you."

Matthew Johnson ran behind a building. Alvin Johnson got back into the cruiser and drove to the other side of the building, where he spotted the teen again. "Stop or I'll shoot," the policeman called out as he gave chase on foot, then fired three warning shots as Matthew disappeared over a hill. Arriving at the top of the incline, the policeman found the teen facedown, a bullet in the left side of his back, and blood pooling around his face. "I'm sure sorry," Alvin Johnson later told reporters, insisting that he meant only to scare the youth, not to kill him. But the policemen didn't make any attempt to evacuate Matthew Johnson's dead body and it lay in the street for almost a half hour before a hearse from a Black funeral home arrived to take it away.

Outraged by the shooting and the disrespect shown to the body, protesters gathered at a nearby job agency office and threatened to march on the closest police station. Alerted to the protest, San Francisco mayor Jack Shelley and police commissioner Harry Nelson rushed to Hunters Point and pleaded for calm. But the crowd was unappeased. "Why did they shoot a kid?" the protesters demanded know. As the sun began to set and the temperatures hung in the sticky mid-eighties, the protest turned violent. "To hell with them, let's go," someone shouted. Bottles and rocks rained down on police cars and smashed the lenses of TV news cameras. Looters broke into a white-owned Rexall drugstore, then went in search of other white businesses to ransack. By dark, protesters were looting and setting small fires from Hunters Point all the way across San Francisco's Mission and Fillmore districts. By midnight, Mayor Shelley imposed a city-wide curfew and prevailed upon Governor Brown to declare a state of emergency and send two thousand National Guardsmen to the city.

The next day, the temperature climbed back into the mid-nineties, and the unrest spread to high schools across the Mission District and Haight-Ashbury. By afternoon, police and National Guardsmen who had amassed at the Candlestick Park baseball stadium marched into Hunters Point and the adjoining Bayview neighborhood. The Guardsmen fired on rioters, who answered with rocks and firebombs. By Wednesday night, armed checkpoints had been set up across the area, but violent flare-ups and sporadic store break-ins continued into the weekend. By Sunday, when the state of emergency was lifted, the toll of the Hunters Point violence had risen to 161 injuries and more than $135,000 in property damage.

That weekend, Ronald Reagan and Pat Brown had agreed to separate interviews on two network news programs, and now reporters pressed them for reaction to the Hunters Point riot. On NBC's *News Conference*, Brown blamed what he characterized as a small "extremist" fringe on San Francisco's streets. On ABC's *Issues and Answers*, Reagan pointed to a "lack of leadership in Sacramento," insinuating that the violence had resulted from Brown's failure to support police and crack down on Black crime. The challenger also predicted that his margin in the polls would widen again once news of the riots sank in. Sure enough, the first survey out after the violence—conducted by the respected California pollster Mervin Field—showed a sudden four-point drop in Brown's support, stretching Reagan's lead to 7 percent.

With the issue of racial violence out in the open and playing to Reagan's advantage, he had every incentive to keep it alive for the rest of the campaign. In mid-October, he saw an opportunity when the press reported that Stokely Carmichael, fresh off his arrest for inciting a riot in Atlanta, had been invited by the Students for a Democratic Society to speak at the University of California at Berkeley. To generate publicity, the SDS issued invitations to Brown and Reagan, knowing that neither would accept. Rather than simply decline, however, Reagan pulled a publicity stunt of his own: he sent Carmichael a personal telegram urging him to stay away. "It is imperative that our election Nov. 8 be held in an atmosphere of calm and good will," Reagan's wire read. "Your appearance on the Berkeley campus so soon before that election will stir strong emotions, and could possibly do damage to both parties. You would be doing a service to your cause and to our state if you decline to appear at this time."

To no one's surprise, Carmichael ignored the telegram. But Reagan's gimmick generated headlines and forced Brown to come up with his own response. The next week, the incumbent announced that he was leaving the campaign trail to fly to San Francisco for talks about preventing unrest during Carmichael's visit. Accusing Reagan of "riding the backlash" by suggesting that "Carmichael wanted to cause panic in the streets," Brown proclaimed that he would ban the use of sound trucks during the Berkeley conference and deny a U.S. Nazi Party petition to hold a counter-rally nearby. "No quarter and no amnesty" would be given "to either 'Black power' advocates or white supremacists," Brown declared.

AS THE POLITICAL POSTURING CONTINUED ON THE WEST COAST, Carmichael was back in the news for a different reason on the East Coast. With America's presence in Vietnam escalating rapidly, the Defense Department announced that it would issue draft notices to forty thousand men previously classified as 1-Y, or required to serve only in the event of a national emergency. Reporters set out to identify prominent figures who fit this category, and two names leapt to the fore: Stokely Carmichael, and George Hamilton, the dashing, perpetually tanned movie star who was dating Lyndon Johnson's elder daughter, Lynda Bird. At the time, Hamilton was in Germany shooting a movie, so reporters focused their attention on Carmichael, who

had received a letter instructing him to appear on the last Thursday
of October at a grimy brick induction center on Whitehall Street in
lower Manhattan.

To the surprise of hovering reporters, the induction examination
took two days. After Carmichael was interviewed by an Army psychiatrist at Whitehall Street, he was quietly transferred to St. Albans
Naval Hospital in Queens for further evaluation. He spent the night
there before being driven back to Whitehall Street for more tests the
next morning. Shortly after noon on Friday, Carmichael tried to sneak
out the back door. Newsmen ran after him, demanding to know if he
planned to go to Vietnam if he was drafted. "I'll go to Leavenworth
first," Carmichael shouted as he hailed a cab to the Harlem apartment
of his Mummy Olga, one of the aunts who had raised him as a child
in Trinidad. After lunching on a plate of Olga's rice and beans, Carmichael emerged on 125th Street to look for a taxi to the airport, announcing to reporters that he would accept a ride only from "a brother."
Then a cabbie pulled up and identified himself as Puerto Rican. "Close
enough," Carmichael quipped as he climbed into the taxi.

Why Carmichael's examination took so long would be revealed
only years later, after records of his surveillance by the FBI were
declassified. According to those records, on the morning of September 19, 1966, FBI headquarters received a phone call from Mildred Stegall, the presidential assistant known around Washington as
Lyndon Johnson's most trusted personal aide. Requesting that her
inquiry be kept in "strictest confidence," Stegall said that Johnson
wanted a report on Stokely Carmichael's draft status and history.
Later that day, FBI agent Sterling Donahoe sent a memo to Deke
DeLoach, J. Edgar Hoover's third-in-command, summarizing what
he had found in the agency's files on Carmichael. "This is not to
be furnished to the Attorney General," Donahoe's memo added, instructing that the contents be kept secret from Ramsey Clark, the
independent-minded deputy attorney general, who had just became
acting head of the Justice Department.

The memo revealed that Carmichael had first registered for the
draft in 1959, shortly after his eighteenth birthday, but received a

student deferment while attending Howard University. Five years later, he reported for a pre-induction physical, including a psychiatric exam. Afterward, the induction center's chief medical officer stamped Carmichael's file with a large "Z"—indicating that he had been classified 4-F, or "not qualified for military service." Although Carmichael showed no evidence of "any inherent anti-social or criminal traits," Donahoe's memo reported, the psychiatrist determined that he was unfit based on a pattern of "disorderly conduct" and "resisting arrest" during civil rights protests. In addition, the memo maintained, "there seems to be homo-sexual tendencies as well as hetero-sexual relationships"—a claim for which no support was given, but whose very mention might have been enough to result in a 4-F designation given the rampant homophobia of the U.S. military at the time.

By early 1966, the military was starting to review 4-F cases for upgrading to I-Y status, and Carmichael was summoned for a second physical in mid-February. This time, the psychiatrist who questioned him found that, since the first exam, Carmichael had suffered "two additional episodes of decompensation"—or temporary nervous breakdowns—"following the shooting of two of his friends." Although the FBI files didn't specify names, those friends almost certainly were Jonathan Daniels, the white seminary student whom Carmichael had befriended in Alabama in the summer of 1965, and Sammy Younge, the Tuskegee student who was gunned down by a white gas station attendant the following January. In that interval, Carmichael had also witnessed the acquittal of Daniels's killer, the highway worker and sheriff's deputy Tom Coleman.

Given the FBI's animus toward Carmichael—and its eagerness to feed President Johnson's appetite for incriminating information about him—its files can hardly be considered definitive evidence of his psychological condition. However, other contemporaneous accounts also testified to Carmichael's fragile state of mind. Carmichael confessed to Jim Forman that he sank into a deep depression and got blind drunk after Sammy Younge's killing. His mother, May Carmichael, told the editor of his autobiography that she had never seen her son more upset and uncommunicative than he was after

Jonathan Daniels's death. Stokely asked May to accompany him to
New Hampshire for Daniels's funeral, but he didn't say a word or
even turn on the car radio during their long drive from New York
City. "Silent, grim, like a heavy, heavy weight was pressing on him,"
was how May described her son's mood. "Even when his father died,
that really hit him, but this was different." Attending the Daniels funeral was "the hardest thing my son had to do in the movement, at
least that I saw," she recalled.

Journalist Jack Nelson, an Alabama native who covered SNCC
for the *Los Angeles Times*, also noticed a marked change in Carmichael
after the Daniels murder. "His attitude toward whites seems to have
hardened—ironically, perhaps—since his friend, Jonathan Daniels,
was shot dead in Lowndes County, Ala. last year," Nelson wrote in
a profile of Carmichael published shortly after the Greenwood, Mississippi, speech. "Daniels' death and the acquittal of his slayer by an
all-white jury seemed to be a traumatic experience for Carmichael."

During his two days of psychological evaluations in October of
1966, Carmichael was likely forced to relive those traumas—and his
response may explain why in the end he was never drafted. Whatever
his mood was when he left the Manhattan induction center, however,
it was lifted the next day when he arrived in San Francisco to another
rock-star-like reception. At a press conference on Saturday morning,
Carmichael was flanked by young admirers, many of them sporting
the dark sunglasses he had helped popularize. From there, he went
to a community meeting at the South San Francisco Opera House in
Bayview, not far from where the Hunters Point riot broke out. The
session was closed to the press, but a correspondent for the local TV
station KQED reported that Carmichael drew a full house, and afterward the station's cameras captured scores of young Blacks beaming
and laughing as they left the auditorium.

Carmichael's speech that afternoon took place at Berkeley's
Greek Theatre. Funded by William Randolph Hearst and modeled
after the ancient theater at Epidaurus, the bowl-like amphitheater was
known for hosting plays, musical concerts, and raucous bonfire rallies

before the annual "Big Game" football showdown between Berkeley and Stanford. The SDS's Black Power conference started at ten in the morning with only a few hundred people in the stands, but the crowd grew steadily through the afternoon. By five in the afternoon, when Carmichael arrived, more than ten thousand people filled the stadium—the largest crowd Berkeley had seen since an appearance the previous year by Senator Robert F. Kennedy.

Dressed in a brown suit and yellow shirt, his hair buzz-cut thin after the army physical, Carmichael loosened up the audience with a playful jab at Berkeley's elite reputation. "It's a privilege and an honor to be in the white intellectual ghetto of the West," Carmichael began, drawing a wave of laughter. Alluding to the role he had played in the governor's race, Carmichael predicted that "our appearance here will win an election in California," and proclaimed "in 1968 I'm gonna run for president of the United States." Loud applause filled the stadium until Carmichael pointed out that he was kidding, since his birth in Trinidad prohibited him from seeking the White House. "I just can't make it cause I wasn't born in the United States," he said. "That's the only thing holding me back."

"BLACK POWER AND ITS CHALLENGES" read a huge banner behind Carmichael, promising a serious discussion of the topic. But for several minutes, Carmichael suggested that the fuss over Black Power was just a way for the media to sell newspapers and get TV ratings. "We wanted to say . . . that we're not ever to be caught up in the intellectual masturbation of the question of Black Power," he claimed. "That's a function of the people who are advertisers that call themselves reporters." After that, however, Carmichael settled into a more substantive critique of racial integration, taunting whites in the audience for supporting it more to prove their own virtue more than to improve the lives of a majority of Blacks. "Are we willing to be concerned about the black people who will never get to Berkeley," he asked the crowd, "who will never get to Harvard, and cannot get an education so you'll get a chance to rub shoulders with them and say, 'Well, he's almost as good as we are. He's not like the others.'"

Midway through the speech, Carmichael turned to the attack that got the most news coverage the next day: on Vietnam and the draft. "I maintain, as we have in SNCC, that the war in Vietnam is an illegal and immoral war," he proclaimed. "And the question is, what can we do to stop that war? What can we do to stop the people who, in the name of our country, are killing babies, women and children? . . . The only power we have is the power to say, 'Hell no to the draft.'" Invoking the names of the president and his secretaries of defense and state, Carmichael continued: "We have to say to ourselves that there's a higher law than the law of a racist named McNamara. There is a higher law than the law of a fool named Rusk. There's a higher law than the law of a buffoon named Johnson. It's the law of each of us . . ."—he waited for loud applause to subside before repeating the punch line—"It's the law of each of us."

Carmichael ended his speech with the slogan of the Black Panther Party in Alabama: "Move on over, or we'll move on over on you." Then he spent the evening hobnobbing and smoking marijuana with white admirers in Haight-Ashbury before flying back to the East Coast. In the end, Carmichael's appearance at Berkeley had not caused another riot, as Ronald Reagan warned. But it had revived talk of a white backlash vote in the final phase of the California race—and as the federal midterm election neared, newspapers across the country were full of stories and opinion columns detecting a similar effect.

In Indiana, Lee Hamilton, a young pro–civil rights lawyer and former college basketball star who had been elected to a first term in Congress in 1964, described hearing resentful murmurs wherever he went on the campaign trail. "Questions are put to you at political gatherings. Haven't we done enough for the Negro? somebody will ask," Hamilton told reporter Robert Semple Jr. of *The New York Times*. "Then there's the whisper approach, in front of plant gates, in local taverns and pool halls. That's where they begin calling me names." Just how big a factor could the backlash be? Semple asked. "It comes up most anywhere, but as far as political impact is concerned it's awfully hard to measure," Hamilton observed. "But I think for the Democrats it's as dangerous as any issue in the election in terms of changing votes."

WHEN LYNDON JOHNSON HAD RUN FOR PRESIDENT IN 1964, PUN-dits speculated about a white backlash in response to his first major civil rights bill. But that factor ultimately paled in comparison to what the Associated Press described as a "frontlash" of moderate Republicans turned off by the hard-line conservatism of their party's nominee, Barry Goldwater. Johnson captured a commanding 61 percent of the popular vote, exceeding Franklin Delano Roosevelt's 1932 record for a first-time candidate at the top of a presidential ticket. He also won a landslide 486 Electoral College votes. In Congress, Democrats picked up thirty-seven seats in the House of Representatives and two in the Senate. Democrats also won seventeen of the twenty-five governorships that were up for grabs, leaving them in control of more than two thirds of America's statehouses.

The day after the 1964 election, the lead editorial in *The New York Times* summed up the near universal consensus: "For the Republican party, the results border on catastrophe." In retrospect, however, the beginnings of a white backlash were detectable in the one area that Goldwater carried, in addition to his home state of Arizona. For the first time since Reconstruction, five states in the heart of the Old Confederacy—South Carolina, Georgia, Alabama, Mississippi, and Louisiana—all went Republican in a presidential race, crumbling what for almost a century had been a Democratic Party bulwark known as the "Solid South."

When Americans went to the polls two years later, on November 8, 1966, that backlash became visible from coast to coast. The Republican Party picked up forty-seven seats in the House of Representatives, three in the U.S. Senate, and seven hundred seats in state legislatures. Out of twenty-five governorships on the line, the GOP won seventeen, an overall gain of nine. In a close race decided several days after the polls closed, Georgians awarded their state's top job to

Lester Maddox, the bat-wielding cafeteria owner who had been dismissed as a white supremacist kook five years earlier when he ran for Atlanta mayor against Ivan Allen.

On a drizzly Election Day in California, the number of registered Democrats who went to the polls exceeded self-declared Republicans by three-to-two, and more than nine out of ten Black voters cast their ballots for Pat Brown. Yet white voters favored Ronald Reagan by such huge margins—particularly in the sprawling suburbs surrounding the state's largest cities—that he won by nearly a million votes. At the Ambassador Hotel in Los Angeles, Reagan left the suite where he had watched the returns to make an acceptance speech in the ballroom. Stopping to chat with reporters, he offered an analysis that winked at white resistance to Black advancement. "It seems to be all over the country," Reagan said. "The people seem to have shown that maybe we have moved too fast, and want to pause and reconsider the course we've been following."

Even in contests that were viewed as exceptions to the white backlash, closer analysis suggested otherwise. In Massachusetts, Edward Brooke, a light-skinned, blue-eyed Republican, became the first Black U.S. senator to win a popular election. (During Reconstruction, two Blacks served in the Senate after being selected by state legislatures.) Brooke won over white voters by campaigning as a fiscal conservative—and by denouncing Black Power. "A vote for me is a vote against Stokely Carmichael," he proclaimed. In the Maryland governor's race, it was the Democrat, George Mahoney, who came out against integrated housing, running on the slogan: "Your home is your castle; Vote to protect it." So reporters hailed it as a blow against racism when Mahoney was defeated by a little known son of a Greek immigrant named Spiro Agnew, who they described at the time as a "Republican moderate."

For Richard Nixon, the results offered the promise of political resurrection. After barely losing the 1960 presidential race to John F. Kennedy, Nixon had run for California governor in 1962 and suffered a humiliating defeat at the hands of Pat Brown. Full of bitterness and self-pity, he seemed to announce his political retirement when he told reporters: "You won't have Nixon to kick around anymore." But now, Nixon saw the makings of a new winning coalition, one that he felt uniquely positioned to assemble. On the one hand, he had stayed on good terms with Republican moderates who swept to victory in 1966, campaigning and raising money for the likes of governors George Romney of Michigan, Nelson Rockefeller of New York, and Winthrop Rockefeller of Arkansas. But Nixon also maintained ties to the conservative wing of the party, which despite Goldwater's drubbing still had enormous grassroots energy. To Nixon, Goldwater's inroads in the Deep South suggested a new path to Electoral College victory in the next presidential year. The strategy entailed holding on to traditional Republican strongholds in the North while fashioning a new "Southern strategy" by exploiting racial resentments. On election night, anchor Walter Cronkite of CBS News invited Nixon to comment on the midterm results. Champing at the bit, Nixon predicted that the 1968 presidential contest was now going to be "a horse race."

Carmichael had planned to spend the week before Election Day back in Lowndes County, stumping for the seven candidates running for local offices under the black panther banner. Instead, he was in a Selma courtroom, insisting on acting as his own attorney after getting arrested for protesting. Released on bail a day before the vote, Carmichael attended a spirited rally at the Mount Moriah Baptist Church, then drove around Lowndes County getting voters to the polls. "Did you vote, right?" he called out to every Black face he saw, waiting to be answered with a nod, or a "Sure did." By nightfall on Election Day, however, it was clear that the dream of a historic triumph for the Lowndes County Freedom Organization was not to be. All seven candidates lost their races, by margins of between two hundred and six hundred votes—enough to qualify the LCFO as an official party under Alabama law, but not to make the dramatic national headlines that Carmichael had envisioned.

Instead, Election Day 1966 in Alabama belonged to a man absent from the ballot: Governor George Wallace. Deprived of the option of running for a second term by the state's constitution, Wallace devised the unlikely stratagem of running his wife, Lurleen, a political novice, in his place. According to *Newsweek* reporter Marshall Frady, who covered the race and would later write a widely admired biography of Wallace, as the state's first lady Mrs. Lurleen Wallace had until then appeared an "obscure and rather lonely figure . . . unassuming and unprepossessing . . . with a fondness for blazers and turtleneck blouses, which made her look like the leader of a girls' college glee club." In the time that her husband had been in office, whispers had spread around the governor's mansion that Lurleen was planning to divorce George, and as the campaign began she was recovering from radiation treatment for uterine cancer and a hysterectomy that she kept secret from voters.

Meanwhile, the passage of the Voting Rights Act of 1965 led to the highest Black turnout in Alabama since the heady days after the Civil War. In the Democratic primary, Blacks had gone to the polls in droves to support Lurleen's opponent, the anti-segregationist state attorney general, Richmond Flowers. Describing the scene on primary day, a *Newsweek* wordsmith wrote: "When morning broke across the new-green land, white men woke goggling to a nightmare torn whole from Reconstruction days: long queues of black men and women snaking out of polling places in courthouse squares and one-room schools and unpainted crossroads stores." That turnout wasn't enough to carry Flowers to victory, but in the general election it produced previously unthought-of results in areas of the state with the highest concentration of Blacks. In Selma, it helped defeat Jim Clark, the thuggish sheriff who had ordered the vicious attack on the Edmund Pettus Bridge. And in Tuskegee's Macon County, where Sammy Younge registered voters on the day he was killed, a Korean War veteran named Lucius Amerson was elected sheriff—the first Black candidate to be win any office in Alabama in almost a century.

Compared with George Wallace's performance four years earlier, Lurleen Wallace received a smaller percentage of the vote in Alabama's cities and Black Belt, thanks to the surge of newly registered Blacks. But she opened even larger margins of victory in the small towns and rural areas around the state where whites were still in a majority, winning more than two thirds of the vote statewide. At a typical campaign rally, she would make a perfunctory ten-minute speech, then introduce her "No. 1 assistant." As a band played "Dixie," George Wallace would take the microphone to rail against leaders of both political parties, big-city newspapers, liberals of all stripes, and the Chase Manhattan Bank. The unconventional campaign further elevated Wallace's profile as national political figure, and positioned him for an outsider presidential candidacy two years later. Like another political outsider nearly fifty years later, Wallace would run not as a conventional candidate of either party, but as the receptacle of racial resentments rooted deeply in America's past and projected far into its future. As pollster Louis Harris put it in analyzing Lurleen Wallace's victory in 1966: "In the end, the election of Mrs. Wallace became synonymous in Alabama with the preservation of rule by the white majority."

In Lowndes County, sympathetic white newsmen who had followed the Freedom Organization experiment described the day's losses in elegiac tones. "Lowndes: A Good Day to Go Voting, But Black Panther Candidates Lose," reported a front-page headline in the liberal weekly *Southern Courier*. Yet at that very moment, another chapter of the black panther story was starting to unfold, thousands of miles and a cultural world away from rural Alabama. In the weeks before Stokely Carmichael's Berkeley speech, hundreds of Lowndes County Freedom Organization pamphlets with the panther logo had circulated around the Bay Area. Some were distributed by the conference's organizers, and others brought back to Oakland by a well-known local activist who had made a pilgrimage to Alabama. One of those pamphlets came to the attention of Huey Newton, the community college student who was dreaming of forming a new organization for the "street brothers" of Oakland. And when Newton saw the image of the prowling, sharp-pawed black feline, the last piece of his plan fell into place.

CHAPTER 15

Ten Points from the Flatlands

In March of 1966, a new weekly newspaper called *The Flatlands* began publishing in Oakland. Founded by an interracial alliance of local activists, the paper covered the distressed area, stretching between the middle-class Oakland Hills and bohemian Berkeley, that was home to much of the city's Black population, which had swelled to almost 100,000 in the years of the Great Migration. "The Flatlands people have no one to speak for them," the editors declared, promising to provide a voice of advocacy for better jobs, housing, schools, and treatment by police. During its brief, two-year existence, *The Flatlands* also became known for profiles of community leaders. In the maiden issue, it celebrated one of the paper's founders and guiding lights: a brawny, broad-faced Black man named Mark Comfort who was known around Oakland for wearing a black beret and dark sunglasses.

Born in Oklahoma, Comfort came to live with his grandmother in West Oakland when he was seven years old. At sixteen, he was sent to San Quentin prison for armed assault after fighting back against white gang members who attacked a Black Halloween party in East Oakland. By the time Comfort got out a year later, he had started reading books about the civil rights movement and had built up his skinny frame to a muscular 210 pounds. After living in Los Angeles for several years, he returned to Oakland and married a white activist named Gloria Black. Speaking at area marches after the 1963 Birmingham church bombing, Comfort discovered a "natural instinct," as he described it, for protest leadership.

Over the next three years, Comfort became Oakland's most visible and innovative Black activist. He helped lead a picketing campaign to demand that the *Oakland Tribune* hire more Blacks. When protesters blockaded the paper's delivery trucks, Comfort was arrested for disturbing the peace and refusing to leave the scene of a "riot," beginning a court battle that dragged on for two years. During that time, he formed an organization called the Oakland Direct Action Committee that monitored how police interacted with local youth. With his wife, Gloria, he also pioneered a program called the Parents Association for Better Schools that lobbied for free lunches in the city's schools.

In May of 1966, Comfort led a delegation that traveled to Hayneville, Alabama, to provide security for the nominating convention of the Lowndes County Freedom Organization. Stokely Carmichael remembered Comfort as a "serious brother, low-key and dedicated" who asked for permission to bring "the Black Panther Party idea" back to Oakland. "We don't got a patent," Carmichael responded. "Feel free. If local conditions indicate, go for it." When Comfort returned to Oakland, he passed out Lowndes Country Freedom Organization flyers and began wearing a pin of the black panther logo on his trademark beret.

When Comfort announced his candidacy for California's state assembly, however, local white authorities moved to take him off the streets. He was fired from a position helping to oversee a summer work program for high school and college students run out of the North Oakland Neighborhood Anti-Poverty Center, a federally funded "Community Action Program" launched as part of President Johnsen's War on Poverty. When a state court upheld Comfort's conviction in the *Tribune* picketing case, a judge ordered him to begin a six-month sentence immediately, despite his plan to appeal to the U.S. Supreme Court. In an emotional plea in *The Flatlands*, Gloria Comfort pointed out that even Dr. Sam Sheppard, an accused wife killer whose trial had caused a media frenzy in 1966, was allowed to remain free pending the final outcome of his case. Providing another model for more famous campaigns to come, Gloria urged the newspaper's readers to flood the governor's office with postcards marked "Free Mark Comfort."

Comfort's legal troubles left a political vacuum on the streets of the Flatlands in the summer and fall of 1966, just as Huey Newton and Bobby Seale were talking about forming an organization of their own. Nowhere in their memoirs or other accounts did either man credit Comfort's influence, although they must have been aware of his activities. Soon after Comfort lost his job with the summer work program, Seale was hired for a similar position at the North Oakland Neighborhood Anti-Poverty Center. Both Newton and Seale boasted about the number of activist publications they read, so it's likely that *The Flatlands* was among them. Although Seale would later maintain that he and Newton got the idea to wear berets from watching a movie about the World War II French Resistance, it's just as probable that they were emulating a style that Mark Comfort had already made fashionable in Oakland.

But if Newton and Seale appropriated Comfort's tactics and clothing style, they didn't heed the lessons that the older activist had learned the hard way about the need for patience and the perils of incarceration. "I'm not a lawyer, but I know what's wrong and what's right," Comfort said in the *Flatlands* profile. "I've been arrested so many times—I finally got hipped to what's going on. We gotta cool it—slow down. We can't win in a day; sitting behind bars you lose everything you built up."

When Bobby Seale started working at the North Oakland anti-poverty center in July, his job was to act as a "foreman" for the summer work program. Every morning, roughly a hundred students reported to the center, and Seale doled out assignments and helped arrange for transportation. Across the Flatlands, boys in white hard hats mowed lawns, pulled up tree stumps, painted fences, and cleaned out rat-infested basements. Girls were assigned to indoor tasks such as sorting donated clothes, babysitting, and doing clerical work.

Seale also viewed the job as an opportunity to "run down a little Black History," as he put it, for the young people. He taught them the two poems he had recited on Telegraph Avenue a few months earlier: "Burn, Baby, Burn," and "Uncle Sammy Call Me Fulla Lucifer." On a tour of a local police station, Seale encouraged the students to describe examples of abuse they had seen on the streets to a roomful of uniformed cops. "Man, those kids tore into the cops," Seale recalled proudly. "They really talked about the police brutality that half of them had actually witnessed. . . . Man, it made the cops mad, and they looked mad."

When Huey Newton also got a part-time job with the North Oakland Neighborhood Anti-Poverty Center, he discovered a legal library on the second floor. He combed through stacks of books looking for more information about California's open carry gun laws. According to his future Black Panther comrade and biographer David Hilliard, Newton also followed news reports that summer about the Community Alert Patrol (CAP), a group of Blacks who had banded together to monitor the police in Watts. So Newton may well have come across a story entitled "A Night with the Watts Community Alert Patrol" in the August issue of the SNCC newspaper *The Movement*. The writer followed a group of CAP volunteers who stationed themselves near a popular taco stand to make sure that police didn't hassle young people who gathered there. Spotting a Lowndes County black panther sticker on the bumper of a car belonging to one of the volunteers, the reporter asked the man what he knew about Black Power. "What is Black Power?" the volunteer exclaimed. "CAP is Black Power."

Yet the Watts experiment also showed how defenseless the CAP volunteers were. After they left the taco stand, police pulled two of them over and issued a speeding ticket. According to Hilliard, Newton saw other accounts of CAP tape recorders and law books being confiscated. Similar harassment had also been faced by Mark Comfort's Direct Action Committee in Oakland. The lesson, as Newton saw it, was that civilian patrols had to do more than stand watch for police to take them seriously. The patrols needed to be armed. The story in *The Movement* also suggested how much attention such an initiative could attract, from the press and from potential recruits on the streets. By late September, Newton was ready to do more than talk about his idea. "It's about time we got the organization off the ground," he told Seale. "And do it now."

IF NEWTON'S AND SEALE'S TENDENCY TOWARD COLORFUL EXAG-geration and selective memory make it hard to rely completely on their version of events before this point, the problem becomes even more vexing in reconstructing the origins of the founding document of the Black Panther Party for Self-Defense known as the "Ten Point Program." As scholars Joshua Bloom and Waldo E. Martin Jr. point out in an award-winning history of the Panthers, no physical trace of this mission statement can be found before it was printed in the first Panther newspaper published in April of 1967. However, in their memoirs and accounts to Panther historian David Hilliard, both Newton and Seale recalled writing a first draft of the program in Oc-tober of 1966.

Crediting thinkers who served as inspirations for the Ten Point Program, Newton cited the French African writer Frantz Fanon, Cuba's Che Guevara, and China's Mao Tse-tung. He gave a nod to *Negroes with Guns*, by Robert F. Williams, the favorite book of his former Merritt College comrades at the Soul Students Advisory Council. But more than anyone, Newton paid homage to Mal-colm X. "Bobby had collected all of Malcolm X's speeches and ideas from papers like *The Militant* and *Muhammed Speaks*," Newton wrote. "These we studied carefully. Although Malcolm's program for the Organization of Afro-American Unity was never put into operation, he has made it clear that Blacks ought to arm. Malcolm's influence was ever-present . . . the words on this page cannot convey the effect that Malcolm has had on the Black Panther Party, although, as far as I am concerned, the Party is a living testament to his life work. I do not claim that the Party has done what Malcolm would have done. Many others say that their programs are Malcolm's programs. We do not say this, but Malcolm's spirit is in us."

Although Newton never mentioned Malcolm X's specific influence on the structure and tone of the Ten Point Program, what he and Seale produced bore marked similarities to the blueprint for the OAAU that Malcolm laid out at the Audubon Ballroom in June of 1964. It featured the same numbered call for action, elaboration of broad principles, and language and tone borrowed from the Founding Fathers—although none of Malcolm's praise for the example of putting aside ideological differences set by the Organization of African Unity.

In Newton's telling, writing the program took only twenty minutes, with Huey "rapping off" ideas and Bobby writing them down. By David Hilliard's more likely account, the process involved drafting, revising, and editing that took place over several weeks, at the North Oakland antipoverty office during the day and at Seale's house at night.

"Now, what's the first thing we want?" Seale recalled Newton asking. "We want freedom."

Seale wrote that down in capital letters: "WE WANT FREEDOM."

"We want the power to determine the destiny of our black community," Newton continued.

"Right, brother, that's good," Seale nodded, scribbling down that point.

As the back-and-forth continued, the two men decided to start each demand with a statement of "what we want," followed by a declaration of "what we believe." They settled on ten points in all, and to get to that round number they ended the statement with a long, almost word-for-word quotation from the Declaration of Independence. Once a draft was complete, according to Hilliard, Seale's wife, Artie, typed up a copy, Newton's brother Melvin proofread it, and Artie created a mimeograph stencil. But Newton and Seale had yet to come up with a name for their new organization, so Artie left a blank space at the top of the stencil.

How and when Newton and Seale chose the black panther name and emblem became another subject of disagreement. Hilliard wrote that it happened on Seale's birthday, October 22, after Newton saw a flyer from the Lowndes County Freedom Organization that Seale had received in the mail. Newton also recalled getting the idea from a Lowndes County pamphlet, but telling Seale about it several days later. It's possible that Newton saw one of the flyers that Mark Comfort brought back from Alabama. Whatever the case, Newton recalled that "the image seemed appropriate" and that Seale "agreed without discussion." In his memoir, Newton described the appeal of the panther in language very similar to that used by Carmichael and John Hulett in interviews with *The Movement*. "The panther is a fierce animal," he wrote, "but he will not attack until he is backed into a corner; then he will strike out."

Once the new party had a name, according to Hilliard's account, Artie Seale filled in the top of the stencil. Newton and Seale printed hundreds copies of the manifesto using a mimeograph machine at the North Oakland center and office paper paid for by federal antipoverty dollars. They filled three empty boxes with flyers and drove to Seale's house, where they stored two boxes in the garage and kept a third in the car to begin distributing on porches and at bars and barbershops across Oakland. The flyers read:

OCTOBER 1966
THE BLACK PANTHER PARTY
PLATFORM AND PROGRAM
WHAT WE WANT
WHAT WE BELIEVE

1. *We want freedom. We want power to determine the destiny of our Black Community.*

   We believe that black people will not be free until we are able to determine our own destiny.

2. *We want full employment for our people.*

   We believe that the federal government is responsible and obligated to give every man employment or a guaranteed income. We believe that if the White American businessmen will not give full employment, then the means of production should be taken from the businessmen and placed in the community so that the people of the community can organize and employ all of its people and give a high standard of living.

3. *We want an end to the robbery by the white men of our Black Community.*

We believe that this racist government has robbed us and now we are demanding the overdue debt of forty acres and two mules. Forty acres and two mules was promised 100 years ago as redistribution for slave labor and mass murder of black people. We will accept the payment in currency which will be distributed to our many communities. The Germans are now aiding the Jews in Israel for the genocide of the Jewish people. The Germans murdered six million Jews. The American racist has taken part in the slaughter of over fifty million black people; therefore, we feel that this is a modest demand that we make.

4. *We want decent housing, fit for shelter of human beings.*

We believe that if the white landlords will not give decent housing to our black community, then the housing and the land should be made into cooperatives so that our community, with government aid, can build and make decent housing for its people.

5. *We want education for our people that exposes the true nature of this decadent American society. We want education that teaches us our true history and our role in the present-day society.*

We believe in an educational system that will give our people a knowledge of self. If a man does not have knowledge of himself and his position in society and the world, then he has little chance to relate to anything else.

6. *We want all black men to be exempt from military service.*

We believe that black people should not be forced to fight in the military service to defend a racist government that does not protect us. We will not fight and kill other people of color in the world who, like black people, are being victimized by the white racist government of America. We will protect ourselves from the force and violence of the racist police and the racist military, by whatever means necessary.

7. *We want an immediate end to POLICE BRUTALITY and MURDER of black people.*

We believe we can end police brutality in our black community by organizing black self-defense groups that are dedicated to defending our black community from racist police oppression and brutality. The Second Amendment to the Constitution of the United States gives a right to bear arms. We therefore believe that all black people should arm themselves for self-defense.

8. *We want freedom for all black men held in federal, state, county and city prisons and jails.*

We believe that all black people should be released from the many jails and prisons because they have not received a fair and impartial trial.

9. *We want black people when brought to trial to be tried in court by a jury of their peer group or people from their black communities, as defined by the Constitution of the United States.*

We believe that the courts should follow the United States Constitution so that black people will receive fair trials. The Fourteenth Amendment of the U.S. Constitution gives a man a right to be tried by his peer group. A peer is a person from a similar economic, social, religious, geographical, environmental, historical, and racial background. To do this the court will be forced to select a jury from the black community from which the black defendant came. We have been and are being tried by all-white juries that have no understanding of "the average reasoning man" of the black community.

10. *We want land, bread, housing, education, clothing, justice, and peace. And as our major political objective, a United Nations–supervised plebiscite to be held throughout the black colony in which only black colonial subjects will be allowed to participate, for the purpose of determining the will of black people as to their national identity.*

When, in the course of human events, it becomes necessary for one people to dissolve the political bands which have connected them with another, and to assume, among the powers of the earth, the separate and equal station to which the laws of nature and nature's God entitle them, a decent respect to the opinions of mankind requires that they should declare the causes which impel them to separation.

We hold these truths to be self-evident, that all men are created equal; that they are endowed by their Creator with certain unalienable rights; that among these are life, liberty, and the pursuit of happiness. That, to secure these rights, governments are instituted among men, deriving their just powers from the consent of the governed; that, whenever any form of government becomes destructive of these ends, it is the right of the people to alter or to abolish it, and to institute a new government, laying its foundation on such principles, and organizing its power in such form, as to them shall seem most likely to effect their safety and happiness. Prudence, indeed, will dictate that governments long established should not be changed for light and transient causes; and, accordingly, all experience hath shown, that mankind are more disposed to suffer, while evils are sufferable, than to right themselves by abolishing the forms to which they are accustomed. But, when a long train of abuses and usurpations, pursuing invariably the same object, evinces a design to reduce them under absolute despotism, it is their right, it is their duty, to throw off such government, and to provide new guards for their future security.

Having produced a founding document, Newton and Seale turned to the issue of organizational structure. According to Seale, Newton proposed two positions—"Chairman," and "Minister of Defense"—and asked which one Seale preferred.

"Doesn't make any difference to me," Seale replied. "What do you want to be?"

Figuring that Seale's gregarious nature was suited to a front man role—and drawn to the aura of strength and mystery conjured up by "Minster of Defense"—Newton opted for the second title and offered the chairmanship to Seale.

Around this time, Newton and Seale also attracted their first recruit: a sixteen-year-old kid from the Flatlands they called "L'il Bobby" Hutton. The nickname was meant to distinguish Hutton from Bobby Seale, but it was also a description of the youth's size and appearance. Just a few inches taller than five feet, Hutton had a round baby face, wide-set eyes, and only the wispy beginnings of an adult mustache. Like the two older men, he was born in the South, in Arkansas, and had moved to Oakland with his parents and two siblings at the age of three after his family was threatened by night riders affiliated with the Klan. That summer, Hutton had applied to the North Oakland antipoverty center jobs program even though he was too young to qualify, and Seale was so impressed with his wiry energy and eagerness to learn that he admitted him anyway. When the summer was over, Hutton kept working at the antipoverty office and spent so much time hanging out with Newton and Seale that he was expelled from school. When he showed up at the center as the two founders were printing the Ten Point Program flyers, they invited Hutton to become an official member the party. They even offered L'il Bobby his own big-sounding title: "Treasurer."

OF NEWTON AND SEALE'S TEN POINTS, MOST WERE SWEEPING demands without any prescription for how to achieve them. Some were ahead of their time, such as the call for repayment in "currency" for the "forty acres and two mules" that foreshadowed a nationwide debate fifty years later over Black "reparations." But one point made an immediate and practical call to action. Newton and Seale assigned the number seven—with its special symbolism in the Black religious tradition—to the matter of guns and the police. Making point seven stand out by using capital letters, they called for "an immediate end to POLICE BRUTALITY and MURDER of black people," and proposed "organizing black self-defense groups that are dedicated to defending our black community from racist police oppression."

To make good on that promise of self-defense groups, Newton and Seale required more weapons, and in late November they discovered where to find them. At Merritt College, they heard about a Japanese American student activist named Richard Aoki who had an extensive stash of firearms for sale. With slicked-back hair and dark sunglasses that he wore everywhere he went, Aoki cut a dashingly radical figure. When Newton and Seale met with him, he agreed to lend them an M-1 rifle and a 9mm pistol free of charge. At the time, Seale flattered himself that he had impressed the gun dealer with an appeal to show that he was a "real revolutionary." Only later was it revealed that Aoki possessed so many weapons and was so generous with them because he was a paid informant for the FBI.

Based on his study of California law, Newton knew that, as a convicted felon on parole, he was prohibited from carrying handguns. So he took the M-1 rifle and let Seale carry the 9mm. With their guns as calling cards, they spent the month of December spreading the word about their police watchdog plan. Newton frequented a bar called Bosn's Locker in North Oakland, where he kept the M-1 rifle on display while holding court. "I used to call it my office because I would sometimes sit in there for twenty hours straight talking with the people who came in," Newton recalled. The duo also began to drive around the city looking for police. When they saw a cop interacting with a Black person on the street, Newton would get out of the car with his M-1 in one hand and a law book in the other. Standing at a distance, he read aloud from the open carry statutes. "Shock-a-buku," he called the ritual, and at first it seemed to work. After taking down Newton's license plate number, the police usually drove away without arresting the suspect they had been questioning.

By the end of December, Newton and Seale had raised $170 to buy more guns by purchasing copies of Mao Tse-tung's "Little Red Book" at a Chinese bookstore in San Francisco for thirty cents a copy and reselling them outside the Berkeley campus for a dollar. They found a vacant storefront on a corner in North Oakland and along with Bobby Hutton pooled their paychecks from the antipoverty program to put down a first month's rent of $150. The three men hung a "Black Panther Party for Self-Defense" sign in the window, and opened for business on New Year's Day 1967. Within weeks, they were attracting enough recruits to launch regular neighborhood police patrols resembling those Newton had read about in Watts.

In April of 1967, Newton, Seale, and Hutton took their armed patrols to the city of North Richmond, sixteen miles north of Oakland, after police there killed an unarmed twenty-two-year-old construction worker named Denzil Dowell. As word spread of their activities, a Republican state assemblyman named Don Mulford introduced a bill to make it illegal in California for civilians to carry firearms in public. On May 2, 1967, Seale and Hutton led a group of twenty-six armed Panthers to the capitol in Sacramento to protest the Mulford Act, which would pass and be signed into law by Governor Reagan two months later. Before the Sacramento protest, the self-defense party had no more than a hundred members, but as soon as images of the rifle-carrying Panthers walking into California's capitol appeared on television and in newspapers, interest in joining the new movement spread across the country.

Still on parole for his assault conviction several years earlier,

Newton stayed behind in Oakland and didn't join the protest. Of the Panthers who were photographed in Sacramento, one of the most striking was a large, muscular figure who wore a large bomber jacket and broad black sunglasses, and held an AK-47 assault rifle in a beefy grip. Although newspaper captions didn't identify him, the man was Mark Comfort, who by then had joined the party and contributed seven of his own firearms to its arsenal.

Comfort would remain on the fringes of the new party for several years, his role in inspiring Newton and Seale never recognized by the media. Yet in an ironic turnabout, just as Comfort's accomplishments had been eclipsed by those two men, something similar was about to happen to Newton and Seale themselves. By the end of 1966, fate conspired to put another older recruit in their path, one who would dramatically alter the direction and image of the new Black Panther Party for Self-Defense before it had a chance to make good on its initial promise of addressing the local problems of the Flatlands.

LIKE NEWTON, SEALE, AND BOBBY HUTTON, LEROY ELDRIDGE Cleaver was a child of the Great Migration from the South to the West. He was born in 1935 in Wabbaseka, Arkansas, a small town on the outskirts of Pine Bluff, to Thelma Robinson, a schoolteacher, and Leroy Cleaver Sr., a railroad waiter and part-time nightclub piano player. A decade later, when Leroy Sr. got a job on the luxury Super Chief sleeping car line that ran from Chicago to Los Angeles, he moved his family to Phoenix, and then to Watts.

Leroy Sr. was a violent and unfaithful man, and soon he left his wife and six children and moved to Chicago. Thelma resorted to working as a high school janitor, and Eldridge, as Leroy Jr. now called himself, drifted into drug use and petty crime. He was sent to reform school for stealing a bicycle, and was sentenced to prison for selling marijuana by the age of eighteen. Radicalized by the news of Emmett Till's lynching in Mississippi, Cleaver emerged from that first jail stint as a rage-filled man of six feet five inches on a twisted mission to seek revenge on white women. At twenty-three, he was arrested and sentenced to serve an extended jail term for "assault with intent to murder" after attempting to rape a white nurse.

During his second prison stay, Cleaver began to keep a diary and write essays as a form of repentance and self-discovery. "That is why I started to write, to save myself," he recalled. Reading accounts of Malcolm X, he became a follower of the Nation of Islam, then sided with Malcolm when he broke with Elijah Muhammad. In early 1965, Cleaver was both shattered and emboldened by the news of Malcolm's murder. Quoting the words of actor Ossie Davis at Malcolm's funeral—"Malcolm was our manhood, our living, black manhood"— Cleaver wrote in his prison diary: "We shall have our manhood. We shall have it or the earth will be leveled by our attempts to gain it."

Soon afterward, Cleaver decided to seek early release, and he came across a story in a local community newspaper called the *Sun Reporter* about a white lawyer named Beverly Axelrod who defended Black clients. The small, dark-haired attorney began to visit Eldridge in prison and to sneak out samples of his writing that she passed along to Edward Keating, publisher of *Ramparts* magazine. Keating was so impressed that he agreed to publish Cleaver's work and to send examples to influential authors such as Norman Mailer and Thomas Merton. With letters of support from Keating and several literary luminaries, Axelrod secured Cleaver's parole—and he walked out of San Quentin Prison on December 12, 1966.

Cleaver didn't encounter Huey Newton and Bobby Seale until several months later, in early 1967. Before the three ever met, however, his *Ramparts* essays showed why he would quickly become a domineering force in the new Black Panther Party, but also how different his talents and motivations were from the two founders. Cleaver's strengths didn't lie in community organizing or understanding the needs of poor neighborhoods in the urban North, given that he had spent his childhood in the South and much of his adult life in prison. His gifts were for using words—and for commanding attention.

What stood out about Cleaver's prison essays was how cleverly crafted they were to shock and seduce at the same time. Writing of his time as a rapist in "On Becoming," he described himself "practicing on black girls in the ghetto . . . [until] when I considered myself smooth enough, I crossed the tracks and sought out white prey." Cleaver called rape "an insurrectionary act," turning indefensible assault into a bid for racial sympathy and a prelude to moral redemption. "After I returned to prison," he wrote, "I took a long look at myself, and for the first time in my life, admitted that I was wrong, that I had gone astray—astray not so much from the white man's law as from being human, civilized—for I could not approve the act of rape."

In his essay "Soul on Ice"—the title he later gave his book—Cleaver confessed to having fallen "in love" with Beverly Axelrod and written her awkward love letters. His ardent tone obscured how inappropriate and manipulative such behavior was in dealing with his own attorney. In "Notes on a Native Son," Cleaver offered a critique of James Baldwin as a self-hating Black man obsessed with white European culture that was heralded at the time. Critic Maxwell Geismar called the essay "the best analysis of James Baldwin's literary career I have read." Decades later, the critique would come across as deeply presumptuous and homophobic. Cleaver was upset that Baldwin had criticized his own literary hero, Richard Wright, in an essay entitled "Alas, Poor Richard." Daring to put himself on the same plane as those two artistic giants, Cleaver concluded that the dispute was the result of Baldwin's homosexuality. "Baldwin's essay on Richard Wright reveals that he despised—not Richard Wright, but his masculinity," he wrote. "He cannot confront the stud in others—except that he must either submit to it or destroy it."

AS SOON AS CLEAVER LEFT PRISON, HE WAS OFFERED A STAFF writer position at *Ramparts*. With his confident strut and watchful green eyes, he exuded "a sense of danger mitigated by an odd introspection and self-irony," recalled Peter Collier, the assistant to the magazine's editor, Robert Scheer. "Talking to him was like playing tennis against a wall," Collier said. "The ball always came back just as hard as you hit it." Imagining himself carrying on the legacy of Malcolm X, Cleaver went on local radio to talk about Malcolm's plans for the Organization of Afro-American Unity, and helped found a San Francisco hangout center called the "Black House" where Malcolm's teachings were studied. According to Cleaver, he first met Newton and Seale when they visited him at the radio station, then started attending meetings at the Black House.

As the second anniversary of Malcolm X's death approached in February 1967, Cleaver had the idea to invite his widow, Betty Shabazz, to the Bay Area for one of her first public appearances since the assassination. Shabazz agreed on condition that she be picked up at the airport and provided with transportation and security. Newton and Seale volunteered for that duty and, on the day of Shabazz's arrival, met her at the airport with a detail of armed Panthers. Having fallen asleep on the plane, Shabazz was startled to see policemen at the gate, then understood why as soon as she rounded a corner and found the Panthers brandishing their weapons and reciting from California law books. "Oh wow," Shabazz recalled thinking. "That's really fantastic." Arriving at the *Ramparts* office in the waterfront Embarcadero neighborhood of San Francisco, the Panthers escorted Shabazz inside the building to be interviewed by Cleaver.

It was the first time Cleaver had seen the Panthers in their full regalia of berets, leather jackets, and firearms, and he was transfixed. After the interview was over, he watched as the Panthers escorted Shabazz out of the magazine's headquarters and Newton clashed with a portly police officer who warned him to lower his rifle.

"Don't point that gun at me!" the officer snapped at Newton.

Newton stared down the policeman. "What's the matter, you got an itchy trigger finger," he taunted. "You want to draw the gun?"

When the officer didn't respond, Newton loaded a shell into his shotgun. "Okay, you big, fat racist pig, draw your gun," he said. "I'm waiting."

After several tense minutes, the policeman backed off and let the Panthers pass by. Cleaver was in awe. "You're the baddest motherfucker I've ever seen," he recalled thinking about Newton, and soon afterward he contacted the Panthers to offer his services for a role that would soon lead to Cleaver joining the party as "Minister of Information."

While still reporting for *Ramparts*, Cleaver also traveled east to profile Stokely Carmichael. He followed Carmichael to a student conference at Fisk University in Tennessee that had been organized by Kathleen Neal, the Barnard student and childhood friend of Sammy Younge's who dropped out of college to join SNCC in 1966. Afterward, Neal wrote Cleaver a love letter, and by the end of 1967 she had moved to the San Francisco area and married him. Taking the position of "Communications Secretary," Kathleen Cleaver went on to make her own sizable contribution to the Panther party's image and message, with her towering Afro, penetrating blue eyes, and forceful speaking presence.

While previous profiles of Carmichael had focused on his appeal, Cleaver's *Ramparts* story slyly exposed Stokely's growing political vulnerability. Less than a year after emerging as the prophet of Black Power, Carmichael was under attack from some Black militants for not being radical enough. In Chicago, Cleaver followed him from a radio interview with white journalists Irv Kupcinet and Studs Terkel to a meeting with a Black group called ACT for Freedom. "What're you doing downtown talking to white folks?" a militant in a Kenyan skullcap asked Carmichael in a confrontational tone. "Why don't you have time for your own people?"

Soon after that profile appeared, Cleaver quit *Ramparts* to devote himself full-time to the Panther party, and he quickly proved a master of provocative marketing. He founded a newspaper called *The Black Panther* that began with a first printing of ten thousand copies and soon attained a nationwide circulation of 100,000. He staged a photograph of Newton sitting on a thronelike wicker chair, clutching his M-1 rifle in one hand and a spear in the other, that was sold as a poster and found its way onto bedroom walls across America. Cleaver also popularized a phrase that became a rallying cry for radicals of all stripes: "You're either part of the problem, or part of the solution."

In October of 1967, Newton was out celebrating the end of his probation in the Odell Lee case when he was pulled over by an Oakland police officer name John Frey. In the ensuing confrontation, gunfire was exchanged, Huey lost consciousness, and Frey was shot dead. Although Newton insisted he didn't fire the fatal bullets, he was sent back to prison, beginning a three-year legal odyssey that would include a conviction for manslaughter, a reversed sentence, and two hung juries, before the charges against him were finally dismissed. As Newton's latest legal ordeal began, Cleaver took control of the Panther's Party's messaging, and amped up the inflammatory rhetoric and image-making. Cleaver produced a newsreel-style film in which uniformed Panthers marched around Oakland in military formation and massed outside the Alameda County Courthouse, where Newton was being held, chanting "Off the pigs!" and "The revolution has come! Time to pick up the gun!"

For a time, the rhetoric was mostly for show, designed to draw media coverage and ensure that no other militant group outflanked the Panthers. But in April of 1968, as rioting swept America two days after Dr. King's assassination, Cleaver put the posturing talk into action by leading a group of fourteen Panthers armed with M-16 rifles and shotguns in a raid on an Oakland police station. When the Panthers found police waiting for them, they took cover in the apartment of two Black sisters in West Oakland, and during a ninety-minute shootout three officers were wounded. Tear-gassed and running out of ammunition, Cleaver finally agreed to surrender, and told the Panthers to strip naked as they were exiting the building. But L'il Bobby Hutton—the party's eager first recruit, who had become like a younger brother to Newton and Seale—was self-conscious about taking off all his clothes and emerged only shirtless.

The Oakland police would later maintain that Hutton was trying to run away when they pumped ten bullets into his small body. But other witnesses, including some of the officers present, insisted that he had his hands up. Six days later twelve hundred people attended L'il Bobby's funeral at a Berkeley church, including James Baldwin and the actor Marlon Brando, but Huey Newton was forced to grieve for his young friend alone in an Alameda County jail cell. Cleaver was detained, then freed on bond, and before he could be sent back to prison he fled the country, first to Cuba and then Algeria, where he was joined by Kathleen. From exile, Eldridge waged an increasingly heated long-distance battle with the imprisoned Newton over the direction and message of the Panther party. He proclaimed himself the head of a revolutionary "International Section, headquartered in Algiers," and denounced the Newton allies who had taken over the party leadership in Oakland as a "right wing . . . breakfast-for-children club" that had "put a muzzle on the Panther." By the time Newton was released in 1970, he had had enough of Cleaver's incendiary bluster. He moved to expel Cleaver from the party and to continue bringing the Panthers back to the more modest mission of serving the people of Oakland with legal aid centers and medical clinics, as well as the free breakfast programs for children.

A year later, in 1971, Newton made an improbable appearance on *Firing Line*, the television interview show hosted by conservative commentator and editor William F. Buckley Jr. In his surprisingly soft, high-pitched voice, Newton expressed remorse for the bloody turn the Panther party had taken during the years he was in prison. Without mentioning L'il Bobby Hutton by name, he confessed sorrowfully: "I contributed so much to almost the destruction of our party and so many fallen comrades who are in their grave or in prison. These are things that I have to live with." But Newton placed even more of the blame on Eldridge Cleaver, the man to whom he had been yoked by accidents of time and place beginning in 1966. Newton sniped that Cleaver turned into an "MF"—a "Media Freak" intent on glorifying violence for its own sake. "With Eldridge's influence, the gun was not just the symbol of revolution, it was the revolution," Newton said, and that image had "led the whole organization down the drain."

The press also bore some responsibility because it had fallen for the spectacle, Newton reminded Buckley. Cleaver "created what I call a media organization," Newton said, in which community organizing took a backseat to doing something provocative anytime "the news reporter comes and puts the camera up." When it came to attracting attention, if nothing else, the strategy had worked with a media increasingly dominated by storytelling through photographs and television imagery. "It's a little different than a paper organization," Newton said with a sardonic smile. "But we're in a push-button world now, right?"

CHAPTER 16

The Peg Leg Bates Purge

On the first day of December 1966, a car carrying two Black women and a white man drove north through New York's Catskill Mountains across a dreary landscape scattered with soot-tinged early-winter snow. One of the women was Ella Baker, the revered civil rights veteran who had encouraged the young pioneers of the sit-in movement and Freedom Rides to form an organization of their own. The other was Joanne Grant, a mixed-race, left-wing journalist and friend of Baker's. The man was Bob Zellner, a lanky twenty-seven-year-old Southerner with warm eyes and a soft drawl who had been one of SNCC's first white recruits. Although Zellner was a longtime friend of both women, on this trip he felt too apprehensive to make conversation. Noticing his somber mood, Baker and Grant treated Zellner as though he had some sort of "illness," he recalled, "and only they could comfort me."

The trio's destination was the Peg Leg Bates Country Club, the only Black-owned hotel in the region known as "the Borscht Belt," with its summer resorts catering mostly to Jewish city dwellers. The facility was owned by the son of a North Carolina sharecropper and childhood tap dance prodigy named Clayton Bates, known as "Peg Leg" because he lost his left leg in a cotton gin accident at the age of twelve and taught himself how to perform with a wooden prosthesis. By the mid-1960s, Bates was known to the broad public mostly for his appearances on *The Ed Sullivan Show*, where he tapped, jumped, and twirled on the wooden leg while mugging for a studio audience. But within Black America, Bates was also respected as a savvy business-man. "Peg," as he was known, had purchased a former turkey farm in the town of Kerhonkson, New York, and transformed it into a resort where Blacks, too, could spend summer vacations lazing around an outdoor pool, stuffing themselves from dinner buffets, and laughing at the salty routines of comedians from the "Chitlin' Circuit."

Negotiating an off-season discount, SNCC booked the Peg Leg Bates hotel for its first staff-wide retreat since the meeting in Kingston Springs. More than a hundred members and longtime allies such as Ella Baker and Joanne Grant attended, and they had much to discuss, including the struggles of SNCC's Southern field offices and the im-pact of Stokely Carmichael's high-profile Black Power and antiwar campaigns. Yet virtually none of those other issues were addressed as the meeting became inflamed with a bitter debate over the role of whites in SNCC. Alcohol, marijuana, and hallucinogenic drugs were consumed in such quantities that many participants later couldn't re-member exactly what was decided. But after six exhausting days, in another middle-of-the-night vote, a small militant faction narrowly prevailed in a motion to expel all the remaining white members of the organization—including two of SNCC's longest-serving and most beloved staffers, Bob Zellner and his wife, the former Dottie Miller.

BORN JOHN ROBERT ZELLNER IN WESTERN FLORIDA, BOB CAME from a family with long ties to the Ku Klux Klan. His grandfather, J. O. Zellner, a dispatcher for the Gulf, Mobile and Ohio Railroad, was one of many in that industry recruited by the Klan to keep South-ern rail travel segregated. Bob's father, James Abraham Zellner, joined the Klan as soon as he turned eighteen, before he became a Methodist minister and renounced the affiliation. The Zellners and their five sons moved from parish to parish across the South before settling in Mobile, Alabama. In high school, Bob was lured by classmates on a joyride attack on Black locals that he recognized as a "test" to see if he, too, was Klan material. Instead of going down that path, he began to follow in his father's footsteps by enrolling at Huntingdon College, a school run by the Methodist Episcopal church in Montgomery.

In his senior year at Huntingdon College, Zellner took a sociology class taught by a professor named Arlie B. Davidson who assigned a research paper on race relations. Since they were in Montgomery, Zellner and five of his classmates proposed to interview Dr. King and other veterans of the Montgomery Improvement Association (MIA), the organization that led the famous bus boycott. "Dr. Arlie B," as the students called him, was aghast. "Go to Martin Luther King, the MIA?" the professor sputtered. "You can't do that, why you'll be arrested!" Ignoring Davidson's warnings, the Huntingdon Five approached Ralph Abernathy, the MIA leader who was then pastor of Montgomery's First Baptist Church. Abernathy started inviting the five to MIA workshops and arranged for them to meet with students from Alabama State University, a local historically Black college.

The activities of the Huntingdon Five soon became the scandalized talk of white Montgomery. At one MIA meeting, police appeared looking for the students and Zellner and his classmates snuck out the back door. Alabama's attorney general summoned the five to the state capitol to warn that they had "fallen in with the wrong crowd" and to accuse the MIA of being controlled by "communist influence." The president of Huntingdon College, Hubert Searcy, chastised the group as "trouble makers" and called them a disgrace to the school. "Don't you realize you have embarrassed this institution?" Searcy scolded.

In May of Zellner's senior year, the Huntingdon Five learned that the Freedom Riders were coming to Montgomery, and they decided to go the bus station downtown to watch their arrival. Two Trailways buses carrying the riders had been attacked in Anniston, Alabama, and then in Birmingham. As the buses reached the city limits of Montgomery, a state trooper patrol pulled back to let city authorities take over. But Montgomery police were nowhere to be seen as a mob of whites converged on the riders and beat them bloody with baseball bats, pipes, and hammers. Arriving at the bus station too late to witness the assault, Zellner and his classmates beheld the gruesome aftermath: a parking lot littered with broken, blood-stained glass, and a crowd of gleeful whites setting fire to the Freedom Riders' suitcases.

By that time, Zellner had caught the eye of Anne Braden, an older white activist who worked for a civil rights group called the Southern Conference Educational Fund (SCEF). Braden invited Zellner and his father to the Highlander Folk School, the renowned labor and civil rights training center in Tennessee. During his stay, Zellner met Ella Baker and Septima Clark, the civil rights legend known as the "Mother of the Movement." Before leaving, he also received a job offer. SCEF had given SNCC a $5,000 grant to hire a staffer to reach out to white campuses, and Braden asked Zellner if was interested in the position. So at the end of that summer of 1961, the Zellner family packed up Bob's belongings into their road-worn Chevrolet sedan and drove him to Atlanta to begin working at SNCC headquarters.

All Zellner knew about the job was a telegram he had received from Jim Forman, SNCC's recently appointed executive secretary. Forman instructed Zellner to check into the YMCA on Auburn Avenue and report to the SNCC office nearby. The headquarters turned out to be no more than a single room, on a hallway opposite a beauty salon, furnished with a desk, a telephone, a metal bookcase, and an empty filing cabinet. No one was in sight until Forman appeared, his bulky frame draped in baggy pants and an ill-fitting blazer. Forman was carrying a reel-to-reel tape recorder and a large duffel bag that contained all of SNCC's existing documents at the time. When Zellner introduced himself in his Alabama accent, Forman frowned and turned on the tape recorder. For the next two hours, he grilled Zellner with questions about his upbringing and family ties to the Klan that seemed designed to determine if he was a spy. "I hope your story holds up," Forman warned.

For the next month, Forman continued to treat Zellner suspiciously until the two shared a bloody baptism by fire in Mississippi. In October, they received word that Herbert Lee, a local activist who was helping to register voters in Amite County, had been murdered. To honor Lee's memory, Forman decided to hold a SNCC summit in the nearby town of McComb. With several other staffers, Forman and Zellner drove South in a used green 1953 Chevrolet. Zellner hid under the floorboards during the day and covered himself with a blanket when the car pulled into gas stations at night. When the group arrived in the middle of the night in McComb, Zellner met the rest of SNCC's early leaders—including the organization's first chairman, Marion Barry; his successor, Chuck McDew; and the legendary organizer from New York City, Bob Moses.

Before the meeting started, some local high school students appeared at the house where the SNCC workers were staying and announced that they intended to march to nearby Magnolia, Mississippi, to protest the arrest of a classmate who had participated in a vigil after Herbert Lee's murder. A group including Zellner volunteered to go with the students to provide support and protection. But as soon as the marchers reached McComb's City Hall, a white mob assaulted them. A group of men that included a Klan member Zellner had known at Huntingdon College surrounded him on the City Hall steps. As Zellner clung to a railing, one Klansman grabbed his belt buckle to pry him loose, while two others pummeled him with a rusty pipe and tried to gouge out his eyeball.

Zellner passed out. When he came to, he was covered with bruises and sitting in the office of McComb's police chief. "I shoulda let them kill ya," the chief snarled, calling Zellner a "dirty, nigger loving son of a bitch" and ordering him out of the office. When Zellner went outside, a pickup truck full of Klansmen was waiting. The Klansmen drove Zellner to an empty field and threatened him with a noose before delivering him to the county jail in Magnolia. Along with Moses and McDew, Zellner was held for "contributing to the delinquency of a minor" before the three posted bail so they could continue the SNCC meeting in Atlanta.

From that point onward, Zellner rarely strayed from the SNCC policy of "jail, no bail." A month after the McComb attack, he traveled to Albany, Georgia, to take part in the Albany Movement desegregation protests led jointly by SNCC and the SCLC. He was arrested as soon as he arrived at the railway station and thrown in a windowless prison cell. For weeks, he was assigned to a work gang during the day and kept awake at night by eleven other prisoners who shared two six-tier metal bunk beds. Soon after Zeller finished the stint in Albany, he joined a protest in Baton Rouge Parish, Louisiana. There, he was sentenced along with Chuck McDew for "attempt to overthrow the government" of the parish. Zellner served two weeks in a dank cell where guards doused prisoners with cold water and beat the soles of their feet at night. For another week, he was moved to a "sweat box" before being set free after thirty-five days.

In the spring of 1962, SNCC sent Zellner to organize in his home state of Alabama. He became a field secretary based in Talladega, and the target of state politicians who, as he put it, "were embarrassed that I was from Alabama." He became a personal obsession for George Wallace, the segregationist who had just been elected governor. Before his inauguration, Wallace instructed a state investigator to find grounds for arresting Zellner. When the FBI found out, it launched an investigation into whether Wallace had exceeded his authority before taking office. Furious, Wallace looked for other charges to pin on Zellner, from passing a bad check at a pawn shop to committing "vagrancy" when he visited his alma mater, Huntingdon College.

BY 1963, ZELLNER HAD BEGUN DATING DOTTIE MILLER, JULIAN Bond's deputy in the Atlanta communications office. That June, the two traveled together to help integrate lunch counters and a library in Danville, Virginia. As an interracial group of more than sixty protesters knelt and prayed at the Danville City Hall, policemen attacked them with nightsticks and water cannons, injuring two thirds of the demonstrators so badly they had to be taken to the hospital. The water cannons washed Miller, who weighed only 106 pounds, under a car and swept away her sandals. When she emerged, a policeman bashed her forehead with a billy club.

Jim Forman rushed to Danville from Atlanta, along with Danny Lyon, the white University of Chicago student who had been hired as SNCC's staff photographer. In one of Lyon's photos, a barefoot Miller gave an account of the attack to Forman, who wrote out an

affidavit. Word reached the church where the organizers were staying that police planned to arrest them under Virginia's "John Brown
statute" barring whites from inciting Blacks. While Miller and Lyon
snuck out the back to return to Atlanta, Zellner volunteered to stay
behind with a Black colleague as a "salt and pepper team" to face the
police. When the two men left the church, they had to duck gunfire
before nearby Black residents helped them escape from Danville.

At that point, it had been three years since Dottie Miller, newly
graduated from Queens College, sat in a Manhattan coffee shop and
read a *New York Times* story about the first lunch counter sit-ins in
Greensboro, North Carolina. Her parents, a British-born dentist
named Barney Miller and his wife, Sara, whom he had met in Canada, were Jewish leftists who had taken Dottie as a child to see Paul
Robeson perform and W. E. B. Du Bois speak. Now Dottie felt inspired to experience the racial justice movement firsthand. She applied to attend a workshop on nonviolent protest organized by CORE
in Miami, then accompanied activists she met there to assist with the
North Carolina sit-ins. Taking a job as a researcher at a civil rights
group called the Southern Regional Council in Atlanta, she began to
hear stories about a new student-run organization several blocks away
called SNCC. When Miller mustered the courage to visit SNCC's
tiny office, accompanying a curious foreign correspondent from Denmark, she met Jim Forman. He greeted her with three words: "Can
you type?" Miller could—sloppily but speedily—so Forman offered
her night work. When she mentioned that she could write, too—she
had been the editor of the student newspaper at Queens College—
Forman perked up and assigned Miller to help his communications
director, Julian Bond.

While Bob Zellner was winning the respect of Black organizers
in the field, Miller became a valued member of the collegial staff at
the Atlanta office. Hired full-time in the summer of 1962, she put in
long days churning out press releases, answering calls from reporters,
and firing off telegrams to politicians in Washington. But she also
cherished lighter moments when everyone stopped work to listen
to SNCC's Freedom Singers, or gathered after hours with visiting

fieldworkers at Paschal's restaurant or the Royal Peacock Club, another SNCC haunt. Looking back decades later, Miller described the sense of interracial fellowship at the Atlanta office with a phrase made famous by Dr. King and adopted by the young civil rights generation. "I was comfortable being in a tiny minority of white people in a black-led organization in a black world," she wrote, "and I enjoyed being a part of 'the beloved community,' the lofty expression that SNCC members used in the early days of the sit-in movement to describe not only the goal they were seeking, but their human relationships."

During his visits to SNCC headquarters, Miller got to know Bob Zellner. She was fascinated, as she put it, by this "unique . . . white Southerner who had broken with segregationists and worked for a predominantly black organization." For his part, Zellner was smitten with Miller's lively mind and dark-haired air of urban sophistication. They became lovers, and before long they were also part of the public face of SNCC. In one image that Danny Lyon captured as SNCC's photographer, Zellner and Miller joined members of the Freedom Singers around a microphone at an outdoor protest. In what became an iconic image captured by the renowned portrait photographer Richard Avedon, Julian Bond stood at the head of a group of SNCC staffers on a street outside the Atlanta headquarters, with Zellner and Miller flanking him on either side.

In August of 1963, Zellner and Miller were married in an impromptu ceremony that was also photographed by Danny Lyon. Bond found a minister to do the honors late on a Saturday night, and an interracial wedding party that also included Jane Bond and Casey and Tom Hayden toasted the newlyweds. For their honeymoon, the Zellners took a cross-country car trip to visit fellow activists in California and to see family in Alabama and New York before making it to the nation's capital in time for the March on Washington. There, they joined SNCC and CORE staffers who sang freedom songs at the base of the Lincoln Memorial.

Once the Zellners were married, Bob decided to take a break from the dangers of fieldwork to pursue a graduate degree at Brandeis University. In September of 1963, he and Dottie moved to Cambridge,

Massachusetts, where she opened a SNCC office in the basement of a church near Harvard's law school. When Bob Moses proposed the idea for Freedom Summer in 1964, Dottie Zellner was put in charge of screening white volunteers from Harvard and other colleges around the region. As she put it, her job was to "weed out . . . thrill seekers who were unappreciative of the seriousness and danger of the work or who might not show the proper respect to the people of the black community."

That June, the couple moved to the small house in Greenwood, Mississippi, that served as a regional hub for Freedom Summer. Bob helped organize voter registration drives and Freedom Schools, while Dottie manned the WATS phone line, taking calls from distressed volunteers, concerned families, and reporters on deadline. The couple also served as a welcoming committee for Hollywood celebrities, and one night even gave up their bed to Harry Belafonte and Sidney Poitier, who had flown in on a private single-engine plane with a medicine bag full of cash to fund the Greenwood operation.

The Zellners were back in Cambridge for much of the tense year that followed Freedom Summer. When the couple returned to Atlanta in the summer of 1965 and Dottie went back to work at the SNCC office two days a week, bringing her newborn baby, Margaret, in a bassinet, the "beloved community" atmosphere she remembered had changed. Research director Jack Minnis and a few other white veterans were still around, but Casey Hayden and other old friends had left, drawn toward the antiwar movement or weary of the tensions over the role of women in SNCC that had surfaced during the Waveland conference.

In February of 1966, the Zellners moved to New Haven, Connecticut, so that Bob could work for a Yale sociology professor who was running for Congress. They didn't attend the Kingston Springs retreat, where it was decided that only Black fieldworkers should work in Black communities. Hearing that news, the Zellners accepted the new policy and began to make plans to organize in white areas of New Haven. But they were unaware of just how vocal and stubborn Bill Ware and his faction had become about ridding SNCC of whites.

As Bob Zellner drove north to the Peg Leg Bates hotel, he recalled, he "didn't fully understand that the die had already been cast. This is somewhat understandable because many in the movement had shielded Dottie and me from the harshest of the anti-white attitudes which had been growing in our organization. Perhaps they wanted to make an exception in our cases because they knew we had been in the movement so long."

IN PLANNING THE PEG LEG BATES AGENDA, STOKELY CARMICHAEL and Ruby Doris Robinson originally planned to devote only half an hour on the first day to the question of white participation. Carmichael's view was that whites should still be allowed to work at the Atlanta headquarters, and perhaps in Northern field offices, but not on the ground in the South. Carmichael was particularly adamant about keeping white women from working alongside Black men in the field, since that, as he put it, "drove white Southerners plumb crazy, killing crazy." But since there were only "seven or so" whites still active in SNCC by late 1966, Carmichael recalled, he thought "the role of whites in the organization was really not a pressing issue."

For her part, Robinson still felt the way she had once described to her SNCC friend Freddie Greene Biddle: tired of staffers who would rather sit around talking about white people than getting to work. She wanted the Peg Leg Bates meeting to move on quickly to addressing the crisis in fundraising and problems in the field offices. As SNCC historian Clayborne Carson put it, Robinson and the other planners hoped that "discussion is a relaxed atmosphere might reverse the decline in SNCC's effectiveness."

From the beginning, however, the atmosphere at the Catskills resort was anything but relaxed. The meeting on the first day took place in the hotel's Casino room, and began with short status reports on various initiatives. The afternoon session was scheduled to go until six o'clock before breaking for an open bar reception and a showing of a movie called *Salt of the Earth* about a labor strike against a zinc mine in Mexico. The last item on the agenda was slated to be a discussion announced as "Role of Whites in the Movement," with Bob Zellner speaking for fifteen minutes, followed by Bill Ware for another fifteen.

In his remarks, Zellner summarized the decision that had been made at Kingston Springs—that whites would stay in SNCC but focus on organizing in white communities. According to Carson's account, at that point a majority of the retreat attendees appeared in favor of maintaining that policy. But then Bill Ware took the floor and demanded that the meeting take an immediate vote on a motion to exclude all whites from SNCC. Ware contended that "the concept of Black Power" itself required that "there would be no white people in the organization at this time." Then he argued that any whites who refused to leave SNCC voluntarily should be kicked out. "Sensitive white people" would recognize that they were no longer welcome, Ware argued. "Those who don't understand that ought to be expelled."

With Ware and his supporters refusing to allow the meeting to move forward without an expulsion vote, the debate dragged into the night and became increasingly ugly over the next five days. When Fannie Lou Hamer tried to strike a conciliatory tone, Jim Forman recalled, the Ware militants snickered. "Mrs. Hamer is no longer relevant," they suggested, or "Mrs. Hamer is not at our level of development." Jim Forman was appalled at the strain of intellectual elitism within the anti-white faction. "Some people with college educations shared their disdain toward people who were slow readers or could not read at all," he recalled. Forman also blamed drugs. "A great deal of marijuana smoking and pill dropping had been introduced into the organization by then," he wrote. In the midst of the retreat, Forman tried to address the drug issue after receiving word that police had raided a SNCC office in Chicago and found a marijuana stash. But "some of the leadership were so high from smoking pot," he recalled, "that they could not participate in any meaningful discussion."

Still loyal to his old friends Bob and Dottie Zellner—and to research director Jack Minnis, who was also present at the Peg Leg Bates retreat—Forman tried to forge a compromise. When all the solutions he proposed were shouted down, he became so frustrated that he made a motion to disband SNCC entirely and donate all its funds to African liberation movements. Behind his back, the Ware faction sniped that Forman had an unspoken personal motive for keeping whites at SNCC: by late 1966, Forman had divorced his wife, Mildred, and married his girlfriend, Dinky Romilly, the white former staffer in the Atlanta office, and now she was pregnant.

Meanwhile, two other SNCC leaders were distracted by their own sexual drama during the Kerhonkson retreat. In his memoir, Cleve Sellers remembered the meeting mostly for a fight that took place there with a girlfriend name Sandy. He had met the tall, smiling eighteen-year-old during the Meredith March, when she volunteered to work at the closing rally in Jackson. Sellers persuaded Sandy to return with him to Atlanta, but he was so busy that he barely saw her. Soon Sellers discovered that Sandy had begun to keep time with his SNCC comrade Hubert Brown, the Louisiana native known by his nickname "Rap." Sellers spotted Sandy with Brown at a bar in Atlanta at a time when she said she was shopping with girlfriends, then discovered on a trip to the South that Brown had been escorting her around Lowndes County, where Rap had succeeded Carmichael as field secretary.

Following an angry confrontation, Sandy agreed to break off with Brown and accompany Sellers to the Peg Leg Bates retreat. But after a few days of being left alone in her hotel room, Sandy took up with Rap again, and this time Sellers threatened "big trouble" if the dalliance continued. The nasty love triangle continued for several weeks after the retreat, until in a shameful moment Sellers slapped Sandy in the face and she fled home to Jackson.

Stokely Carmichael remained uncharacteristically passive during much of the retreat. Years later, when he was interviewed about the Peg Leg Bates meeting by Ekwueme Michael Thelwell, the SNCC veteran who helped him write his autobiography, Carmichael was evasive. He offered praise for several white veterans who had come under attack. Jack Minnis was a "very good struggler," Carmichael said, and Bob Zellner was a "real soldier." In typical fashion,

Carmichael recalled joking with Zellner about the move to expel him. "Used to be Africans who were the last hired and first fired," Carmichael quipped. "In SNCC, you were the first [white] hired and the last fired."

But Carmichael refused to talk about how and why Bill Ware and his supporters had gained the upper hand. In a note to readers, Thelwell wrote that Carmichael made "passing references" that could be "cobbled together" to suggest some remorse about letting Ware have his way. Carmichael recalled "an organized faction," Thelwell wrote, that "came into the 'Peg Leg' Bates meeting determined to make the question of the role and presence of whites an *ideological* one" and "generated anger, confusion, frustration." But when Thelwell tried to go into greater detail, Carmichael brushed him aside. "I didn't sense a reluctance so much as impatience, even boredom," Thelwell wrote. Carmichael's attitude was: "Why even belabor that dead horse now?"

As the debate dragged on, the whites at the retreat felt "handcuffed," Zellner recalled. As far as Zellner was concerned, SNCC's white veterans had always understood that Blacks were in charge. "Old hands were clear that this was proper leadership for a primarily black organization working on mainly a black agenda," he wrote. Since there so few whites staffers left by 1966, Zellner also wondered why Ware kept warning about their undue influence. "My question was: What white people?" Zellner recalled. But since he and Minnis didn't want to look like they were pleading their own case, they weighed in only "very carefully and mildly," Zellner wrote. "We wanted to make our position clear, but we didn't want to 'fight' for it. We felt if we lobbied and organized and cajoled and maneuvered against the vote to become all-black, our work in the movement would be rather meaningless."

The expulsion vote came at last in the early-morning hours of December 8, the last day of the retreat. In a replay of the scene in Kingston Springs seven months earlier, the pre-vote debate dragged on so long that many of the attendees had gone to bed. Almost half of the Black staffers who remained abstained. So did the handful of white staffers present, not wanting to be accused of tipping the outcome in their favor. When the vote occurred around two in the morning, only thirty-seven staffers took part, and the motion passed by just one vote: 19-to-18. Heartsick and exhausted, Zellner and the other whites immediately left the room. Among the black staffers who voted for the measure, some celebrated, while others had sudden pangs of guilt. Ethel Minor, a Chicago native who had once worked as an office manager for Malcolm X and had joined SNCC's communications department, felt badly about Bob Zellner in particular. "Here was someone who had been on the front lines long before I came into the organization," Minor recalled. "No one wanted to look at Bob afterwards."

JUST AS BOB AND DOTTIE ZELLNER WERE ABOUT TO FACE DIS-missal from SNCC, ironically, they received good news about the reversal of another expulsion. Three days before the vote, on December 5, their friend Julian Bond finally prevailed in a year-long battle to overturn his ouster by the Georgia state House of Representatives. After that drama the previous January, Bond won another special election in his Atlanta district, only to have the state's lawmakers again bar him from taking his seat. At that point, a host of prominent political and entertainment figures made him a cause célèbre. "Will you join the defenders of Bond's right to dissent?" asked a full-page advertisement in The New York Times signed by Harry Belafonte, comedian Woody Allen, novelist Joseph Heller, and bestselling pediatrician and author Benjamin Spock. On a visit to New York City, Bond was invited to lunch at the United Nations with ambassadors from fifteen African countries and offered a warm patrician endorsement by liberal Republican mayor John V. Lindsay. "If I were still in the private practice of law, I would be pleased to take on the case and argue it," Lindsay told reporters about Bond's pending lawsuit.

In taking his case to court, however, Bond demonstrated the same lofty disregard for political expediency that had gotten him in trouble in the first place. At the state level, a three-judge panel ruled two-to-one against Bond, with one of the adverse rulings coming from

Griffin Bell, the Atlanta jurist later appointed U.S. attorney general by Jimmy Carter. Then Bond risked his celebrity darling status by hiring two left-wing lawyers from New York, Leonard Boudin and Victor Rabinowitz, both of whom had past ties to the Communist Party and made no secret of their own strong opposition to the Vietnam War. The American Civil Liberties Union withdrew its support, leaving Bond's brother-in-law Howard Moore, who had been defending him on behalf of the ACLU, to stay on his team as a private adviser. From then on, Boudin and Rabinowitz took over the case officially known as *Bond v. Floyd*—after James H. Floyd, a white Georgia legislator who went by the nickname "Sloppy" Floyd.

Sloppy also turned out to be a good description of the oral argument that Georgia's attorney general, Arthur Bolton, made on behalf of Floyd and the other Georgia lawmakers when the case went before the U.S. Supreme Court in November. Representing Bond, Leonard Boudin made a straightforward argument that the Georgia legislature had unjustly punished his client for exercising his constitutional right to free speech in expressing opinions about Vietnam and the draft. In response, Bolton maintained that Bond had relinquished that right by showing sympathy for draft card burners. Bolton contended that those statements violated an elected official's oath to support the Constitution—even though Bond had never directly advocated card burning, and had yet to be allowed to take his oath as an elected official in Georgia.

"Are you telling us that there is a requirement to support a war that Congress hasn't even declared?" Justice Potter Stewart asked. "You're differentiating legislators from other people?"

"Yes," Bolton replied.

One after another, the nine Supreme Court justices expressed bewilderment at Bolton's circular constitutional logic. "Is that all you have?" Justice Byron White blurted out when Bolton finished. "You come all this way and that's all you have?" Less than a month later, the court issued a unanimous verdict in Bond's favor, the first time the high court had ever overruled a state legislature's sanction of one of its own elected officials. Writing the opinion, Chief Justice Earl

Warren suggested that Bolton had done his defendants no favor by conceding that the Georgia legislature would not have been justified in discriminating against Bond simply because he was Black. "We are not persuaded by the State's attempt to distinguish, for the purposes of our jurisdiction, between an exclusion alleged to be on racial grounds and one alleged to violate the First Amendment," Warren wrote with visible disdain. Bond learned the news in an Indianapolis airport when he was summoned over the public address system. A radio reporter had tracked him down and was calling to get comment on the Supreme Court victory—the same scenario that had started Bond's ordeal ten months earlier when a radio newsman asked for his views about SNCC's anti–Vietnam War statement.

IN ANOTHER IRONY, THE MONTHS AFTER THE PEG LEG BATES meeting brought Bill Ware's own expulsion from SNCC, as his arrogance and insubordination at last went too far for the organization's new leadership. The showdown came not over a matter of policy but over a car—a vehicle from SNCC's Sojourner Motor Fleet that Ware had borrowed and refused to return. After Sellers fired off several angry letters, he and Carmichael went to confront Ware at his cramped headquarters in Vine City. Acting surly and "obviously jealous of Stokely," Sellers recalled, Ware refused to disclose the whereabouts of the car. On the way back to headquarters, Sellers convinced Carmichael that they had to report the missing vehicle to the police, so SNCC wouldn't be held liable if it was involved in an accident. "This is business," Sellers argued.

When the police contacted Ware about the missing car, he became enraged. He fired off a blistering telegram to Jim Forman, who was in Boston receiving treatment for his ulcers. The wire took vicious swipes at Carmichael and Atlanta mayor Ivan Allen, and threatened to leak embarrassing information about SNCC's leadership to the press—likely a veiled reference to Forman's marriage to Dinky Romilly and her pregnancy. "Your hand-picked Chairman, the alleged hope of Black America," Ware informed Forman, "has descended to the level of calling a racist henchman cop of the white Master Allen of Atlanta to settle an internal dispute between the supposedly black people of SNCC. Beware of going to the man to deal with supposedly internal conflicts. It can work both ways. We have tapes and other information that could fall into black people's hands across the country. There are several magazines lined up to publish our writing."

Unaware of the car dispute, Forman called the Atlanta office to find out what was going on. When he read the telegram to Carmichael, Carmichael decided he had finally had enough of Ware and his tactics. He sent a one-sentence letter to Ware and the rest of the Vine City staff: "You have been fired from the Student Nonviolent Coordinating Committee." To make sure that the decision received support from the broader staff, Sellers asked Fay Bellamy to write a report documenting the extent of Ware's disobedience. Although some of the Vine City militants stayed in Atlanta for a time, hoping to get the decision reversed, ultimately Ware accepted its "finality," according to historian Clayborne Carson. Later, Ware even went so far as to tell Carson that he had dissuaded some of his comrades from bringing guns to a central committee meeting where the expulsion was ratified.

Even after Ware's firing, however, the top SNCC leaders refused to reconsider the purge he had precipitated. By the following May, when the Central Committee met for the first time after the Peg Leg Bates retreat, Carmichael had stepped down as chairman, explaining to the public that he wanted to return to fieldwork. Rap Brown had been elected chairman, and he presided over a meeting that included Jim Forman, Fay Bellamy, Stanley Wise, and several others. As the date approached, Dottie Zellner told her husband that she wanted to resolve their own status with SNCC once and for all. She drafted a one-page proposal for Bob Zellner to present to the Central Committee. Bob and Dottie would agree to stay in New Haven and organize only in white communities, she proposed, but they wanted to remain staff members with voting privileges.

When Bob Zellner flew to Atlanta to address the Central Committee, its members at first couldn't agree on what had actually happened in Kerhonkson. Some accurately remembered a vote to expel whites entirely; others claimed to recall that the decision was simply to exclude whites from policymaking, or to make them work on contract. After listening to the confused back and forth, Zellner made one final plea. "I feel, and have always felt, that SNCC was as much a part of me as anybody else and that I was SNCC and I will always be SNCC," he said, his voice full of wounded pride. "I will not accept any sort of restrictions or special categories because of race. We do not expect other people to do that in this country and I will not accept it for myself."

At that point, Zellner agreed to leave the room, and the members of the Central Committee fell into more bickering. When Fay Bellamy regretted that Zellner had brought "emotionalism" into the discussion, Jim Forman shot back: "I know that [if] I were he, I would be emotional too." In the end, however, the committee decided that it couldn't reverse a vote that had been taken at a meeting of the entire SNCC membership, and that it needed to stand up for the principle of Black control even if it meant shutting the door on loyal friends like the Zellners. "It is absolutely crucial that we strike the first blow," said Stanley Wise. "If Bob does not wish to be, as he terms it, second-class . . . understanding that there is not racism involved . . . if he is not willing to do that, then I see no alternative that this group has but to say that he is fired."

Brought back into the room and informed of that verdict, Zellner grudgingly accepted it. He asked only for a written transcript of the meeting so that he could show Dottie that he had stood up for the two of them. Otherwise, Zellner promised to keep the matter private. "I think it is a mistake, but that is among us," he told the group. "As far as the press is concerned, I don't have anything to say to them about this." Twenty-five years later, photographer Danny Lyon would come into possession of a transcript of that Central Committee meeting and publish parts of it in a collection of his SNCC photography. Having left the organization in 1965 because of his own growing sense that he was no longer welcome, Lyon added a biting reflection on Zellner's submission. "Like a loyal Bolshevik," Danny quipped, "he goes before the firing squad praising the revolution."

Zellner honored his commitment to stay quiet about the details of the Central Committee meeting, and later shared only his feelings of devastation. "I realized it was my last day in SNCC," he wrote in a memoir. "It was huge for me, because I had been on the staff since 1961. SNCC was our life. It was our existence. It was our total identity. . . . It was like being cast into outer darkness, because SNCC was our family in a very strong sense."

With their bid to remain with SNCC at an end, the Zellners agreed to join their old friend Anne Braden as the Southern Conference Educational Fund in New Orleans, where they lived and worked for the next decade before separating. For Dottie Zellner, even that painful personal ordeal didn't compare with the hurt she felt after the rupture with SNCC. "It was the worst thing that ever happened to me," she recalled, "including my divorce."

SADLY, THE ONE SNCC LEADER WHO MIGHT HAVE CAUSED A RE-consideration of the Peg Leg Bates decision was too ill to attend the Central Committee meeting in 1967. In January of that year, just weeks after the Kerhonkson retreat, Ruby Doris Robinson flew from Atlanta to New York City for a fundraiser. At the airport awaiting the flight back, she became suddenly weak and pale. Friends took her to New York's Beth Israel Hospital, where she would remain for the next six months. Her spleen was removed and she contracted hepatitis from a blood transfusion. Then she was diagnosed with terminal cancer.

From her hospital bed, Robinson summoned the strength to draft a letter to her friend Charlotte Carter for discussion at the Atlanta meeting. Ruby Doris proposed that SNCC designate a category of members who would be considered staff but be ineligible to serve on the Central Committee. Under those by-laws, whites could have remained without any possibility that they might become part of leadership. But without Robinson at the meeting to make the case in person, and to wield her blunt authority to help her colleagues see the logic of the proposal, the letter was mentioned only briefly without further debate.

As it happened, Dottie Zeller's parents lived a short distance from Beth Israel Hospital. Once Zellner learned that Robinson was sick, she started visiting her every time she came to New York from New Haven. As Zellner held Robinson's hand and brought her news of the outside world, their previous relationship of mutual respect deepened into a warm friendship. For Robinson, it was a bittersweet irony that, after all her years of racial wariness, it was a white woman who bothered to visit her bedside. As for Zellner, it touched her heart to see the once fearsome Ruby Doris Robinson become so weak that she could speak only in a whisper. "I saw a side of her that I had never seen before, and that most people never had seen, in that vulnerable state," Zellner recalled.

Once Beth Israel could do no more for her, Robinson was transferred to a hospital in Atlanta. On the night of Saturday, October 7, 1967, she passed away at the age of twenty-six, leaving behind her husband, Clifford, and their two-year-old son, Kenneth. A week later, several hundred people crowded into Atlanta's modest, red-brick West Mitchell Christian Methodist Episcopal Church to honor her memory. Present were the other young leaders who had taken command of SNCC in Kingston Springs: Stokely Carmichael and Cleve Sellers, along with their allies Willie Ricks and Courtland Cox. There, too, were the SNCC veterans the young leaders had displaced: Jim Forman, John Lewis, and Julian Bond. In a sign of the respect with which Robinson was held throughout the spreading Black Power movement, Eldridge Cleaver, now minister of information for the Black Panther Party for Self-Defense, came all the way from Oakland.

Barely visible among all the Black bodies in the plain wooden pews was the petite figure of Dottie Zellner. It was the last time Zellner would see most of the people in the church for twenty years, until SNCC veterans came together for a reunion in 1988, and started a process of forgiving and forgetting. Zellner herself would come to take her expulsion less personally over time, and to see it from the perspective of Black friends who had nursed deep wounds over white betrayal going back to the 1964 Democratic convention in Atlantic City and had never fully come to terms with that trauma. "I don't believe now that the Black people in SNCC were culpable," she said. "It was racism that did it."

Yet on that October day in the Atlanta church, gazing at the high school photograph of Robinson on the cover of the funeral program—her hair straightened and curled, in the days before she helped to pioneer the "natural look"—Zellner broke into sobs. Seeing some expressions of annoyance as well as sympathy on the Black faces around her, Zellner composed herself and sat quietly through the rest of the service, silently mourning her friend Ruby Doris and her faded memories of "the beloved community."

In a wild, all-night election for leadership of the Student Nonviolent Coordinating Committee (SNCC) in May of 1966, firebrand Stokely Carmichael (left) was chosen to replace John Lewis (below), the more moderate hero of "Bloody Sunday." During the Meredith March in Mississippi a month later, Carmichael unleashed the slogan "Black Power" and roused a crowd of thousands at a closing rally at the capitol in Jackson.

The new guard at SNCC also included "tough as nails" Ruby Doris Smith Robinson (top right), who took over as executive secretary from Jim Forman (top left), as well as program director Cleveland "Cleve" Sellers (top middle). Gone was the original self-effacing spirit of SNCC personified by its "godmother," Ella Baker (bottom right), and legendarily modest and brave voting rights organizer Bob Moses (bottom left).

6

ONTGOMERY POLICE DEP'T.

Two of SNCC's first and most respected white staffers were Alabama-bred Bob Zellner and New York City–born Dorothy "Dottie" Miller (above), who fell in love and were married in Atlanta in 1963. But in 1966, a year-long campaign that ended with their emotional ouster was waged by Bill Ware (left), an aggressively militant Black organizer from Mississippi who wrote a "position paper" calling for the expulsion of all whites from SNCC.

Black disillusionment with mainstream politics deepened when SNCC veteran Julian Bond (above, seated) was voted out of the Georgia state legislature after publicly criticizing the Vietnam War and draft. Meanwhile, Martin Luther King Jr. and his wife, Coretta (below), rented a slum apartment in Chicago in what became a frustrating and violently opposed bid to move the civil rights movement north and take on a new battle over housing.

When civil rights icon James Meredith (above) was shot by a white gunman during his march across Mississippi in June of 1966, talks over carrying on the Meredith March led to a split among the Big Five civil rights groups. They included SNCC and four organizations whose leaders met in 1964 with President Lyndon Johnson (below, with Roy Wilkins of the NAACP, James Farmer of CORE, Dr. King of the SCLC, and Whitney Young of the Urban League).

In Oakland, California, the Black Panther Party for Self-Defense was born when community college students Bobby Seale (above, left) and Huey Newton (above, right) wrote a "Ten Point Program" and adopted berets and guns as their calling cards. Meanwhile, their future partner—and eventual rival—Eldridge Cleaver was released from prison and took a magazine assignment that introduced him to Kathleen Neal, his future wife (below, in 1968, flanked by a reporter on the left and lawyer Charles Garry and Cleaver on the right).

Inspired by the memory of Malcolm X (below), other increasingly visible young Black leaders called for a cultural and psychological revolution of Black Consciousness. Chief among them were Ron Karenga (top left), founder of a Los Angeles group called US and creator of the African-inspired holiday Kwanzaa, and LeRoi Jones (bottom left), the poet and playwright who spearheaded the Black Arts Movement and later changed his name to Amiri Baraka.

"White backlash" against Black Power and urban unrest propelled a sharp rightward swing in the 1966 midterm elections with profound implications for America's political future. Ronald Reagan (above) was elected governor of California, while in Alabama the appeal of a blatantly white nationalist message was evident when term-limited segregationist governor George Wallace was succeeded by his wife, Lurleen (below).

Black Studies and the First Kwanzaa

I n the spring of 1966, Jimmy Garrett arrived at San Francisco State College determined to win a bet. Just turned twenty-three, Garrett until recently had been SNCC's chief fundraiser in Los Angeles, charged with raising as much as $150 million a year from civil rights sympathizers in Hollywood. Garrett was young for the job, and looked even younger, with a skinny frame and a dark, boyish face made only slightly more mature-looking by a thin mustache. But he was an effective envoy to white liberals, Garrett recalled, because "I didn't have a threatening look. . . . I looked like everybody's nephew or baby cousin. . . . 110 pounds soaking wet . . . all nose and ears." While not busy fundraising, Garrett had been watching the spread of the SDS and other white activist groups at colleges across the country, and he had a wager with his SNCC comrade Courtland Cox about whether Black students could pull off something comparable. "The bet was that you could build a black student movement on a predominantly white campus," Garrett recalled. "I bet that it could happen."

Garrett inherited his knack for thinking big and working hard from his parents. His father came from a family of Black Texans who had acquired their own land after the Civil War and tilled it to sell crops to a rich white rancher. His mother hailed from a line of Black women who worked as domestics in the Dallas area, where his parents met and where Garrett was born in 1942. But just as Garrett was entering his teens, his parents moved the family to Los Angeles after a Black Texan they knew was lynched, and another was executed on charges of raping a white woman whom the man had never met.

While in high school in L.A., Garrett got mixed up with a street gang, and his worried parents sent him back to Texas to stay with family for the summer. In Texas, Garrett participated in sit-in protests and became swept up in the civil rights movement. He participated in one of the last Freedom Rides in 1961 and worked for CORE in Southern California. By 1964, he had become a member of SNCC and organized under Bob Moses in rural Mississippi. At a protest in Madison County toward the end of Freedom Summer, Garrett was beaten so badly by local police that he ended up in a local hospital. After that, he decided to go back to L.A. and accept the challenging but less perilous job of raising money in the entertainment world.

Before Garrett got the L.A. job, however, he had to survive a stern interview with Ruby Doris Robinson. As Garrett recalled, "Ruby Doris said if I screw up even a bit, she's gone kick my ass. And I was more afraid of Ruby Doris then I was of Jim Forman, so I did my best." Garrett moved into the SNCC office in the skid row section of Hollywood Boulevard, and began working with white volunteer Peggy Penn, the wife of film director Arthur Penn. Together, they organized fundraisers at the homes of Hollywood celebrities which attracted the likes of movie star Jane Fonda and ventriloquist Edgar Bergen and his daughter, Candice, a college student embarking on her own acting career.

Such a fundraiser was planned at the home of movie superstars Elizabeth Taylor and Richard Burton on the night of August 11, 1965, when violence erupted in the South-Central Los Angeles neighborhood of Watts. It started early in the evening when a state motorcycle patrolman pulled over a twenty-one-year-old Black man named Marquette Frye for drunk driving, and Frye's mother came to the scene to question the arrest. As a crowd gathered to watch the confrontation,

Frye was struck with a police baton, his mother was shoved, and onlookers claimed they saw a pregnant woman get knocked to the ground.

The national press labeled what came next "the Watts riots." Thousands of Blacks poured into the streets in waves of protest and looting that lasted for the next five days, escalating into bloody battles with the National Guard and leaving thirty-four people dead and more than $40 million worth of property destroyed. But among Black Americans, the convulsion earned a different name: "the Watts Rebellion." They saw the violence as a deeper reaction to the myriad hardships and heartbreaks suffered by so many children of the Great Migration to the West. In Watts, the pent-up fury was also specifically directed at the imperious and frequently abusive way that Blacks had come to be treated by the Los Angeles Police Department during the sixteen-year reign of the LAPD's leader, Chief William Parker.

Expected at the Elizabeth Taylor fundraiser for SNCC, Garrett joined the Watts protest instead. "I was gone," he recalled. "I was in the streets." Peggy Penn was so furious that she stopped talking to Garrett and soon quit working for SNCC. In the wake of the unrest, Garrett also noticed a sudden change in other longtime white supporters, who seemed less enthusiastic about bankrolling Black protest now that it had erupted so close to their homes. "You could taste it," he recalled. "You could feel it. Their thing was, 'Wait a minute. Wait a minute. You can't disrupt my lifestyle. You can take all the money.'"

Atlanta headquarters was also unhappy with Garrett for joining in the uprising, although Robinson was privately sympathetic. As Garrett recalled, her attitude was: "What the hell do you expect [him] to do? Run away from the black community when it's in motion?" But other SNCC leaders thought Garrett had compromised his effectiveness, and he concluded that it was time to "get out of Dodge," as he put it. He quit the SNCC job, accepted an opportunity to travel to Japan, and applied to several colleges to avoid getting drafted to serve in Vietnam.

When Garrett returned to America, he had acceptances from two schools—Michigan State University and San Francisco State College.

With his bet on campus organizing in mind, he looked into the status of Black students at both schools, and concluded that San Francisco State was best suited for his experiment. The student population of eighteen thousand included only 150 Blacks. Most of them congregated in Black fraternities and sororities, or on athletic teams, and a small Negro Student Union had little impact. The ground was ripe for an attempt to unite the groups and pressure the administration to admit more Black students. Even more ambitiously, Garrett dreamed of demanding something that had never existed at a white institution of higher learning before: an official course of study devoted to the history and concerns of Black people.

A SPRAWLING CAMPUS OF POSTWAR BUILDINGS ARRAYED CLOSE to Lake Merced on the western edge of the city, San Francisco State College had grown so large by 1966 that not long afterward it would be renamed San Francisco State University. As soon as Garrett enrolled as a second-term freshman that spring, he began telling anyone who would listen about his plans for forming a Black Student Union. At a frat party, he made his first convert: Jerry Varnado, a Black twenty-year-old Mississippi native who had just finished a stint in the Navy. Varnado was already feeling out of place on the virtually all-white campus, and he immediately embraced Garrett's vision of uniting and organizing the tiny Black student population. "When I got to San Francisco State, I felt a little bit of an inferiority complex," Varnado recalled. "I would sit in the back of the class, and I thought that the white students knew more than us—but in time I found out that they didn't."

By April, Garrett and Varnado had enlisted a half dozen more recruits, and they began tossing around names for the new organization. After weeks of debate, they settled on the Black Student Union, regarding it as celebration of "the national consciousness that was developing . . . [of] the validity of blackness," as Garrett put it. The two founders also agreed that the Black Student Union should be open to any Black person on campus who wanted to join—not only students, but also professors and employees, including groundskeepers, janitors, and cleaning ladies. "If they were black," Garrett said, "then they were members of the BSU."

Accustomed to dealing with white liberals after his work in Hollywood, Garrett sought the support of the college's new president, a forty-one-year-old, curly-haired Canadian named John Summerskill. An avid traveler and wine lover, Summerskill was the kind of worldly do-gooder, Garrett sensed, who would think "it was good for the white students to have an expanded connection with diverse people." Garrett persuaded Summerskill to introduce a "special admissions" program under which the college would accept Black applicants who were vetted by the BSU. Over the next two years, 416 new students were admitted under the program, helping to expand the number of Black undergraduates from 150 in 1966 to 600 by the spring of 1968, and then to 900 the following fall.

Handed the power to all but guarantee admission, the Black Students Union set out to find applicants who showed potential but didn't fit the middle-class model of Black achievement described by W. E. B. Du Bois's phrase "the talented tenth." One such recruit was a bright but troubled son of a San Francisco postal worker who had all but dropped out of a local city college when BSU members found him hanging out on the streets of Haight-Ashbury. They befriended the young man and arranged for Danny Glover—who would go on to become one of America's most acclaimed Black actors—to enroll at San Francisco State.

In the fall of 1966, Garrett began to circulate an outline of his ideas for a new kind of curriculum that he entitled "Justification for Black Studies." At first, he viewed the manifesto mostly as a way to introduce his fellow students to the notion of Black Consciousness. Previously, as Garrett saw it, the smattering of Blacks at San Francisco State had exhibited "Negro consciousness, or petit bourgeois consciousness, or personal independent individual aggrandizement consciousness, but they didn't have collective consciousness." Starting in

1966, however, that began to change. Across the college, Black students displayed a new sense of solidarity, exchanging nods and smiles as they crossed paths on campus, and calling one another "my sister" and "my brother."

By November of 1968, Jimmy Garrett had left San Francisco State to organize in Washington, D.C, when his vision of a Black Studies program became the focus of the longest student strike in U.S. history. It began after John Summerskill resigned and a new, more conservative college president named Robert Smith took over. When Smith fired a Black teaching assistant named George Murray who had joined the Black Panther Party, hundreds of members of the BSU and other minority student groups poured into the center of campus calling for Murray's reinstatement. They also demanded that a program called "the experimental college," which had begun to offer individual courses in Black culture and history, be expanded into a full-fledged department.

After three weeks of protests, Smith resigned as well, and was replaced by a Japanese American semantics professor named S. I. Hayakawa who was recognizable by his thick black glasses and fondness for wool tam o'shanter caps. Hayakawa took a hard line with the demonstrators, cutting their loudspeakers at one protest and calling in city police to keep order. The protest continued for the next four months, attracting support from other Bay Area activists and up-and-coming local Black politicians such as Ron Dellums and Willie Brown. Governor Ronald Reagan, who had jurisdiction over the state college, publicly backed Hayakawa's tough stance and genially dismissed the protesters, telling reporters that "the strike is failing; it's on the way out." But after several more violent clashes, Hayakawa relented and agreed to the creation of a department named the College of Ethnic Studies. Over the following years, protests inspired by the San Francisco State strike would lead to the establishment of hundreds of similar Black and Ethnic Studies programs across the country. They also forced a gradual—if often hard-won—expansion of Black faculty hiring at white colleges and universities. As Jimmy Garrett later boasted: "I would fully say that probably 80 to 85 percent of Black faculty members on white college campuses are there as a direct result of our struggle."

IN FEBRUARY OF 1968, A YEAR AND A HALF AFTER THE CRY FIRST made national headlines, *The New York Review of Books* published an issue with the provocative cover line: "The Trouble with Black Power." The cover story, written by white social critic Christopher Lasch, was a long essay presented as a review of several books that had just come out, including one coauthored by Stokely Carmichael and Black scholar Charles V. Hamilton called *Black Power: The Politics of Liberation in America.* In his sweeping essay, Lasch picked apart the *political* case for Black Power. He dismissed Carmichael's vision of a "common struggle" with Third World liberation movements by pointing out that Blacks didn't represent a majority of the U.S. population or have armed control of any territory. Lasch also questioned Carmichael's appeal for Blacks to use their economic clout to force a "total revamping of the society" by wondering why corporate America would care about the Black "lumpenproletariat" in the inner city. "Would self-determination for the ghetto threaten General Motors?" Lasch asked.

At the same, however, Lasch gave more serious attention than any other prominent white critic to the *cultural* appeal of Black Power. He cited the argument of Black historian E. Franklin Frazier that the "primary struggle" of Blacks in America had been "to acquire a culture." First, slavery stripped them of much of the culture they had known in Africa. After the Civil War, Southern Blacks developed a distinct culture centered largely around the church. But then millions moved north in the Great Migration, and found themselves in worlds defined by rootless poverty or Black middle-class emulation of white social institutions. This cultural drift was one reason, Lasch argued, that the Nation of Islam, with its strict behavioral codes, had made such inroads among the urban poor, while the civil rights movement led by Dr. King had faltered in its bid to move north.

"The civil rights movement does not address itself to the question of how Negroes are to acquire a culture, or to the consequences of their failure to do so," Lasch wrote. "It addresses itself to legal inequalities. In so far as it implies a cultural program of any kind, the civil rights strategy proposes to integrate Negroes into the culture which already surrounds them." By contrast, Lasch argued, Carmichael and his followers were at least speaking to the longing for a separate cultural identity, one that went far deeper than all their improbable talk of political revolution. "Black Power represents, among other things, a revival of Negro-American nationalism and therefore cannot be regarded simply as a response to recent events," Lasch wrote. "Black Power has secularized the separatist impulse which has usually (though not always) manifested itself in religious forms."

In the wake of the example set by San Francisco State, the Black Power generation would also now have a laboratory for the creation of this new Black culture. Instead of the church, it was the campus. That insight was underlined in another seminal essay by Eugene Genovese, one of the foremost white historians of American slavery. In the Spring 1970 issue of the quarterly *Daedalus*, Genovese argued that Black intellectuals could play a key role in reconciling the historic tension between assimilation and separatism, by defining a culture that would allow Blacks to feel at home in America even in the absence of significant racial integration. "The emergence of a black intelligentsia, conscious of the historical evolution of a community of interest, has within itself the power to forge a separate culture out of a tradition that has been both of America and a thing apart," Genovese wrote. "In view of the white-racist resistance to integration, the victory of this tendency seems probable."

Almost a half century before "The 1619 Project"—the widely read and hotly debated attempt to recast the white-centered narrative of America's founding—Genovese made a prescient prediction about the role of Black historians in particular. "We may expect to arrive, therefore, at a new view of Afro-American history, whatever the political outcome of the present turmoil," he wrote. "If the nationalist movement scores substantial gains, this view will be immensely strengthened; if it is crushed or substantially beaten back, the strategic position of the young nationalist intelligentsia is still likely to guarantee the consolidation of a considerable portion of its interpretation of the historical record."

For already well-known Black intellectuals and the upcoming student generation alike, discussion of the new Black Consciousness almost always came back to Malcolm X. Although Malcolm had been dead for a year by 1966, the release of the paperback edition of his posthumous memoir, *The Autobiography of Malcolm X*, extended awareness of his life and legacy to every corner of the country. The original deal to publish that book, written in cooperation with author Alex Haley after Haley interviewed Malcolm for *Playboy* magazine, was with the publisher Doubleday. But after Malcolm was assassinated in February of 1965, Doubleday got cold feet, even though the book was already typeset and ready to print.

Haley's agent shopped the manuscript to as many as a dozen other publishers. The only taker was Grove Press, the small iconoclastic imprint whose authors ranged from Beat poets to Che Guevara. Grove ordered a first printing of ten thousand hardcover copies—a healthy number, but hardly an indicator of bestseller hopes. Yet beyond expectations, the hardcover edition of *The Autobiography of Malcolm X* was a critical and commercial success. So when Grove came out with a paperback edition in the summer of 1966, priced at $1.25, it invested in a substantially larger print run and marketing campaign. For the book cover, Grove replaced the staid photograph on the hardcover edition with an image of Malcolm defiantly thrusting his finger in the air. Above the title was a tease worthy of a detective thriller: "He rose from hoodlum, thief, dope peddler, pimp . . . to become the most dynamic leader of the Black Revolution. He said he would be murdered before this book appeared."

Ever since, questions have been raised about the reliability of Alex Haley's depiction of Malcolm X—about whether it embellished his early life of crime, or softened the still sharp edges of his later Pan-African message. But it was precisely this revision of Malcolm's image that made him so widely attractive as a cultural icon. He could be remembered for his celebration of Black self-love and embodiment of Black "manhood" without the necessity of dwelling on his years of divisive racial rhetoric or obedience to the dogmatic and corrupt Nation of Islam leader Elijah Muhammad. Explaining his decision to buy the manuscript after reading it in one night, Grove Press founder Barney Rosset stressed the appeal of Haley's uplifting narrative. "On the whole, I liked the whole feeling of the strong activist viewpoint of Malcolm," Rosset recalled. "Religiously, he left me cold, but he had a strong attitude on behalf of black people—his call to self-reliance and equality."

BY 1966, MALCOLM'S INFLUENCE COULD ALSO BE FELT THROUGH-out the nascent Black Arts Movement, a phenomenon that one of its early pioneers, playwright Larry Neal, described as "the aesthetic and spiritual sister of Black Power." The movement's most promi-nent trailblazer was the poet and playwright LeRoi Jones, who later converted to Islam and changed his name to Amiri Baraka. Born to a post office supervisor and social worker in Newark, New Jersey, Ev-erett Leroy Jones was a bright but rebellious youth who dropped out of Howard University after concluding that it was an assimilationist "employment agency" for middle-class Blacks, then was dishonor-ably discharged from the Air Force after he was found with reading material that made the military suspect he was a communist. Mov-ing to Greenwich Village in the late 1950s, Jones took the pen name "LeRoi" and threw himself into writing poetry and plays. He became part of the beatnik scene and married a white writer, Hettie Cohen, with whom he founded a literary magazine that published the likes of Allen Ginsberg and Jack Kerouac.

In 1964, Jones became one of four founders of the Black Arts Repertory Theatre in Harlem, a space dedicated to producing plays and staging poetry readings and concerts to showcase the work exclu-sively of Black artists. After Malcolm X's assassination in 1965, Jones took this embrace of Black identity a step further by leaving his white wife and two biracial children and moving to Harlem. Later that year, he published a collection of essays entitled *Home* that ended with a meditation entitled, in all lower case letters, "the legacy of malcolm x, and the coming of the black nation." In the essay, Jones interpreted Malcolm as calling for Blacks not to seek a separate homeland, as Black nationalists such as Marcus Garvey had done in the past, but to reimagine themselves as a race reborn on American soil. "The point is that Malcolm had begun to call for Black National Consciousness," Jones wrote. "We do not want a Nation, we are a Nation. . . . The land is literally ours. And we must begin to act like it."

Jones went on to describe the role of Black artists in this process, capitalizing the word "black" in a way that was fifty years ahead of its time. "The Black artist, in this context, is desperately needed to change the images his people identify with, by asserting Black feeling, Black mind, Black judgment," Jones wrote. "The Black intellectual, in this same context, is needed to change the interpretation of facts toward the Black Man's best interests, instead of merely tagging along reciting white judgments of the world."

Elsewhere in 1966, homages to the influence of Malcolm X appeared again and again in the work of other Black Arts Movement pioneers. In an essay for the February edition of the literary journal *Liberator 6*, Larry Neal declared "behind black doors we are all Malcolm X." In Denver, dramatist William Wellington Mackey entitled a play *Requiem for Brother X*. The poet Sonia Sanchez was also in the process of honing a poem called "Malcolm" that she would eventually publish in 1969, after joining LeRoi Jones as a guest lecturer invited by the students of San Francisco State. Capturing Malcolm's charisma and appeal to intellectuals and prison inmates alike, Sanchez wrote: *"He was the sun that tagged/ the western sky and/ melted tiger-scholars/ while they searched for stripes . . ."*

Sanchez had first experienced Malcolm's blazing presence in the early 1960s, when he was running the Nation of Islam mosque in Harlem. Raised in Birmingham, Alabama, in the neighborhood that would later become the heart of that city's famous civil rights battles, Sanchez was teaching high school English in New York City, volunteering for CORE, and working toward the integrationist dream she had heard Dr. King conjure up when she attended the March on

Washington. On a drizzly day on 125th Street, she went out to hear Malcolm speak out of wary curiosity, and found herself slowly nodding at his words and thinking, she recalled: "Yeah, that's right. That makes sense. That's logical."

After Malcolm finished, Sanchez approached him, and he pushed aside his bodyguards to shake her hand.

"I didn't agree with all that you said, but I liked some of what you said," Sanchez ventured in a quiet voice that hid the effort of a former child stutterer.

"One day you will, sister," Malcolm replied in a gentle voice. "One day you will, sister."

From then on, Sanchez came out to hear Malcolm whenever he spoke in the neighborhood, and in the crowds she noticed the broadest cross section of Black Harlem she had ever seen. "The joy of Malcolm," she recalled, "is that he could have in an audience college professors, schoolteachers, nurses, doctors, musicians, artists, poets, and sisters who were housewives. Sisters who worked for people in their houses. Brothers who were out of prison. Brothers who were on drugs and were coming off drugs. Brothers who were workers. Brothers who were just hanging on the streets or were waiting outside the temples to get inside. And he understood the better line is that if you tell people the truth, then it will appeal to everyone. If you tell them all about their oppression, in a fashion they ain't never heard before, then they will all gravitate towards you."

That oppression, as Malcolm described it, was as much psychological as political. Malcolm had a unique ability to describe a mental and cultural "enslavement," as he called it, that endured a century after Emancipation—and to offer a personal model of how to escape it. "He cut through all the crap," Sanchez recalled. "You see, what he said out loud is what African-American people had been saying forever behind closed doors. . . . He said it out loud. Not behind closed doors. He took on America for us. He assumed the responsibility of father, brother, lover, man. . . . The man that we needed to see in the North and in the South. He became the man that most African-American women have wanted their men to be: strong. . . . That's why we all loved him so very much. Because he made us feel holy. And he made us feel whole. He made us feel loved. And he made us feel that we were worth something finally on this planet Earth. Finally we have some worth."

In a story for the Sunday *New York Times Magazine* in December 1966, critic Nat Hentoff set out to explain a musical extension of the Black Arts Movement that became known as "Free Jazz." Entitled "The New Jazz: Black, Angry and Hard to Understand," the story captured the bewilderment of white swing era and bebop fans with the latest offerings from musicians such as John Coltrane, Ornette Coleman, and Charles Mingus, with their lack of traditional chord structures and dissonant melodies. If white jazz enthusiasts felt "insulted," Hentoff observed, it was because these "experimenters are writing music which, more consciously than ever before, is an attempt to underline their collective identity with black people." Saxophonist Archie Shepp, one of the most experimental and political of the Free Jazz pioneers, entitled one of his new compositions "Malcolm, Malcolm—Semper Malcolm." As Shepp explained to Hentoff: "Malcolm knew what it is to be faceless in America and to be sick and tired of that feeling. And he knew the pride of black, that negritude which was bigger than Malcolm himself."

For years, the soundtrack to the civil rights movement had been folk songs and spirituals such as "We Shall Overcome." But in November of 1966, Julius Lester, a SNCC activist and writer, took to the pages of a folk music journal called *Sing Out!* to explain to its largely white readership why young Blacks were through with that kind of music. Entitled "The Singing Is Over: The Angry Children of Malcolm X," Lester's essay conjured up the image of civil rights protesters holding hands and "swaying gently" in the face of white vigilantes "with guns, tire chains, baseball bats, rocks, sticks, clubs and bottles, waiting as you turn the corner singing This Little Light of Mine." By contrast, Lester captured the searing effect that Malcolm had on young Blacks by telling them that they no longer had to be submissive. "More than any other person Malcolm X was responsible for the new militancy that entered The Movement in 1965," Lester wrote. "Malcolm X said aloud those things which Negroes had been saying among themselves. He even said those things Negroes had been afraid to say to each other. His clear, uncomplicated words cut through the chains on black minds like a giant blowtorch."

Along with reading Malcolm X, listening to Free Jazz, and adopting the label Black rather than Negro, the other major expression of Black pride and identity in 1966 was the growing popularity of the Afro hairstyle. In June, *Ebony* magazine granted its stamp of approval with a cover story entitled "The Natural Look: New Mode for Negro Women." The author was Phyllis Garland, a onetime editor of the Black-owned *Pittsburgh Courier.* Garland described the practical reasons women had for abandoning chemical hair straighteners and stifling wigs, but she also explored the trend's cultural and psychological meaning. "Though hair has become the focal point in this muted rebellion against prevailing beauty standards," Garland wrote, "it cannot be separated from other changes taking place in the psyche of the American Negro."

IN THE JULY ISSUE OF *LIFE* MAGAZINE, MEANWHILE, WHITE READers read about an entire new movement devoted to the cultural assertion of Black Power. On the cover was a photograph of a dark-skinned man in a green African shirt called a *buba* shouting orders to four Black boys dressed in sweatshirts decorated with images of lions with their Swahili name: *Simba.* Inside, the *Life* story reported that the drill sergeant and youths were members of a Los Angeles group called "US." In August, *Newsweek* profiled the movement's leader: Ron Karenga, a twenty-four-year-old graduate student at UCLA with a shaved head, a mouth-circling mustache, and thick-framed black glasses. Since forming US the previous September, *Newsweek* reported, Karenga had attracted some three hundred followers to a strict regimen that included studying Swahili, adopting Africa-inspired dress, and conducting drill sessions for children on the weekends. His inspiration, the magazine noted, was Malcolm X, whose picture hung on the wall behind Karenga in a photograph that accompanied the story.

The young man who had changed his last name to Karenga—or "Keeper of the Tradition," in Swahili—was born Ronald McKinley Everett in the small town of Parsonsburg, Maryland. He was the youngest of fourteen children born to Levi Everett, a farmer and part-time preacher, and his wife, Addie. A modern-day sharecropper, Levi Everett rented a patch of land from a local white property owner and paid for it with half of his output of crops and chickens. Like all of his siblings, Ron went to work on the farm at a young age. But according to superstition, as the "seventh son" in the family, he was considered destined for bigger things. So after an older brother moved to Los Angeles, his parents blessed Everett's decision to drop out of high school and travel west, where he took advantage of an open enrollment policy to enter the two-year community college program at Los Angeles City College (LACC).

Soon after Everett arrived, LACC became one of the first community colleges in the nation to offer a class in African history. He became so caught up in the subject that he started studying Kiswahili, the Bantu tongue of Africa's Swahili people. Everett adopted his Swahili name and was elected student body president—the first Black student ever to hold that position—before transferring to UCLA. There, he met Malcolm X when he came to speak in the fall of 1962. Still a member of the Nation of Islam, Malcolm spent much of the speech heaping praise on the Honorable Elijah Muhammad and urging total Black separation from white America. But it was Malcolm's cultural message that registered with Karenga. "The American Negro is a Frankenstein, a monster who has been stripped of his culture and doesn't even know his name," Malcolm lamented. Afterward, Karenga sought out Malcolm, and the visitor invited his new disciple to "eat bean pie and talk abstract," as Karenga put it, at a restaurant near L.A.'s Muslim mosque.

Shortly after Malcolm's appearance, another animated young Black leader came to speak at UCLA: Donald Warden, the Berkeley law school graduate who had founded the Afro-American Association, the San Francisco–area group that would also briefly attract Huey Newton. Karenga asked for a meeting, and Warden was so impressed that he offered Karenga a position as head of the AAA's Los Angeles chapter. Karenga began to hold Sunday study meetings in a Methodist church, and attracted local press attention for his own vivid pronouncements about the importance of Black culture. "The Negro battling for equality without first acquiring pride in his racial heritage and an adequate education is like a man ringing the doorbell while leaning against the door," Karenga told a reporter. "He'll fall flat on his face when someone answers."

Around the time that Malcolm was killed in early 1965, Karenga quit the AAA and allied himself with Hakim Jamal, a cousin and supporter of Malcolm's who had moved to Los Angeles. Karenga and Jamal hosted a study group to explore the ideas surrounding the Organization of Afro-American Unity that Malcolm had begun to expound after severing ties with the Nation of Islam. Word quickly spread of their weekly meetings held at the Aquarian Bookstore, a beloved institution in South-Central L.A. founded by a former railway porter and crammed with seventy thousand volumes about Black history and society.

The Watts Rebellion gave Karenga and Jamal's project even greater urgency. Less than a month later, on September 7, 1965, they announced the formation of a new organization dedicated to the proposition that Blacks needed to prepare for political struggle by first undergoing a cultural transformation. As Karenga put it: "You must have a cultural revolution before the violent revolution. The cultural revolution gives identity, purpose and direction." Suggested by Jamal, the title "US" was meant to carry a triple meaning: to serve as an acronym for "United Slaves"; to stand for "us blacks, versus them whites"; and to offer an implicit indictment of the United States of America for failing to live up to that name. To announce the group's arrival, the two men put out a newsletter entitled *Message to the Grassroots*, after one of Malcolm X's most famous speeches, that listed Jamal as the "founder" of US and Karenga as its "chairman."

Although both men had emulated their hero in repudiating the Nation of Islam, US copied much of that sect's "organizational structure," as Scot Brown, a scholar of the movement, pointed out. "Full membership in both organizations," Brown observed, "required the complete acceptance of an alternative lifestyle." Karenga and Jamal gave their prescribed way of life a Swahili name: *Kawaida*, or "Tradition." Their wives were put in charge of an "US School of Afro-American Culture" that instructed followers in how to behave, how to dress in African garb, and how to choose new African names for themselves and their children. Weekly drill sessions in marching and martial arts were organized for the boys of followers, to prepare them for service in a paramilitary wing called the *Simba Wachanga*, or "Young Lions."

The founders also laid out a year-long calendar of holidays. It included commemorations of Malcolm's X's birthday in May (*Kuzaliwa*, or "Birth"), the Watts Rebellion in August (*Uhuru*, or "Freedom"), and the founding of US in September (*Kuanzisha*, or "Foundation"). To complete the calendar, Karenga set out to create a holiday for the Christmas season. He looked into African agricultural rites, borrowing from the Umkhosi festival of the Zulu people and the Ikore ceremony of the Yoruba tribe. As a name for the holiday, he chose the Swahili word *Kwanza*, or "First Fruits," and added an extra "a" to make it Kwanzaa so that it would have seven letters, the sacred number in the Black religious tradition that Karenga had first learned as the seventh son of Maryland Baptists.

By the summer of 1966, Hakim Jamal had split with US, and Ron Karenga became identified as the organization's sole leader and public face. He bestowed on himself the Swahili title of *Maulana*, or "Master Teacher"—and issued a green-bound book of sayings that he entitled *The Quotable Karenga*. When Watts activists formed the Community Alert Patrol, the police-monitoring program that would serve as a model for Huey Newton in Oakland, Karenga was quoted in the press as CAP's spokesman. In October, he traveled to Atlanta to attend the funeral of Ruby Doris Robinson. A few weeks later, he was on the roster of warm-up speakers for Stokely Carmichael at Berkeley's Greek Theatre.

In November, Karenga was on the bill with Carmichael again when Stokely delivered an incendiary address in Will Rogers Memorial Park in Los Angeles. Accounts of the speech suggest that sharing

the stage with Karenga and other California militants pushed Carmichael to new rhetorical extremes. He held forth for more than
forty minutes, whipping up the mostly Black crowd of 6,500 people
in a way that at least one prominent white reporter at the scene interpreted as inciting violence against him personally. Pointing into
the crowd from the back of a pickup truck, Carmichael shouted that
his generation of Black leaders "is going to deal with white people
whether they like it or not."

In the coming years, US would increasingly take on the trappings
of a "cult of personality," as Scot Brown put it. The Young Lions security detail assigned to Karenga grew more menacing, and his list
of lifestyle commandments stretched to more than twenty, including
such petty rules as prohibiting "side conversations during meetings"
and "talking homespun knowledge" not sanctioned by his little green
book. Karenga began to make ominous predictions of seven years of
racial conflict that would culminate in a civil war he labeled the Year
of the Guerrilla. Quietly, Karenga began to encourage male followers
to have children with more than one woman, justifying polygamy as
a way of compensating for a scarcity of reliable male partners outside
the movement. To female followers, he sent a disturbing command
of subservience. "What makes a woman appealing is femininity, and
she can't be feminine without being submissive," he wrote in *The
Quotable Karenga*.

That dark side of Karenga's movement had yet to become fully
apparent on the clear, crisp day after Christmas 1966 when a group of
some fifty US followers met to celebrate the first Kwanzaa. Dressed
in colorful African tunics and headdresses, they gathered in the Jefferson Park neighborhood of Los Angeles at the home of an US
follower that was decorated with wicker baskets full of fruit and a
large wooden candelabra called a *Kinera*, akin to a Jewish menorah.
They welcomed one another with a Swahili greeting—*Hahari gani*, or
"What's new?"—then lit a candle and sat on the floor holding hands,
singing songs, and recounting African folk tales.

For the next week, the participants repeated the ritual, focusing on a different theme each day. Karenga called them the "Seven Principles"—or *Nguzo Saba*. On the first day, the theme was Unity, or *Umoja*. Next came Self-Determination (*Kujichagulia*), Collective Responsibility (*Ujima*), Cooperative Economics (*Ujamaa*), Purpose (*Nia*), Creativity (*Kuumba*), and Faith (*Imani*). On the last night, the celebrants shared a holiday meal called *Karamu*, or "Feast of Faith," passing dishes laden with spicy delicacies around in a circle and eating with their hands as their ancestors had in Africa.

For the next several years, awareness of the new Kwanzaa holiday was limited mostly to US followers in Los Angeles and a small network of Black nationalists in other American cities. But over time, the celebration came to be embraced by more mainstream, middle-class Blacks, many of them living in predominantly white environments, who were looking for a way to affirm their Black identity and instill a sense of racial pride and responsibility in their children. In 1991, Vickie Butcher, a fifty-year-old lawyer living in the town of El Cajon on the outskirts of San Diego, told a reporter from *Time* magazine why she had begun to celebrate Kwanzaa with her husband, a physician, and their five kids. "My children grew up in a fairly white community, and that motivated me to teach them the value of the African-American heritage," Butcher explained.

By the mid-1990s, the U.S. Postal Service had issued a Kwanzaa stamp, and the Smithsonian Institution in Washington, D.C., was staging annual Kwanzaa performances and poetry readings. A Kwanzaa cookbook had gone on sale for $25, and the Hallmark company was shipping tens of thousands of Kwanzaa cards each year along with their Christmas and Hanukkah offerings. As Kwanzaa's visibility rose, so did inevitable questions about commercialization. It was unclear how many people observed all the rituals that Karenga laid out, in addition to exchanging gifts and greeting cards at post-Christmas discounts. But at least by the measure of consumer behavior, the National Association of Realtors estimated that some five million Americans celebrated the holiday in one fashion or another in 2015.

WHILE STOKELY CARMICHAEL AND RON KARENGA WERE MAKING national headlines in 1966, and Huey Newton and Bobby Seale were founding a new Black party, millions of young Blacks were experiencing a quieter personal transformation. One was Vern Smith, a twenty-year-old student at San Francisco State College. Smith came from Natchez, Mississippi, deep in the southwest corner of the state, the same town where SNCC's Bill Ware grew up. With dozens of former plantation mansions scattered around the area, Natchez had a veneer of antebellum charm. But during Smith's childhood, it was still the kind of place where Black fathers patrolled their neighborhoods at night communicating with citizens band radios and kept guns at the ready to defend against the Klan. Natchez was "an armed camp," Smith recalled. "Everybody I knew had guns. My daddy had two shotguns. They were all hunters, but they also had those guns to protect themselves, because they knew people who had been assaulted by night riders, and you couldn't call the police or the sheriff's department."

Vern's father, Eddie Smith, was an auto mechanic at a Chevy dealership and his mother, Rosetta, worked in a box factory. They attended Baptist church on Sundays, and arranged for Vern and his older and younger sisters go to a church-run day school. His parents worked their way up from half of a two-family house to a three-bedroom in a suburban-style neighborhood called College Heights where Vern sometimes played with white children. But that all changed in his high school years when white kids shunned Black peers and it became clear how limited his future would be if he stayed in Natchez. "I just wanted to get out of Mississippi," Vern recalled. "It was just so stifling."

During World War II, two of Rosetta Smith's sisters had joined the Great Migration to Northern California. Vern grew up watching his mother write long letters to his aunts, firing his own ambition be a writer and filling him with curiosity about life in "the non-segregated world," as he thought of it. Most of his Natchez friends were planning to attend nearby historically Black colleges such as Alcorn University and Jackson State. But Vern set his sights on San Francisco State College. He enrolled in 1964, at a time when "you could go whole days without seeing a Black face," he recalled. Until Jimmy Garrett formed the Black Student Union, the only other Blacks Smith knew well were fellow members of the basketball team and a woman who worked for the campus newspaper.

Then came the indelible moment when the Black students of San Francisco State watched Stokely Carmichael shout "Black Power!" in Greenwood, Mississippi. Smith remembered it happening in the fall of 1966, which suggested that he saw the footage on the CBS news special on Black Power that September. "It was electrifying," he recalled. "Especially in Mississippi, the word "black" had always had such a pejorative context. In the early '60s and late '50s, calling somebody black, those were fighting words. To see that word being embraced like that—as a positive—was just such an aha! moment." Smith and his friends were also instantly taken with Carmichael, he recalled, at how "fearless" he seemed, and what a "showman" he was. "Stokely was the image that a lot of young brothers embraced," he said. "The fact that the establishment was railing against him only made him more popular with us."

The Black students at San Francisco State used words like "metamorphosis" and "mind transformation" to describe what happened to them in that school year of 1966 and 1967. "It was almost like a born-again experience," Smith recalled, "like becoming a new you. You were shedding off all that negative baggage that the culture had forced on you. We were no longer Negroes. We didn't even want to look like we used to look." As a badge of their new identity, the women stopped straightening their hair and the men abandoned the close-cropped look with the part on the side. Afros sprouted everywhere. Colorful African dashiki tunics became the new fashion statement. "I mean, we didn't even know what dashikis were before then," Smith recalled with a chuckle.

Until that year, the music that Smith and his friends listened to was Motown. The Temptations were his favorite, along with Smokey

Robinson's love ballads. But now they started to seek out musicians who spoke to their new sense of Blackness, like the Impressions and their song "People Get Ready," written by lead singer Curtis May-field. In 1968, James Brown would record the most famous anthem of Black Power: "Say It Loud, I'm Black and I'm Proud." But as far as Smith and his friends were concerned, by then Brown was just responding to a mood that had been spreading for two years. "The masses were already there," Smith pointed out. "What Brown did was to masterfully capture what he was seeing out there."

When Smith went home to Natchez in the summer of 1967, the signs of white backlash to Black advancement were palpable. In 1965, the local head of the NAACP had barely survived a car bomb attack. Two years later, a truck bomb exploded and killed a thirty-six-year-old NAACP treasurer who had a wife and five children at home. Andrew Young came to explore the possibility of Dr. King visiting Natchez to protest the attack, but decided against it after seeing the .50 caliber machine gun mounted on the roof of the town's small airport terminal.

Despite the tense atmosphere in Natchez, the new spirit of Black pride and defiance had also taken hold among Smith's high school friends. They formed their own activist group, called the "Student Action Movement," and gathered over backyard barbecues to talk, as Smith put it, "about what was happening to us, explaining to each other what it meant." A few years later, one of those Natchez friends, who had gone to Alcorn State, became the first of the group to start a family of his own, and he gave all of his children African names. "His thinking was that he was arming them," Smith explained. "He was giving them proud Black names from which they could derive some sense of self-worth just by saying their names."

Fueled by this new faith himself, Vern Smith returned to San Francisco State to graduate and fulfill his dream of writing for a living. In 1969, he became part of a new wave of Black journalists hired by white-run news organizations that realized the previous generation of white civil rights reporters would never have the same feel for or access to a world of urban unrest and Black Power. Smith started at the

Long Beach *Press-Telegram* and was then hired by *Newsweek* magazine and sent to the racial front lines of Detroit. From there, he moved to Atlanta, where he was promoted to bureau chief and then national correspondent. With cool discernment, he reported on the role that the changing dynamics of race and politics in the South played in the rise of Jimmy Carter, the triumph of Barack Obama, and the showdowns between Donald Trump and Joe Biden. Yet no matter what his assessment of Black Power as a political force, Smith would never forget the impact it had on him personally in that fateful year of 1966.

"The media took it as a threat, as something sinister to white folks," he recalled. "In our minds, what it really meant was Black *empowerment*—that what we wanted was the power to control and affect our own destiny. It seems quaint when you look back at it, but the sense of inferiority that had been pushed down on people for generations was just not thought about until that moment. We began to look at ourselves differently, and really, for the first time in my life, and for most of the people I was hanging with, we were seeing things in ourselves that we had been shunning or denying and beginning to embrace them as a positive, as a strength."

Thinking about the generation of his grandson, a late teen on the verge of adulthood named Malcolm, Smith concluded: "If you are a twenty- or twenty-five-year-old Black person today and you call yourself Black or African American, it seems just like the most natural thing in the world to do. I guess that's a testament to the success that Black Power had in terms of making people not feel bad about themselves and really embrace who they were."

Of Allies and Messiahs

In the second week of 1967, with his mother watching from the gallery, Julian Bond was finally sworn in as a Georgia state assemblyman. This time the only drama came when Sloppy Floyd, the white lawmaker on the losing side of Bond's unanimous Supreme Court ruling, stalked out of the state House chamber in protest. Bond went on to serve for two decades as a state representative and senator before announcing a run for the U.S. House of Representatives in 1986. He began that race as an apparent shoo-in, with support from most of the local Black political establishment and outside luminaries, from Massachusetts senator Ted Kennedy to New York City mayor Ed Koch. But Bond was challenged by none other than John Lewis, his former SNCC colleague, who by then was an Atlanta city councilman. With his lifelong combination of quiet ambition and determination not to be limited by his Alabama sharecropper roots, Lewis concluded that he was more deserving than the more well-born Bond, whom he had come to view as overly cautious, lazy, and enamored of his celebrity status.

Working out of a tiny, drab storefront and brushing aside criticism that he was a race traitor for opposing Bond, Lewis spent long days campaigning across Georgia's 5th Congressional District, recounting tales of his civil rights era heroism, and won enough votes to force Bond into a second-round primary runoff. Stunned that Lewis had gotten that far, Bond challenged him to a series of debates, thinking he would show up his less polished opponent. But Lewis hired a media consultant and submitted to a grueling debate preparation that reminded him of his early training in nonviolent resistance. When Bond questioned his integrity as a city councilman in the third debate, Lewis brought up a sensitive issue that another candidate had raised in the first primary round. "Mr. Bond," Lewis said. "My friend. My brother. We were asked to take a drug test not long ago, and five of us went and took that test. Why don't we step out and go to the men's room and take another test?"

Bond refused—passing up the opportunity to put to rest rumors that he had become a recreational cocaine user, a charge that he denied but that his wife, Alice, later repeated, then retracted, during a messy divorce. On election night, Bond captured a clear majority of Black votes in the Atlanta district, but an early lead evaporated as some 90 percent of the white vote went to Lewis. It would end a career in politics for Bond, who went on to teach and serve as chairman of the NAACP and first head of the Southern Poverty Law Center before his death in 2015. Although Lewis later maintained that the two men patched up their differences and became friends again, remarks made by Bond in later years suggested otherwise. "It was a break in our relationship that never healed," Bond said in 2002. "We see each other from time to time, and I would like to think we're cordial. But it has never healed."

Lewis held that U.S. congressional seat for the next thirty-three years until his death in 2020, becoming a revered national icon and sweeping away public memories of the nasty contest with Bond. But that 1986 race demonstrated a hard political reality that would hold true for more than half a century after the first Black Power experiment in rural Alabama in 1966: Black politicians needed to appeal to white voters to win office. Even in Lowndes County, John Hulett, the founder of the original Black Panther Party, was elected county sheriff in 1970 only after the party merged with white state Democrats who had split from George Wallace's segregationists. Across America, winning some white support while counting on strong Black turnout proved a successful formula for scores of Black mayors, and the growing ranks of the Congressional Black Caucus. In 2008, it was key to the election of America's first Black president, as Barack Obama lost the overall white vote by twelve points but still received enough white support to forge a winning coalition with Black voters who supported him by more than 95 percent.

Among the Black Power leaders who continued to work outside the electoral system after 1966, how much to rely on whites also continued to be a major point of contention. After stepping down as SNCC chairman in early 1967, Stokely Carmichael embarked on a tour of Cuba, Vietnam, China, and Guinea. He returned arguing that Black Americans should sever all ties to whites at home and instead cast their lot with radical regimes of color abroad. Hoping to capitalize on Carmichael's stardom, the Black Panther Party for Self-Defense bestowed on him an honorary title of prime minister, only to have Stokely break with the Panthers over their desire to work with sympathetic white radicals. In 1969, Carmichael accepted an invitation from Guinea's increasingly autocratic leader Ahmed Sekou Touré to relocate to his country. Changing his name to Kwame Ture, Stokely supported himself as a traveling speaker who conjured up a vague and futile promise of a global Pan-African uprising. Until he died of prostate cancer at the age of fifty-seven, he answered phone calls with the greeting "Ready for revolution!"—a slogan that, as usual with Stokely, was partly a rallying cry and partly a joke.

Hoping to turn down the bright spotlight that Carmichael had attracted, SNCC's Central Committee replaced him as chairman with Hubert "Rap" Brown, the little known, bushy-haired Louisiana native who had succeeded Stokely as SNCC's field secretary in Alabama. But Brown quickly proved to have his own penchant for loose inflammatory rhetoric, without any of Carmichael's charm or sense of humor. Brown made headlines with statements such as "violence is as American as cherry pie" and "if America chooses to play Nazis, black folks ain't going to play Jews." Without checking with SNCC's Central Committee, a rogue staffer further alienated former Jewish supporters by publishing a pro-Palestinian, anti-Israel diatribe after the 1967 Six-Day War. What little white financial support SNCC still had all but disappeared, along with the protection that white backing had provided against police and FBI persecution. As SNCC historian Clayborne Carson put it: "Without fully understanding the consequences, SNCC willingly relinquished the undependable but still vital buffer of white liberal support that previously had restrained its opposition."

For H. Rap Brown, as he came to be known, that opposition arrived fast and hard. Only months into his tenure as SNCC chairman, violence broke out and several buildings were burned after Brown gave a fiery speech in Cambridge, Maryland. State prosecutors charged him with inciting a riot and added a trumped-up count of arson to justify putting the FBI on his tail. In Washington, meanwhile, previous liberal opposition collapsed to a new federal law against crossing state lines to incite violence that would be used to hound Brown and other Black Power leaders. As his trial dragged on, Brown vanished underground, and several years later was sent to prison when he resurfaced to rob a bank. Even after he converted to Islam in prison and took on a new identity as a cleric living in Atlanta, Brown's rap sheet followed him. When a Black Atlanta policeman tried to detain him for missing a court date in 2000, Brown shot the officer dead and then fled into hiding in Lowndes County, where the FBI found him in a rural shack and sent him back to Georgia for sentencing to life in prison.

In keeping with their Ten Point Program, the Panthers portrayed themselves as class warriors as well as race warriors, and thus open to alliances with whites with a similar agenda of bringing "all power to the people," as their slogan went. But soon after 1966, they also began to clash over motives for courting whites. After the Panther gun law protest in Sacramento in May of 1967, Bobby Seale was arrested and sent to prison for several months, and soon afterward Huey Newton was put on trial for shooting Oakland police officer John Frey. Eldridge Cleaver suddenly became the Panthers' most visible spokesman. As Cleaver explained it, "we got a whole slew of invitations from all the radical, liberal forums in California, and we were really short on people who knew how to handle that kind of public speaking task. So it kind of fell to me to do that." But for Newton and Seale, it was the beginning of suspicions that Cleaver was spending so much time seeking out white radicals and journalists only to get more attention for himself.

IN THE YEARS AFTER 1966, J. EDGAR HOOVER AND THE FBI ALSO dramatically escalated a campaign to undermine the Black Power movement by fanning those internal ideological and personal disputes. In August of 1967, Hoover sent a letter to twenty-three FBI field offices instructing them "to expose, disrupt, misdirect, discredit or otherwise neutralize activities of black nationalist, hate-type groups," among which he listed SNCC and even Dr. King's SCLC. In March of 1968, Hoover turned up the heat on this counterintelligence initiative—now known as COINTELPRO-BLACK HATE— by urging forty-one field offices to do everything they could to prevent the emergence of a "messiah" who could "unify and electrify" Black Americans. After Dr. King was assassinated a month later, and as SNCC ceased to be a national force, the FBI trained its sights on the Black Panthers. In the FBI's 1969 annual report, Hoover declared that the Panthers had become "the greatest threat to the internal security of the United States" of all the Black protest groups, and eventually the Panthers would be the target of 233 of the 296 covert actions unleashed under the COINTELPRO-BLACK HATE program.

Once Eldridge Cleaver had fled into exile after the Oakland shootout in 1968, the bureau did everything it could to inflame his long-distance feud with the imprisoned Huey Newton. Taking advantage of the two men's isolation and paranoia, FBI agents manufactured letters from rank-and-file Panthers to each of them, accusing the other of taking the party in the wrong direction. As Bobby Seale became ensnared in more high-profile legal battles—first as a defendant in the Chicago Eight trial (later Seven, after he was separated from the trial), then as an alleged accomplice in the murder of New Haven Panther suspected of being an FBI snitch—a dynamic new leader named Fred Hampton emerged in the Panther Chicago chapter. But the FBI ensured that Hampton never fulfilled his potential to become the "messiah" that Hoover feared. A local FBI agent cultivated an informant who provided evidence of an arms cache used to justify a predawn raid on Hampton's house—as well as a floor plan that led Chicago police to a bedroom where they killed Hampton in a barrage of gunfire as his pregnant fiancée looked on.

In Los Angeles, FBI agents worked to turn the local Panther chapter and Ron Karenga's US movement against each other. They disseminated derogatory cartoons about the Panthers that they attributed to US, while spreading whispers that Karenga was cooperating with the government after he accepted an invitation to meet with Governor Reagan following Dr. King's murder. Enflamed by the FBI smear tactics, the feud came to a head when members of both groups who were enrolled at UCLA clashed in a gun battle that left two popular Panthers dead. When police raided a weapons-stocked Panther lair the following day, the Panthers accused US of setting them up, and Karenga became convinced that he would be targeted for assassination. Two years later, he was convicted of trying to torture a confession out of two female US followers who he thought were plotting to slip poison crystals into his food. After serving a four-year prison term, Karenga carried on as a Black Studies professor, rising to chair the Africana Studies Department at California State University, Long Beach, but his days as a leader of full-fledged cultural nationalist movement were over.

Even after Newton was released from prison in 1970—following a three-year, high-profile "Free Huey" campaign—neither he nor any of the other founders were able to establish control over what had become a sort of Black Panther Party franchise operation. Across the country, militants took it upon themselves to launch chapters, organize free breakfast programs, and adopt the beret-and-leather-jacket dress code. Newton spiraled into drug and alcohol addiction and continued to get into hotheaded armed clashes that sent him fleeing into exile for a period and led to his death by gunfire, at age forty-seven, on a West Oakland street corner. After becoming a born-again Christian in exile, Eldridge Cleaver returned to the United States to face trial, eventually cutting a plea deal and taking a bizarre turn into designing men's codpieces, getting hooked on crack cocaine, and converting to right-wing Republicanism before he passed away at the age of sixty-two. Of the original Panther leaders, only Bobby Seale would survive to the 2020s, making occasional public appearances in his trademark beret and spinning versions of the Panther glory days in which he made himself out to be the principal hero.

Like Ruby Doris Robinson at SNCC, women were left to do most of the work at what was left of the Black Panther Party in Oakland, taking over when Newton went into exile and running a Panther elementary school. But given the times, only one woman of the Black Power generation was seen by the FBI or anyone else as having "messiah" potential. Brilliant, statuesque, and possessed of the most magnificent Afro most people had ever seen, UCLA philosophy professor Angela Davis became an international icon after she was discovered to have supplied guns used in a fatal attempt to free George Jackson, one of the so-called Soledad Brothers serving time for armed robbery in the San Francisco prison of that name. Davis fled into hiding, was put on the FBI's Most Wanted List, and graced the cover of *Newsweek* when she was caught. During a sixteen-month trial that ended with her acquittal, she became the focus of a global "Free Angela" campaign and was celebrated by luminaries from James Baldwin to John Lennon and Yoko Ono. But Davis remained a scholar by temperament, and went on to have far more influence in a long career of studying race and the criminal justice system than in a brief flirtation with politics as vice presidential candidate for the American Communist Party.

HOBBLED BY THE FBI'S DIRTY TRICKS AND THEIR OWN PERSONAL fights and failings, the first Black Power generation seemed to have played itself out by the late 1970s. Yet not long afterward, in the full-circle way that history often works, the conditions for a rebirth were laid during the presidency of Ronald Reagan, the former California governor first elected in part by a "backlash vote" against Black

Power in 1966. The dramatic increase in income inequality, draconian drug laws, and punitive prison sentencing ushered in during the Reagan era—with their starkly disproportionate impact on inner-city Black communities—brought forth a counterreaction from a new generation of radicalized Black political and cultural activists. By the 1990s and 2000s, a revived spirit of Black Consciousness could be detected in everything from hip hop music and racially charged films, television shows, and books to the academic explorations of "critical race theory" in law schools and revisionist American history pioneered by Black scholars and later popularized by *New York Times* reporters in their controversial "1619 Project."

In the 2010s, two factors that had led to the Black Power movement almost a half century earlier resurfaced to give rise to the Black Lives Matter movement. One was the unending nightmare of violence against unarmed Black Americans, either committed or condoned by the police, and now captured on smartphone and police cam video and broadcast across social media platforms that made household names of victims such as Trayvon Martin, Michael Brown, and Eric Garner. The other was a hangover of disappointment in conventional politics that resembled the bitterness felt after the betrayal of Fannie Lou Hamer and the Mississippi Freedom Democratic Party at the Atlantic City convention in 1964. Many young Blacks and their progressive white peers who turned out in droves for Barack Obama in 2008 ended up feeling badly let down that America's first Black president didn't do more to address issues about which they cared deeply, from climate change and environmental racism to police and criminal justice reform.

In the summer of 2020, the Black Lives Matter movement took on even greater force when the police murders of George Floyd in Minneapolis and Breonna Taylor in Louisville brought millions of Blacks and whites together into the streets of America in the most impressive moment of interracial protest since the height of the civil rights era. But just as they had in 1966, arguments over control and leadership quickly rose to the surface. In a memoir published that year, Alicia Garza, the Oakland-based activist who first coined the phrase "Black

Lives Matter" on Facebook, responded to those disagreements by advocating for a model of "decentralization" that called for "distributing leadership throughout an organization rather than concentrating it in one place or in one person or even a few people."

That idea sounded noble enough, but the past offered a different perspective. To produce lasting change, consequential social and political movements around the world had always demanded more than decentralized armies of young foot soldiers. If not messiahs, who could often prove false, they required visible leaders of exceptional charisma, maturity, and vision. At the height of the first chapter of the civil rights era, before Black Power, sit-in protesters and Freedom Riders such as John Lewis and Ruby Doris Robinson needed the support of Dr. King, just as he needed them to push him into battles he might not otherwise have fought. For all the contributions of others, before and after, the early American women's rights movement could not have gained the momentum it did without the guiding partnership of Susan B. Anthony and Elizabeth Cady Stanton. The Salt Marchers of India needed Mahatma Gandhi, and vice versa, just as the Soweto rioters of South Africa needed Nelson Mandela.

The first Black Power generation might have had such a transcendant leader, who could have channeled their demands and energy and kept them on a more constructive course, but he was cut down in a burst of shotgun fire at the Audubon Ballroom a year before they found their voice. So like children clinging to the memory of a lost father without the benefit of his helping hand, that generation raised themselves, sometimes for better but often for worse. The presence of Malcolm X hovered over them in 1966—but so, too, did his absence. And so the story still went a half century later, even after the first Black president. The latest heirs to the Black Power tradition were left to carry on the struggle by themselves, their rhetoric defiant but with no commanding presence to guide them forward.

Acknowledgments

A number of the central figures in this book wrote autobiographies, including Stokely Carmichael, James Forman, John Lewis, Bob Zellner, and Huey Newton. For the purposes of historical study, these accounts presented both a gift and a challenge. They were rich in narrative detail and access to private thoughts, but also prone to self-justification, score-settling, and selective memory. Before relying on these personal remembrances, therefore, I did my best to establish points of agreement, or to find corroboration in news accounts from the time and other contemporaneous sources. When versions of events conflicted or were clearly erroneous in significant ways, or when a reconstruction was unavoidably based on one subjective source, I tried to indicate as much. As an author, I was also thankful for the collaborators, some credited and some not, who helped bring these accounts to the printed page.

Among biographies of major characters in the book, I was indebted in particular to portraits of Stokely Carmichael by Peniel E. Joseph; of Ruby Doris Smith Robinson by Cynthia Griggs Fleming; of Bob Moses by Laura Visser-Maessen; and of the Reverend Martin Luther King Jr. by David J. Garrow and Taylor Branch. Valuable background and insight about key organizations and locations were contained in studies of SNCC by Clayborne Carson; of the Black Panther Party for Self-Defense by Joshua Bloom and Waldo E. Martin Jr.; of Lowndes County, Alabama, by Hasan Kwame Jeffries; of the West Side of Chicago by Beryl Satter; and of the Black community of Oakland, California, by Donna Jean Murch. Peniel Joseph and

Clayborne Carson were also kind enough to read advance copies of the book and to offer their expert feedback.

Since much of my research was conducted during a pandemic that made travel and visiting libraries extremely difficult, I was grateful for the online archives of *The New York Times*, *The New Yorker*, and the hundreds of papers represented on Newspapers.com, as well as less well-known and short-lived publications such as *The Southern Courier* and *The Flatlands*. Of immense usefulness was also the Civil Rights Movement Archive in San Francisco, the SNCC Digital Gateway at Duke University, the archives of Dr. King and photographer Bob Fitch at Stanford University, and several oral history projects organized by other universities.

Of the dozens of interviews I conducted for the book, the most revelatory were with surviving figures who hadn't previously given detailed accounts of their roles during this time period. I was fortunate to speak at length with Bob Moses, the legendarily brave and self-effacing former SNCC organizer, before he passed away in 2021. I gained essential information and perspective from Dorothy Miller Zellner, who along with her then husband, Bob Zellner, was among the last remaining white staffers who were expelled from SNCC at the end of 1966. Some of the most prominent journalists who covered the events of that year—Gene Roberts, for *The New York Times*; James S. Doyle, for *The Boston Globe*; and Renata Adler, for *The New Yorker*—were generous with their time and sharp and pointed in their recollections.

My former *Newsweek* colleague Vern Smith provided vivid background and moving personal reflections on events in two of the book's key settings: the Ku Klux Klan–infested world of Natchez, Mississippi, where he grew up; and Vern's alma mater, San Francisco State College (now University), where he was present at the creation of America's first Black Student Union and Black Studies department. Of the many other friends who encouraged me on this journey, I was assisted in particular by the Reverend Eugene Rivers, who pointed me to essays on Black Power by Christopher Lasch and

Eugene Genovese; by Bennett Freeman, a University of California at Berkeley graduate and expert on the history of activism in the Bay Area and around the globe; and by Peter Goldman, another former *Newsweek* colleague who is also one of America's foremost authorities on the life and legacy of Malcolm X.

My editor at Simon & Schuster when I embarked on this project was the legendary Alice Mayhew, who sadly passed away in early 2020. The last time I saw Alice, over lunch several months before her death, she encouraged me to reread the historian Barbara Tuchman. It was revisiting Tuchman's classic book on the first month of World War I, *The Guns of August*, that led me to narrow my then somewhat amorphous focus on the Black Power movement to the pivotal year of 1966. The rest of the way, Bob Bender guided me with warm encouragement, incisive suggestions, and a keen editing eye. At S&S, my thanks also go to Fred Chase, Johanna Li, Lisa Healy, Cat Boyd and Stephen Bedford for their help with copyediting and promotion; to Alison Forner for designing the book cover; and to CEO Jonathan Karp, for seeing the potential for a book on Black Power in my initial flurry of book proposals. My literary agent, Lynn Nesbit, was her usual fount of good cheer and wise advice.

As always, I was blessed with the love and insightful feedback of my wife, Alexis Gelber, and of our children, Rachel and Matthew Whitaker. This book is dedicated to my late parents—C. Sylvester Whitaker Jr., and Jeanne Theis Whitaker—whose influence I felt throughout its creation. My fascination with Black Power began in the late 1960s when my father, who had divorced my mother and largely abandoned our family in 1963, resurfaced in my life as an Afro-sporting, dashiki-wearing director of a new Afro-American Studies program at Princeton University. Although we had a very difficult relationship at that time—which I wrote about in my book *My Long Trip Home*—my father provided me with an example of how to think about issues of race, politics, and culture with independence, empathy for different perspectives, and a healthy sense of irony. To my mother, I'll always be grateful for her encouragement of all my writing endeavors, and for how she kept her two biracial sons connected with my father's family and our Black heritage. Until she passed away in October 2021, at the age of ninety-five, my mother never failed to ask me how things were going with the latest book. For the first time, she isn't here to see the final result, but I hope she would have approved.

Notes

AUTHOR'S NOTE

xi *widely accepted practice:* Nancy Coleman, "Why We're Capitalizing Black,"
    New York Times, July 5, 2020; Kwame Anthony Appiah, "The Case for
    Capitalizing the B in Black," *The Atlantic,* June 18, 2020.

PROLOGUE: DECEMBER 31, 1965 - THE ROAD TO BLACK POWER

1 *one of the scariest in the South:* Renata Adler, "Letter from Selma," *The New
   Yorker,* April 10, 1965.

1 *One car didn't make it:* Donna Britt, " 'They Killed a White Woman':
   Fifty-four Years Later, Leroy Moton Looks Back at the Killing That
   Changed the Civil Rights Movement," *Washington Post,* February 27,
   2019; Jonathan Yardley review of *The Informant: The FBI, the Ku Klux
   Klan, and the Murder of Viola Liuzzo,* by Gary May, *Washington Post,* July 3,
   2005.

2 *five young Black organizers:* Stokely Carmichael, *Ready for Revolution: The
   Life and Struggles of Stokely Carmichael (Kwame Toure)* (New York: Scribner, 2003), 459; Peniel Joseph, *Stokely: A Life* (New York: Basic Civitas,
   2014), 85.

2 *armed with hunting rifles:* Hasan Kwame Jeffries, *Bloody Lowndes: Civil
   Rights and Black Power in Alabama's Black Belt* (New York: New York
   University Press, 2009), 108.

2 *a blue Volkswagen Beetle drove up:* James Forman, *Sammy Younge, Jr.: The
   First Black College Student to Die in the Black Liberation Movement* (New
   York: Grove, 1968), 181–82; Gwen Patton, "Born Freedom Fighter," in
   Faith S. Holsaert et al., eds., *Hands on the Freedom Plow: Personal Accounts
   by Women in SNCC* (Urbana: University of Illinois Press, 2012), 581.

2 *Drunk on pink Catawba wine:* Forman, *Sammy Younge, Jr.,* 139.

3 *"we had a talk":* Ibid., 181.

3 *"What's happening, baby?"*: Ibid., 183–84.

3 *already had a name:* "Lowndes County Forms Local Political Group," *Student Voice*, December 20, 1965.

5 *"Black Consciousness":* Cleveland Sellers, *The River of No Return: The Autobiography of a Black Militant and the Life and Death of SNCC* (New York: William Morrow, 1973), 164–66.

5 *reject the label "Negro":* John Kifner, "Substitute Word for 'Negro' Argued," *New York Times*, December 11, 1966.

6 *a running battle:* Author interview with Gene Roberts, January 14, 2019.

6 *"The Natural Look":* *Ebony*, June 1966.

6 *bestselling $1.50 paperback:* "Dell Best Seller List," *Chicago Tribune*, August 19, 1966; Tim Warren, "The Rocky Road to the Publication of Book on Malcolm X," Baltimore *Sun*, November 16, 1992.

6 *commissioned pollster Louis Harris:* "The Negro in America," *Newsweek*, July 29, 1963.

6 *another such poll:* "Black and White: A Major Survey of U.S. Racial Attitudes Today," *Newsweek*, August 22, 1966.

6 *"They're asking too much":* "Black and White," *Newsweek*.

7 Soul on Ice: Eldridge Cleaver, *Soul on Ice* (New York: McGraw-Hill, 1968).

8 *two insightful white scholars:* Christopher Lasch, "The Trouble with Black Power," *New York Review of Books*, February 29, 1968; Eugene Genovese, "The Influence of the Black Power Movement on Historical Scholarship: Reflections of a White Historian," *Daedalus* (Spring 1970).

CHAPTER 1: JANUARY 3 - A MURDER IN TUSKEGEE

13 *a succession of girlfriends:* Forman, *Sammy Younge, Jr.*, 133–34.

13 *stately Alabama city:* Ibid., 29; Gene Roberts, "A Negro Student Slain in Alabama," *New York Times*, January 5, 1966.

13 *Sammy's mother, Renee:* Forman, *Sammy Younge, Jr.*, 32–38.

14 *"Brains, prosperity and character":* Booker T. Washington, "The Educational Outlook in the South," July 16, 1884: https://teachingamerican history.org/library/document/the-educational-outlook-in-the-south/.

14 *fictionalized description:* Ralph Ellison, *Invisible Man* (New York: Modern Library, 1994), 34.

14 *the* Pittsburgh Courier: "Red Cross Volunteers," *Pittsburgh Courier*, March 28, 1964.

14 *"getting into it with the Sisters":* Forman, *Sammy Younge, Jr.*, 49.

15 *"the Unbelievables":* Ibid., 60–62.

15   *disappointing his parents:* Ibid., 64–65.

15   *a congenital ailment:* Ibid., 70–72.

15   *coverage of "Bloody Sunday":* Ibid., 79.

15   *Lewis had grown up:* "John Lewis," SNCC Digital Gateway: https://sncc digital.org/people/john-lewis/; John Lewis official SNCC biography, crmvet.org: "Chairman John Lewis," SNCC staff biography, wisconsin history.org: https://content.wisconsinhistory.org/digital/collection/p15 932coll2/id/24299.

15   *dreamed of becoming a preacher:* John Lewis, *Walking with the Wind: Memoirs of the Movement* (New York: Simon & Schuster, 1998), 27, 53, 156–57.

16   *chose him by acclamation:* Ibid., 199–200.

16   *approached by a TV reporter:* "Selma, Alabama: The Role of the News Media in the Civil Rights Movement," pbslearningmedia.org: https:// ny.pbslearningmedia.org/resource/mr13.socst.us.selma/selma-alabama -the-role-of-news-media-in-the-civil-rights-movement/

17   *"I thought I was going to die on that bridge":* Sydney Trent, "John Lewis Nearly Died on the Edmund Pettus Bridge. Now It May Be Renamed for Him," *Washington Post,* July 26, 2020.

17   *Younge was chosen:* Forman, *Sammy Younge, Jr.,* 79–81.

17   *"a picnic":* Ibid., 102–3.

18   *walls of picket signs:* Ibid., 86–90.

18   *James Forman:* James Forman, *The Making of Black Revolutionaries* (Seattle: University of Washington Press, 1997), 3–110; Julian Bond, Foreword, xi–xiii; M. W. Newman, "Rugged, Ragged 'Snick': What It Is and What It Does," *Chicago Daily News,* July 20, 1963.

20   *"Everybody sit down":* Forman, *Sammy Younge, Jr.,* 88.

20   *didn't know what to make of him:* Ibid., 111.

20   *"Mr. Say ain't the man":* Clayborne Carson, *In Struggle: SNCC and the Black Awakening of the 1960's* (Cambridge: Harvard University Press, 1995), 199.

20   *"baptized" in the struggle:* Forman, *Sammy Younge, Jr.,* 113.

21   *caught the eye of Stokely:* Ibid., 115–16.

21   *one of the most visible activists:* Ibid., 117–29.

21   *"a little hum in his voice":* Ibid., 119.

21   *the city swimming pool:* Ibid., 142–43.

21   *integrate three white churches:* Ibid., 157–59.

22   *lose interest in the struggle:* Ibid., 174.

22   *a dorm fire escape:* Patton, "Born Freedom Fighter," in Holsaert et al., eds., *Hands on the Freedom Plow,* 580.

22   *"the Tuskegee system got to him":* Forman, *Sammy Younge, Jr.,* 176.

22　*a twenty-first birthday party:* Ibid., 181, 182.

22　*"We had some good talks":* Carmichael, *Ready for Revolution*, 466.

22　*released without explanation:* Ibid., 467–70.

23　*Younge was so upset:* Forman, *Sammy Younge, Jr.*, 179–80.

23　*ready to plunge back:* Ibid., 182–83.

23　*showed up at the courthouse:* Ibid., 185–88.

24　*new Black voters:* Roberts, "A Negro Student Slain in Alabama."

24　*his blue Volkswagen Beetle:* Patton, "Born Freedom Fighter," in Holsaert et al., eds., *Hands on the Freedom Plow*, 581.

24　*"I want to use the restroom":* "Civil Rights Division: Notice to Close File," March 28, 2011: https://www.justice.gov/crt/case-document/file/9490 26/download.

25　*bus driver stepped down:* Mary Ellen Gale, "The Trial . . . And After," *Southern Courier*, December 17–18, 1966.

25　*Segrest fired another bullet:* "Civil Rights Division: Notice to Close File," March 28, 2011.

25　*the phone rang:* Forman, *Sammy Younge, Jr.*, 89–190.

26　*"What's that body?":* Ibid., 191.

26　*a gruesome sight:* Ibid., photo insert.

26　*a front-page story:* Roberts, "A Negro Student Slain in Alabama."

26　*wire service account:* "Slaying of Negro Upsets Tuskegee," (Eau Claire, Wisconsin) *Daily Telegram*, January 5, 1966.

26　*an all-white jury:* "Civil Rights Division: Notice to Close File," March 28, 2011.

27　*Forman was in New York City:* Forman, *Sammy Younge, Jr.*, 19.

27　*"1966 was going to be decisive":* Ibid., 20.

27　*he had lost the heart:* Ibid., 21–25.

28　*"The absolute absurdity":* Sellers, *The River of No Return*, 157.

28　*Gloria Larry:* Cheryl Lynn Greenberg, ed., *A Circle of Trust: Remembering SNCC* (New Brunswick: Rutgers University Press, 1998), 104; Gloria House, "We'll Never Turn Back," in Holsaert et al., eds., *Hands on the Freedom Plow*.

29　*compounded by indignation:* "Civil Rights Division: Notice to Close File, March 28, 2011"; Forman, *Sammy Younge, Jr.*, 194.

29　*reached Kathleen Neal:* Forman, *Sammy Younge, Jr.*, 44–45.

29　*found college boring:* Kathleen Cleaver interview for the Civil Rights History Project of Library of Congress, September 16, 2011: https://www.loc .gov/collections/civil-rights-history-project/?fa=segmentof:afc2010039 .afc2010039_crhp0051_cleaver_transcript/&sb=shelf-id&st=gallery.

30 *an Army therapist:* FBI Records: The Vault, Stokely Carmichael, Part 4, 3–5, PDF at: https://vault.fbi.gov/Stokely%20Carmichael/Stokely%20 Carmichael%20Part%204%20of%205/view.

30 *the long car ride:* Carmichael, *Ready for Revolution*, 470.

30 *"I didn't have the strength, man":* Forman, *Sammy Younge, Jr.*, 184.

CHAPTER 2: JANUARY 10 – HUMILIATED IN ATLANTA

31 *local radio reporter:* Edwin D. Spivia Obituary: https://obits.funeralinno vations.com/obituaries/view/386886/2/.

31 *stood on the war:* "Burn Draft Cards, Negro Rights Leader Proposes," UPI/*Pensacola News Journal*, January 7, 1966.

32 *When Julian was five:* Marshall Frady, *Southerners: A Journalist's Odyssey* (New York: New American Library, 1980), 171.

33 *his own poems:* Roy Reed, "Pacifist Rights Aide: Horace Julian Bond," *New York Times*, January 12, 1966.

33 *advertising poster:* Ibid.

33 *Donaldson convinced Bond:* Clayborne Carson, *In Struggle*, 166.

33 *$500 entry fee:* Sellers, *The River of No Return*, 156.

33 *the highest turnout:* Frady, *Southerners*, 173.

33 *front-page headline:* Bill Shipp, "Defiance of Draft Call Urged by SNCC Leader," *Atlanta Constitution*, January 7 1966.

34 *"un-American attitude":* Sam Hopkins, "Rep.-Elect Bond Facing an Ouster Fight After Urging Draft-Dodging," *Atlanta Constitution*, January 8, 1966.

34 *Roy Wilkins:* "NAACP Disavows Part in Anti-Viet Blast," *Tampa Tribune*, January 9, 1966.

34 *Eugene Patterson:* Gene Roberts and Hank Klibanoff, *The Race Beat: The Press, the Civil Rights Struggle, and the Awakening of a Nation* (New York: Vintage, 2007), 351–52, 370–71.

34 *a scathing editorial:* Eugene Patterson, "SNCC Reaches End of the Line," *Atlanta Constitution*, January 8, 1966.

34 *Plotting over a meal:* "Two-Time Loser," *Newsweek*, January 24, 1966; Frady, *Southerners*, 167.

34 *"really shaken":* Lewis, *Walking with the Wind*, 377.

34 *"a balancing patriotic statement":* "Two-Time Loser," *Newsweek*.

34 *"just plain beg a little":* Roger F. Williams, *The Bonds: An American Family* (New York: Atheneum, 1972), 224.

35 *Georgia state capitol:* Edwin L. Jackson, "Georgia State Capitol," *New Georgia Encyclopedia*: https://www.georgiaencyclopedia.org/articles/arts-culture

/georgia-state-capitol/; "Controversial State Capitol Statues," AJC.com: https://www.ajc.com/news/photos-controversial-georgia-state-capitol -statues/RmmBlmnmO406uXvwQBAzgM/.

35 *"Mr. Doorkeeper":* "Two-Time Loser," *Newsweek.*

35 *a small metal name plate:* "Will This House Desk Be Occupied Monday?," *Atlanta Constitution,* January 10, 1966.

35 *"a college dance":* Roy Reed, "Pacifist Rights Aide," *New York Times,* January 12, 1966.

36 *attempted to take a nap:* Bill Shipp, "Bond Naps in Back Office as Aides Work on Defenses," *Atlanta Constitution,* January 11, 1966; Frady, *Southerners,* 167, 176.

36 *"My God, I didn't raise my boy":* Frady, *Southerners,* 171.

36 *resembled a criminal trial:* "Two-Time Loser," *Newsweek.*

37 *Pafford came to the dais:* Frady, *Southerners,* 177–78.

37 *"a disgrace":* "Two-Time Loser," *Newsweek.*

37 *"outhouse door":* Frady, *Southerners,* 178.

37 *"a blur of tears":* John Neary, *Julian Bond: Black Rebel* (New York: William Morrow, 1971), 124.

37 *"state of shock":* Taylor Branch, *At Canaan's Edge: America in the King Years, 1965–68* (New York: Simon & Schuster, 2006), 411, 882.

38 *tomato sandwich:* Frady, *Southerners,* 178.

38 *"worst thing I've ever been through":* "Two Time Loser," *Newsweek.*

38 *a $200,000 deficit:* Gene Roberts, "Fund Lag Plagues Rights Movement," *New York Times,* January 10, 1966.

38 *"The irony hit me":* Lewis, *Walking with the Wind,* 374.

38 *"we were getting screwed":* Ibid., 387.

39 *Fannie Lou Hamer:* Jerry DeMuth, " 'Tired of Being Sick and Tired,' " *The Nation,* June 1, 1964.

39 *Although Hamer lost:* "MFDP Challenge at Democratic National Convention," SNCC Digital Gateway: https://snccdigital.org/events/mfdp -challenge-at-democratic-national-convention/.

40 *the biggest news story:* "Fannie Lou Hamer's Powerful Testimony," *American Experience,* PBS, YouTube: https://www.youtube.com/watch?v=07P wNVCZCcY.

40 *President Johnson was irate:* Ibid.; Laura Visser-Maessen, *Robert Parris Moses: A Life in Civil Rights and Leadership at the Grassroots* (Chapel Hill: University of North Carolina Press, 2016), 218–44; Taylor Branch, *Pillar of Fire: America in the King Years, 1963–65* (New York: Simon & Schuster, 1998), 456–76.

41 *"We didn't come all this way":* "MFDP Challenge at Democratic National

Convention," SNCC Digital Gateway: https://snccdigital.org/events
/mfdp-challenge-at-democratic-national-convention/.

42 *"Never again were we lulled":* Sellers, *River of No Return*, 117.

42 *one of his friends in particular:* Author interview with Dorothy Zellner,
July 6, 2020; Dorothy Zellner interview for Julian Bond Oral History
Project, American University, September 28, 2018: https://www.julian
bondoralhistoryproject.org/dorothy-zellne.

42 *Bill Ware:* "Bill Ware," SNCC Digital Gateway: https://snccdigital.org
/people/bill-ware/; Ware family tree and documents, Ancestry.com:
https://www.ancestry.com/discoveryui-content/view/281869002:754;
Dick Cunningham, "Ex–St. Paulite Risks Life in Mississippi," *Minneapolis Tribune*, July 5, 1964; "The Movement in Natchez—Narrative Time-
line," mscivilrightsproject.org: https://mscivilrightsproject.org/adams
/event-adams/the-movement-in-natchez-narrative-timeline/.

44 *"the Vine City Project":* "Bill Ware," SNCC Digital Gateway; "Purpose
of the Atlanta Project," SNCC News Service, crmvet.org: https://www
.crmvet.org/docs/660000_sncc_atlproj.pdf; Douglas Martin, "Mendy
Samstein, 68, Dies; Championed Civil Rights," *New York Times*, January 25, 2007.

CHAPTER 3: JANUARY 26 – A NEW FRONT IN CHICAGO

45 *complicated history:* "North Lawndale History," Steans Family Founda-
tion: http://www.steansfamilyfoundation.org/lawndale_history.shtml;
Beryl Satter, *Family Properties: How the Struggle over Race and Real Estate
Transformed Chicago and Urban America* (New York: Picador, 2009), 17–19.

46 *"contract selling":* Satter, *Family Properties*, 1–13.

46 *Chicago Daily News:* John Culhane, "I Was Hired to Sell Slums to
Negroes," *Chicago Daily News*, May 24, 1963; John Culhane, "His First
Day 'Selling Slums,' " *Chicago Daily News*, May 25, 1963.

46 *"The Case for Reparations":* Ta-Nehisi Coates, "The Case for Reparations," *The Atlantic*, June 2014.

46 *James Bevel:* "James Bevel," SNCC Digital Gateway: https://snccdigital
.org/people/james-bevel/.

46 *"It didn't sell":* Satter, *Family Properties*, 181–82.

48 *"miscalculation":* Ibid., 183.

49 *he traveled to Chicago:* David J. Garrow, *Bearing the Cross: Martin Luther
King, Jr. and the Southern Leadership Conference* (New York: William Morrow, 1986), 432.

49 *King tested the waters:* Ibid., 433–37.

50　*"the equivalent to Wallace":* Ibid., 432.

50　*"You don't know what Chicago is like":* Ibid., 455.

50　*"If northern problems":* Ibid., 443–44.

51　*Betty Washington:* Ethan Michaeli, *The Defender: How the Legendary Black Newspaper Changed America* (Boston: Houghton Mifflin Harcourt, 2016), 398–99.

51　*a fifteen-page document:* Donald Janson, "Drive in Chicago Begun by Dr. King," *New York Times,* January 8, 1966.

51　*"the verbosity of the document":* Garrow, *Bearing the Cross,* 457.

51　*rent on the South Side:* Branch, *At Canaan's Edge,* 427.

51　*"epitome of filth":* Satter, *Family Properties,* 182.

52　*"I'm delighted to have him":* Ibid., 185.

52　*"It Wasn't the Plan":* Michaeli, *The Defender,* 401.

52　*dingy enough:* Coretta Scott King, *My Life with Martin Luther King, Jr.* (New York: Holt, Rinehart & Winston, 1969), 276.

52　*Ralph Abernathy's wife:* Branch, *At Canaan's Edge,* 429; Satter, *Family Properties,* 185.

52　*elegantly dressed couple:* Photo, *Chicago Tribune,* January 27, 1966.

52　*cheerfully waved:* Photo, *Pittsburgh Courier,* February 12, 1966.

52　*"for One Day":* *Chicago Tribune,* January 27, 1966.

52　*Orlando Wilson:* *Chicago Tribune,* January 28, 1966; Branch, *At Canaan's Edge,* 427.

53　*steal King's thunder:* Branch, *At Canaan's Edge,* 428.

53　*1320 South Homan Avenue:* James Sullivan, "Dr. King Takes Over Slum Building," *Chicago Tribune,* February 24, 1966.

53　*sanitation crew jumpsuits:* Photo, *Chicago Tribune,* February 24, 1966; Garrow, *Bearing the Cross,* 465.

53　*eighty-on-year-old invalid:* Sullivan, "Dr. King Takes Over Slum Building."

53　*"King is doing the right thing":* "Civil Rights Groups Become 'Trustees' of City Tenements," (Muncie, Indiana) *Star Press,* February 24, 1966.

53　*"We're with you":* Satter, *Family Properties,* 185.

54　*Robert Weaver:* Robert B. Semple, "Johnson Names Weaver to Head Housing Agency," *New York Times,* January 14, 1966.

54　*dismissed as too small:* Austin C. Wehrwein, "Dr. King Occupies a Flat in Slum," *New York Times,* January 27, 1966.

54　*State of the Union Address:* "January 12, 1966: State of the Union," transcript, UVA Miller Center: https://millercenter.org/the-presidency /presidential-speeches/january-12-1966-state-union.

54　*Stokely had been born:* Carmichael, *Ready for Revolution,* 22–43.

55　*When he was eleven:* Ibid., 44–59; "Stokely Carmichael Interviewing

His Mother in 1967," YouTube.com: https://www.youtube.com/watch
?v=cXKZdw49b3I.

55　*"serious, serious dump"*: Carmichael, *Ready for Revolution*, 61–62.

55　*"These were working people"*: Ibid., 538–39.

CHAPTER 4: MARCH 17 - TWO TOUGHS FROM OAKLAND

57　*Thursday, March 17*: Bobby Seale, *Seize the Time: The Story of the Black
Panther Party and Huey P. Newton* (Baltimore: Black Classic Press, 1991),
2728; Joshua Bloom and Waldo E. Martin, *Black Against Empire: The
History and Politics of the Black Panther Party* (Oakland: University of California Press, 2013), 35.

59　*"doesn't let anyone mess over"*: Seale, *Seize the Time*, 28.

59　*understand Frantz Fanon*: Ibid., 25–26.

60　*It was Newton's family*: Huey P. Newton, *Revolutionary Suicide* (New York:
Penguin Classics, 2009), 10–12; David Hilliard, *Huey: Spirit of the Pan-
ther* (New York: Basic Books, 2006), 8; Donna Jean Murch, *Living for the
City: Migration, Education and the Rise of the Black Panther Party in Oakland,
California* (Chapel Hill: University of North Carolina Press), 45.

60　*"Huey P. Long had been a great man"*: Newton, *Revolutionary Suicide*, 11.

60　*"you can take a killing"*: Bloom and Martin, *Black Against Empire*, 19.

60　*"If you hit me a lick"*: Newton, *Revolutionary Suicide*, 30–31.

61　*"My father's father"*: Ibid., 9.

61　*diet of "cush"*: Ibid., 15.

61　*"preoccupation with bills"*: Ibid., 39–40.

61　*Armelia often seemed*: Ibid., 10.

61　*By junior high school*: Hilliard, *Huey*, 7–8.

62　*He was able to recite*: Newton, *Revolutionary Suicide*, 33.

62　*learned to use his fists*: Ibid., 21–22.

62　*take after Sonny Man*: Ibid., 24

62　*went to Oakland Tech*: "History & Alumni," oaklandtech.com: https://
oaklandtech.com/staff/history-alumni/.

62　*Stanford-Binet IQ test*: Newton, *Revolutionary Suicide*, 53.

63　*"diploma was a farce"*: Ibid., 50.

63　*Plato's Republic*: Ibid., 54–55.

63　*Oakland City College*: Murch, *Living for the City*, 97–105.

64　*in open rebellion*: Newton, *Revolutionary Suicide*, 56–59; Hilliard, *Huey*, 11.

64　*charismatic mixture*: Murch, *Living for the City*, 77–79.

65　*book study groups*: Newton, *Revolutionary Suicide*, 63.

65　*weekly radio program*: Murch, *Living for the City*, 94.

65 *old acquaintance from childhood:* Hilliard, *Huey,* 12–13.

65 *disillusioned with Donald Warden:* Newton, *Revolutionary Suicide,* 63–65.

66 *McClymonds High School:* Ibid., 71–72; "Oakland Conclave Is Attracting Top Negro Celebrities," *San Bernardino County Sun,* August 8, 1963.

66 *Malcolm instantly impressed Newton:* Newton, *Revolutionary Suicide,* 71–72.

67 *"You must be an Afro-American":* Ibid., 88–90.

67 *frequent the law library:* Ibid., 79, 85–88.

67 *act as his own lawyer:* Ibid., 90–92.

68 *"Soul Breaker":* Ibid., 103–10.

69 *Revolutionary Action Movement:* Bloom and Martin, *Black Against Empire,* 31.

69 *Robert F. Williams:* "From Robert F. Williams," King Papers, Stanford University: https://kinginstitute.stanford.edu/king-papers/documents/robert-f-williams.

69 *Kenny Freeman:* Seale, *Seize the Time,* 25.

69 *The SSAC spread word:* Ibid., 29–30.

69 *a final rupture:* Newton, *Revolutionary Suicide,* 111–14; Seale, *Seize the Time,* 29–33.

70 *"We resign":* Seale, *Seize the Time,* 33.

70 *"been all along: nowhere":* Newton, *Revolutionary Suicide,* 114.

71 *"guns are key":* Seale, *Seize the Time,* 34.

CHAPTER 5: MAY 3 – THE BLACK PANTHERS OF LOWNDES COUNTY

72 *Adolphus Carmichael died:* Carmichael, *Ready for Revolution,* 246.

72 *days without seeing him:* Howard Zinn, *SNCC: The New Abolitionists* (Chicago: Haymarket, 2017), 55.

72 *phonograph records:* Carmichael, *Ready for Revolution,* 81–82.

72 *dock in Ghana:* Ibid., 101.

73 *angry commentary:* Lerone Bennett, Jr., "Stokely Carmichael: Architect of Black Power," *Ebony,* September 1966.

73 *"I want to remember our father":* Carmichael, *Ready for Revolution,* 247.

74 *tall, imposing Black figure:* Ibid., 95.

75 *changed his life:* Ibid., 112–13.

75 *Rustin's essays:* Bayard Rustin, "The Negro and Non-Violence," *Fellowship: The Journal of the Fellowship of Reconciliation,* October 1942; Bayard Rustin, "Non-Violence and Jim Crow," *Fellowship,* July 1942.

75 *Bayard stayed up:* Sellers, *The River of No Return,* 63.

75 *debate Malcolm X:* Carmichael, *Ready for Revolution,* 256–61.

76 *become "respectable":* Sellers, *The River of No Return,* 64–67.

77 *"You're a traitor":* Branch, *Pillar of Fire,* 473.

77 *self-interested motive:* Author interview with Bob Moses, February 7, 2019.

78 *Raised in Harlem:* Ibid.

78 *"taking the initiative":* Zinn, *SNCC*, 17.

78 *Jane Stembridge:* "Jane Stembridge," SNCC Digital Gateway: https://snccdigital.org/people/jane-stembridge/.

78 *communist spy:* Visser-Maessen, *Robert Parris Moses*, 43.

79 *Parchman Farm:* Carmichael, *Ready for Revolution*, 210.

79 *hearing about Bob Moses:* Ibid., 240–43.

79 *soft-spoken organizer:* Ibid., 310–11.

80 *"It took all night":* Author interview with Bob Moses.

80 *Camus' The Rebel:* Visser-Maessen, *Robert Parris Moses*, 124.

80 *"a phenomenal organizer":* Carmichael, *Ready for Revolution*, 312.

80 *Moses made a special trip:* Author interview with Bob Moses.

81 *"the greatest honor":* Carmichael, *Ready for Revolution*, 313.

81 *"Stokely had all three":* Author interview with Bob Moses.

81 *At a workshop:* Sellers, *The River of No Return*, 88.

82 *search party:* Ibid., 88–98; Carmichael, *Ready for Revolution*, 373–81.

82 *"superior firepower":* Carmichael, *Ready for Revolution*, 379.

82 *"media person":* Author interview with Bob Moses.

83 *"needed to leave":* Lewis, *Walking with the Wind*, 366.

83 *"I felt a responsibility":* Carmichael, *Ready for Revolution*, 437.

83 *"Bob Moses bag":* Visser-Maessen, *Robert Parris Moses*, 280.

83 *evolution that Malcolm X:* Peniel E. Joseph, *The Sword and the Shield: The Revolutionary Lives of Malcolm X and Martin Luther King, Jr.* (New York: Basic Books, 2020), 25–54, 168–69.

84 *Malcolm's speech that day:* Ibid., 196–97; "Malcolm X Repeats Call for Negro Unity on Rights," *New York Times*, June 29, 1964; "(1964) Malcolm X's Speech at the Founding Rally of the Organization of Afro-American Unity," blackpast.org: https://www.blackpast.org/african-american-history/speeches-african-american-history/1964-malcolm-x-s-speech-founding-rally-organization-afro-american-unity/.

85 *Malcolm ran into John Lewis:* Lewis, *Walking with the Wind*, 295–98; Carmichael, *Ready for Revolution*, 440.

85 *Fannie Lou Hamer joined:* Carmichael, *Ready for Revolution*, 440–41.

85 *As a college student:* Ibid., 253–61.

86 *a more strategic role:* Ibid., 440.

86 *Silas Norman:* "Selma Voting Rights Campaign," SNCC Digital Gateway: https://snccdigital.org/events/selma-voting-rights-campaign/.

86 *newspaper reports:* George Carmack, " 'Bama Negroes Face 2 Routes to Freedom," Scripps-Howard/*Pittsburgh Press*, February 5, 1965.

86 *raves about Malcolm:* Carmichael, *Ready for Revolution*, 440.

86 *bulletin on the car radio:* Ibid., 439–41.

87 *two of the men were exonerated:* Ashley Southall and Jonah E. Bromwich, "2 Men Convicted of Killing Malcolm X Will Be Exonerated After Decades," *New York Times*, November 17, 2021.

87 *evidence of a plot:* Troy Clossen, "These Are the People Scholars Believe Really Killed Malcolm X," *New York Times*, November 17, 2021.

87 *"the only figure of that generation":* Carmichael, *Ready for Revolution*, 441.

87 *Jimmie Lee Jackson:* "Selma Voting Rights Campaign," SNCC Digital Gateway: https://snccdigital.org/events/selma-voting-rights-campaign/.

88 *man of few words:* Beth Wilcox, "John Hulett: Man on the Go in Lowndes County," *Southern Courier*, January 13–14, 1968.

88 *"very heart of darkness":* Andrew Kopkind, *The Thirty Years' Wars: Dispatches and Diversions of a Radical Journalist, 1965–1994* (London: Verso, 1995), 49.

89 *Daylight Savings Club:* Jeffries, *Bloody Lowndes*, 41–43.

89 *"Don't you know how to knock?":* Ibid.; "John Hulett," SNCC Digital Gateway: https://snccdigital.org/people/john-hulett/.

89 *LCCMHR:* Kopkind, *The Thirty Years' Wars*, 50.

90 *"people looove Dr. King":* Carmichael, *Ready for Revolution*, 455–56.

90 *"virgin territory":* Ibid., 457–58.

90 *Bob Mants:* Ibid., 455–56.

90 *Robert Strickland:* Kopkind, *The Thirty Years' Wars*, 53.

91 *Carmichael and Mants did return:* Carmichael, *Ready for Revolution*, 458–60; Greenberg, ed, *A Circle of Trust*, 100–101.

92 *At the jailhouse:* Jeffries, *Bloody Lowndes*, 75–78.

92 *sharecropper's shack:* Kopkind, *The Thirty Years' Wars*, 51.

93 *federal "examiners":* John Herbers, "9 Counties to Get Vote Aides Today," *New York Times*, August 10, 1965.

93 *on the ground:* Gene Roberts, "Voting Officials Sign 1,144 Negroes First Day of Drive," *New York Times*, August 11, 1965.

93 *Fort Deposit:* Jeffries, *Bloody Lowndes*, 79.

93 *impassioned speech:* Ibid., 153.

94 *asked Jack Minnis:* Carmichael, *Ready for Revolution*, 462; "Jack Minnis," SNCC Digital Gateway: https://snccdigital.org/people/jack-minnis/.

94 *spelled out the details:* Jeffries, *Bloody Lowndes*, 147–48.

94 *animal symbols:* Benjamin Hedin, "From Selma to Black Power," *The Atlantic*, March 6, 2015.

94 *assigned Ruth Howard:* Ibid.; "The Black Panther Symbol: An Email Discussion," May–June, 2006, crmvet.org: https://www.crmvet.org/disc/panther.htm.

95 *announced the founding:* "Lowndes County Forms Local Political Group," *Student Voice*, December 20, 1965.

95 *"Freedom City":* Jeffries, *Bloody Lowndes*, 106–11.

95 *Hosea Williams:* John Klein, "Civil Rights Leaders Disagree on Using Votes in Black Belt," *Southern Courier*, January 22–23, 1966.

96 *the Alabama Democrats:* "Panther on the Prowl," *Newsweek*, February 7, 1966.

96 *declared their candidacies:* "Mass Meeting Day Tuesday for Lowndes County Party," *Southern Courier*, April 30–May 1, 1966.

97 *didn't have to wait long:* Jeffries, *Bloody Lowndes*, 171–73.

97 *Charles Nesson:* Ibid.; Branch, *At Canaan's Edge*, 461.

97 *voted for the first time:* Gene Roberts, "Negroes in Alabama Explain 'Defections,' " *New York Times*, May 8, 1966; Roy Reed, "Alabama Negro Candidates Lead in 2 Legislative Elective, 3 Sheriff's Votes," *New York Times*, May 4, 1966.

98 *First Baptist Church:* Larry Freudiger, "Lowndes Third Party Attracts 900, Nominates Logan to Face Sheriff," *Southern Courier*, May 7–8, 1966; Reed, "Alabama Negro Candidates Lead in 2 Legislative Elective, 3 Sheriff's Votes."

98 *passed out balloons:* Jeffries, *Bloody Lowndes*, 175.

98 *as the sun was setting:* Freudiger, "Lowndes Third Party Attracts 900, Nominates Logan to Face Sheriff."

CHAPTER 6: MAY 13 – A COUP IN KINGSTON SPRINGS

100 *Carmichael drove:* Carmichael, *Ready for Revolution*, 477–78.

100 *Bethany Hills:* "SNCC Names New Leaders," *The Tennessean*, May 17, 1966.

100 *"wasn't paying that much attention":* Carmichael, *Ready for Revolution*, 478.

101 *a different memory:* Lewis, *Walking with the Wind*, 372–73, 380–81.

102 *only one biography:* Cynthia Griggs Fleming, *Soon We Will Not Cry: The Liberation of Ruby Doris Smith Robinson* (Lanham, MD: Rowman & Littlefield, 2000).

102 *"plain features":* Sellers, *The River of No Return*, 25.

102 *earliest childhood photos:* Cynthia Griggs Fleming, *Soon We Will Not Cry*, photo insert.

102 *Smith's parents:* Ibid., 16–21.

102 *"I didn't recognize their existence":* Harry G. Lefever, *Undaunted by the Fight: Spelman College and the Civil Rights Movement, 1957–1967* (Macon, GA: Mercer University Press, 2005), 24–25,

103   *at Price High School:* Cynthia Griggs Fleming, *Soon We Will Not Cry*, 32, 38.

103   *less conformist influence:* Josephine Carson, *Silent Voices: An Intimate Study of Southern Black Women During the Civil Rights Struggle* (New York: Delacorte, 1969), 201.

103   *Ruby Doris entered Spelman:* Cynthia Griggs Fleming, *Soon We Will Not Cry*, 44–48.

103   *pleaded to be included:* Ibid., 52–68; Lefever, *Undaunted by the Fight*, 34–36, 63–65.

104   *the Rock Hill protest:* Cynthia Griggs Fleming, *Soon We Will Not Cry*, 72–77; Lefevre, *Undaunted by the Fight*, 85–91.

104   *conquer her physical insecurities:* Josephine Carson, *Silent Voices*, 202; Cynthia Griggs Fleming, *Soon We Will Not Cry*, 74–75.

105   *resenting white women:* Josephine Carson, *Silent Voices*, 202.

105   *greeted as a hero:* Lefever, *Undaunted by the Fight*, photo, 107.

105   *eighteen pounds:* Sellers, *The River of No Return*, 25.

105   *"African kind of beauty":* Josephine Carson, *Silent Voices*, 202.

105   *second wave of Freedom Riders:* Zinn, *SNCC*, 45–48, 54–55.

106   *week-long workshop:* Cynthia Griggs Fleming, *Soon We Will Not Cry*, 88.

106   *"not believing in non-violence":* Ibid.

107   *"above reproach":* Lefevre, *Undaunted by the Fight*, 130.

107   *at SNCC's headquarters:* Ibid., 92–96.

107   *impose order:* Foreword by Julian Bond, in Forman, *The Making of Black Revolutionaries*, xi.

107   *deserved as much credit:* Cynthia Griggs Fleming, *Soon We Will Not Cry*, 94–101; Dorothy M. Zellner, "My Real Vocation," in Holsaert et al., eds., *Hands on the Freedom Plow*, 316.

108   *Then came Freedom Summer:* Cynthia Griggs Fleming, *Soon We Will Not Cry*, 109–12, 130, 134, 209.

109   *Dottie Miller met her:* Author interview with Dorothy Zellner, July 6, 2000; Zellner, "My Real Vocation."

109   *arm-in-arm:* Cynthia Griggs Fleming, *Soon We Will Not Cry*, photo insert.

109   *joined a sit-in:* Lefever, *Undaunted by the Fight*, 214.

109   *the issue of women's roles:* "SNCC Position Paper (Name Withheld Upon Request)," crmvet.org: https://www.crmvet.org/docs/6411w_us_women.pdf; Cynthia Griggs Fleming, *Soon We Will Not Cry*, 152.

110   *bothered by sexual politics:* Ibid., 137–38, 151.

110   *most notorious incident:* Lefever, *Undaunted by the Fight*, 211–12; Mary E. King, *Freedom Song: A Personal Story of the 1960's Civil Rights Movement* (New York: William Morrow, 1987), 451–52; Cynthia Griggs Fleming, *Soon We Will Not Cry*, 153.

110 *African country of Guinea:* Cynthia Griggs Fleming, *Soon We Will Not Cry*, 148–49; Jonathan C. Randel, "Empty Palace Catches Tenor of Toure's Rule," *Washington Post*, May 25, 1984.

111 *factional battle:* Clayborne Carson, *In Struggle*, 155, 169.

111 *personal reasons:* Cynthia Griggs Fleming, *Soon We Will Not Cry*, 103–8, 160.

112 *another rebellious faction:* Clayborne Carson, *In Struggle*, 195–98.

112 *"position paper":* "Black Power: A Reprint of a Position Paper for the SNCC Vine City Project," United States National Students Association: https://www.crmvet.org/docs/6604_sncc_atlanta_race.pdf.

113 *cold reception:* Clayborne Carson, *In Struggle*, 199–200.

113 *"sit around talking about white people":* Cynthia Griggs Fleming, *Soon We Will Not Cry*, 179.

114 *moving images:* Danny Lyon, *Memories of the Southern Civil Rights Movement* (Chapel Hill: University of North Carolina Press, 1992), 162–65.

114 *future was limited:* Author interview with Danny Lyon, January 18, 2020.

114 *Bethany Hills religious camp:* Bethany Hills website: https://www.bethany hills.org; "Fanny Battle Day Home Records," Nashville Public Library: https://bucket.library.nashville.org/findingaids/Special_Collections_Division_Finding_Aid_Fannie_Battle.pdf.

115 *prickly memo:* John Lewis memo, crmvet.org: https://www.crmvet.org /docs/660000_sncc_lewis_europe.pdf.

115 *more than 120 Black participants:* Sellers, *The River of No Return*, 164–66.

116 *pragmatic argument:* Clayborne Carson, *In Struggle*, 201–2.

117 *tense experience:* Ibid., 201; Lewis, *Walking with the Wind*, 382; Sellers, *The River of No Return*, 166–67.

117 *On the last full day:* Lewis, *Walking with the Wind*, 382–83; Carmichael, *Ready for Revolution*, 480.

119 *burst into the mess hall:* Sellers, *The River of No Return*, 167–68; Lewis, *Walking with the Wind*," 383–85; Clayborne Carson, *In Struggle*, 202–3.

119 *"handkerchief head":* Carmichael, *Ready for Revolution*, 481.

120 *ironic twist:* Ibid.; Sellers, *The River of No Return*, 168.

120 *circumstances of his rise:* Carmichael, *Ready for Revolution*, 482; Lewis, *Walking with the Wind*, 199–200.

120 *"fussing and cussin' ":* Sellers, *The River of No Return*, 168.

121 *Dazed and drained:* Lewis, *Walking with the Wind*, 385.

121 *"I'm here today":* Gene Roberts, "Militants Take Over Student Coordinating Committee," *New York Times*, May 17, 1966.

121 *score-settling feud:* Lewis, *Walking with the Wind*, 383–84; Forman, *The Making of Black Revolutionaries*, 452–53.

122 *more power in the hands:* "Motions, Recommendations, Mandates of SNCC Central Committee," crmvet.org: https://www.crmvet.org/docs /660514_sncc_centcom-decs.pdf.

122 *Carmichael took questions:* Transcript of SNCC press conference, May 21, 1966, crmvet.org: https://www.crmvet.org/docs/660521_sncc_whc_qa.pdf.

122 *tracked down Dr. King:* Austin C. Wehrwein, "Dr. King Disputes Negro Separatist," *New York Times*, May 28, 1966.

123 *"special bulletin":* " 'What's Happening in SNCC?': A Special Bulletin from the New York Office," June 3, 1966, crmvet.org: https://www .crmvet.org/docs/660521_sncc_whc_qa.pdf.

123 *in Little Rock, Arkansas:* Sellers, *The River of No Return*, 169; Carmichael, *Ready for Revolution*, 488.

CHAPTER 7: JUNE 7 – SHOWDOWN AT THE LORRAINE MOTEL

124 *Peabody Hotel:* Roy Reed, "Meredith Begins Mississippi Walk to Combat Fear," *New York Times*, June 6, 1966.

125 *dressed the part:* Ibid., AP photo.

125 *African blessing:* Edward C. Burks, "Meredith Begins Vote March Today," *New York Times,* June 5, 1966.

125 *stage an ambush:* Roy Reed, "Meredith Is Shot in Back on Walk into Mississippi," *New York Times*, June 7, 1966.

126 *erroneous news report:* "Meredith Death Report on TV in Error," *New York Times*, June 7, 1966.

126 *wasn't the only reporter:* Roy Reed, *Beware of Limbo Dancers: A Correspondent's Adventures with the New York Times* (Little Rock: University of Arkansas Press, 2012), 149–50.

127 *his wife, Mary June:* Bernard Weinraub, "Meredith, in Call to His Wife, Says 'Everything's All Right,' " *New York Times*, June 7, 1966.

127 *"a Negro's life":* Martin Luther King, Jr., *Where Do We Go from Here: Chaos or Community?* (New York: Harper & Row, 1967), 23.

128 *number 511B:* "The Meredith March Began," *Newsweek,* June 20, 1966.

128 *a new visitor:* Martin Luther King, Jr., *Where Do We Go from Here*, 24–25.

128 *knew he should check:* Carmichael, *Ready for Revolution*, 489–90.

129 *seated by Dr. King's side:* AP photo, *Boston Globe*, June 8, 1966.

129 *"Don't call us for help!":* Sellers, *The River of No Return*, 171.

129 *to SNCC's advantage:* Carmichael, *Ready for Revolution*, 489–90.

129 *caravan of four cars:* Martin Luther King, Jr., *Where Do We Go from Here*, 25.

130 *Dick Gregory:* "3 Civil Rights Leaders Resume Meredith March," AP/ *Burlington Free Press*, June 8, 1966.

130 *ordered them off the road:* Garrow, *Bearing the Cross*, 474; "Police Force King to Side of Road as Rights Group Takes Up Meredith March," Louisville *Courier-Journal*, June 8, 1966.

130 *"I restrained Stokely":* Carmichael, *Ready for Revolution*, 503; Joseph, *Stokely*, 106, Garrow, *Bearing the Cross*, 476; Branch, *At Canaan's Edge*, 477.

131 *a unity rally:* Joseph, *Stokely*, 197, "The Meredith March Began," *Newsweek*.

131 *"So, you expect any problems?":* Carmichael, *Ready for Revolution*, 491–93.

132 *respect for Dr. King:* Joseph, *Stokely*, 82, 105.

132 *Lorraine Motel:* Allyson Hobbs, "The Lorraine Motel and Martin Luther King," *The New Yorker*, January 18, 2016.

133 *reserved a conference room:* The rest of the re-creation of the meeting is drawn from the following: Carmichael, *Ready for Revolution*, 494–99; Martin Luther King, Jr., *Where Do We Go from Here*, 26–28; Garrow, *Bearing the Cross*, 476–78; "The Meredith March Began," *Newsweek*; Gene Roberts, "Troops Shove Group Resuming Meredith March," *New York Times*, June 8, 1966.

134 *given the bill new momentum:* John Herbers, "Attack on Meredith Spurs Rights Bill," *New York Times*, June 8, 1966.

138 *took the private skirmish public:* James Driscoll, "Young Fears Rights Unity Only Temporary," Louisville *Courier-Journal*, June 9, 1966.

139 *even Malcolm X:* Gene Roberts, "Rights March Disunity," *New York Times*, June 28, 1966.

CHAPTER 8: JUNE 16 – A CRY IN THE MISSISSIPPI NIGHT

140 *a pale imitation:* Gene Roberts, "March's Leaders Demand Action by U.S. on Rights," *New York Times*, June 9, 1966; Gene Roberts, "Mississippi March Gains Momentum," *New York Times*, June 10, 1966.

140 *soured the mood:* Paul Good, "The Meredith March," *New South*, Summer 1966.

141 *fresh story angles:* Gene Roberts, "Whites' Role Splits Leaders of March," *New York Times*, June 12, 1966.

141 *pace picked up:* "The Meredith March Began," *Newsweek*; Roy Reed, "Marchers Detour for Voting Drive," *New York Times*, June 12, 1966.

142 *reached Grenada:* Good, "The Meredith March"; Gene Roberts, "Negros Win Voting Gains on Stop in Grenada, Miss.," *New York Times*, June 15, 1966; "The Meredith March Began," *Newsweek*.

143 *After sunset:* Joseph, *Stokely*, 111.

144 *closer than ever before:* Carmichael, *Ready for Revolution*, 511–12.

144 *"he began to agree":* Sellers, *The River of No Return*, 173.

145 *"There he is!":* Ibid., 174.

145 *seven elderly Black women:* Carmichael, *Ready for Revolution*, 513.

145 *King informed reporters:* Jack Nelson, "Police Show Tolerance on Mississippi March," *Los Angeles Times*, June 16, 1966.

145 *forty-eight documented lynchings: Lynching in America: Confronting the Legacy of Racial Terror*, third edition, Equal Justice Initiative, 2017.

146 *magical memories:* Joseph, *Stokely*, 48.

146 *governor Paul Johnson:* "The Meredith March Began," *Newsweek*.

147 *Byron de la Beckwith:* Ibid.; Carmichael, *Ready for Revolution*, 506.

147 *Stone Street High School:* Carmichael, *Ready for Revolution*, 506–7; Joseph, *Stokely*, 14.

148 *approached Hammond:* Branch, *At Canaan's Edge*, 485–86.

148 *a photo of the scene:* The Bob Fitch Photo Archive, "Meredith March Against Fear, June 1966, Stanford Library Digital Archive: https://exhibits.stanford.edu/fitch/catalog/vb997nv5376.

148 *"What's a man going to do?":* Bill Crider, "Marchers Defy Policemen; Three Leaders Are Arrested," AP/*The Paducah* (Kentucky) *Sun*, June 17, 1966.

149 *For Willie Ricks:* Willie Ricks interview, January 24, 2006, Atlanta History Center: https://www.youtube.com/watch?v=kZpUak4YLyA; Mary Claire Comperry, "Willie Ricks biographical sketch," UTC Scholar: https://scholar.utc.edu/cgi/viewcontent.cgi?article=1010&context=racial-justice-biographies.

150 *a protest in Tuskegee:* Gene Roberts, "500 at Tuskegee Protest Slaying," *New York Times*, January 9, 1966.

150 *got under his skin:* Branch, *At Canaan's Edge*, 128–29.

150 *"What do you want?":* "Chapter 19: 'Freedom Now,' " Stanford U. King Institute: https://kinginstitute.stanford.edu/chapter-19-freedom-now.

151 *"going wild for it":* Clayborne Carson, *In Struggle*, 209.

151 *Forman took credit:* Forman, *The Making of Black Revolutionaries*, 456.

151 *Carmichael became convinced:* Clayborne Carson, *In Struggle*, 209; SNCC Central Committee Meeting minutes, June 10, 1966, crmvet.org: https://www.crmvet.org/docs/660612_sncc_min.pdf.

152 *a makeshift stage:* Carmichael, *Ready for Revolution*, 507; Footage of speech in "Black Power, White Backlash," September 27, 1966, CBS News: https://www.cbsnews.com/news/from-the-vault-Black-power-white-backlash/.

153 *uncomfortable silence:* " 'Black Power!,' " *Newsweek*, June 27, 1966.

CHAPTER 9: JUNE 23 - TEAR GAS OVER CANTON

157   *Richard Wright:* Richard Wright, *Black Power: Three Books from Exile*, harpercollins.com: https://www.harpercollins.com/9780061449451/Black -power/.

157   *Adam Clayton Powell Jr.:* "Seek Audacious Black Power by Adam Clayton Powell," Keyamsha.com: https://keyamsha.com/2016/05/30/seek-auda cious-power-by-adam-clayton-powell/.

157   *Bruce Biossat:* Bruce Biossat, "Fiery Militants Damage the Negro's Cause," AP/(Greenwood, South Carolina) *Index-Journal*, June 3, 1966.

157   *history-bending story:* James Bossey, "Mississippi Marchers Chant 'We Want Black Power!,' " AP/(Owensboro, Kentucky) *Messenger-Inquirer*, June 7, 1966.

158   *more than two hundred American newspapers:* Based on a count of stories archived by Newspapers.com.

158   *at least seven hundred more:* Ibid.

158   *next issue of* Newsweek: "Civil Rights: 'Black Power!,' " *Newsweek*, June 27, 1966.

158   *a likeness from Jacob Lawrence:* Wil Haygood, "This Powerful Stokely Carmichael Portrait Never Made It to the Cover of Time Magazine," *Smithsonian*, June 2016.

159   *a more disapproving take:* "Civil Rights: The New Racism," *Time*, July 1, 1966.

159   *a guest appearance:* Transcript of *Face the Nation*, June 19, 1966, crmvet .org: https://www.crmvet.org/nars/660619_sncc_stokely_ftn.pdf.

159   *Doyle would later admit:* Author interview with James S. Doyle, January 8, 2019.

160   *interview to a socialist weekly:* "Interview with New SNCC Chairman," *Militant*, May 23, 1966.

161   *Jim Doyle thought:* Author interview with James S. Doyle.

161   *Doyle's editors:* "Rights Violence Can Be Justified, SNCC Man Says," *Boston Globe*, June 20, 1966.

161   *more nuanced language:* David K. Underhill, "The Cry Changes to 'Black Power,' " *Southern Courier*, June 25–26, 1966.

162   *a mood of festive unity:* Gene Roberts, "Mississippi March Puts Rights Drive into Evangelical Phase," *New York Times*, June 19, 1966.

162   *atmosphere grew tense:* Underhill, "The Cry Changes to 'Black Power.' "

162   *statement distancing himself:* "Dr. King Deplores 'Black Power' Bid," UPI/ *New York Times*, June 21, 1966.

162   *Philadelphia was the seat:* Joseph Lelyveld, "A Stranger in Philadelphia, Mississippi," *New York Times Magazine*, December 27, 1964.

163 *marchers led by Dr. King:* Roy Reed, "Philadelphia, Miss., Whites and Negroes Trade Shots," *New York Times*, June 22, 1966; "The March—In Step and Out," *Newsweek*, July 4, 1966.

164 *violence continued that night:* Reed, "Philadelphia, Miss., Whites and Negroes Trade Shots."

165 *"We are armed":* Courtland Milloy, "A Namesake Worthy of His Name," *Washington Post*, May 30, 1999.

165 *Reconstructing the scene:* Kopkind, *The Thirty Years' Wars*, 60.

165 *fueled the growing arguments:* Roy Reed, "Dr. King Bids U.S. Guard New March," *New York Times*, June 22, 1966.

165 *Trying to save face:* Gene Roberts, "Dr. King Plans Return," *New York Times*, June 21, 1966.

165 *King sent a telegram:* Branch, *At Canaan's Edge*, 488–89.

166 *Canton was known:* "Our History," cantontourism.com: https://www.cantontourism.com/history#our-history.

166 *a Delta bluesman:* "Mississippi Blues Trail," cantontourism.com: https://www.cantontourism.com/history#our-history"; "Jan. 27: The Great Elmore James Was Born 100 Years Ago Today—1918," borntolisten.com: https://borntolisten.com/2018/01/27/jan-27-the-late-great-elmore-james-was-born-100-years-ago-1918/.

166 *Shortly after six:* Paul Good, "The Meredith March," *New South*, Summer 1966; Carmichael, *Ready for Revolution*, 508.

166 *"we're going to do it now!":* Joseph, *Stokely*, 118; Gene Roberts, "Mississippi Police Use Gas to Rout Rights Campers," *New York Times*, June 24 1966.

167 *the protesters scattered:* Good, "The Meredith March."

167 *defiance dissolved into desperation:* Ibid.; Carmichael, *Ready for Revolution*, 345–46; "Notes and Comments," *The New Yorker*, July 16, 1966.

168 *showed little sympathy:* Roberts, "Mississippi Police Use Gas to Rout Rights Campers"; Good, "The Meredith March."

169 *without major incident:* Gene Roberts, "Marchers Defy Crowd of Whites, Hold Rally in Philadelphia, Miss.," *New York Times*, June 25, 1966.

169 *more generational discord:* Kopkind, *The Thirty Years' Wars*, 60.

169 *Meredith rejoined the march:* Gene Roberts, "Meredith Leads the March on Eve of Rally in Jackson," *New York Times*, June 26, 1966; "Mississippi March Nears Final Phase," AP/ *Poughkeepsie Journal*, June 25, 1966.

170 *march reached Jackson:* Gene Roberts, "Meredith Hailed at Rally at Mississippi Capitol," *New York Times*, June 27, 1966; "Hot Day," *Southern Courier*, July 2–3, 1966; Kopkind, *The Thirty Years' Wars,* 59–60.

171 *even older Black residents:* Gene Roberts, "12,000 End Rights March to Jackson," *New York Times*, June 27, 1966.

172 *deepening misunderstanding:* "Notes and Comments," *The New Yorker,* July 16, 1966.

172 *when he arrived in Vietnam:* Author interview with Gene Roberts, January 14, 2019.

CHAPTER 10: JULY AND AUGUST – "STARMICHAEL" ON TOUR

174 *"all over shy":* "Notes and Comments," *New Yorker,* July 16, 1966.

174 *a different adjective:* Nicholas von Hoffman, "Dividing Rights Groups," *Boston Globe,* July 3, 1966.

175 *Moses decided to travel:* Author interview with Bob Moses, February 7, 2019

175 *showed support for the cry:* Forman, *The Making of Black Revolutionaries,* 457.

175 *more appropriate than ever:* Joseph, *Stokely,* 138.

176 *Adler's novelistic description:* "Notes and Comments," *The New Yorker,* July 16, 1966.

176 *master of the "put-on":* Jacob Brackman, "The Put-On," *The New Yorker,* June 24, 1967.

177 *"child of Camus":* Kopkind, *The Thirty Years' Wars,* 92.

177 *cover of* Jet: *Jet,* July 28, 1966.

177 *At* Ebony: Lerone Bennett Jr., "Stokely Carmichael: Architect of Black Power," *Ebony,* September 1966.

179 *Lewis abruptly announced:* "Lewis Quits SNCC, Shuns 'Black Power,' " *New York Times,* July 1, 1966.

179 *the reporters lost interest:* "Carmichael Scores Bill," AP/*New York Times,* July 2, 1966.

179 *CORE's annual convention:* M. S. Handler, "CORE Hears Cries of 'Black Power,' " *New York Times,* July 2, 1966.

180 *Roy Wilkins responded:* M. S. Handler, "Wilkins Assails CORE and SNCC, Hints Bill Break," *New York Times,* July 6, 1966; M. S. Handler, "Humphrey Backs NAACP in Fight on Black Power," *New York Times,* July 7, 1966.

180 *with Nina Simone:* "Negro Business, Housing Co-Ops Urged by SNCC," AP/*Delaware County Daily Times,* July 18, 1966; Joseph, *Stokely,* 128–29.

181 *In Washington:* Marjorie Hunter, "Powell Defends Rights Militants," *New York Times,* July 19, 1966; "Reverend Adam Clayton Powell, Jr. and Stokely Carmichael," National Portrait Gallery: https://npg.si.edu /object/npg_NPG.94.220.

181 *Elijah Muhammad:* Carmichael, *Ready for Revolution,* 521–23.

181 *"join hands":* Austin C. Wehrwein, "Carmichael Plans Black Unity Talks with Muslims," *New York Times,* July 29, 1966.

181 *eccentric ramblings:* Carmichael, *Ready for Revolution,* 522.

182 *met briefly with Dr. King:* Joseph, *Stokely,* 130.

182 *summit would fall apart:* Drew Pearson, "Powell Dodges Wife, She Leaks News of Her Errant Paychecks, *Tampa Tribune,* September 1, 1966; "Black Power Parley Is Canceled," *Sacramento Bee,* November 17, 1966.

182 *Cobo Hall:* "Negroes Urged Not to Fight in Vietnam," *Chicago Tribune,* July 31, 1966; photo and transcript in "Stokely Carmichael Speaks on Black Power in Detroit, July 30, 1966," panafricannews.com: http://panafricannews.blogspot.com/2006/06/stokely-carmichael-speaks-on-Black.html; Stokely Carmichael, "Definitions of Black Power," BlackPast.org: https://www.Blackpast.org/african-american-history/1966-stokely-carmichael-definitions-Black-power/.

182 *NBC's* Today *show:* "Distorted Cry?," *Newsweek,* August 8, 1966.

183 *columnist Russell Baker:* Russell Baker, "The Treacheries of Washington," *New York Times,* August 4, 1966.

184 *"Man in the News" profile:* "Black Power Prophet," *New York Times,* August 5, 1966.

184 *On the front page:* Gene Roberts, "Black Power Idea Long in the Making," *New York Times,* August 5, 1966.

185 *trouble with the* Times *scoop:* "New York Times Publishes Atlanta Project Statement," SNCC Digital Gateway: https://snccdigital.org/events/new-york-times-publishes-atlanta-project-statement/.

185 *suspiciously printed:* "Black Power" pamphlet, crmvet.org: https://www.crmvet.org/docs/6604_sncc_atlanta_race.pdf.

185 *funded by the CIA:* Juan de Onis, "Ramparts Says CIA Received Student Report," *New York Times,* February 16, 1967.

CHAPTER 11: AUGUST 5 - A ROCK IN MARQUETTE PARK

186 *blistering heatwave:* Walter Sullivan, "1966 Heat Wave Linked to Fatal Strokes," *New York Times,* August 11, 1971; "Record Hot Spell Lingers at 101°; Death Rate Rises," *New York Times,* July 14, 1966; Fred Robbins, "Air Conditioner Sellers Happy," *Dayton Daily News,* July 1, 1966; "94° Heat Chases Throngs to City's Beaches, Parks," *Chicago Tribune,* June 28, 1966.

186 *returned to Chicago:* "Dr. King to Stage Big Rally Today," *New York Times,* July 10, 1966.

187 *"militantly non-violent":* Gene Roberts, "Dr. King Declares Rights Movement Is 'Close' to a Split," *New York Times,* July 9, 1966.

187 *day of the Soldier Field rally:* Austin C. Wehrwein, "Dr. King and CORE
Chief Act to Heal Rights Breach," *New York Times*, July 11, 1966;
Branch, *At Canaan's Edge*, 501; Liam T. A. Ford, *Soldier Field: A Stadium
and Its City* (Chicago: University of Chicago Press, 2009), 209.

187 *Coretta, agreed to move:* Coretta Scott King, *My Life with Martin Luther
King, Jr.*, 279–82; Wehrwein, "Dr. King and CORE Chief Act to Heal
Rights Breach."

188 *Daley invited King:* Austin C. Wehrwein, "Dr. King Declares Daley Balks
Him," *New York Times*, July 12, 1966; Garrow, *Bearing the Cross*, 492–93.

188 *"a riot starting":* Coretta Scott King, *My Life with Martin Luther King, Jr.*,
283–84; Garrow, *Bearing the Cross*, 493.

188 *opened the fire hydrants:* "Fire Hydrant Riots," in "The Near West Side
and the Jane Addams Homes: Chicago's Ellis Island," National Public Housing Museum: https://www.vamonde.com/posts/fire_hydrant
_riots/1170; "West Side Story," *Newsweek*, July 25, 1966; Donald Jensen,
"Armed Negroes Fight the Police in Chicago Riots," *New York Times*,
July 15, 1966; Branch, *At Canaan's Edge*, 502–4; Garrow, *Bearing the
Cross*, 493–94.

189 *couldn't find a babysitter:* Coretta Scott King, *My Life with Martin Luther
King, Jr.*, 286–87; Charles Krohn, "Want Your Head Shot Off?," UPI/
Billings Gazette, July 16, 1966.

189 *King's apartment:* Branch, *At Canaan's Edge*, 504–5; Roger Wilkins, *A
Man's Life* (New York: Simon & Schuster, 1984), 208.

190 *sniping between Daley and King:* "West Side Story," *Newsweek*, July 18,
1966; Branch, *At Canaan's Edge*, 505–6.

190 *described his challenge:* Gene Roberts, "Dr. King on the Middle Ground,"
New York Times, July 17, 1966.

190 *full-page advertisement:* Martin Luther King, Jr., "It Is Not Enough to
Condemn Black Power," *New York Times*, July 26, 1966; Garrow, *Bearing
the Cross*, 496–97.

191 *working-class immigrant area:* Gene Roberts, "Rock Hits Dr. King as
Whites Attack March in Chicago," *New York Times*, August 6, 1966; Garrow, *Bearing the Cross*, 498.

191 *unsettling start:* Garrow, *Bearing the Cross*, 498–99; Branch, *At Canaan's
Edge*, 507–8.

192 *King returned to Chicago:* Roberts, "Rock Hits Dr. King as Whites Attack
March in Chicago"; Branch, *At Canaan's Edge*, 509–10.

192 *on his right temple:* Roberts, "Rock Hits Dr. King as Whites Attack March
in Chicago"; "The Touchiest Target," *Newsweek*, August 15, 1966.

193 *Jackson got carried away:* Branch, *At Canaan's Edge*, 514–15.

194   *a face-saving deal:* Garrow, *Bearing the Cross*, 517–24.

194   *cut off repeatedly:* Henry Hampton and Steve Fayer, eds., *Voices of Freedom: An Oral History of the Civil Rights Movement from the 1950s Through the 1980s* (New York: Bantam, 1991), 317.

194   *couldn't hide his disappointment:* Garrow, *Bearing the Cross*, 524.

194   *Bob Lucas:* Hampton and Fayer, eds., *Voices of Freedom*, 317–19; Donald Janson, "Guards Bayonet Hecklers in Cicero's Rights March," *New York Times*, September 5, 1966.

195   *comprehensive new national poll:* "Black and White: A Major Survey of U.S. Racial Attitudes Today," *Newsweek*, August 22, 1966.

195   *Osborn Elliott:* Michael T. Kaufman, "Osborn Elliott, Father of Newsweek's Rebirth, Dies at 83," *New York Times*, September 28, 2008.

195   *first of a series:* The Negro in America," *Newsweek*, July 29, 1963.

196   *thirty-two-page* Newsweek *cover story:* "Black and White: A Major Survey of U.S. Racial Attitudes Today," *Newsweek*, August 22, 1966

CHAPTER 12: AUGUST 13 - A DYNAMITE BUST IN PHILADELPHIA

199   *Frank Rizzo:* Timothy J. Lombardo, "Civil Rights and the Rise of Frank Rizzo in 1960's Philadelphia," *Pennsylvania Legacies*, Fall 2018.

199   *dramatic announcement:* Paul S. Good, "Out to Get SNCC: A Tale of Two Cities," *The Nation*, November 21, 1966.

200   *reporters went to North Philadelphia:* "Police Grab Dynamite in SNCC Spot Raid," AP/*Dayton Daily News*, August 13, 1966.

200   *only one of the arrested suspects:* Good, "Out to Get SNCC: A Tale of Two Cities."

200   *quickly fell apart:* Ibid.; "Three Held, Three Dismissed in SNCC Dynamite Case," AP/(Hanover, Pennsylvania) *Evening Sun*, August 23, 1966.

201   *on the bureau's payroll:* FBI Records: The Vault, Stokely Carmichael, Part 1, 57–59.

201   *The search warrant:* Good, "Out to Get SNCC: A Tale of Two Cities."

201   *heated phone call:* Joseph, *Stokely*, 132–33.

202   *Watson told DeLoach:* FBI Records: The Vault, Stokely Carmichael, Part 1, 57–59.

202   *immigration files:* Ibid., Carmichael, Part 5, 51.

202   *tangential revelation:* Ibid., Carmichael, Part 1, 1.

202   *reprinted a letter:* Ibid., Carmichael, Part 3, 36.

203   *Baumgardner sent a memo:* Ibid., Carmichael, Part 1, 57.

203   *"Addendum" was added:* Ibid., Carmichael, Part 1, 59.

203   *edition of* Meet the Press: Transcript of *Meet the Press*, August 21, 1966,

crmvet.org: https://www.crmvet.org/info/660821_mtp_ckmmwy.pdf; "Civil Rights Discussion," NBC Universal Archives: https://www.you tube.com/watch?v=lj0D9BKqo6c.

CHAPTER 13: SEPTEMBER 6 - RIOT COMES TO SUMMERHILL

206   *"city too busy to hate":* Virginia H. Hein, "The Image of 'A City Too Busy to Hate': Atlanta in the 1960's," *Phylon,* Fall 1972, 205–21.

206   *in Summerhill were strivers:* Cynthia Griggs Fleming, *Soon We Will Not Cry,* 18–19, 34–35.

207   *Braves played their first game:* "The History of the Atlanta Braves," braves historyblog: https://braveshistoryblog.wordpress.com/2018/08/07/first -ever-game-at-atlanta-fulton-county-stadium-tuesday-april-12-1966/.

207   *approved for patrol duty:* "History of the APD," atlantapd.org: https:// www.atlantapd.org/about-apd/apd-history.

207   *two white police officers:* Winston A. Grady-Willis, "Black Power in the South: Urban Protest and Neighborhood Activism in Atlanta, Georgia, 1966–1969," *Présence Africaine,* 2000, 328–44.

207   *resident of Ormond Street:* "Eyewitness to the Atlanta Riots," *The Movement,* December 1966.

207   *Allen had met that morning:* Joseph, *Stokely,* 139.

208   *gather a crowd:* Ibid., 140; Stephen E. Cotton, "What's Going on in Atlanta?," *Southern Courier,* September 17–18, 1966; Gene Roberts, "Atlanta Negroes Riot After Police Wound a Suspect," *New York Times,* September 7, 1966.

208   *fresh political image:* Reese Cleghorn, "Allen of Atlanta Collides with Black Power and White Racism," *New York Times Magazine,* October 16, 1966, 251.

209   *Allen arrived in Summerhill:* Ibid.; Roberts, "Atlanta Negroes Riot After Police Wound a Suspect."

210   *deteriorating war of words:* Roy Reed, "SNCC Assailed on Atlanta Riot," *New York Times,* September 8, 1966.

210   *circulate flyers:* "Statement by Stokely Carmichael," crmvet.org: https:// www.crmvet.org/docs/660908_sncc_stokely.pdf.

210   *Prominent local journalists:* Ralph McGill, "Story of a Man and of SNCC," *Atlanta Constitution,* September 8, 1966; Eugene Patterson, "For Negroes and Whites Only," *Atlanta Constitution,* September 8, 1966; "Allen Gets Humphrey Applause," *Atlanta Constitution,* September 8, 1966.

211   *less militant Black residents:* Patterson, "For Negroes and Whites Only"; "Eyewitness to the Atlanta Riots," *The Movement.*

211 *went door-to-door:* "Eyewitness to the Atlanta Riots," *The Movement.*

211 *"political prisoner":* "Carmichael Held in Riot Aftermath," *New York Times,* September 9, 1966; Roy Reed, "Carmichael Refuses to Post Bail and Is Held for Jury in Atlanta," *New York Times,* September 10, 1966.

212 *For Julian Bond:* Bill Shipp, "Julian Bond Gets Out of Snick," *Atlanta Constitution,* September 9, 1966.

212 *two Black sixteen-year-olds:* Roy Reed, "Negro Is Slain in Atlanta, Setting Off New Violence," *New York Times,* September 11, 1966; Roy Reed, "New Violence Breaks Out in a Negro Area of Atlanta," *New York Times,* September 11, 1966; "White in Atlanta Held in Slaying," *New York Times,* September 14, 1966.

212 *final demise:* Robert B. Semple Jr., "Rights Bill Dies as Closure Fails," *New York Times,* September 20, 1966; "Rights Leaders React Bitterly," *New York Times,* September 20, 1966.

213 *pen his own answer:* Stokely Carmichael, "What We Want," *New York Review of Books,* September 22, 1966.

214 *prime-time CBS news special:* "Black Power, White Backlash," September 27, 1966, CBS News: https://www.youtube.com/watch?v=otMQe JFOAzM.

215 *"I saw it that night:"* The *African-Americans: Many Rivers to Cross, with Henry Louis Gates Jr.,* Youtube.com: https://www.youtube.com/watch ?v=YyoWG7SGPnc; Aram Goudsouzian, *Down to the Crossroads: Civil Rights, Black Power, and the Meredith March Against Fear* (New York: Farrar, Straus & Giroux, 2014).

217 *moment of decision:* Ruby Doris S. Robinson, "Organizational Report," October 21, 1966, crmvet.org: https://www.crmvet.org/docs/661021_ sncc_org-rpt.pdf.

219 *note of contrition:* "Minutes of the Central Committee," October 22–23, 1966, crmvet.org: https://www.crmvet.org/docs/661023_sncc_cc-min.pdf.

219 *Ralph Featherstone:* Ibid.

CHAPTER 14: OCTOBER 29 - BERKELEY AND THE BACKLASH VOTE

221 *thirty-minute TV ad:* Peter Bart, "Reagan Enters Gubernatorial Race in California," *New York Times,* January 5, 1966.

222 *avoided direct racial appeals:* Lawrence E. Davies, " 'White Backlash' Becomes a Major Coast Issue," *New York Times,* September 28, 1966.

222 *Brown closed the polling gap:* Lawrence E. Davies, "Reagan's Margin Declines in Polls," *New York Times,* September 3, 1966.

222 *he grew more forward:* Lawrence E. Davies, "Reagan Wooing the Farm Voters," *New York Times*, September 6, 1966.

222 *a sleepy stretch:* Gary Kamiya, "Officer's '66 Killing of Black Teen Sparked Hunters Point Riot," *San Francisco Chronicle*, September 16, 2016.

223 *the unrest in Hunters Point began:* Ibid.; "Policeman 'Begged Youth to Stop,' Fired Fatal Shot," *Oakland Tribune*, September 28, 1966.

224 *the unrest spread:* Gary Kamiya, "The SF Riots That Brought Out the National Guard," *San Francisco Chronicle*, September 3, 2016.

224 *pressed them for reaction:* "Candidates Clash over Coast Riots," *New York Times*, October 2, 1966.

224 *the first survey out:* Lawrence E. Davies, "New Poll Finds Brown Slipping," *New York Times*, October 12, 1966.

225 *a publicity stunt of his own:* "Reagan Shuns Black Power Rally," *San Francisco Examiner*, October 19, 1966.

225 *the incumbent announced:* Lynn Ludlow, "Crisis on 'Power' Rally," *San Francisco Examiner*, October 25, 1966.

225 *two names leapt to the fore:* "Draft Spotlight Put on Stokely, Lynda's George," AP/ *Cincinnati Inquirer*, October 29, 1966.

226 *process took two days:* Thomas A. Johnson, "Carmichael Says He Won't Go if Drafted," *New York Times*, October 29, 1966.

226 *records of his surveillance:* FBI Records: The Vault, Stokely Carmichael, Part 4, 3–5.

227 *acquittal of Daniels's killer:* Robert E. Smith, "Coleman Tried Among Friends," *Southern Courier*, October 3–4, 1965; Robert E. Smith, "Lowndes County Justice," *Southern Courier*, October 9–10, 1965.

227 *other contemporaneous accounts:* Forman, *Sammy Younge, Jr.*, 184; Carmichael, *Ready for Revolution*, 470.

228 *noticed a marked change:* Jack Nelson, "The 'Color Line' Closes on King," *Los Angeles Times*, September 3, 1966.

228 *At a press conference:* "Before Campus Rally," *New York Times*, October 30, 1966.

228 *a community meeting:* "Stokely Carmichael to Speak About Black Power in Hunters Point," sfsu.edu: https://diva.sfsu.edu/collections/sfbatv /bundles/238932.

228 *Berkeley's Greek Theatre:* Carol Hyman, "U.C. Berkeley's Greek Theatre Turns 100 Years Old This Month," *U.C. Berkeley News*, September 11, 2003; Lawrence E. Davies, "Carmichael Asks Draft's Defiance," *New York Times*, October 30, 1966.

229 *when Carmichael arrived:* "Stokely Lashes at Whites in UC Rally," *San Francisco Examiner*, October 30, 1966; "Stokely Carmichael, Speech at

University of California, Berkeley, October 29, 1966," americanradio works.com: https://americanradioworks.publicradio.org/features/black speech/scarmichael.html.

230 *got the most news coverage:* Davies, "Carmichael Asks Draft's Defiance."

230 *hobnobbing and smoking marijuana:* Peniel E. Joseph, "Ronald Reagan Meets Black Power: Stokely Carmichael, Civil Rights and the 1960s," *Salon,* March 9, 2014.

230 *Lee Hamilton:* Robert B. Semple Jr., "In Tight Races, the Backlash Vote May Mean Victory," *New York Times,* October 17, 1966.

231 *When Lyndon Johnson had run:* "All Races, Ethnic Groups, Economic Levels Support Johnson for Landslide," AP/*Pensacola News,* November 4, 1964; "The Johnson Landslide," *New York Times,* November 4, 1964.

231 *visible from coast to coast:* "Republican Party: Back from the Brink," *Time,* November 18, 1966.

232 *Election Day in California:* Lawrence E. Davies, "Reagan Elected by a Wide Margin," *New York Times,* November 9, 1966.

232 *viewed as exceptions:* Tim Wicker, "House Seats Shift," *New York Times,* November 9, 1966; "Republican Party: Back from the Brink," *Time.*

232 *For Richard Nixon:* Wicker, "House Seats Shift."

233 *in a Selma courtroom:* "Carmichael Gets 60-Day Sentence," *New York Times,* November 30, 1966.

233 *drove around Lowndes County:* Viola Bradford, "Lowndes: A Good Day for Voting, But Black Panther Candidates Lose," *Southern Courier,* November 12–13, 1966.

234 *running his wife, Lurleen:* Marshall Frady, *Wallace* (New York: Meridien, 1968), 187–93.

234 *to the polls in droves:* "Alabama's New Era: The Negro Votes," *Newsweek,* May 16, 1966; "Selma Rejects Bid by Sheriff Clark," *New York Times,* November 10, 1966.

234 *Compared with George Wallace's performance:* Louis Harris, "Analyzing the Vote—and Its Lessons," *Newsweek,* May 16, 1966.

235 *"Lowndes: A Good Day to Go Voting":* Bradford, "Lowndes: A Good Day for Voting, But Black Panther Candidates Lose."

CHAPTER 15: OCTOBER - TEN POINTS FROM THE FLATLANDS

236 *new weekly newspaper:* "Flatland Says," *The Flatlands,* March 12, 1966.

236 *one of the paper's founders:* "The Flatlands Profiles," ibid.

237 *Carmichael remembered Comfort:* Carmichael, *Ready for Revolution,* 475–76.

237   *take him off the streets:* "Labor Council Runs Scared," *The Flatlands*, May 7, 1966; Gloria Comfort, "No Comfort for Knowland," *The Flatlands*, June 18, 1966.

237   *North Oakland Neighborhood Anti-Poverty Program:* Alondra Nelson, *Body and Soul: The Black Panther Party and the Fight Against Medical Discrimination* (Minneapolis: University of Minnesota Press, 2011), 55.

238   *Newton and Seale boasted:* Hampton and Fayer, eds., *Voices of Freedom*, 352.

238   *idea to wear berets:* Nancy MacDowell, "How Berets Became a Part of Black History, from the Black Panthers to Beyoncé," *Wall Street Journal*, February 2, 2022.

238   *didn't heed the lessons:* "The Flatlands Profiles," *The Flatlands*.

238   *act as a "foreman":* Seale, *Seize the Time*, 35.

238   *Across the Flatlands:* Sue Lohman, "Hard Hats, Hard Cash," *The Flatlands*, July 30, 1966.

239   *"a little Black History":* Seale, *Seize the Time*, 37, 48–54.

239   *a legal library:* Newton, *Revolutionary Suicide*, 120–21.

239   *Community Alert Patrol:* Hilliard, *Huey*, 39–40; Terence Canada, "A Night with the Watts Community Alert Patrol," *The Movement*, August 1966.

240   *"And do it now":* Seale, *Seize the Time*, 59.

240   *"Ten Point Program":* Bloom and Martin, *Black Against Empire*, 70–73, 417; Newton, *Revolutionary Suicide*, 122; Hilliard, *Huey*, 28–29; Seale, *Seize the Time*, 60–61.

240   *Crediting thinkers:* Newton, *Revolutionary Suicide*, 116–18.

241   *In Newton's telling:* Ibid., 122.

241   *chose the black panther name:* Hilliard, *Huey*, 29; Newton, *Revolutionary Suicide*, 118–19.

242   *Once the new party had a name:* Hilliard, *Huey*, 30–35.

246   *organizational structure:* Seale, *Seize the Time*, 62; Newton, *Revolutionary Suicide*, 125–26.

246   *first recruit:* Hilliard, *Huey*, 29–30; "Bobby Hutton (1950–1968)," black past.org: https://www.blackpast.org/african-american-history/hutton-bobby-1950-1968/.

247   *Richard Aoki:* Seale, *Seize the Time*, 72–73; Seth Rosenfeld, "New FBI Files Show Wide Range of Black Panther Informants Activities," *Monterey Herald*, June 9, 2015.

247   *spreading the word:* Newton, *Revolutionary Suicide*, 129, 134.

248   *By the end of December:* Seale, *Seize the Time*, 77–81.

248   *In April of 1967:* Bloom and Martin, *Black Against Empire*, 50–62.

248   *one of the most striking:* Ibid., 58–62; photo, sacbee.com: https://en.wikipedia.org/wiki/Mark_Comfort#/media/File:Mark_Comfort.jpg.

249   *Leroy Eldridge Cleaver:* "Eldridge Cleaver," in Henry Louis Gates Jr.
       and Evelyn Brooks Higginbotham, eds., *African-American Lives* (Ox-
       ford: Oxford University Press, 2004), 173–75; John Kifner, "Eldridge
       Cleaver, Black Panther Who Became G.O.P. Conservative, Is Dead at
       62," *New York Times*, May 2, 1998.

249   *Leroy Sr. was a violent:* Eldridge Cleaver, "My Father & Stokely Carmi-
       chael," *Ramparts*, April 1967.

249   *keep a diary:* Cleaver, *Soul on Ice*, 15, 61.

250   *Cleaver didn't encounter:* Kifner, "Eldridge Cleaver, Black Panther Who
       Became G.O.P. Conservative, Is Dead at 62."

250   *Cleaver's prison essays:* Cleaver, *Soul on Ice*, 15–16, 19–22.

251   *critique of James Baldwin:* Ibid., Introduction by Maxwell Geismar.

251   *position at* Ramparts: Peter Richardson, *A Bomb in Every Issue: How the
       Short, Unruly Life of Ramparts Magazine Changed America,* (New York: The
       New Press, 2002), 71.

251   *went on local radio:* Hampton and Stayer, eds., *Voices of Freedom*, 363–65.

252   *on the day of Shabazz's arrival:* Ibid., 365–66.

253   *organized by Kathleen Neal:* Joseph, *Stokely*, 180.

253   *Cleaver's* Ramparts *story:* Cleaver, "My Father & Stokely Carmichael."
       Ramparts, April 1967.

253   *a newspaper:* Hampton and Stayer, eds., *Voices of Freedom*, 367.

253   *staged a photograph:* "Black Panthers: Arts and History," nyhistory.org, June
       24, 2015: https://www.nyhistory.org/blogs/black-panthers-art-history.

253   *popularized a phrase:* Kifner, "Eldridge Cleaver, Black Panther Who Be-
       came G.O.P. Conservative, Is Dead at 62."

254   *newsreel-style film:* "Off the Pigs!," blackfilmarchive.com: https://black
       filmarchive.com/Off-the-Pigs.

254   *posturing talk into action:* Karen Grisby Bates, "Bobby Hutton: The Killing
       That Catapulted the Black Panthers to Fame," npr.org, April 6, 2018.

254   *The Oakland police:* "Black Panther Chief Demands Indictment," *Los
       Angeles Times*, April 13, 1968; Eldridge Cleaver interview by Henry
       Louis Gates Jr., 1997, pbs.org: https://www.pbs.org/wgbh/pages/front
       line/shows/race/interviews/ecleaver.html.

255   *"International Section":* Brown, *A Taste of Power*, 220.

255   *appearance on* Firing Line: "Firing Line With William F. Buckley, Jr.:
       How Goes It with the Black Movement," January 23, 1973, *youtube.com*:
       https://www.youtube.com/watch?v=XUicVnx1UKU

CHAPTER 16: DECEMBER 8 - THE PEG LEG BATES PURGE

256 *On the first day of December:* Bob Zellner, *The Wrong Side of Murder Creek: A White Southerner in the Freedom Movement* (Montgomery, AL: New South Books, 2008), 292–93.

256 *the Peg Leg Bates Country Club:* Jennifer Dunning, "Peg Leg Bates, One-Legged Dancer, Dies at 91," *New York Times*, December 8, 1998; *Ed Sullivan Show*, youtube.com: https://www.youtube.com/watch?v=NXesFCMwys0.

257 *bitter debate:* Forman, *The Making of Black Revolutionaries*, 475–81.

257 *Born John Robert Zellner:* Bob Zellner, *The Wrong Side of Murder Creek*, 17–18, 40–42.

258 *Huntingdon College:* Ibid., 47–49, 61.

258 *the Huntingdon Five:* Ibid., 64–68, 73.

258 *the Freedom Riders:* Ibid., 89–96; "May 20, 1961," eji.org: https://calendar.eji.org/racial-injustice/may/20.

259 *Anne Braden:* Bob Zellner, *The Wrong Side of Murder Creek*, 101–19.

259 *All Zellner knew about the job:* Ibid., 131–39.

259 *bloody baptism by fire:* Ibid., 150–72.

260 *Zellner rarely strayed:* Ibid., 174–85, 190–206.

261 *home state of Alabama:* Ibid., 207–16, 217–33.

261 *Danville, Virginia:* Ibid, 234–45; Dorothy M. Zellner, "My Real Vocation," in Holsaert et al., eds., *Hands on the Freedom Plow*.

262 *three years since Dottie Miller:* Ibid.

263 *joined members of the Freedom Singers:* Lyon, *Memories of the Southern Civil Rights Movement,* 66.

263 *an iconic image:* Richard Avedon mural, *acpinfo.org:* https://acpinfo.org/blog/2019/02/06/sheila-pree-bright-richard-avedon-mural/.

263 *Zellner and Miller were married:* Lyon, *Memories of the Southern Civil Rights Movement*, 85, 112–13; Bob Zellner, *The Wrong Side of Murder Creek*, 244–45.

264 *Dottie Zellner was put in charge:* Dorothy M. Zellner, "My Real Vocation."

264 *welcoming committee:* Bob Zellner, *The Wrong Side of Murder Creek*, 268.

264 *the tense year:* Dorothy M. Zellner, "My Real Vocation"; Bob Zellner, *The Wrong Side of Murder Creek*, 286–92.

265 *"the die had already been cast":* Bob Zeller, *The Wrong Side of Murder Creek*, 292.

265 *Peg Leg Bates agenda:* "From Kingston Springs to Peg Leg Bates," crmvet.org: https://www.crmvet.org/docs/661200_sncc_staffmtg_agenda.pdf; Clayborne Carson, *In Struggle*, 239-41; Carmichael, "Ready for Revolution," 566–56.

266 *"Sensitive white people":* Clayborne Carson, *In Struggle*, 240.

266 *increasingly ugly:* Forman, *The Making of Black Revolutionaries*, 476–77.

266 *tried to forge a compromise:* Ibid., 477; Clayborne Carson, *In Struggle*, 240.

267 *own sexual drama:* Sellers, *The River of No Return*, 182–91.

267 *uncharacteristically passive:* Carmichael, *Ready for Revolution*, 567.

268 *felt "handcuffed":* Bob Zellner, *The Wrong Side of Murder Creek*, 295.

268 *vote came at last:* Clayborne Carson, *In Struggle*, 240–41.

269 *Ethel Minor:* "Ethel Minor," SNCC Digital Gateway: https://snccdigital. org/people/ethel-minor/.

269 *Bond finally prevailed:* Neary, *Julian Bond*, 128–40; Fred P. Graham, "High Court Voids Refusal of Seat to Bond," *New York Times*, December 6, 1966.

271 *Ware's own expulsion:* Sellers, *The River of No Return*, 195–97.

272 *Ware accepted its "finality":* Clayborne Carson, *In Struggle*, 241.

272 *Dottie Zellner told her husband:* Author interview with Dorothy Zellner, July 6, 2000.

272 *address the Central Committee:* Lyon, *Memories of the Southern Civil Rights Movement*, 176–81.

274 *feelings of devastation:* Bob Zellner, *The Wrong Side of Murder Creek*, 296–98.

274 *"the worst thing":* Author interview with Dorothy Zellner.

274 *too ill to attend:* Cynthia Griggs Fleming, *Soon We Will Not Cry*, 183–84.

274 *draft a letter:* Lyon, *Memories of the Southern Civil Rights Movement*, 181.

275 *Once Zellner learned:* Author interview with Dorothy Zellner.

275 *honor her memory:* Cynthia Griggs Fleming, *Soon We Will Not Cry*, 1–12.

276 *"racism that did it":* Author interview with Dorothy Zellner.

276 *funeral program:* Cynthia Griggs Fleming, *Soon We Will Not Cry*, photo insert.

CHAPTER 17: DECEMBER 26 – BLACK STUDIES AND THE FIRST KWANZAA

277 *Jimmy Garrett arrived:* Sam Whiting, "The Black Student Union of SFSU Started It All," February 1, 2010, SFGate.com: https://www.sfgate. com/news/article/The-Black-Student-Union-at-SFSU-started-it-all -3274175.php; "From the Streets of LA . . . ," U.C. Berkeley oral panel, September 30, 2018, crmvet.org: https://www.crmvet.org/nars /1809jimy.htm.

277 *Garrett inherited his knack:* "From the Streets of LA . . . ," crmvet.org; Ibram Rogers, "Remembering the Black Campus Movement: An Oral History Interview with James P. Garrett," *Journal of Pan African Studies*, June 2009.

278 *when violence erupted:* "Watts Rebellion," History.com: https://www.his tory.com/topics/1960s/watts-riots.

279 *joined the Watts protest:* "From the Streets of LA . . . ," crmvet.org; Rogers, "Remembering the Black Campus Movement."

279 *acceptances from two schools:* Rogers, "Remembering the Black Campus Movement."

280 *made his first convert:* Mary Roaf, "Trailblazing a Movement: An Interview with Black Student Union Co-founders Jerry Vernado and James Garrett," *Ethnic Studies Review*, 2019.

280 *tossing around names:* Rogers, "Remembering the Black Campus Movement."

281 *college's new president:* Roaf, "Trailblazing a Movement."

281 *new kind of curriculum:* Rogers, "Remembering the Black Campus Movement."

282 *longest student strike:* Roaf, "Trailblazing a Movement."

282 *"the experimental college":* Author interview with Vern Smith, August 1, 2020.

282 *local Black politicians:* Ibid.

282 *Governor Ronald Reagan:* "Police/Alioto/Reagan on the SFS Strike," diva .sfsu.edu: https://diva.sfsu.edu/collections/sfbatv/bundles/187272.

283 *"a direct result":* Rogers, "Remembering the Black Campus Movement."

283 *Christopher Lasch:* Christopher Lasch, "The Trouble with Black Power," *New York Review of Books*, February 29, 1968.

284 *another seminal essay:* Eugene D. Genovese, "The Influence of the Black Power Movement on Historical Scholarship: Reflections of a White Historian," *Daedalus*, Spring 1970.

285 *paperback edition:* Tim Warren, "The Rocky Road to Publication of Book on Malcolm X," Baltimore *Sun*, November 16, 1992.

286 *Rosset stressed the appeal:* Ibid.

286 *Larry Neal:* Larry Neal, "The Black Arts Movement," *Drama Review*, Summer 1968.

286 *LeRoi Jones:* Margalit Fox, "Amiri Baraka, Polarizing Poet and Playwright, Dies at 79," *New York Times*, January 9, 2014; LeRoi Jones, *Home: Social Essays* (New York: William Morrow, 1966), 238–50.

287 *influence of Malcolm X:* William L. Van Deburg, *New Day in Babylon: The Black Power Movement and American Culture, 1965–1975* (Chicago: University of Chicago Press, 1992), 6–8.

287 *Sonia Sanchez:* Sonia Sanchez, *Home Coming: Poems by Sonia Sanchez* (Detroit: Broadside Press, 1969), 15; Hampton and Fayer, eds., *Voices of Freedom*, 252–55; "Sonia Sanchez: How I Overcame Stuttering," you tube.com: https://www.youtube.com/watch?v=l3rRclOBUDY.

289 *"Free Jazz":* Nat Hentoff, "The New Jazz: Black, Angry, and Hard to Understand," *New York Times Magazine*, December 25, 1966.

289   *folk music journal:* Julius Lester, "The Singing Is Over: The Angry Children of Malcolm X," *Sing Out!*, October–November 1966.

290   *Afro hairstyle:* Phyl Garland, "The Natural Look: Many Negro Women
Reject White Standards of Beauty," *Ebony*, June 1966.

290   *entire new movement:* "There's Still Hell to Pay in Watts," *Life*, July 15,
1966; " 'We Have Only One Power—To Disrupt Things,' " *Newsweek*,
August 22, 1966.

291   *Ronald McKinley Everett:* Scot Brown, *Fighting for US: Maulana Karenga,
the US Organization, and Black Cultural Nationalism* (New York: New
York University Press 2003), 7–12.

291   *met Malcolm X:* David Shaw, " 'Negro a Monster Stripped of His
Culture'—Malcolm X," *UCLA Daily Bruin*, October 29, 1962;
"Maulana Karenga Remembers Malcolm X," October 18, 2001, the
historymakers.org: https://www.thehistorymakers.org/biography/maulana
-karenga-39.

291   *animated young Black leader:* Scot Brown, *Fighting for US*, 26–27; Austin Conniver, "Negro Seeks to Install Pride in Race," *Hollywood Citizen
News*, July 25, 1963.

292   *Hakim Jamal:* Scot Brown, *Fighting for US*, 38–42; Douglas Martin, "Al-
fred Ligon Is Dead at 96; Owned Renowned Bookstore," *New York
Times*, August 23, 2002.

292   *"cultural revolution":* Keith A. Mayes, *Kwanzaa: Black Power and the Making
of the African-American Holiday Tradition* (London: Routledge, 2009), 65;
Scot Brown, *Fighting for US*, 21, 34, 38–42, 68–70.

293   *calendar of holidays:* "Maulana Karenga Deals How He Created Kwanzaa," October 18, 2001, thehistorymakers.org: https://www.thehistory
makers.org/biography/maulana-karenga-39.

293   *sole leader:* Scot Brown, *Fighting for US*, 42–44; "Rights Patrol Will Begin
in South LA Areas," *Sacramento Bee*, June 21, 1966; Cynthia Griggs
Fleming, *Soon We Will Not Cry*, 6; photo of Karenga, douglaswachter
.com: https://www.douglaswachter.com/1965-black-power-rally-uc
-greek-the.

294   *Will Rogers Memorial Park:* Fred Hanlin, "Police Gear to Handle Outbreak," *Long Beach Independent*, November 26, 1966; Ray Rogers, "Defiant Carmichael Declares Goals of Negro Generation," *Los Angeles
Times*, November 27, 1966.

294   *violence against him personally:* Karl Fleming, *Son of the Rough South: An
Uncivil Memoir* (New York: PublicAffairs, 2005), 1–20. Fleming, the for-
mer L.A. bureau chief for *Newsweek* magazine, remembered attending
Carmichael's speech in Will Rogers Park, but reported that it happened

six months earlier, on May 17, 1966. Later that day, L.A. rioters attacked Fleming and left him with bloody, near fatal head injuries, and Fleming suggested that Carmichael had incited the attack by singling him out as a white reporter at the park. However, there is no other record of Carmichael speaking at Will Rogers Park on May 17, which was just days after he was elected SNCC chairman in Kingston Springs, Tennessee, and proceeded immediately from there to a meeting of SNCC's Central Committee in Atlanta.

294 *"cult of personality"*: Scot Brown, *Fighting for US*, 45–48, 56, 65–67.

294 *first Kwanzaa:* Ibid., 70–71; "Maulana Karenga Deals How He Created Kwanzaa," thehistorymakers.org.

295 *mainstream, middle-class Blacks:* Janice C. Simpson, "Tidings of Black Pride and Joy," *Time*, December 23, 1991; Camilo Hannibal Smith, "Making a Case for Kwanzaa," *Houston Press*, January 2, 2015.

295 *quieter personal transformation:* Author interview with Vern Smith.

EPILOGUE: AFTER 1966 – OF ALLIES AND MESSIAHS

300 *Bond was finally sworn in:* Duane Riner, "Bond Sworn In, Mother Watches," *Atlanta Constitution*, January 10, 1967.

300 *none other than John Lewis:* Lewis, *Walking with the Wind*, 461–79.

301 *put to rest rumors:* Dorothy Gilliam, "A Woman Scorned," *Washington Post*, April 16, 1987.

301 *"never healed":* Michael G. Long, ed., *Race Man: Julian Bond, Selected Works, 1960–2015* (San Francisco: City Lights Books, 2020), 166–68.

301 *even in Lowndes County:* "Blacks Score Gains," AP/*Anniston* (Alabama) *Star*, November 4, 1970.

302 *America's first Black president:* Tom Rosensteil, "Inside Obama's Sweeping Victory," November 5, 2008, Pew Research Center: https://www.pew research.org/2008/11/05/inside-obamas-sweeping-victory/; "Dissecting the 2008 Electorate: Most Diverse in History," April 30, 2009, Pew Re search Center: https://www.pewresearch.org/hispanic/2009/04/30/dissect ing-the-2008-electorate-most-diverse-in-us-history/.

302 *Carmichael embarked on a tour:* Clayborne Carson, *In Struggle*, 278–82; Michael T. Kaufman, "Stokely Carmichael, Rights Leader Who Coined 'Black Power,' Dies at 57," *New York Times*, November 16, 1988.

302 *Hubert "Rap" Brown:* Clayborne Carson, *In Struggle*, 253–57; "Rap Brown Case to Be Reviewed," *New York Times*, March 20, 1971, 23; David Firestone, "For Former Radical, Old Battleground Became Refuge," *New York Times*, March 22, 2000.

304 *"fell to me"*: Hampton and Fayer, eds., *Voices of Freedom*, 369–70.

304 *Hoover and the FBI*: Gerald D. McKnight, Introduction, *Supplemental Detailed Staff Reports on Intelligence Activities and the Rights of Americans, Book III, Final Report of the Select Committee to Study Governmental Operations with Respect to Intelligence Activities, United States Senate, April 23, 1976* (Ipswich, ME: Mary Ferrell Foundation Press), 20–22, 188; FBI Records: The Vault, COINTELPRO Black Extremist, Part 1, 3.: https://vault.fbi .gov/cointel-pro/cointel-pro-black-extremists/cointelpro-black-extrem ists-part-01-of/view

304 *manufactured letters:* McKnight, Introduction, *Supplemental Detailed Staff Reports on Intelligence Activities and the Rights of Americans, Book III, Final Report of the Select Committee to Study Governmental Operations with Respect to Intelligence Activities, United States Senate*, 201–8.

304 *Fred Hampton:* Ibid., 222–23.

305 *In Los Angeles:* Ibid.,188–90; Scot Brown, *Fighting for US*, 93; Elaine Brown, *A Taste of Power: A Black Woman's Story* (New York: Anchor, 1994), 156–70.

305 *Karenga became convinced:* Scot Brown, *Fighting for US*, 120–22, 128.

305 *Newton spiraled:* "Huey Newton Killed; Was a Co-Founder of Black Panthers," *New York Times*, August 23. 1989.

306 *bizarre turn:* Kifner, "Eldridge Cleaver, Black Panther Who Became G.O.P. Conservative, Is Dead at 62."

306 *principal hero:* Examples of Bobby Seale's self-promoting versions of early Panther history—which are at odds with accounts written by Huey Newton, David Hilliard, and Seale himself closer to the time of events—can be found in Stephen Shames and Bobby Seale, *Power to the People: The World of the Black Panthers* (New York: Abrams, 2016).

306 *women were left:* Elaine Brown, *A Taste of Power*; "Biography," ericahug gins.com: https://www.erickahuggins.com/bio.

306 *Angela Davis:* "Angela Davis: Black Revolutionary," *Newsweek*, October 26, 1970; "Angela Davis," womenofthehall.org: https://www.womenof thehall.org/inductee/angela-davis/.

307 *"1619 Project":* "The 1619 Project," newyorktimes.com: https://www .nytimes.com/interactive/2019/08/14/magazine/1619-america-slavery .html.

307 *Black Lives Matter movement:* Jelani Cobb, "The Matter of Black Lives," *The New Yorker*, March 2, 2016.

307 *Alicia Garza:* Alicia Garza, *The Purpose of Power: How We Come Together When We Fall Apart* (New York: One World, 2020), 163.

Bibliography

Assante, Molefi Kete. *Maulana Karenga: An Intellectual Portrait*. Cambridge: Polity, 2009.

Barbour, Floyd B., ed. *The Black Power Revolt*. New York: Collier, 1969.

Bloom, Joshua, and Waldo E. Martin Jr. *Black Against Empire: The History and Politics of the Black Panther Party*. Oakland: University of California Press, 2013.

Branch, Taylor. *At Canaan's Edge: America in the King Years, 1965–68*. New York: Simon & Schuster, 2006.

———. *Parting the Waters: America in the King Years, 1954–63*. New York: Simon & Schuster, 1988.

———. *Pillar of Fire: America in the King Years, 1963–65*. New York: Simon & Schuster, 1998.

Brown, Elaine. *A Taste of Power: A Black Woman's Story*. New York: Anchor, 1994.

Brown, Scot. *Fighting for US: Maulana Karenga, the US Organization, and Black Cultural Nationalism*. New York: New York University Press, 2003.

Carmichael, Stokely. *Ready for Revolution: The Life and Struggles of Stokely Carmichael (Kwame Ture)*. In collaboration with Edwueme Michael Thelwell. New York: Scribner, 2003.

Carmichael, Stokely, and Charles V. Hamilton. *Black Power: The Politics of Liberation in America*. New York: Random House, 1967.

Carson, Clayborne. *In Struggle: SNCC and the Black Awakening of the 1960's*. Cambridge: Harvard University Press, 1995.

Carson, Josephine. *Silent Voices: An Intimate Study of Southern Black Women During the Civil Rights Struggle*. New York: Delacorte, 1969.

Cleaver, Eldridge. *Soul on Ice*. New York: McGraw-Hill, 1968.

———. *Target Zero: A Life in Writing*. New York: Palgrave, 2006.

D'Emilio, John. *Lost Prophet: The Life and Times of Bayard Rustin*. Chicago: University of Chicago Press, 2004.

Du Bois, W. E. B. *The Souls of Black Folk*. Oxford: Oxford University Press, 2007.

Ellison, Ralph. *Invisible Man*. New York: Modern Library, 1994.

Fanon, Frantz. *The Wretched of the Earth*. New York: Grove, 1968.

Fleming, Cynthia Griggs. *Soon We Will Not Cry: The Liberation of Ruby Doris Smith Robinson*. Lanham, MD: Rowman & Littlefield, 2000.

Fleming, Karl. *Son of the Rough South: An Uncivil Memoir*. New York: Public-Affairs, 2005.

Ford, Liam T. A. *Soldier Field: A Stadium and Its City*. Chicago: University of Chicago Press, 2009.

Forman, James. *The Making of Black Revolutionaries*. Seattle: University of Washington Press, 1997.

———. *Sammy Younge, Jr.: The First Black College Student to Die in the Black Liberation Movement*. New York: Grove, 1968.

Frady, Marshall. *Southerners: A Journalist's Odyssey*. New York: New American Library, 1980.

———. *Wallace*. New York: Meridien, 1968.

Garrow, David J. *Bearing the Cross: Martin Luther King, Jr. and the Southern Leadership Conference*. New York: William Morrow, 1986.

Garza, Alicia. *The Purpose of Power: How We Come Together When We Fall Apart*. New York: One World, 2020.

Gates, Henry Louis Jr., and Evelyn Brooks Higginbotham, eds. *African-American Lives*. Oxford: Oxford University Press, 2004.

Goudsouzian, Aram. *Down At the Crossroads: Civil Rights, Black Power, and the Meredith March Against Fear*. New York: Farrar, Straus & Giroux, 2014.

Greenberg, Cheryl Lynn, ed. *A Circle of Trust: Remembering SNCC*. New Brunswick: Rutgers University Press, 1998.

Hamilton, Charles V. *Adam Clayton Powell, Jr.: The Political Biography of an American Dilemma*. New York: Atheneum, 1991.

Hampton, Henry, and Steve Fayer, eds. *Voices of Freedom: An Oral History of the Civil Rights Movement from the 1950's Through the 1980's*. New York: Bantam, 1990.

Hannah-Jones, Nikole. *The 1619 Project: A New Origin Story*. New York: One World, 2021.

Hilliard, David. *Huey: Spirit of the Panther*. In collaboration with Keith and Kent Zimmerman. New York: Basic Books, 2006.

Holsaert, Faith S., et al., eds. *Hands on the Freedom Plow: Personal Accounts by Women in SNCC*. Urbana: University of Illinois Press, 2012.

Jeffries, Hasan Kwame. *Bloody Lowndes: Civil Rights and Black Power in Alabama's Black Belt* (New York: New York University Press, 2009).

Jones, LeRoi. *Home: Social Essays*. New York: William Morrow, 1966.

Joseph, Peniel E. *Stokely: A Life*. New York: Basic Civitas, 2104.

————. *The Sword and the Shield: The Revolutionary Lives of Malcolm X and Martin Luther King, Jr.* New York: Basic Books, 2020.

————. *Waiting 'Til the Midnight Hour: A Narrative History of Black Power in America*. New York: Henry Holt, 2006.

King, Coretta Scott. *My Life with Martin Luther King, Jr.* New York: Holt, Rinehart & Winston, 1969.

King, Martin Luther Jr. *Where Do We Go from Here: Chaos or Community?* New York: Harper & Row, 1967.

King, Mary E. *Freedom Song: A Personal Story of the 1960's Civil Rights Movement*. New York: William Morrow, 1987.

Kopkind, Andrew. *The Thirty Years' Wars: Dispatches and Diversions of a Radical Journalist, 1965–1994*. London: Verso, 1995.

Lefever, Harry G. *Undaunted by the Fight: Spelman College and the Civil Rights Movement, 1957–1967*. Macon, GA: Mercer University Press, 2005.

Lewis, John. *Walking with the Wind: A Memoir of the Movement*. In collaboration with Michael D'Orso. New York: Simon & Schuster, 1998.

Long, Michael, ed. *Race Man: Julian Bond, Selected Works, 1960–2015*. San Francisco: City Lights Books, 2020.

Lyon, Danny. *Memories of the Southern Civil Rights Movement*. Chapel Hill: University of North Carolina Press, 1992.

Marable, Manning. *Malcolm X: A Life of Reinvention*. New York: Viking, 2011.

Mayes, Keith A. *Kwanzaa: Black Power and the Making of the African-American Holiday Tradition*. London: Routledge, 2009.

McKnight, Gerald D., Introduction. *Supplemental Detailed Staff Reports on Intelligence Activities and the Rights of American, Book III, Final Report of the Select Committee to Study Government Operations with Respect to Intelligence Activities, United States Senate, April 23, 1976*. Ipswich, ME: Mary Ferrell Foundation Press.

Michaeli, Ethan. *The Defender: How the Legendary Black Newspaper Changed America*. Boston: Houghton Mifflin Harcourt, 2016.

Murch, Donna Jean. *Living for the City: Migration, Education and the Rise of the Black Panther Party in Oakland, California*. Chapel Hill: University of North Carolina Press, 2010.

Neary, John. *Julian Bond: Black Rebel*. New York: William Morrow, 1971.

Nelson, Alondra. *Body and Soul: The Black Panther Party and the Fight Against Medical Discrimination*. Minneapolis: University of Minnesota Press, 2011.

Newton, Huey P. *Revolutionary Suicide*. New York: Penguin Classics, 2009.

Payne, Les, and Tamara Payne. *The Dead Are Arising: The Life of Malcolm X*. New York: Liveright, 2020.

Reed, Roy. *Beware of Limbo Dancers: A Correspondent's Adventures with the New York Times*. Little Rock: University of Arkansas Press, 2012.

Reporting Civil Rights: Part Two, American Journalism, 1963–1973. Library of America, 2003.

Richardson, Peter. *A Bomb in Every Issue: How the Short, Unruly Life of Ramparts Magazine Changed America*. New York: The New Press, 2002.

Roberts, Gene, and Hank Klibanoff. *The Race Beat: The Press, the Civil Rights Struggle and the Awakening of a Nation*. New York: Vintage, 2007.

Sanchez, Sonia. *Home Coming: Poems by Sonia Sanchez*. Detroit: Broadside Press, 1969.

Satter, Beryl. *Family Properties: How the Struggle over Race and Real Estate Transformed Chicago and Urban America*. New York: Picador, 2009.

Seale, Bobby. *Seize the Time: The Story of the Black Panther Party and Huey P. Newton*. Baltimore: Black Classic Press, 1991.

Sellers, Cleveland. *The River of No Return: The Autobiography of a Black Militant and the Life and Death of SNCC*. In collaboration with Robert Terrell (New York: William Morrow, 1973).

Shames, Stephen, and Bobby Seale. *Power to the People: The World of the Black Panthers*. New York: Abrams, 2016.

Smith, Stephen Drury, and Catherine Ellis, eds. *Free All Along: The Robert Penn Warren Civil Rights Interviews*. New York: The New Press, 2019.

Van Deburg, William L. *New Day in Babylon: The Black Power Movement and American Culture, 1965–1975*. Chicago: University of Chicago Press, 1992.

Visser-Maessen, Laura. *Robert Parris Moses: A Life in Civil Rights and Leadership at the Grassroots*. Chapel Hill: University of North Carolina Press, 2016.

Wilkins, Roger. *A Man's Life*. New York: Simon & Schuster, 1984.

Williams, Robert F. *Negroes with Guns*. Eastford, CT: Martino Fine Books, 2020.

Williams, Roger F. *The Bonds: An American Family*. New York: Atheneum, 1972.

Wright, Richard. *Black Power: Three Books from Exile*. New York: Harper Perennial Modern Classics, 2008.

X, Malcolm. *The Autobiography of Malcolm X*. New York: Grove, 1966.

Zellner, Bob. *The Wrong Side of Murder Creek: A White Southerner in the Freedom Movement*. Montgomery, AL: New South Books, 2008.

Zinn, Howard. *SNCC: The New Abolitionists*. Chicago: Haymarket, 2017.

Photo Credits

Index

Page numbers beginning with 313 refer to endnotes.

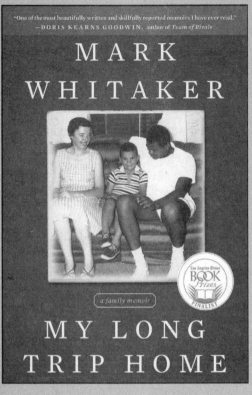

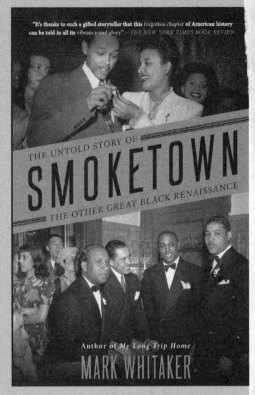

"[Whitaker] brings his gifts as a journalist and ultimately, his deep compassion as a human, to shed light on his own unique and very moving family story."

—Anna Deavere Smith, playwright and performer, author of *Fires in the Mirror*

"Fascinating... *Smoketown* will appeal to anybody interested in black history and anybody who loves a good story. In short, anybody."

—*Washington Post*